Free Labor

Free Labor

Workfare and the Contested Language of Neoliberalism

JOHN KRINSKY

The University of Chicago Press
Chicago and London

John Krinsky is associate professor of political science at City College of
New York (CUNY). This is his first book.

The University of Chicago Press, Chicago 60637
The University of Chicago Press, Ltd., London
© 2007 by The University of Chicago
All rights reserved. Published 2007
Printed in the United States of America

16 15 14 13 12 11 10 09 08 07   1 2 3 4 5

ISBN-13: 978-0-226-45365-1 (cloth)
ISBN-13: 978-0-226-45366-8 (paper)
ISBN-10: 0-226-45365-0 (cloth)
ISBN-10: 0-226-45366-9 (paper)

Library of Congress Cataloging-in-Publication Data

Krinsky, John.
   Free labor : workfare and the contested language of neoliberalism / John
Krinsky.
      p. cm.
   Includes bibliographical references and index.
   ISBN-13: 978-0-226-45365-1 (cloth : alk. paper)
   ISBN-10: 0-226-45365-0 (cloth : alk. paper)
   ISBN-13: 978-0-226-45366-8 (pbk. : alk. paper)
   ISBN-10: 0-226-45366-9 (pbk. : alk. paper)   1. Welfare recipients—
Employment—New York (State)—New York.   2. Welfare rights movement—
New York (State)—New York.   3. Employee rights—New York (State)—
New York.   4. New York (N.Y.)—Social policy.   5. New York (N.Y.)—
Politics and government—1951–   6. Neoliberalism.   I. Title.
   HV99 .N59K75 2007
   362.5'84097471—dc22
                                                           2007015186
⊗ The paper used in this publication meets the minimum requirements of
the American National Standard for Information Sciences—Permanence of
Paper for Printed Library Materials, ANSI Z39.48-1992.

For Keren, Maya, and Adam

CONTENTS

ACORN	Association of Community Organizations for Reform Now	National organization of membership-based community groups with roots in the welfare rights movement
ACT-UP	AIDS Coalition To Unleash Power	Premier AIDS activist organization of the late 1980s and early 1990s
AFDC	Aid to Families with Dependent Children	Federal welfare program for families prior to August 1996
AFSCME	American Federation of State, County, and Municipal Employees	Principal public employees' union
BEGIN	Begin Employment Gain Independence Now	Name of local program in New York City under FSA
CATE	Coalition for Access to Training and Education	Advocacy group made up of WRI, FAC, and other anti-WEP groups
CETA	Comprehensive Education and Training Act	Federal employment program of 1970s
CFRC	Community Food Resource Center	Advocacy and service organization focusing on hunger and poverty
CHAT	Cultural Historical Activity Theory	Program of research in cognitive and developmental psychology

COW	Count Our Work	Campaign begun by CVH in 1999
CSS	Community Service Society	Charity and advocacy organization with roots in nineteenth-century social work and reform movements
CVH	Community Voices Heard	Membership-based poor people's organization in New York City, founded in 1996
CWA 1180	Communications Workers of America Local 1180	Labor union representing white-collar workers and supervisors in New York City government, typically in the middle-range civil service categories, especially in the HRA
DCAS	Department of Citywide Administrative Services	City department with responsibility for maintaining City property; successor to Department of General Services
DC 37	District Council 37 of AFSCME	Main municipal workers' union in New York City, with fifty-six locals organized under the district council
EFCB	Emergency Financial Control Board	State agency founded during New York City's fiscal crisis to oversee the City's budget
FAC	Fifth Avenue Committee	Community organizing and development group founded in Park Slope, Brooklyn, in 1977
FPI	Fiscal Policy Institute	Union-backed research and advocacy organization

FSA	Family Support Act of 1988	Welfare reform legislation authored by Sen. Daniel Patrick Moynihan (D-NY) that established work requirements
FUREE	Families United for Racial and Economic Equality	Successor to WWT
HANNYS	Hunger Action Network of New York State	Antihunger advocacy group
HR	Home Relief	New York State's welfare program for adults without dependent children prior to 1997, when it was re-formed and renamed Safety Net Assistance
HRA	Human Resources Administration	Welfare and social services department in New York City
KWRU	Kensington Welfare Rights Union	Philadelphia-based organization emphasizing human rights violations under welfare reform; worked in coalition with UJC in late 1990s
LACH	Legal Action Center for the Homeless	Center founded in 1984 to provide public benefits advocacy to homeless people; precursor to UJC
NELP	National Employment Law Project	Nonprofit law practice, formerly part of Legal Services, that provides legal expertise on issues of low-wage employment
NOW–LDEF	NOW Legal Defense and Education Fund	Offshoot of the National Organization of Women founded in 1970 to pursue litigation, legislation, and education; now called Legal Momentum

NWRO	National Welfare Rights Organization	Main welfare-rights advocacy organization (1967–74); parent organization of ACORN, founded in 1970
NYC–WAY	New York City–Work, Accountability, and You	Name of New York City's welfare reform program (and of the computer application to manage the caseload)
OCB	Office of Collective Bargaining	New York City department responsible for administering and enforcing the New York City collective bargaining law
PESH	Public Employees Safety and Health	New York State office responsible for investigating grievances on workplace health and safety concerns
POP	Parks Opportunity Program	Temporary job program for welfare recipients nearing the end of their five-year limits on federal welfare receipt, enacted in 2001
PRWORA	Personal Responsibility and Work Opportunity Reconciliation Act of 1996	Federal welfare reform legislation passed by the 104th Congress and signed into law by President Bill Clinton on August 22, 1996
PWP	Public Works Program	Workfare program begun in 1971 and then expanded in 1986 by New York City mayor Ed Koch
TANF	Temporary Aid to Needy Families	Program of block-granted money to the states that replaced AFDC as part of the PRWORA
TEP	Transitional Employment Program	Five-year pilot project for transitional job placement

UJC	Urban Justice Center	Multi-issue advocacy organization with independent projects focusing on economically disadvantaged New Yorkers, begun as the Legal Action Center for the Homeless in 1984
WEP	Work Experience Program	New York City's principal "workfare" program
WFP	Working Families Party	Political party formed by several unions, including ACORN and CWA 1180
WLC	Welfare Law Center	Nonprofit law firm specializing in advocacy around public benefits law; formerly part of Legal Services as the Center for Welfare Policy and Law; now called the National Center for Law and Economic Justice
WRI	Welfare Rights Initiative	Organization founded in 1996 to safeguard educational opportunities for welfare recipients
WRN	Welfare Reform Network	Contact group of New York City's welfare-, hunger-, and homeless-advocacy groups formed in response to FSA
WWT	WEP Workers Together	Organization founded jointly in 1996 by the Fifth Avenue Committee, the Urban Justice Center, and Community Voices Heard in order to organize WEP workers

In early 1996, I was working with the Community Service Society of New York, a venerable nonprofit organization, conducting a study of low-income cooperative housing models. My study took me to the Fifth Avenue Committee, a neighborhood-based tenant organizing and community development group in Brooklyn, where the executive director, Brad Lander, mentioned a new project the group was starting. The group was beginning to organize welfare recipients forced to "work off" their benefits in the city's newly expanded "workfare" program. The challenge, Brad told me, was that since workfare workers were doing work previously done by municipal workers but were not defined as municipal employees, it was not clear whether they should be organized as welfare recipients, with activism directed at welfare offices, or as workers, with unionlike structures agitating for reform at the workplace.

This challenge stuck with me. I had previously worked as an organizer in Chester, Pennsylvania, with a homeless advocacy group. In the homeless movement of the late 1980s and early 1990s, I found that the identity of "the homeless" was a terribly slippery thing. "The homeless" were frequently subject to spells of homelessness, becoming by turns homeless and low-income tenants. Since the homeless movement was rooted in a different set of institutions than the tenants' movement and since the respective statuses of homeless people and tenants were separated by a gulf of stigma, it was as difficult as it was necessary for the homeless movement to form coalitions across these divides if it was to succeed in making the case that homelessness was a structural feature of housing poverty in the United States rather than the result of the moral shortcomings of the very poor. A ready analogy between this problem and the one faced by antiworkfare organizers formed in my head.

Shortly after returning to graduate school in late 1996, I began to examine the movement against workfare. This book is the result of these investigations over the course of nearly a decade.

In addition to expanding workfare, New York mayor Rudolph Giuliani also tightened eligibility restrictions on welfare, making it more difficult to apply for benefits. In a local economy in which more than one in four New Yorkers lived below the poverty line and in which the bottom fifth of the income distribution had lost real income since the early 1980s, these moves seemed unforgiving. They were also among the most popular of Giuliani's policies, and they remain a touchstone of his admirers' claims that he turned New York City's declining fortunes around. Today, fewer than half as many people receive welfare benefits as did in 1994. In the eyes of Giuliani's admirers, this figure vindicates the tough and often paternalistic approach of his reforms.

People who were forced into the program, however, often considered it little better than slavery. Though made to work in municipal agencies for up to thirty-five hours a week, they worked for welfare benefits valued well under the federal poverty level. For roughly the equivalent of minimum wage, they did work that was often nearly identical to that done by unionized municipal employees making three times as much money. At welfare offices, they were harangued by caseworkers instructed to get people off the welfare rolls and into jobs, no matter what the jobs paid, or the conditions of employment. Work was simply seen as the salve for all possible problems. Gloria, a workfare worker I met, who had fled an abusive husband and became homeless, had a typical antipathy, though perhaps atypical response, to the program. She told me that when asked by a caseworker—who had just ordered her into workfare—why she was crying, she responded, "I'm crying because it's the only thing keeping me from throwing you up against that wall and whipping your ass!"

However important the workfare workers' responses were to the formation and maintenance of resistance to the program's expansion and administration, this book is not so much about these responses as it is about the process of political claim-making. Three largely academic, rather than expressly political, interests inform my approach. First, I am interested in understanding the ways in which the movement against workfare is affected by workfare itself, which is neither exactly employment nor welfare. To understand this effect, I believe, we need to understand workfare's place in welfare-state politics and in urban political economy. Second, I am also taken with questions about how public debates take shape as cultural fields, that is, as intersecting interactions among political actors and the political claims they make. In such fields, public definitions of particular, focal actors, such as workfare workers or the homeless, can become more or less consensual and more or less segmented among various institutional sites. For example, I am interested in what different ways the credibility is established among speakers and listeners of a claim that workfare is akin to slavery when workfare workers say it at rallies, lawyers say it in courtrooms, and religious leaders say it in the mass media. The third interest I have is in how various political actors come to understand their political strategies and learn from their interactions with others. Taken together, however, these academic interests point to parts of an answer to how to think about urban movements against neoliberalism and how they may be able to fight against the ideological dominance of hyperindividualist, moralistic public policies that impose austerity on the poor and, in the name of the ostensible efficiency of markets, redistribute our social surplus to those who already enjoy it most.

This book is, accordingly, a cultural and political analysis of workfare politics in New York, underpinned with theoretical and methodological ideas that I think have application beyond the case. It is not a book that "gives voice" to workfare workers, nor is it written so that it can be immediately put to use by opponents of workfare. Instead, if this book has any positive consequences for the movement whose activists have so generously lent me their time, it should come in the form of things to think about that may spur new strategic thoughts, and perhaps greater strategic capacity, sometime in the future.

In the course of my work, I have also benefited greatly from the guidance, inspiration, criticism, and encouragement of Charles Tilly, Francesca Polletta, and Peter Bearman, who, as my dissertation committee and as important intellectual guides, helped influence my perspectives on social analysis. Many teachers, colleagues, and friends have also influenced, prodded, and criticized my work, including Ellen Reese, Chad Goldberg, David Stark, Herb Gans, Jennifer Lena, Tammy Smith, Galit Shashoua-Goldblatt, Carlos Costa-Ribeiro, Fernanda Wanderley, Balázs Vedres, Cecelia Walsh-Russo, Amanda Damarin, Ira Katznelson, Susan Fainstein, Frances Fox Piven, Michael Paris, Joyce Gelb, Andy Rich, Eileen McDonaugh, Ricky Blum, Lesley Wood, Daniel Skinner, Chik Collins, Ines Langemeyer, Laurence Cox, Kevin Ward, and Ann Mische. Members of the Center for Place Culture and Politics at the Graduate Center of the City University of New York, convened by Neil Smith and Omar Dahbour, offered helpful criticism at a crucial juncture. The always-patient and friendly members of the Workshop on Contentious Politics at Columbia University, convened by Chuck Tilly and which has been as close as anything to an intellectual home for me, have provided invaluable help at many stages of this book's development. Andy Perrin, Robin Wagner-Pacifici, and Joe Razza have been my most precious interlocutors since my days as a student and organizer. Even when they're not present, I imagine how they might respond. Colin Barker, too, plays this role. Since meeting him in 1998, his generous but pointed criticism has always led me to think of new directions in which to take my work.

I have been particularly fortunate to work at the City College of New York in the Political Science Department, where my students and colleagues have always been a source of support. As chair, Vince Boudreau helped me adjust to teaching in a new discipline. As a colleague, serious reader, and critic of my work and a partner in thinking through contentious politics, he has been as wonderful as I have been lucky. Thanks are also due Paula Oyebisi, our department administrator, who keeps everything running smoothly.

Thanks to Lesley Wood, Mac Scott, Lesley Wood, Ye Zhou, and Shannyn Morse, who performed critical transcription and data entry work for various pieces of this project. Daniel Skinner did invaluable coding work for the analysis in chapter 5.

Doug Mitchell and Tim McGovern at the University of Chicago Press have provided uplifting encouragement along the way. Lori Meek Schuldt's eagle eye improved the manuscript's readability. The suggestions of two anonymous reviewers have made this a much better book than might otherwise have been the case. I am extremely lucky to have gotten as serious, engaged, and constructive criticism as these reviewers gave me. More-experienced colleagues to whom I showed the reviews marveled at their detail and rigor. Any failure to follow their advice has probably resulted in shortcomings in the book.

I owe an enormous debt of thanks to the workfare workers and activists who stood up to a bullying mayor to argue, passionately, for a better, more-humane city. They helped me through various stages of this research to gain access to information and to understand the information I received. I would have been simply at sea without the help and comradeship they gave me. Paul Getsos, the late—and missed—Gail Aska, Elaine Kim, Lynn Lewis, Rusia Muhiuddin, Nathan Smith, Lionel Ouellette, Heidi Dorow, Keren Zolotov, Milagros Silva, Diomaris Maya, Maurice Emsellem, Liz Krueger, and especially Peter Colavito, Benjamin Dulchin, and Ricky Blum deserve particular recognition from among the many, many people who eased this project's realization.

Teachers Lisa Galeano and Irene Martinez of P.S. 163 and the entire staff at Purple Circle Day Care have enabled me to work with the knowledge that my kids are in great hands. My kids, Maya and Adam, are a constant source of love, humor, music, noise, and intellectual stimulation. Both have been patient with me. Rami and Miriam Osman have supported me in countless ways, from helping me think through ideas to taking the kids so I could work. My parents, Robert and Carol Krinsky, have also been terrifically supportive. My mother is a sensible, patient, and graceful editor who can turn around 250 pages of text in three days. Finally, for eighteen years, my partner, Keren Osman, has tried, with varying degrees of success, to talk sense into me when I have needed it most and has inspired me with her combination of intellectual toughness and sensitivity and her fierce compassion.

CHAPTER ONE

Free Labor?

"If they can make me work for free, they will downsize you and they won't hire me." So read a banner carried by welfare recipients marching in chains in the Labor Day Parade in New York City in 1996, just weeks after President Clinton signed the welfare reform act that required welfare recipients to work as a condition of receiving welfare. The welfare recipients were protesting New York City's expansion of its existing welfare work or "workfare" program, the Work Experience Program (WEP). WEP had been on the books in some form for more than twenty years. But Mayor Rudolph W. Giuliani began a fourfold expansion of WEP in 1995, and by 1997, more than thirty-eight thousand workfare workers were toiling in city agencies and nonprofit organizations at between half- and full-time hours in order to receive welfare checks that rarely yielded more than twenty dollars a day per person covered. WEP's proponents claimed that for welfare recipients with shallow work histories, rapid attachment to the labor force—even in a WEP placement with little to no hope for being hired into their jobs—was the best training. WEP's critics often derided it as a dead end and a waste of time at best and slavery at worst. They complained that WEP workers were working in the same jobs as regular workers but without the full panoply of workers' rights. Their very presence in municipal workplaces eroded these rights and was a way of circumventing unions. The banner's slogan ended with a demand: Real Jobs, Not WEP.

The appearance of a group of WEP worker activists in the Labor Day Parade marked one of the first large public appearances of opposition to workfare. The opposition continues more than ten years later, having grown and peaked in its first five years. During that time, a variety of community groups, antipoverty advocates, legal advocates, labor unions, religious leaders, politicians, editorialists, and workfare workers themselves made public claims about WEP and the need to reform it. They walked picket lines, sued, held press conferences, organized at worksites and welfare offices, and proposed, drafted, and argued for legislation. Each of these efforts was met by equivalent actions by WEP's proponents among politicians, municipal financiers, and conservatives, both organized and not. Between the poles of indignant opposition and stubborn support were a range of positions on details and aspects of the program that sometimes blurred the lines between supporters and opponents. Thus, though WEP workers marched in the Labor Day Parade as the guests of one municipal union, their signs were "directed at the City unions and at the Mayor;"[1] to the former for their quiescence and to the latter for what WEP's opponents perceived as his punitive policies toward the poor.

This book traces the development of the politics of workfare in New York City in the 1990s and into the first decade of the current millennium. In particular, it focuses on the ways in which political claims entered into public discourse through and among various institutionally situated actors, defining the often-slippery political meanings of workfare along the way. In doing so, it argues that current models of theorizing about policy and political movements that address it are inadequate, on their own, to understand the formation and change of insurgent political identities through the political process. In proposing my own synthesis, I draw on urban political economy, political and cultural sociology, literary and linguistic theory, and developmental psychology in an effort to respecify these dynamics. The movement that developed against workfare in New York gives specific expression to more-general problems of political action and opposition: How do political actors define their interests and preferences? How do they define and identify their allies and adversaries? How do they decide on political claims to make on the state and on other claimants? How are these decisions shaped through existing institutional contexts? Where, as in New York City's workfare program—and increasingly under conditions of state-led market liberalization—uncertainty reigns about basic categories of workplace and community rights, these questions are thrown into sharp relief. They take on, therefore, both theoretical importance and practical significance.

Movements through "City Trenches"

In 1981, Ira Katznelson published *City Trenches*, a masterful study of the development of working-class politics in the New York City neighborhood of Washington Heights. Writing at the end of the 1970s, he remarked that the radical political projects that had "defined debated alternatives" were supplanted by "managerial and fiscal matters [wherein] the new terminology defines action in terms of balancing budgets, bondholder confidence, service cutbacks, wage freezes, municipal employee layoffs, the erosion of the tax base, and making do with less."[2] The fragmentation of the response to these changes was, Katznelson argued, symptomatic of a deeper divide in working-class politics in the United States. This divide split workers' consciousness and political activity into two spheres of activity, one suited to the home and community and the other to the workplace. "The links between work and community-based conflicts have been unusually tenuous," Katznelson wrote, due to the coincident timing of immigrant incorporation through political machines and parties and the channeling of worker organization into narrow class unionism through the nineteenth century.[3] These institutional frameworks—Katznelson calls them "trenches" that shape the contests of urban politics—are remarkably resilient and, while periodically challenged, reassert themselves once more-radical challenges, like those of the 1960s, pass.

In this light, the workfare workers' march marked an anomaly. A coalition of community-based and antipoverty organizations organized the workfare workers, who marched at the invitation of a union. They marched in chains, and they cast their demands both to other municipal unions and to the City administration. What was curious about workfare workers was that they were not straightforwardly *workers* or *welfare recipients*. They cast their demands as both and also as neither: their marching in chains suggested they were *slaves*, and their demand for "real jobs" suggested that they were unemployed, or *potential* workers.

This semiotic stew is enriched by a further ingredient of uncertainty, namely, that beyond a basic claim for working-class solidarity, there is little in the way of an articulated and encompassing ideology expressed by the WEP workers. Katznelson suggests that encompassing ideologies can sometimes help bridge the gaps between community and labor politics. But here, WEP workers' and their organizations' *uncertainty* about what it means politically to be a workfare worker is more on display than is any clear analysis of the question.

One of the many strengths of *City Trenches* is that it synthesizes two literatures in a novel way. It explains the patterns of urban politics in the United States by way of class formation and vice versa. In its skillful blend of institutional analysis and political economy, it produces a

historical narrative that elucidates the ease with which urban retrenchment in the 1970s and 1980s was accomplished.

The urban policies Katznelson described in their infancy have become
the backbone of urban politics—and, indeed, of international development policy—nearly three decades later. In part through the crucible
of New York City's fiscal crisis in the 1970s, *neoliberalism* became the
dominant style for social and economic policy development. Neoliberalism includes changes in the scale and manner of capital accumulation
and employment to favor "flexibility" for employers and local and trans-
national rather than national regulation; changes in welfare-state provisions from enhancing social equity toward increasing austerity for the
poor; increasing privatization of social services, either through contracting or through the sale of public assets; and the application of "market"
principles of efficiency for a wide range of public goods to which these
principles had not been applied previously.

Workfare in New York City during the 1990s reflected all these trends.
By studying the ways in which the social and political meanings of workfare were forged by, in, and through the movement against WEP over the
course of a ten-year span, we can better understand the ways in which
both neoliberalism and those excluded from its hollowed-out form
of social citizenship have been shaped, and reshaped by the enduring
divides of urban politics.

Synthesizing Theory and Method

Four years before the publication of *City Trenches*, Frances Fox Piven and
Richard Cloward published *Poor People's Movements: How They Succeed,
Why They Fail.* This book extended an argument they began in 1971, in
Regulating the Poor: The Functions of Public Welfare, that claimed that public poverty relief expanded under conditions of mass unemployment not
because of the compassion of the economically fortunate for the plight of
the poor but rather when the threat or actuality of social disorder became
palpable. The form of poor relief was dictated by the fear of disorder,
too. Public relief programs were attached to stigmatizing claims about
their beneficiaries and were designed to reach only those among the poor
whose support could be co-opted into restoring order. Relief programs
contracted when the economic crises causing mass unemployment subsided, thus providing anew a supply of laborers who would work at "any
job at any wage." The corollary for poor people's movements was that
movements succeed to the extent that they create disorder and uncer-

tainty among the elite and resist co-optation. But given the propensity of poor people's movements to form formal, mass-membership organizations and thus a leadership susceptible to co-optation, poor people's movements' gains are frequently stymied, leaving only a "residue of reform."

Like *City Trenches*, *Poor People's Movements* stood out for its synthesis of political economy with questions of oppositional organizing and for its direction to contemporary political concerns. Its comparison of two major waves of welfare-state reform in the 1930s and the 1960s set political sociologists down a new path of inquiry that engaged and sometimes challenged Piven and Cloward's arguments and extended their reach. Writing at the birth of what is now the vibrant subdiscipline of social movement studies in sociology and comparative political science, Piven and Cloward helped set the stage for a wide range of work that took seriously the efforts of ordinary people trying to resist the conditions of their subordination, treating them as thinking, deliberating, and strategizing instead of simply irrationally and spasmodically reacting to oppression.

Poor People's Movements, *City Trenches*, and work such as Charles Tilly's *From Mobilization to Revolution* share a period of development in the mid- to late 1970s in which scholars interested in social protest were also interested in arguments that synthesized insights from several fields of study into more-encompassing explanations of why popular politics took the forms it did and how these forms related to the developing relations of state institutions to a capitalism that was itself in flux. Under the more or less explicit influence of Marxist arguments, these works resulted in broadly structuralist explanations of political stability and change. Produced amid a realignment of capital, state, and social relations, they set the agenda for a new generation of scholarship that nevertheless attempted little of the synthetic scope of its progenitors.

In this book, I address the dynamics of antiworkfare politics by recrafting a synthesis appropriate both to the deepening and broadening of neoliberal political economy *since* the 1970s—one paradigmatic expression of which is workfare—and to the increased attention given by scholars to the ways in which political actors make sense of their own action. By steering between structuralism and pragmatism, I offer a series of studies that move in stepwise fashion through levels of analysis, from a discussion of changes in welfare policy set against larger questions of urban political economy, through analyses of organizational strategies to oppose workfare within particular institutional settings, and from analyses of political claim-making among institutional settings to a close study of how actors within anti-WEP organizations changed their minds about their claim-making strategies. Each specific investigation should offer new insights or novel applications to readers within the respective subfields of welfare and urban policy; social and labor movement studies; the sociology of culture; and developmental psychology. By moving stepwise along levels of analysis, each successive analysis is built on the foundation of the previous one, so that the synthesis—to which I will return at the end of the book—is made as clearly as possible.

Like the syntheses of the late 1970s and early 1980s, the synthesis I offer draws on broadly Marxian themes in state theory, while attending to the importance of institutional constraints on and resources for action. It also draws on theoretical and research programs that were less well known—or nonexistent—at that time but which have contributed to research in cultural sociology in the study of political culture, and in studies of culture and cognition. In addition to tying together substantive subfields of research, I also suggest methodological paths through the synthesis, drawing on the social-network application of blockmodeling, on theories of language derived from the Bakhtin circle and from Antonio Gramsci's work, and on a program of research in cognitive and developmental psychology called Cultural Historical Activity Theory, or CHAT.

Substantive Questions

How do we understand the definitional ambiguities of workfare in light of the larger push for labor market flexibility as part of an emerging repertoire of neoliberal governance? How do movements—especially when not dominated by single organizations—define the objects of their claims and organize coalitions to support their public interpretations? How do they play off dominant discursive repertoires to improvise changes, and how and when do they simply repeat the performances of authorities without challenging them? What determines how emerging labor-community coalitions respond to retrenchment in the local welfare state? What potential for reorganizing policy agendas do such coalitions have? And, how, finally, do political actors gain and lose dominance over the terms of debate over an issue?

The need for a methodologically catholic and theoretically synthetic approach to both the general and specific questions I set out should be evident. Consider an example. If we want to understand why labor and community groups were unsuccessful in achieving a recognition of the workers' rights of workfare workers—for example, securing for them the right to collectively bargain, the right to be paid in wages rather than in welfare benefits, and so on—we could point to Mayor Giuliani's infamous ruthlessness in dealing with critics; the corruption of the principal municipal workers' union, District Council 37 of AFSCME (DC 37), and its political support for Giuliani; or we could point to the failure of anti-WEP organizing groups to mount disruptive challenges to the program in the form of strikes or other mass action. All would contain some truth, but all would elide several crucial distinctions.

Foremost among these distinctions is that winning workers' rights for workfare workers might simply have confined WEP workers to the lowest segments of the labor market, enforcing their poverty, and left other aspects of welfare reform untouched. Therefore, it is difficult to see anti-WEP activists' failure to secure these rights as an unequivocal failure. Moreover, we would still want to know how WEP developed *before* Giuliani and what the stakes were in defining the WEP placements as they were defined. Put differently, we would want to know why Giuliani was ruthless on this issue. To figure that out, we will want to put workfare into a fuller political-economic context at a local level and at state and national levels, too. Workfare's outlines were, after all, a matter of state law, and though WEP's expansion predated federal welfare reform by more than a year, the program was enabled by the Clinton administration's commitment to local-level welfare reform experiments and has become a template for further national-level reforms inscribed in the little-debated Deficit Reduction Act of 2005.[4] Similarly, we should ask why DC 37's corruption prevented it from challenging Giuliani on the issue of WEP. One could postulate, as Chad Goldberg did in an early paper on anti-WEP organizing, that union reluctance to organize WEP workers was due in part to municipal workers' distancing strategies with respect to lower-status welfare recipients doing the same work they did.[5] Or, one can point to historical precedents in which efforts to organize workfare workers into DC 37 threatened the power of incumbent leaders, as Vanessa Tait has done.[6] Finally, one ought to be able to account for why a mass mobilization and disruption strategy was not a cornerstone of opposition to WEP and why rallies and shows of solidarity took more-predictable, less-threatening forms. Simple, parsimonious explanations, while attractive, will obscure more than they elucidate here. What the late urbanist Jane Jacobs wrote of the complexity of cities applies here, too: "There is no use wishing it were a simpler problem, or trying to make it a simpler problem, because in real life, it is not a simpler problem."[7]

Like urban political economists drawing on neo-Marxist state theory, I understand workfare to be part of a larger-scale restructuring of contemporary welfare states in a way that also reworks the local state's regulation of labor. Yet, unlike much of this work, I emphasize that this restructuring cannot be, and is not, simply imposed on the existing infrastructure of civil society without some resistance.[8] Drawing on recent research on "actually existing neoliberalism," I argue that workfare was both a money-saving and a labor-disciplining device and a performance of "good government" by the Giuliani administration to an audience of evaluators of public finance. It also restructured relations between nonprofit organizations and the City in such a way as to call into being its own opposition.

Like most students of labor-community coalitions, I take the historical separation of labor and community organizing to be an impediment to a broader politics of social equity and to building trade unionism beyond a narrow "business unionism" and toward a "social-movement unionism" model.[9] In this light, even though activists rarely expressed their goals in this way, anti-WEP organizing challenged the repertoires and routines of organization, claim-making, and action that distinguish labor and community politics in the United States and were an attempt to organize broader-based solidarity against local neoliberalism. Most of this literature does not, however, specify the kinds of coalitions that labor and community groups might form, and much of the scholarship focuses on community support for union drives or against plant closings.[10] Like Frege, Heery, and Turner,[11] I am particularly interested in the substance of the ties within coalitions that determine what *kinds* of coalitions are formed. Moreover, I am interested in the ways in which coalitions among labor and community organizations form and dissolve around particular issues and in a political field populated by complementary or competing coalitions. I find, as the political-cultural sociologist Margaret Somers suggests, that the ability to organize an encompassing class-based political identity bridging the workplace and community relies on a peculiar confluence of relations among anti-WEP activists and authorities in and across specific "relational settings" such as workplaces, the courts, legislatures, and the media.[12] That this confluence is rare does not mean that it is impossible or that failure is overdetermined. Rather, there may be several possible "workable" confluences and several ways in which coalitions may be organized to bring them into being. For students of urban movements, this means, too, that neoliberal urban restructuring has not banished movements of the poor in favor of movements for cultural recognition; rather, it means that movements of the poor must strive for recognition on new grounds, and there is evidence that this is occurring both in anti-WEP politics and in organizing among the low-wage service workers who make up an increasing proportion of the contemporary metropolitan proletariat.[13]

Taking a cue from recent studies of social movements and political claim-making, I understand the importance of relational settings to mean, further, that the ability to make broadly authoritative claims of identity, for rights, and against policies requires the organization within and across settings of coalitions that will provide what the Russian literary theorist Mikhail Bakhtin called "choral support" for these claims.[14] Meaning, therefore, is a relational and situated organizational accomplishment as much as it is a phenomenological occurrence within individuals' heads. It may also be an accomplishment of *disorganization*, where public meanings become secure by default, with their stability relying on their proponents' ability to interfere with potential opponents' attempts to coalesce around reevaluations of available political terms.

If we return to the example of claims for workfare workers' rights *as workers*, it is possible to identify multiple ways in which these rights *were* secured but failed to become hegemonic—that is, to organize political claim-making within and across multiple institutional settings. WEP workers were entitled to workers' compensation if injured at the worksite. They were entitled to use the Public Employee Safety and Health procedure to grieve workplace hazards. They were—after a long court battle—granted the right to protection from sexual and racial harassment under equal employment opportunity law. Nevertheless, their work is still legally defined as compensation for the welfare benefits they receive rather than that which they exchange for remuneration, as are wages. They must still report to worksites designated for them rather than choose their place of work. They are still not recognized as employees for the purposes of collective bargaining. To understand what workers' rights claims *mean* in the context of workfare requires understanding the ways in which the various political actors involved in the debate over workfare position themselves with respect to these institutional venues and to other claims being made within them. For understanding this positioning, Durkheimian approaches to meaning creation that emphasize the negotiation of the boundaries between dualistically defined categories (e.g., "work" and "welfare") are only partially useful. If definitions of work do not always depend on an "other" in welfare, while there is still plenty of negotiation of boundaries, the boundaries multiply well beyond those assumed in a dualistic framework.[15]

The need for more-complex analytical frameworks, in turn, suggests something deeper about cognition that is routinely missed by students of social movements and political claim-making. Studies of "framing," whether in social movements or in more-general political venues (e.g., party politics and elections), frequently treat cognitive processes as a black box, wherein individuals hold socially learned schematas and stories in their heads and match them to their observed experiences and others' claims about them.[16] A view of meaning that emphasizes its dynamic, organizational, and coalitional aspects highlights the *distribution* of cognitive processes within "cultural-historical activity systems" composed of actors, the objects of their actions, the tools or artifacts they use to mediate action toward their objects, *and* the rules and divisions of labor by which their communities operate.[17] If this view is true, controlling the terms of debate requires far more than strategically finding the "right frame." Indeed, activists' own interpretations of what is going on and what is to be done become subject to the structuring influences of the dynamics of the activity system. Nevertheless, lest this seem too overdetermined, it is important to emphasize that these dynamics are shaped by activists' own action and the actions of others. Here, cognition does not precede political action but rather exists in a dynamic, dialectical relation with it.

In the rest of the book, I expand on these themes, and I do so by drawing together a range of mainly neo-Marxist theories that span disciplinary boundaries but which often do not address one another. Though I draw widely from cultural and political sociology, political science, cognitive psychology, and political economy, I find that a strand of thinking that developed in the first half of the twentieth century that joined Marxism with other philosophical, political, linguistic, and cultural inquiry in the early Soviet Union and among Communist activists in Western Europe provides a particularly useful thread with which to stitch together a synthetic analysis of anti-WEP politics. This work includes that of Mikhail Bakhtin and his associates in the early Soviet Union to develop a "dialogical" approach to linguistics and literary theory; the work of Antonio Gramsci, developed mainly in a Fascist prison cell in the 1920s and 1930s in Italy, which sets the groundwork for contemporary urban political economy and critical cultural theory; and the work of Lev Vygotsky, also in the Soviet Union, who pioneered a broadly sociological approach to cognitive development and whose theories form one basis for contemporary approaches in educational theory and even in artificial intelligence. All of these thinkers attempted to understand the ways in which the history of institutions both weighs upon and is remade by the creative interaction of people who do not, and cannot, stand outside that history.

I will return to these issues later in the chapter and throughout in the book. For now, it will be most useful to turn to the development of the politics of workfare in New York, in order to anchor both the theory and the analysis.

Workfare and Contention in New York City, 1995–2004

Few policy changes during the 1990s more clearly revealed the sea change in the role of the federal government in social welfare than the welfare reform act signed into law by President Bill Clinton in August 1996. The Personal Responsibility and Work Opportunity Reconciliation Act of 1996 (PRWORA) codified many aspects of welfare-state change that neoliberals had promoted in theory and through smaller-scale examples for more than ten years: PRWORA ended national entitlements to income support; devolved administrative power and funding to state and local governments; encouraged rapid reduction of welfare expenditures through fiscal incentives to state governments; and enforced work and administrative obstacles to aid—in a word, austerity—on the poor.[18]

By the time PRWORA was signed into law, dozens of states had already experimented with welfare reforms of their own, through waivers granted by the Department of Health and Human Services under the administrations of both George H. W. Bush and Bill Clinton. One of the most radical and far-reaching reforms occurred in New York City, where Mayor Rudolph Giuliani's administration instituted a workfare, or "work experience," program that put welfare recipients to work in city agencies and nonprofit organizations to an unprecedented extent. WEP is a mandatory program requiring welfare recipients to work as a condition of receiving welfare. No other state or city embarked on as ambitious a public-sector workfare program as did New York during the Giuliani years. Since then, WEP and its complement of administrative reforms emphasizing labor-force attachment to the exclusion of other aspects of welfare provision (e.g., education and training) have become one of several models for a new round of national welfare reforms that promise to build on the state and local experiments of the 1990s.[19]

Prologue

Workfare has existed in New York City since the early 1970s, when small-scale experiments with work requirements accompanied President Nixon's welfare reform plans. But it was only after New York's notorious fiscal crisis of the 1970s, when the city nearly went bankrupt, that workfare expanded under the mayoral administration of Edward I. Koch. In the late 1970s, the Koch administration instituted a wider-scale application of a 1971 workfare program, called the Public Works Program (PWP), an expansion which put welfare recipients into city agency jobs alongside municipal workers. The main municipal workers' union, District Council 37 (DC 37) of the American Federation of State, County, and Municipal Employees (AFSCME), cried foul and attempted to win collective bargaining and representation rights for PWP workers from the City's Office of Collective Bargaining.[20] Though the effort failed, the program was scaled back as the city's finances began to recover, and the Koch administration found it more useful to build political support among municipal workers than to save money by using welfare recipients to displace them.

Workfare expanded again, along with some new conditions for receiving it, under Koch's successor, David Dinkins. Under Dinkins, the program enlisted mainly adults without dependent children in the state's Home Relief (HR) program. During the early 1990s, about ten thousand HR workers were engaged in workfare activities, many doing clerical tasks in the Human Resources Administration (HRA), the city's welfare department. In 1988, before Dinkins was elected, Congress passed the Family Support Act (FSA), which required adults with children in the Aid to Families with Dependent Children (AFDC) program—unlike HR, partially federally funded—to work, enter job training, or engage in educational activities. Under Dinkins, the FSA program, known as BEGIN (Begin Employment Gain Independence Now), encumbered the receipt of welfare with obligations on the part of welfare recipients but did not involve mandatory work assignments.

Dinkins, however, faced a steep recession after the stock market decline of 1987, and by 1989, the city had acute financial problems. Moreover, the city's bond raters and creditors, concerned that Dinkins's electoral coalition—which included African Americans, Latinos, and large city unions, the groups that they blamed for the profligacy that led to the fiscal crisis in the 1970s—would demand too much of the city's money, forced Dinkins to abandon his base and lay off more than fifteen thousand city employees. These layoffs contributed to Dinkins's failed reelection bid and to the subsequent election of Rudolph Giuliani as mayor.[21]

Fishy Beginnings

In the late 1980s, Westchester County, New York City's generally affluent suburban neighbor, instituted a workfare program inspired by a mass fish kill. Mary Glass, the county's welfare commissioner, could not mobilize a program fast enough to clean up the thousands of dead fish that washed up on Westchester's beaches. She realized then, however, that the county could use welfare recipients to do nasty tasks that nobody else wanted to do. Soon, with the blessing of county executive Andrew O'Rourke (who received welfare benefits in childhood), Westchester County had a burgeoning workfare program that O'Rourke credited for rapid caseload reductions and labor savings.[22]

Giuliani immediately took interest in the program and began to talk in public about emulating it. New York City, whose income distribution was becoming more unequal by the day,[23] also had the largest number of welfare recipients in the country, surpassing 1.2 million, or just under one-sixth of its population. In late 1994, the mayor undertook plans to expand the workfare program. First, he co-opted the weak and increasingly corrupt leadership of DC 37, an umbrella organization of fifty-six locals representing city employees of all sorts. The two large unions at its core are made powerful by a bloc-voting system that gives the two largest unions the controlling votes in the district council. One large local represents clerical workers. It had had many workfare workers in its shops for years. Giuliani targeted the leader of the other local as an ally in a workfare-based apprenticeship program in which welfare recipients would move into vacancies in union jobs where possible.[24] Though the program remained minuscule, the union president, Dr. Charles Hughes, who was in the process of embezzling from his union, was loath to criticize workfare locally, even as it expanded greatly throughout the municipal labor structure.

When, in 1995, the Giuliani administration rolled out the NYC-WAY (New York City-Work, Accountability, and You) program, its package of welfare reforms, it met little immediate opposition, and hardly any from DC 37, which had opposed more vigorously Koch's similar program. NYC-WAY included mandatory workfare assignments for able-bodied single adults, with a phasein of parents within the year. Assignments were in municipal agencies and in a handful of state agencies and non-profits with contracts with the City.[25] The required hours were calculated by dividing the total value of the recipient's cash benefits, shelter allowance (the portion of the welfare check set aside for housing), and food stamps and then dividing this result by the minimum wage, which was then $4.15 per hour. The average workweek was roughly twenty hours for an HR recipient, thirty-five for an AFDC recipient. Education and training programs were curtailed and could not count toward work requirements. Community college and university students on welfare were no longer able to count their internships or work-study jobs toward BEGIN work credits. The application process was encumbered by finger imaging and more-intrusive eligibility investigations with inspectors trained from an adapted detective manual, and sanctions for noncompliance with rules both at the workplace and in the welfare administration process were more widely applied.

Contention Begins

By late 1995, welfare recipients had become acutely aware of the changes in the program. By the spring of 1996, when parents began to be called into WEP, the program had already expanded nearly twofold from its pre-Giuliani incarnation. Welfare recipients began to seek help from community organizations and antipoverty groups. Three organizations, whose organizers knew one another through previously established activist networks, combined resources to form a WEP worker-organizing project called WEP Workers Together, or WWT. The three groups were the Fifth Avenue Committee (FAC), Community Voices Heard (CVH), and the Urban Justice Center (UJC). FAC, founded in 1977, is a community group in Brooklyn formed to organize tenants to fight landlord abandonment and to fight gentrification during the fiscal crisis; it had become a leader in nonprofit affordable housing and community development. Community Voices Heard, formed in 1996 as a membership-based organization, spun off from a statewide antihunger group. The lead organizer and director of CVH had spent years organizing homeless people in the city's shelter system in order to press for improvements in it. UJC is the reorganized version of the Legal Action Center for the Homeless, founded in 1984 in an East Harlem storefront. As UJC, it branched out from homeless advocacy and litigation to broader efforts on behalf of immigrant workers, sex workers, and other underrepresented groups. It also launched a grassroots-organizing project. Together, as WWT, the groups began by organizing workfare workers at their worksites. Cognizant of its limited resources, WWT sought, at first, to show unions that WEP workers were *organizable,* hoping that a union might devote the requisite resources either to engage in joint organizing or to take over the organizing altogether.[26]

By the end of 1996, two other groups were organizing workfare workers at worksites. The most prominent was the Association of Community Organizations for Reform Now (ACORN), a national organization of community-based groups that advocates for low- and moderate-income urbanites. Founded in 1970 as a membership-building project of the National Welfare Rights Organization, ACORN spread to twenty-eight states and became a leader in affordable housing campaigns throughout the 1980s.[27] The other group, Work*fairness,* was an all-volunteer effort by activists involved in the International Action Center and Workers World Party. Using some long-standing ties to black radicals and to some union leaders, Work*fairness* initially held large rallies of workfare workers to demand an end to the program.[28]

Nevertheless, the program expanded apace. Several unions, including DC 37, cried foul when the Metropolitan Transit Authority reached an agreement with the Transport Workers' Union to replace five hundred union cleaners with WEP workers—a deal ultimately torpedoed by Mayor Giuliani, who did not want direct displacement of public employees to be a rallying cry for a labor-community alliance.[29] But neither DC 37 nor many other unions actively joined in the organizing, taking a wait-and-see approach.

By early 1997, a complex field of organizations had developed around the politics of workfare. Antipoverty advocacy groups, the organizing groups, several city unions, several progressive religious congregations, some DC 37 staff (and inconsistently, its leaders), and the local chapter of Jobs with Justice—a community-labor alliance-building organization—had all expressed opposition to WEP and particularly its tendency to use welfare recipients to replace unionized workers. They protested in a variety of forums, including the press and city council committee hearings chaired by Stephen DiBrienza, a frequent critic of Giuliani. Working closely with the organizing groups to find plaintiffs, legal advocates such as the National Employment Law Project (NELP), the Welfare Law Center (WLC), and the Legal Aid Society brought class-action lawsuits challenging the use of minimum wages to calculate WEP workers' hours, conditions at WEP worksites, assessment procedures for welfare recipients, and denial of educational and training opportunities.

Hot Summer, Chilly Spring

In mid-1997, the New York State government began to finalize welfare reform legislation that would bring it into compliance with PRWORA, signed by President Clinton the year before. Though DC 37 failed in its effort to get the state legislature to adopt language giving WEP workers the rights of "employees," it won stronger antidisplacement language and a legal commitment for the City to give the union data on WEP placements throughout City agencies.[30] At the same time, welfare reform at the state level ratified nearly all of NYC-WAY, some of which had earlier been of dubious legality.[31] The state's refusal to grant workfare workers "employee" rights meant that unions had little incentive to participate in workplace organizing. Without the collective bargaining framework that employee status would impart, there was little apparent net benefit in having a union, rather than a community-based organization, represent WEP workers.

Though worksite-based organizing continued, it began to be challenged as the preeminent strategy for fighting WEP. Under a new organizing director, UJC switched its focus from worksite organizing to mobilizing a conscience-based constituency. Working closely with Judson Memorial Church, a progressive congregation with a pastor who had long experience in the labor movement, UJC launched a WEP Campaign of Resistance. In this campaign, nonprofit service providers and congregations were asked to sign a Pledge of Resistance committing them to resist City pressure to become WEP worksites in what was widely expected to be the next frontier of WEP's expansion. In July, the inaugural press conference of the Pledge of Resistance campaign made front-page news in the *New York Times*, setting off several weeks of inconclusive but spirited debate in local and national newspapers about the morality of WEP and of workfare in general.

Meanwhile, ACORN pressed ahead with its own campaign to organize WEP workers *as workers* regardless of its ability to involve unions. By far the largest among the organizing groups, ACORN had already exported this strategy to other cities' antiworkfare activities. In July, it delivered sixteen thousand cards to city hall expressing support for an ACORN-led WEP workers' union, signed by workfare workers encountered primarily at worksites. In October, continuing to mimic a union drive mediated by the National Labor Relations Board, ACORN held an election seeking authorization from workfare workers to represent them as a union.

A blue-ribbon panel of politicians, clergy, and labor leaders recruited by ACORN and Jobs with Justice oversaw the election, held in October 1997, just before Giuliani's election to a second term. Already, by August, however, many municipal unions—including DC 37 and most of its locals—were lining up to support the mayor's reelection, mainly out of a conviction that his challenger could not win and that it was important to support Giuliani if they hoped to bargain with him productively in the future. The unions' support for Giuliani both heightened the implicit critique of unions within the ACORN vote and reduced the impact that the vote might have in terms of the public debate about WEP workers' rights as workers.

At the same time, chastened by state welfare reform and facing internal differences in organizing strategy, WWT split apart and became a project supported by FAC alone. Nevertheless, CVH and FAC worked in concert and on parallel tracks toward legislative programs that would create "transitional jobs" that were alternatives to WEP. CVH, working with NELP and a union-backed research and policy advocacy group in Albany, put together a statewide coalition for community-based job creation that managed to win funding but no programmatic outlines within a year and a half. WWT led the formation of a citywide coalition to push similar legislation through city council, a coalition in which both NELP and CVH were central members, too.

By the end of 1997, a focus on WEP workers' rights and identity *as workers* was giving way to, or at least increasingly coexisting with, a focus on WEP workers as *potential workers*, whose primary needs were education, training, and child care.

During this period, in the spring of 1998, the Giuliani administration also lost its union allies and some of its friendly support in the local press. First, it announced layoffs at City hospitals in which WEP workers were still working. Though the hospital workers' union leader was a DC 37 local president who was critical of Giuliani, it put Stanley Hill, DC 37's executive director and a Giuliani ally, on the spot. As Giuliani's relationship with Hill soured, anger over workfare escalated within the union and became a symbol of Hill's poor leadership. In its media relations, the Giuliani administration's incessant touting of its success in trimming its welfare caseload invited questions about how welfare recipients had fared. Here, the administration was so secretive that the *Times* and other news outlets took it to court to gain basic information on program outcomes.

Shifting the Focus and Running Out the Clock

Also in the spring of 1998, the Giuliani administration replaced the longtime civil servant at the helm of HRA, bringing in Jason A. Turner, Wisconsin's welfare chief, who led that state's dramatic, nationally acclaimed reductions in welfare caseloads.[32] Accompanied by a team of welfare reformers tied to conservative think tanks, Turner pledged to remake New York's welfare system so as to hasten the demise of welfare altogether.[33] Rather than focusing on expanding workfare, Turner and Giuliani sought to encumber the application process for welfare. Though workfare placements continued to grow, the number of new recipients declined. More dramatic was the increased number of applicants for welfare who were rejected or "diverted." Many of them were also prevented from applying immediately for federal entitlements such as Medicaid and food stamps.[34] The administration's efforts to block the front end of the welfare pipeline and Giuliani's renewed efforts (he had tried early in NYC-WAY's expansion) to require WEP as a condition of receiving emergency homeless shelter landed the administration in court opposing legal advocates for welfare recipients.

The advocates resorted to court when, in 2000, Giuliani refused to implement the transitional jobs program that the WWT-led coalition finally passed through the city council, withstanding a mayoral veto. In the meantime, too, dramatic changes in the DC 37 leadership, following a wide-ranging corruption scandal, led the union—now under trusteeship from its national affiliate—to take a more dramatic stance against WEP than it had under Stanley Hill. Worksite organizing had already been nearly eclipsed in 1999, so DC 37 launched a series of lawsuits that drew on the state social services law's antidisplacement language in order to enjoin WEP.[35] Yet, by inviting all this litigation, the Giuliani administration was able to defer decisions about workfare for a long time, often until after the mayor anticipated leaving office. He withdrew from a U.S. Senate campaign in 1999, as prostate cancer and a publicly failing marriage undermined his ability to campaign.

Giuliani did, however, implement his own jobs program, the Parks Opportunity Program (POP), after being taken to court over his failure to implement the city council's transitional jobs bill in early 2001. Over the next year, POP created nearly ten thousand 11 1/2-month jobs for welfare recipients, primarily those whose federal welfare benefits were expiring due to PRWORA's five-year lifetime limit on federal benefits receipt. POP workers had employee rights and were unionized even though they were seasonal employees. Pay was nearly ten dollars an hour. Though it provided no education or training, POP provided better pay for more welfare-recipients-turned-workers than did the city council bill. The program was mainly funded by using federal funds left over from PRWORA block grants. Therefore the City maintained its workforce in the Parks and other agencies, without having to rely solely on state and local funds.

The Aftermath of Disaster and a Policy Shift

The fall of 2001 was, of course, marked by disaster. The attacks on the World Trade Center plunged the city into economic and emotional depression for months. Politically, the attacks created several odd local effects. First, the attacks boosted Mayor Giuliani's political fortunes, which had severely declined in the previous two years. Second, the attacks came on primary election day for the Democratic mayoral candidates. The vote had to be rescheduled for the next month. In that month, the Democratic Party imploded in racial recriminations, and some of its black and Latino base either stayed home on Election Day or supported the liberal Republican, Michael Bloomberg, who was endorsed by Giuliani.

Just before leaving office, the Giuliani administration sought to transfer POP contracts to a for-profit temporary employment agency, which would mean that workers in the POP program would take a two-dollar-per-hour pay cut and lose union status. CVH, DC 37, and other groups successfully mobilized to block such a transfer as Bloomberg took office and withdrew the contract.[36]

Encouraging as this victory was, it did not augur a sea change in welfare policy. Nevertheless, the City's approach began to appear less ideological than it had under Mayor Giuliani. Bloomberg did not rehire Turner or most of his top aides for jobs in his HRA. Turner, who had a history of questionable ethical dealings with respect to contracting, became a fellow at the Heritage Foundation, a conservative policy organization in Washington, D.C. Bloomberg turned to Verna Eggleston, a Republican, African American, nonprofit social service agency head, to run HRA. Under Eggleston, HRA created a client advisory group, which introduced at least some semblance of corporatism, as it included representatives from CVH and ACORN.

Yet, Eggleston was still hostile to welfare and, like her predecessor, saw even food stamps as fostering a culture of dependency. Nevertheless, she was more open to the inclusion of educational and training activities in workfare programs. As a result, opportunities opened for the

Welfare Rights Initiative (WRI), a group of welfare recipient-students at Hunter College in the City University system. WRI was founded in 1996 to safeguard educational opportunities for welfare recipients in the face of mounting workfare requirements. In 2000, WRI successfully led a coalition to pass state legislation allowing student internships and work-study jobs to count toward workfare requirements. With FAC and other anti-WEP groups, it then became a key player in CATE, the Coalition for Access to Training and Education, which sought city council legislation to allow education and training activities themselves to count toward workfare requirements. Though the council passed the bill, Bloomberg vetoed it. After the council overrode the veto, the case went to court, where it was eventually decided in the mayor's favor, as was earlier litigation over transitional jobs. In both cases, the crux of the legal decision rested not on the merits of the program but on the balance of powers between the mayor and city council.

At the same time, the administration settled a lawsuit begun in 1996, challenging the assessment process for welfare recipients and the denial of education and training possibilities to them. The settlement in the *Davila* case, as it was called, required the City to inform welfare recipients of their rights to education and training and to give them a list of approved service providers.

POP, however, fared less well. Taking advantage of renewed internal conflict between reformers and union officials at DC 37, the Bloomberg administration sought to cut POP workers' pay in the face of large deficits. While the union local president, Mark Rosenthal, a reformer, was willing to negotiate, the new executive director of DC 37, Lillian Roberts, was not. As a result, POP workers took a pay cut, jobs were transferred to six-month status, and the jobs were lost to the union.[37]

In general, however, under Bloomberg, fewer welfare recipients have been put into "pure WEP"—that is, WEP assignments without training or educational supplements—which continues a trend begun under Turner. No longer stressing "work first," the mantra of early workfare advocates, the new model stresses "full engagement," or maintaining a work-program-job-search regimen for all welfare recipients in a somewhat less-uniform manner. Nevertheless, WEP as a form of labor contract still exists; WEP still has nearly twenty thousand participants in New York City; and work-first programs remain the keystone of further rounds of welfare reform. These reforms, including those touted by Turner, were quietly worked into a budget bill in 2006, passing, as many Bush administration initiatives have, with little debate and little public fanfare.[38]

Yet, locally, the enthusiasm for increased work requirements for welfare recipients is muted, even within the Bloomberg administration; it is also muted among many governors, even Republican ones, because it will create enormous administrative problems, be insensitive to local labor market conditions, and change the ways in which these governors can divert welfare funds to other uses.[39]

Thus, the terms of debate have changed since 1995 and NYC-WAY's expansion. Opponents of workfare speak much less than they did in the idiom of workers' rights; proponents speak in less-universalistic terms about the morality of work and social contractualism. A decade after its expansion, workfare (the Work Experience Program in particular) remains essentially contested and blurrily defined politically.

Theoretical Concerns

This book is organized around a basic question in political sociology: How are political subjects defined? The case of contention over workfare's expansion in New York City convinced me that many of the ways of answering this question were inadequate, either because they treated cultural processes as disembodied from the contexts within which contending and cooperating political actors communicated or because they treated these definitional processes as flowing directly from rational responses to these contexts. The former problems are fairly typical of "framing" approaches in the study of social movements (in spite of this perspective's pragmatist roots) and of structuralist approaches to identity formation, such as Jeffery Alexander's neo-Durkheimian sociology. The latter problems are typical of formalistic approaches to social movements, such as the increasingly depoliticized political process model and the more-encompassing rational-choice theories to which it is related.[40] I was faced with more complexity than any of these approaches could handle well.

The history I have just presented is complex, but it is one of obvious interest to scholars of welfare policy, welfare-state restructuring, urban politics, and political movements. Yet it is also a history that, in its complexity, can help cultural analysts untangle the mediations between public representations and actors' attempts to make meaningful claims and the institutional settings within which these attempts occur. Conversely, the complexity allows political economists interested in neoliberalism to understand the mediations between larger trends in the regulation of capitalism and capitalist societies and the cultural consequences of the institutions created or reformed to achieve new regulatory projects. For those interested in organizational features of social movement coalitions, the history allows analysis of both the larger institutional environment within which such coalitions form and the cultural material that ties coalitions of political claim makers together. Put differently, the analysis of complexity I propose here approaches the history of anti-WEP organizing from the "standpoint of totality," so that each part of the analysis—which must proceed by means of heuristic simplifications—preserves rather than banishes complexity by methodological sleight of hand.

Relations, Regulation, and Repertoires

What is workfare? Why does it take the form it does? How does the form it takes influence the strategies that others use to oppose it? On one reading, there is little new about workfare. The requirement to work as a condition of receiving aid—the least-eligibility principle, so called because even the meanest work was meant to be preferable to receiving relief—has been a mainstay of public-relief efforts since at least the seventeenth century in Europe. Times in which public relief was not conditioned on work have been relatively rare, in large part because there is a fundamental link between the expansion and contraction of public relief and the relative need of capital for labor. When capital needs more labor, relief contracts, and vice versa. Of course, this is a tendency realized over the long term rather than an automatic response to fluctuations in markets. Nevertheless, as Frances Fox Piven and Richard A. Cloward argued in 1971, the arrangements of public relief are such that even part of their geographic variability can be understood as responses to the geographic scope of labor markets.[41]

If work requirements for relief are understood as labor-regulatory programs, however, this gives analytical leverage for answering what *is* new about workfare. Here, it is useful to think in terms of what is called *regulation theory* in political economy. Based originally on Gramsci's insights into the development of distinctive cultures of economic governance in his essay "Americanism and Fordism," regulation theory focuses on the institutions of economic regulation and their cultural and legal consequences.[42] Specifically, like other neo-Marxist state theory, it suggests that there is an inherent tension or contradiction between the requirement that capitalist states foster private capital accumulation (if for no other reason than the functional one that states require capital to tax) and the requirement that the state claim *general* legitimacy, even as the fostering of capital accumulation often works against the immediate interests of the majority. Since this is a fundamental tension, it cannot be resolved once and for all.[43] Instead, regulation theorists identify core sets of institutional performances (e.g., national collective bargaining regimes, welfare programs, business-development tax incentives, regulatory devolution) and cultural performances (e.g., antidrug crusades, ethnonationalist rhetoric) by state actors that are meant to stabilize periodic "crises of accumulation" or "crises of legitimation." These "modes of regulation" are contingent matches with "regimes of accumulation"—that is, the form of the latter does not dictate the former—but do, over time, congeal into identifiable repertoires of governance. Hence, regulation theorists identify a period of "Atlantic Fordism" in industrialized countries—marked by the institution of collective bargaining regimes, high wages, industrial discipline, and Keynesian, countercyclical welfare policy—that entered into crisis in the early 1970s. Regulation theorists argue about the particular configurations of "post-Fordism" and about whether any clear set of regulatory performances has congealed into a post-Fordist repertoire. Nevertheless, it is clear that the imposition of workfare as a way of (1) scaling back long-run welfare-state expenditures on income support and (2) preparing workers to accept increasingly contingent labor contracts is part of many analytic formulations of post-Fordism. The British sociologist Bob Jessop has written about the replacement of the Keynesian welfare state by the "Schumpeterian Post-national Workfare Regime." In doing so, he highlights the emphasis within a new regulatory repertoire on economic flexibility, geographic restructuring of capital and labor flows, workfare, and the importance of coalitional composition to the actual formulation of policy on multiple levels of governance. As a result, Jessop indicates that there are multiple coalitional possibilities under post-Fordism, only one of which is a hard neoliberalism, or a reductive market orientation combined with an eviscerated welfare state, even though it appears as the dominant direction that the post-Fordist "solution" is now taking.[44]

With these ideas in the background, it is easier to make sense of why workfare in New York City was implemented in the manner it was in 1995. Two principal factors contributed to the program's form. First, municipal unions were weakened by layoffs during the City's second acute fiscal crisis in twenty years. Public-sector workplaces were thus a soft target for workfare placements. Second, the mounting national criticism of welfare, and triangulating acceptance of this criticism by centrist Democrats touting government "reinvention," cleared the way for workfare to appear as a cutting-edge social policy, touted by good-government reformers.

Locally, however, workfare met with little demand from New York City's business leaders for large wage savings, perhaps since the value of wages and real income had been on a steady decline for the lower quintile of workers in the City for a quarter century. Together, these factors fostered the rapid expansion of workfare in the *public sector,* where it could further undermine union power. Thus, what Jessop has called "neocorporatist" power sharing, typified by previous levels of public-sector union power, was undermined on the urban scale.

Peck has gone further to speculate that where labor markets are slack—that is, where there are a lot of jobs for fewer applicants—workfare tends to be implemented in the private sector, where it has the ability to depress wages and foster capital accumulation; and that where labor markets are tight, workfare oriented toward the public sector or nonprofit sector is the norm. He further notes that the sectoral placement of workfare activates different kinds of oppositional strategies: private-sector placements may produce boycotts but few organizing drives due to the difficulty in concentrating many workfare workers dispersed among worksites; nonprofit-sector placements may generate moral protest and noncooperation campaigns; and public-sector placements are most susceptible to union-like organizing drives.[45] To a large degree, this prediction (or distillation of experience) holds true for New York, as the history I outlined earlier in this chapter suggests. Certainly, public-sector placements generated worksite-based organizing, and the threat of expanded nonprofit-sector placements generated moral campaigning against the program. On the other hand, it is most useful for predicting starting positions, since this history shows considerable change in the strategies, claims, and coalitional orientations of anti-WEP activists as debates around the program developed. Moreover, as Peck and Jessop indicate, to the extent that local policy entrepreneurs promote their welfare policies as "good governance" practices to larger audiences, policies may be transferred to places in which the economic precursors no longer hold. Therefore, for example, the increased work requirements in the reauthorization of federal welfare reform may push more localities to implement public-sector workfare programs where they had not done so before.[46]

Coalitions, Cohesion, and Claims

How, then, do we understand the ways in which economic and social regulation articulates with oppositional politics? Can we link broad questions about political-economic regulatory repertoires with more micro-

or mesolevel processes of political claim-making? How, for example, do we understand the ways in which claims about WEP changed from ones focused initially on workers' rights to a more diffuse set of claims that prominently featured claims for education and training? To some degree, one can argue that this shift was occasioned by shifts, undertaken by the Giuliani and Bloomberg administrations from 2000 onward, away from five-day WEP workweeks. But the shifts in discourse happened before then and arguably resulted in policy shifts, rather than the other way around.

A more promising approach comes from work both in linguistic- and literary-theoretically informed cultural sociology and in the study of movements. The first premise of the approach I take here is that social movements are best understood as multiorganizational phenomena rather than as unitary movements.[47] As such, they occupy what some sociologists have taken to calling a "field," in which organizations interact and in which symbolic and material resources are distributed, usually unevenly, resulting in varying types and degrees of power both in the field as a whole and among the various actors. David Meyer insists that the baseline unit of analysis for social movement studies should be the coalition rather that the single social movement organization (SMO).[48] Moreover, he urges analysts to focus on the ways in which these coalitions reshape the coalitions that political scientists have long understood form to develop and implement public policies. To understand what binds multiorganizational coalitions and the claims they make, therefore, is to begin to ask a deeper question about the ways in which particular political claims gain or lose broader currency among a diverse range of political actors.

Clearly, this is not a new question for students of social protest. Nevertheless, it is one that still requires development. The dominant lenses for the analysis of political culture and cultural dynamics in politics have been in transition for nearly ten years. One such lens has been *framing theory* in the study of social movements. Framing theory focuses on the ways in which social movement actors use symbols to mobilize participants and spur them into action. Early pivotal articles in this vein emphasized the ways in which social movement actors "aligned" their frames—focused on diagnosing, prognosticating, and building identity around social injustices—with the experiences and cultural frameworks of potential audiences.[49] Framing theory has been criticized—mainly sympathetically—from two principal angles. First, Francesca Polletta and others interested in *narratives* have emphasized the importance of storytelling in mobilization, and they have argued that narratives—which place actors in space and time—are both more ambiguous and more compelling than the specifically targeted, often categorical statements of framing.[50] In the context of WEP politics, therefore, one might argue that claims for education and training located WEP workers in a developmental narrative, in which—at the sacrifice of clarifying their current status as workers, welfare recipients, and so on—it is argued that they would gain the status of independent workers in the future. This narrative strategy would help mobilize a coalition because it would reduce the potential costs of staking a definitional claim up front.

A second, related line of critique of framing theory is that it is insufficiently attentive both to the historical development of political claims and to the interactive dynamics of framing activity. Exponents of this criticism, such as Marc Steinberg and Colin Barker,[51] have relied on the literary and linguistic theory of the Bakhtin circle. Bakhtin and his collaborators—most notably Valentin Vološinov—argued that meanings were neither a question of mapping claims onto others' templates nor one of activating associations that were "out there" in an objective structure of culture. Instead, they asserted, people operate within institutionalized settings, in which certain kinds of claims are *already* more likely to be made and understood by their interlocutors. These institutionalized collections of claims or speech acts, which Bakhtin calls "genres," are conventions to which interlocutors generally adhere but with which they can always improvise.[52] Within genres, there is always a tug-of-war between specificity and ambiguity, between new uses of words and the blurring of genre boundaries and conventional speech that reconfirms them, between "centrifugal" and "centripetal" forces of dialogue. Bakhtin thus occupies a ground between the pragmatism of framing theory and the structuralism of more objective, structuralist approaches to culture that might, for example, point to the enduring dualism of the welfare-work distinction as a key structuring force in meaning making about WEP. For those working with Bakhtinian theory—as I will in this book—the objective will be to track the development, within and across what Margaret Somers has called concrete "relational settings" of consensus and dissensus around claims about WEP,[53] rather than to try to discern whether these claims either resonate with the phenomenological, experientially based templates of political actors or approach one or another ostensibly more stable pole of meaning about welfare and work.

Understanding meaning to be generated from interactions rooted in institutionalized genres within concrete settings clarifies two problems.

First, it shows what network-analytical sociologists have called the "duality" of culture and practice, that is, the ways in which claims, to become authoritative at all, must be used in similar ways by coalitions of actors and, conversely, the ways in which coalitions are bound together and defined—at least in part—by their common use of claims.[54] Second, it draws a link back to Gramsci by suggesting that the ways in which the relational settings of workfare take shape—for example, what the characteristics of WEP placements are in spatial (e.g., dispersion of workers) or temporal (e.g., rate of turnover) terms—may play a large role in the ability of particular genres of claim-making to gain traction in particular settings.

This link to Gramsci raises two further issues that I will address later in the book but to which I will just gesture now. First, Gramsci, like Bakhtin, was concerned with authorities' ability to determine the terms of debate by exerting considerable "centripetal" force on public dialogue through the manipulation of settings and their cultural content. *Hegemony,* a term most closely associated with Gramsci's cultural writings, is therefore not just another term for dominant ideology that secures consent from the masses for their own oppression. Rather, it is a configurational outcome—Gramsci uses metaphors of trench warfare—in which actors with a coalitional project (e.g., a neoliberal project) organize in such a way as to have their claims be important reference points, even for opponents' attempts to make counterclaims. By making their claims indispensable elements of others' attempts to make public sense, hegemonic actors interfere with the organization of alternatives. Second, Gramsci's attention to political configurations suggests that we can understand the ways in which social and economic regulation articulates with oppositional politics by gauging the extent to which authorities and challengers can populate one another's discourse and hold their own together. It is therefore important, too, to take into account another aspect of social movement coalitions, namely, the strength of the ties that bind them and their consequent ability to organize sets of claims within and among relational settings and across genres and to resist being pushed into new positions or buried in the trenches they occupy.

Katznelson's classic application of Gramsci's trench-warfare metaphor in *City Trenches* makes the point that working-class interests have set public agendas when more-encompassing ideologies have helped bridge the gulf between the genres or repertoires of workplace politics (in the United States, a language of class combined with trade or, more rarely, industrial unionism) and those of the home community (a combination of religious and ethnic languages and institutions, including electoral coalitions).[55] This point is repeated elsewhere in labor history and in the emerging literature on labor-community coalitions in the United States. For WEP's opponents, finding the links that could bind labor unions with welfare recipients, antipoverty advocates with community organizations, and all of these to bridging institutions such as courts, elected officials, and the mass media, was an ongoing, fractured project of coalition building.

Genres, Positions, and Mechanisms

Steinberg quotes Bakhtin: "The life of the word is contained in its transfer from one context to another, from one social collective to another, from one generation to another . . . [but it] cannot completely free itself from the power of the concrete contexts into which it has entered."[56] The Bakhtinian concept of genre includes the concept of a "chronotope" or the temporal and spatial profiles that genres accumulate as they are used and refashioned through dialogue.[57] This idea can make tractable, in more specific terms than can framing theory, the difficulty that anti-WEP activists from community organizations and unions had in making workers' rights claims even when DC 37's leadership changed in 1999 and the new leaders showed considerably more willingness to make them a cornerstone of their opposition to WEP. By then, workers' rights claims, as a genre of oppositional claims, were too confined to worksite organizing and thus also too confined to the temporal constraint of ameliorating workfare workers' short-term worksite conditions, as opposed to their long-term access to income, to be the coalitional glue they once had been. At the same time, workers' rights claims had been limited in their effectiveness in part because they were not made consistently by DC 37, the group that most observers believed had the greatest stake—with the possible exception of WEP workers—in rolling back the program.

The several factors pushing and pulling on the importance of workers' rights claims, finally, illuminate the complexity of the theoretical problems posed by the complex history of workfare politics. There is an interplay among the spatiotemporal aspects of claim-making repertoires or genres, the relational settings within which they form the basis of interaction among WEP's opponents, bystanders, and supporters, and the coalitional dynamics that result in wider or narrower support one or another set of claims. In order to get a handle on this play of forces, I turn to network-analytical methods, which, though often understood as static and overly structural, can help organize our analysis of changing configurations of claims, settings, and organizational actors. Following Charles Tilly's work on changing repertoires of protest in Great Britain and Ann Mische's work on the intersection of network relations and the pragmatics of claim-making, and combining these with a concern for the creation of centrifugal and centripetal forces of claim-making within the field of WEP politics, I draw on these methods to map the developing dialogues about WEP over time.[58] In so doing, I identify a set of "mechanisms," or patterned sets of interaction, that result in changes in the configuration of genres and in the power of actors and claims in the field. While drawing on the language of mechanisms from Tilly's, Mische's, and others' work in social movements, I draw these moments of structured agency that result from the interaction of multiple actors out of their narrowly relational context and back into a broader analysis of their generation within settings nested in larger hegemonic and regulatory projects. Therefore, on the level of discursive interaction, I can chart the ways in which the Pledge of Resistance's moral claims about workfare give way to ones emphasizing efficient program management as hegemonic; I can also work backward into the case to understand why the coalition pushing moral protest broke apart and why the settings within which its members connected were eclipsed in importance by others.

Claims, Cognition, and Contradictions

The danger of a broadly synthetic project is that it can easily appear that all the action in the history I tell is "overdetermined" and that actors' consciousness is beside the point, at best. This is particularly true when network methods are introduced and actors and claims are reduced mathematically to cold, unfeeling data points. Nevertheless, this reduction is a useful heuristic, a methodological stab at complexity, rather than an ontological elision of it. Yet framing theorists and proponents of Bakhtinian dialogic theory might still be aghast. All of the habitual and strategic action, and the creative action occurring between them, within dialogue among actors who evaluate—often emotionally—the speech of others at every turn, could simply be understood to be determined at a higher level of analysis, one in which macrosocial forces shape the relational settings within which these actors operate.

I hope not to convey this impression. Consciousness counts, and people create aspects of their own settings. But they also change their interpretations of these settings, the limitations they impose, and the creative possibilities they enable. They often do so, moreover, without consciously knowing it. In other words, even for politically savvy, engaged activists, changes of mind occur, *to some degree*, behind their backs. Framing theory does not contemplate the possibility that people can be creative without their completely understanding their creative processes or extent of their creations. The reason is that it—like many theoretical tendencies in sociology—treats cognition as process that unfolds in people's heads.

The Gramscian-Bakhtinian approach that I develop here suggests important links not only with recent work in cognitive sociology[59] (some of which shares the same pitfalls as the dualist, objective cultural sociology I mentioned earlier) but also with a sociological approach to cognition pioneered by Gramsci and Bakhtin's contemporary Lev Vygotsky and by the inheritors of his program. Many writers have noted the analytical links between Bakhtinian dialogic theory and Vygotsky's cognitive psychology. I will mention a few of these links when I develop the argument later in the book. My main concern, however, is to emphasize the importance of understanding consciousness and cognition without reducing our inquiry to psychological states or intracranial processes and thus political or any other kind of creativity to a sort of unexplainable grace.

In the service of this goal, I introduce one strand of Vygotskian theory, called Cultural Historical Activity Theory, or CHAT, which emphasizes, above all, the activity of actors toward objects or goals. Like pragmatism, CHAT focuses on interaction among actors who have objectives and who identify and try to solve problems. The unit of analysis, however, is the "activity system," which includes artifacts, rules, and divisions of labor that mediate this activity, rather than the individual "mind." Accordingly, CHAT does not begin with an individualist notion of cognition but rather treats cognition as inherently social and linked to inherently social activities. CHAT allows us to begin to understand, in a way difficult to do otherwise, what happens when activists or authorities change their minds, change tactics, and blend or adhere to central tendencies in repertoires. The second basic premise after the social nature of cognition is that elements of an activity system do not fit perfectly together and will eventually come into conflict or be unable to help actors solve problems. Solutions to these potential contradictions within the system produce, over time, their own new contradictions. Thus, there are dialectical tensions produced within the dialogic contexts of problem solving that result in changes of mind among activists, influencing both their reconstructions and their prospective considerations of their activity.[60]

This kind of inquiry becomes important for explaining the reasons that various actors adopt, drop, or try to modify the claims they make.

The language of mechanisms, introduced earlier, also suggests that there is a range of specific, patterned interactions that can describe the ways in which we attempt to fix the contradictions that occur in our activity systems. The CHAT framework helps clarify why, for example, ACORN organizers found that they could not organize WEP workers at worksites in the same way that they conducted community-organizing campaigns in public-housing projects. They found that the tools they had at their disposal—an ACORN organizing model—fit only partially with the high turnover rates at WEP worksites that were a product both of WEP rules and of the generally high turnover in welfare rolls. They therefore made adjustments in the time they expected to be able to build their organizations and, eventually, in their definition of the problems they were addressing. If, as the lead organizer of ACORN said in a 1998 interview, "The terms of debate [were] going to change in the next few years,"[61] this was equally true for ACORN's own efforts: while ACORN made progress in rolling back some of WEP's most onerous practices, it also ceased to organize on the basis of broad workers' rights.

The Plan of the Book

All of these lines of inquiry get developed further in subsequent chapters. My aim here is to introduce them as the principal pillars of my analysis. Translating a case study into a broader theoretical case—and back—is a famously tricky task. In combining four distinct types of analysis—political-economic, organizational, cultural, and cognitive—I hope to paint a more complete picture than is currently available of the process by which political claims gain currency, policy debate agendas are set, and political identities bounded. I begin in chapter 2 with an analysis of WEP that explicates welfare reform policies and their changes in light of a broader analysis of New York City's political economy. The chapter draws together contemporary urban theory (some of which has roots in Gramscian observations about political and economic regulation) with a careful assessment of New York's workfare policies as they have unfolded over the ten-year span between 1994 and 2004. I also discuss the workfare labor contract in comparative terms, concluding that workfare policies' emblematic status as symbols of neoliberal welfare-state change is largely deserved.

In chapter 3, I reintroduce political claim-making around workfare by introducing the actors and focusing on the institutional contexts of struggle over workfare. Chapter 2 locates workfare within New York

City's political economy; chapter 3 does the same for the advocates and organizers who opposed WEP. Only by understanding the ways in which community organizations, antipoverty advocacy groups, and unions weathered, in more general terms, the storm of neoliberal policies issuing from the 1970s fiscal crisis and whipping across the following two decades can we understand their initial approaches—ranging from confrontational to accomodationist—to WEP's expansion in 1995 and 1996.

Chapter 4 explains why it is so difficult to assemble stable sets of claims about workfare within key institutional sites of protest. Bakhtinian theory led me to find that the spatial and temporal dimensions of workfare itself—along with specific, long-term features of New York's political economy—limited WEP's opponents' ability to generate "choral support" for their claims, or relatively stable sets of associations among a range of speakers. Drawing on interviews with participants in the field of workfare politics; observation of organizing and of meetings and demonstrations; and on texts generated within the field by activists, advocates, lawyers, courts, newspapers, and policymakers, I explain why certain claim-making strategies were engaged and why these strategies met with success and failure within the institutional settings under study.

In chapter 5, I emerge from the "trenches" of legal struggles, legislative campaigns, Pledges of Resistance, and worksite-organizing drives to track the development of workfare-related politics *across* institutional contexts over the study period. Drawing more closely on Gramsci's discussions of political strategy and on commonalities between Gramsci's linguistic theories and those of the Bakhtin circle, the chapter expands on a framework for studying positions of discursive power within political debates and for explaining change in the incumbency in these positions. Using the language of "mechanisms" to describe both regular patterns of changing relations and network-analytic methods, it groups together actors, claims, and institutional contexts according to the correlation of their appearance in the debate with other actors, claims, and settings, and it describes how these groupings and their ability to shape the field change over the course of the debate.

Chapter 6 deals more explicitly with the problem of cognition and the adoption of political claims. It shows why political actors choose the claims they do and why they understand particular claims in particular ways. Since the strategic question in the background of this study asks how movements try to redefine their subjects against dominant definitions, this chapter asks how actors decide which are dominant claims and which dominant claims they can resituate, repackage, or challenge, and when. Drawing together the arguments in previous chapters, and on CHAT, I argue that the only way in which these matters of cognition are tractable is if cognition—like culture—is taken out of people's heads and is treated as distributed among actors and their settings of interaction. More concretely, I focus on two claims that anti-WEP activists used in different ways over the course of the ten-year public debate under study: that WEP was akin to slavery and that what was needed instead was "real jobs." By focusing on these claims, we can begin to see more clearly the ways in which the meanings of claims are coalitional, in a dual fashion: they depend on coalitions of speakers who fashion common arguments with particular claims, and they are the "glue" of these coalitions. Only when we see how meaning-making coalitions form, dissolve, and re-form can we understand the ways in which particular, dominant claims can be reclaimed and revalued to become oppositional.

Taken together, the chapters move from political economy, through intra- and interinstitutional strategic claim-making, to microlevel studies of political cognition and cultural formation. The focus throughout is on workfare policy in New York City and the ways in which movement challenges shifted the terms of debate over workfare but often in ways that anti-WEP movement actors did not anticipate. By tracing the relations that lead to particular meaning formations, cognitions, and dominant claims, I hope to show that the very process of organizing in social movements is a more complex matter than mobilizing people and their resources according to the people's self-interest or than coming up with a frame or narrative that will sway target publics once and for all. In the final chapter, therefore, I synthesize and extend the theoretical concerns that motivate each chapter, and I suggest a more general framework for studying urban political contention under neoliberal social and political regulation, as well as other potential applications of the approach to contentious claim-making I outline here.

CHAPTER TWO

The Workfare Contract in the Workfare State

What Is Workfare?

Workfare is the name given to nearly any work requirement entailed by welfare benefits. Coined in 1970 by William Safire, then a speechwriter in the Nixon administration, the word runs together *work* and *welfare* and is ambiguous enough to include diverse programs.[1] The focus in this chapter is on *work experience* or *community work experience* programs. Work experience programs, including New York City's eponymous one, known as WEP, put welfare recipients to work as a condition of receiving benefits, and the programs stress attachment to the labor force. In work experience programs, welfare recipients are not defined legally as employees or as earning their incomes. Instead, they are defined as compensating the government through their labor for the benefits they receive. The rhetorical blurring between work and welfare on the one hand and the distinctive legal construction of the labor contract on the other hand makes workfare programs, and particularly work experience programs, battlegrounds for competing claims about the similarity or dissimilarity of workfare workers to regular workers; the justice of the labor contract; the extent to which workfare workers displace workers with more-extensive rights; and those who benefit from workfare programs. In a larger perspective, workfare programs blur the distinction between the deserving and industrious working poor and the supposedly undeserving, work-averse, tax-wasting welfare poor. They may also extend the stigma of welfare outward to municipal employees and contingent workers.

This chapter will not judge these claims. Rather, it introduces the Work Experience Program in greater detail and traces its development in the context of New York City's welfare reform policies between 1994 and 2004.

Then, I discuss the workfare assignment in comparison to other labor contracts and examine WEP's relation to municipal employment. Finally, I extend the discussion to examine municipal employment and WEP in the context of post-fiscal-crisis urban governance and political economy.

The image of WEP that emerges from this chapter will likely not win the program any admirers. But the point of the chapter is to show the ways in which it created problems, both of and for governance and for welfare recipients and their organizational allies by extracting them from previous interactive networks around policy and reembedding them in new ones. As we see WEP assignments creating crises around child care, for example, or WEP workers taking their workplace grievances to the organizers they know—who are housing and homeless organizers—we can discern the outlines of transformation in the local political field.

By showing the ways in which WEP created changes both in the institutions of government and in the routines of welfare recipients and their allies, the chapter addresses neoliberalism at a lower level of abstraction than is often the case in studies of political economy. Though this chapter draws on these studies, what is most important is that workfare is understood as part of a larger shift in governance that has effects that cannot sensibly be confined to welfare policy or even to "poor relief." Workfare displays similar effects on the temporal and spatial environments in which opposition might grow as do other quintessential neoliberal policies, such as those promoting "flexible," spatially dispersed production and short-term labor contracts. In comparison to the "Fordist" ideal of larger-scale, spatially concentrated production and long-term labor contracts (only partially realized in actuality), neoliberal policies make collective action more difficult to organize. This difficulty, combined with an approximately thirty-year legacy of attempts to resist the implementation of neoliberal austerity, makes giving a mesoinstitutional description of workfare policy a critical first step in a broader synthetic account of the development of political claims and coalitions addressing it.

Workfare in New York City

Defined most broadly, *workfare* simply involves making people work in exchange for welfare benefits. This exchange can be accomplished in many ways, with greater or lesser emphasis on job training, education, public- or private-sector work, penalties and job discipline, and with several methods of treating the welfare income resulting from the expenditure of effort on the part of the recipient.

While work relief programs have characterized welfare states from their inception in the Elizabethan Poor Law, contemporary workfare programs began during the Nixon administration. Work requirements, such as those in the Work Incentive Program (WIN), created obstacles to the Johnson administration's Great Society welfare programs and pushed poor women into the labor market in very disadvantageous positions.[2] Work requirements demanding reciprocity from able-bodied welfare recipients reinforced the normative—if not actual—nuclear family headed by the male breadwinner. They did so by forcing a recipient to find a wage-earning spouse or to enter the labor force. Yet until recently, workfare programs rarely required commitment of substantial work time, and they still were skewed toward active labor market programs that applied education and training and, where applicable, job creation to the project of reducing welfare rolls. Now, however, workfare has taken on the connotation of "work-first" workfare programs. Work-first workfare regimes insist that work itself—rather than the more active labor market programs—at any job and at any wage has salubrious effects for the recipient's development of good work habits and thus for integration into the mainstream of society.[3]

New York City's Program Expands

New York City's first post-Great Society workfare programs were small in scale in the early 1970s, funded through President Nixon's WIN program. First, the Public Works Program (PWP) for childless adults was begun in 1971. The Work Relief Employment Project, which began in 1973 and lasted until 1976, used welfare funds to pay wages and benefits to welfare recipients.[4] PWP formed the basis of an expanded program and would eventually turn into WEP. PWP's expansion began in 1976, as New York was in the midst of its epochal fiscal crisis, at the instigation of the new, pro-growth mayor, Edward I. Koch. In the early 1980s, PWP met similar criticism to that levied against WEP a dozen years later. Welfare recipients called it slavery, municipal unions denounced it as undercutting regular workers' power, and progressive politicians decried the Koch administration's failure to track the job-finding fortunes of program participants. PWP targeted Home Relief (HR) recipients; few recipients of Aid to Families with Dependent Children (AFDC) worked in the program. In the face of efforts on the part of District Council 37 of the American Federation of State, County, and Municipal Employees (DC 37 of AFSCME) to represent PWP workers in 1980, the Koch administration successfully argued in court "that the program was not really a job, and the participants were not really workers, and were thus not entitled to union representation."[5] Moreover, Koch's view—echoed later by Mayor Rudolph W. Giuliani— was that workfare was a character-building exercise and that "even if they are not learning skills that are transferable, they're working—and that's a work skill."[6] At its height, PWP pushed fifteen thousand welfare recipients into work, typically in part-time positions in city agencies. After Koch was replaced by David N. Dinkins, the program shrank by nearly a third and was focused nearly exclusively on clerical work in the welfare department, the Human Resources Administration (HRA).

In 1994, when Mayor Giuliani began to raise in earnest an expansion of WEP, he therefore had the basic structure of the program already in place. Elected by the resurgent white ethnics and professionals who formed Koch's winning coalitions, Giuliani also looked for help during the mayoral transition from Koch-era insiders, some of whom were keen to make an effective workfare program.[7] In the first year of its expansion, starting in 1995, WEP doubled, from just over ten thousand to just over twenty-one thousand WEP workers in March 1996. The program covered adults without dependents in the Home Relief program and only expanded to AFDC recipients in March 1996. Thereafter WEP nearly doubled again and by 1997 had more than thirty-eight thousand participants.[8]

WEP's expansion was part of a program called New York City-Work, Accountability, and You (NYC–WAY), a larger package of welfare reforms that also included tightened Eligibility Verification Reviews (EVRs), finger imaging, and the increased application of sanctions for administrative infractions by welfare recipients. New York State does not have a "full-family sanction"; unlike many other states, it does not cut off the entire family grant for a period as a sanction. It reduces the cash portion of the grant for the parent (usually the mother) *only* and does not touch the portion of the grant set aside for housing. Nevertheless, in family budgets that never reach more than three-quarters of the federal poverty level, the widespread use of sanctions early in the program's expansion greatly increased the punitive force of reforms as perceived by welfare recipients.[9]

Shifting the Core

New York City's commitment to WEP was only partial. Though WEP formed the core of NYC–WAY during the 1990s, at least for those who remained on the welfare rolls, it began to decline in relative importance beginning in 1999.[10] Five factors account for this decline. First, the Personal Responsibility and Work Opportunity Reconciliation Act of 1996 (PRWORA) gives credits to states that reach caseload reduction milestones. When they do, a greater proportion of those remaining on the welfare rolls become exempt from work activities, the coordination of which takes valuable resources that might otherwise be directed somewhere else. As caseloads in New York City declined by over half between 1994 and 2004, less emphasis needed to be placed on WEP. Second, beginning in 2001, nearly four thousand welfare recipients reaching their five-year lifetime limits imposed on welfare by PRWORA were transferred out of WEP and into the Parks Opportunity Program (POP), which used surplus money from the Temporary Aid to Needy Families (TANF) program to pay wages to welfare recipients to do essentially the same jobs they had been doing without wages in WEP. Third, New York City's economy began to climb out of a prolonged recession in the late 1990s, and the addition of jobs helped absorb the large number of people leaving the welfare rolls. Fourth, the expanding economy also increased employment opportunities for people still reliant on welfare, and, as long as recipients worked in a nonworkfare job, they could be exempt from WEP, regardless of whether they worked the same number of hours as they would be required to work in the program. Liberal State-legislated earned-income disregards contained in the 1997 welfare reform law enabled welfare recipients to keep more of their earnings even when they still needed to rely on public assistance, thus providing an incentive to enter the workforce. Fifth, due in part to activist publicity around the issue of barriers to employment, but also to a softening of the stridency against welfare in the Michael R. Bloomberg administration, increasing numbers of welfare recipients were tracked into substance-abuse treatment programs as well as remedial educational programs, as part of their work requirements. By 2004, there were fewer than two thousand welfare recipients in "basic" WEP, that is, where WEP is the only activity required in the range of work requirements, outside of job-search activities, though the number of WEP workers neared twenty thousand. In contrast, basic WEP had accounted for twenty-nine thousand of just over thirty-five thousand workfare placements in the last week of November 1999. One large part of the change is that WEP placements have largely shifted from the "simulated workweek," trumpeted by Jason Turner in 1998, to part-time assignments for three days a week, supplemented by job-search, treatment, or basic education activities on the other two days.[11]

WEP and Institutional Spillover

The decline of the welfare rolls under NYC–WAY, and associated with WEP, resulted in billions of dollars of savings for New York City.[12] New York State is one of few states that require localities to contribute to the cost of federal programs that otherwise require only cost sharing with states. As a result, New York City and New York State each pay one-quarter of the cost of welfare and Medicaid, and federal funds pay one-half. Accordingly, as the caseload fell, the City was able to save hundreds of millions of dollars in welfare payments a year relative to prereform levels. Moreover, WEP assigned welfare recipients to tasks normally done by municipal employees. But because their hours were calculated by dividing their welfare and food stamp benefits by the minimum wage, and because the City only contributed a quarter of the value of their checks, they cost the City only $1.80 an hour for their labor. Though there are various ways to determine the value of the work WEP workers did for the City, several estimates put the labor cost savings to the City in hundreds of millions of dollars.[13]

Though the cost savings of WEP has its own independent importance in my political analysis of the program (to be detailed subsequently), the issues of cost and program are separable and should be considered separately. Programmatically, WEP pushed tens of thousands of AFDC—and then TANF—recipients into work assignments, and NYC–WAY pushed tens of thousands more into the labor force, as eligibility restrictions and grant cutoffs reduced welfare rolls, which resulted in several spillover effects.

Education

In addition to increasing hardship among welfare recipients immediately, the work-first emphasis of NYC–WAY often interferes with recipients' ability to improve their skills and credentials through education. One of the first major issues raised in the New York City Council on NYC–WAY regarded the implementation of workfare requirements among students at the City University of New York (CUNY). It became clear very early that students on welfare faced enormous barriers to staying in school if compelled to fulfill workfare assignments taking twenty-five to thirty-five hours per week. Often, these students worked in internships and work-study jobs on campus and could not fulfill these tuition-remitting assignments and workfare assignments together. Additionally, until both legislative and legal pressure forced the administration to start solving this problem, many welfare recipients at CUNY were assigned to jobs that interfered with their school schedules.[14] The enrollment of welfare recipients at CUNY quickly began to drop. In 1995, twenty-eight thousand CUNY students received public assistance. By 1997, the figure had dropped by nearly ten thousand, and it has since then declined as much again.[15] WEP's interference with education was so great that bipartisan state legislation in 1997 required CUNY students who were in WEP to be placed in positions on or near campus and in accordance with their academic schedules. Nearly a year of mayoral inaction followed passage of this law. Then, under pressure from state lawmakers, several pilot programs began at community college campuses. Another state bill, passed by both houses and signed by Governor George Pataki in the period leading up to the 2000 elections (in which the Republicans in the state senate faced several major challenges to their control) allows internships and work-study jobs to count toward work activities.[16]

Finally, a lawsuit brought by legal advocates in 1996 charged that the City was violating the law by assigning welfare recipients to WEP without first assessing their needs and barriers to employment. The City finally settled the lawsuit in 2003 and agreed to inform welfare recipients about educational and training options and give them a list of qualified providers. Though compliance with the settlement is reported to be mixed, the advocates' victory in the case, called *Davila*, means that the City is no longer able arbitrarily to assign welfare recipients to thirty-five-hour weeks of WEP.[17]

Child Care

Another area in which NYC–WAY's more stringent requirements were quickly felt was in child-care services. Beginning in 1996, the flood of AFDC recipients into WEP assignments precipitated a child-care crisis. Four factors characterized this crisis: (1) an absolute increase in the need for child care; (2) the informalizing of child-care services; (3) competition between welfare recipients and other poor people for available child-care vouchers; and (4) the City's ignoring laws regarding its obligation to inform welfare recipients about their child-care options.

The absolute increase in the need for child care is an obvious outcome of pushing thousands of women into the nondomestic workforce. New York City already faced a shortage of licensed child-care slots for poor parents, whether on welfare or not. By 1998, if the City were to have licensed child care for all welfare recipients in workfare, it would have needed an additional twenty-nine thousand day-care slots. A report by HRA found that 61 percent of parents in workfare would not have licensed child care available to them.[18]

That the shortage of licensed child-care services did not create an enormous obstacle to placing parents in WEP reveals the ongoing trend of informalizing child-care provision for the poor. New York has strict health and safety standards for licensed, regulated child care. Yet, as the population of school-age children in the city has increased without corresponding increases in the number of licensed child-care slots, increasing numbers of parents are turning to relatives, friends, and neighbors to look after their children. Even if these arrangements work out well, three aspects of this shift are particularly important. First, while there is no reliable way to ascertain the quality of informal care arrangements, one study found that welfare recipients presented with choices were likely to abandon their informal arrangements in favor of formal, regulated care.[19] A second, perhaps related, issue is that informal child-care arrangements—which are still subsidized by the City—are potentially less stable as personal relations are transformed into ones mediated by money.[20] Third, formal child-care providers often resisted taking the children of parents on welfare because HRA was often late in reimbursing the providers for care given and often failed to notify them when a case was closed, so that the providers would continue to care for a child even when they could not expect payment.[21]

Because the informal arrangements were often unpredictable and makeshift, the City came under increasing pressure to prioritize child-care slots for children of workfare workers. Such prioritization quickly set up competition between workfare workers and working-class parents who both depended upon subsidized child care. During the period between 1997 and 1999, the City nearly doubled the budget for workfare-related day care, while cutting the budget for working families. This development was exacerbated by the fact that in 1997, an increase in the availability of child-care vouchers was directed primarily to Orthodox Jewish neighborhoods in Brooklyn, which, though needy, were also politically important to City Hall and far from the neediest communities in the city.[22]

The fourth factor characterizing child care under NYC–WAY was the City's regular practice of ignoring laws requiring the notification of child-care rights. With the expansion of NYC–WAY, many mothers on welfare were being pressured—in direct contravention of the law—to accept any child-care provisions offered to them so that they could fulfill their work-fare requirements and not lose their benefits. New York state law makes a broad exception to the work requirements for parents who are unable to secure child care that is suitable *in their own estimation* for the needs of their children. Moreover, the administrative code requires casework-ers actively to help parents locate child care. In a survey of ninety-two mothers on welfare in New York City, the National Organization for Women Legal Defense and Education Fund (NOW–LDEF; now called Legal Momentum) found that 81 percent were not told that they could *not* be sanctioned for failing to report to a work assignment if suitable care was unavailable. Forty-six percent were told that they *would* be sanc-tioned if they did not find child care.[23] No one knows how many parents did not contest sanctions they received for not placing their children in care of which they disapproved. It is thus unknown how many parents wrongly lost benefits. It is also unknown how many parents found care they did not approve of but merely settled for. In any event, of the respon-dents to the NOW–LDEF survey, fully 83 percent used informal child-care arrangements.

In 1999, the City began to move aggressively to remedy the crisis, using TANF surplus money to fund large increases in subsidized child-care vouchers. By 2001, the State allocated money for about twenty-six thousand child-care slots to the City from the TANF surplus, and this number has been increased nearly fourfold since then as the surplus has grown. Nevertheless, the level of funding of these vouchers by the State is subject to the vicissitudes of the State budget and to the other possible uses of the surplus.[24]

Homelessness and Food Security

WEP and NYC–WAY may also have had an effect on housing instability, homelessness, and food insecurity. Though there is not much evidence of the direct relationship between the plummeting welfare rolls and the rise in homelessness during the late 1990s and early 2000s, and in the rising demand on the city's emergency food providers, the relationship is suggested.[25]

Since NYC–WAY was implemented, food pantries and soup kitchens have reported unprecedented use, even when the local economy was gen-erally expanding. Between 1995 and 1997, the New York City Coalition Against Hunger, an association of food pantries, reported that demand at its members' soup kitchens had jumped nearly 70 percent. The central food bank in New York reported a 38 percent increase in the amount of food it gave out.[26] Moreover, the coalition reported in early 1998 that it was turning away nearly nineteen hundred people per month at its food programs.[27] By 2002, the number of people receiving emergency food assistance from New York's food pantries and soup kitchens had nearly doubled since 1995—just as the welfare rolls had been cut in half.

Part of the problem has to do with underenrollment in the food stamp program, a fact that has been reinforced by City policy, in spite of the millions of dollars higher enrollment would add to the local economy. One feature of the conversion of welfare centers to so-called Job Centers under Jason Turner when he became the HRA commissioner in 1998 was the imposition of procedural barriers to applying for food stamps and Medicaid. Though these barriers were later found to be illegal, HRA's antipathy to food stamp enrollment as a form of dependency continued under the Bloomberg administration. Only recently has HRA become more encouraging of people signing onto the program, and even then, it declined to apply for federal waivers allowing unemployed people seeking work to collect food stamps.[28]

Curtailment of welfare benefits prompting absolute hardship in households often makes rent difficult to pay. Cutting people off welfare removes the institutional framework within which many welfare recipients remain housed in New York City. Because welfare rental allowances are typically more than $250 per month less than the rents that welfare recipients in privately owned housing pay, a judge mandated that the City pay the difference in reasonable cases of discrepancy. This relief—called "Jiggetts' relief," after the lead plaintiff in the class-action suit challenging the adequacy of welfare rent allowances—is thus tied explicitly to the receipt of welfare. Getting pushed off welfare and into a low-wage job (at best, and into an utter lack of support at worst) that fails to boost a family's income sufficiently to pay the rent might trigger an eviction for which no safety net exists.[29] To date, however, few data are available about evictions resulting from the loss of Jiggetts' relief. Beyond Jiggetts, however, there is the simpler problem that people who leave welfare do not necessarily enter stable employment or gain steady incomes. As reported by Peter Rossi in 1989, it takes an average of four years for people to become homeless after losing their means of support. Though the relationship may be spurious and is doubtless complicated by the acute loss of affordable housing in New York City during the late 1990s, the homeless shelter population increased dramatically from 2000 onward.[30]

The WEP Assignment

There are numerous ways to understand the WEP assignment, especially as it looked from 1995 through 2000, when WEP was expanding and at its height. In what follows, I describe the WEP assignment as a labor contract, locating it in statutory and legal contexts and in comparison to other types of labor contract.

At a basic level, however, the workfare assignment consists of a requirement that a welfare recipient participate in a range of possible activities relating to work deemed appropriate by the government social service agency in charge of issuing the benefits.

Statutory Basis

Specific requirements for work are not given in state or federal law. Rather, guidelines for programs that will fulfill federal conditions of aid have been contained in federal welfare legislation, and state law limits what is allowable. For example, PRWORA mandated that by fiscal year 2002, 50 percent of each state's caseload had to participate in work activities or have left the welfare rolls. Accordingly, as more people leave the welfare rolls, fewer people have to work as a condition of receiving welfare. Allowable work activities under the law include "unsubsidized or subsidized employment, on-the-job training, work experience, community service, 12 months of vocational training, or [a position] provid[ing] child care services to individuals who are participating in community service. Up to 6 weeks of job search (no more than 4 consecutive weeks) . . . count toward the work requirement.[31] Welfare recipients—here, only TANF recipients, since HR programs were state and local affairs—were required to work at least thirty hours by 2002.[32]

These programmatic outlines at the federal level meant that women with children were more likely to work longer workweeks than were (mostly male) welfare recipients without dependents since the children's benefits were included in the income that the mother had to work off. New York City and State typically calculated required working hours by conforming to federal regulations, which set the allowable workfare hours at the point at which a welfare recipient would be earning the minimum wage if his or her work were treated as employment. Until 1997, however, New York State's Social Services Law required that work relief program participants' hours be calculated at the *prevailing wage* paid for the specific work being done. In May 1997, a court therefore found that the City was improperly assigning WEP workers' hours, but in July, the state legislature passed a welfare reform bill that removed this more generous provision. Without it, WEP assignments could, and did, continue to dominate the work activities of welfare recipients.

As noted earlier, in 1981, DC 37 failed in its effort to persuade the City's Office of Collective Bargaining (OCB) to recognize PWP workers as employees with collective bargaining and union representation rights. During WEP's expansion fifteen years later, no one imagined that the OCB would reconsider its previous ruling. WEP workers were covered by workers' compensation insurance in the event that they were injured on the job, and they were entitled to engage the grievance process on workplace health and safety concerns through the Public Employees Safety and Health board (PESH). Nevertheless, they had no other apparatus to file grievances about conditions, harassment, or supervision at their worksites. Moreover, the PESH procedure was awkward, if not impossible, for WEP workers to use: WEP assignments are characterized by a good deal of turnover; but PESH investigations can take months to activate, so that a WEP worker will likely not be at a worksite when the requested inspection takes place. In addition, PESH hearings typically allow a representative from the aggrieved worker's union to be present and to assist in the complaint. But WEP workers do not have this possibility because the OCB had ruled in 1981 against union representation.[33]

Nevertheless, as litigation played out in WEP-related cases, interpretations of the statute blurred, revealing competing definitions of the WEP placement. In her ruling in *Brukhman v. Giuliani* (1997), the prevailing wage case, the lower court judge deemed WEP workers to be entitled to a "day's work for a day's pay,"[34] although subsequent appellate rulings in the case emphasized that WEP workers are not "employees" because they are not "in the employ" of anyone.[35] In other words, although the higher courts found that WEP workers were not selling their labor for wages but were in some form of unfree labor contract, the courts did not say so outright, nor did they suggest a remedy. In fact, the only time in which the unfreedom of the WEP labor contract became an issue in the *Brukhman*—or any other—litigation was when the City cited a Thirteenth and Fourteenth Amendment case from 1916 to bolster its claim that WEP workers did not have a property right in their labor and were therefore not owed back pay.[36]

In 1998, however, a group of WEP workers, working with the NOW–LDEF, later joined by the Clinton administration, sued the City for not protecting them against racial and sexual harassment at worksites. Again, the City responded that WEP workers were not "employees" and that therefore the City had no legal obligation to protect them against harassment under the equal employment opportunity framework of Title VII of the Civil Rights Act of 1964. A federal court of appeals ultimately ruled in favor of the plaintiffs, though the ruling was only rendered in 2004. In its ruling, the court agreed with the plaintiffs' position in *Brukhman*, namely, that whatever it is called, WEP is enough *like* the employer-employee relationship that it should be treated in the same way under the law. In a stinging dissent, one justice wrote that

> the only likely impact of this case will be to frustrate important welfare reforms by impairing the flexible and temporary nature of WEP assignments. PRWORA was designed, *inter alia*, to assist state programs that allow welfare recipients to move from dependency to gainful employment via training and workplace experience. If WEP participants are "employees" under federal common law, it may then follow—and it will certainly be argued—that they have a right, like other employees, to unionize, ("Employees shall have the right to self-organization, to form, join, or assist labor organizations, to bargain collectively through representatives of their own choosing . . ."), a development incompatible with the statutory goal of a transitional work experience. And there are no doubt other implications under state law of turning thousands of WEP participants into City employees . . .[37]

Relational and Comparative Perspective

Though the question of flexibility will be treated more intensively later on, it is important to note here that this part of the judge's dissent was based largely on extrinsic justifications for structuring the assignment as it was. While I hesitate to adjudicate among competing definitions in a book about the process of *arriving* at competing definitions and political claims, it will be useful to clarify what WEP workers do and did, comparing this to what regular municipal employees do and to other kinds of labor contracts.

WEP workers were, and are, engaged in a broad range of activities. The agencies in which WEP workers were placed most often—Parks and Recreation, Citywide Administrative Services, Sanitation, and HRA—used them to clean and do routine maintenance work and to perform clerical

duties. Other WEP workers worked as school aides, in nonprofit organizations as receptionists, as clerical workers, or in maintenance. On
occasion, WEP workers with skills in electrical work, carpentry, or other
trades would do skilled jobs. Nevertheless, the modal WEP work was in
maintenance and clerical jobs.

WEP assignments varied in their conditions. Clerical work tended
to be less onerous than indoor maintenance work, and both were less
punishing than outdoor jobs picking up litter or cleaning toilets in parks
or cleaning highways and sidewalks. Moreover, WEP workers tended to
complain less about conditions in clerical jobs than they did about doing
work that someone else, with full pay and benefits, should have been
doing. By contrast, WEP workers in outdoor assignments complained
about the work itself, which was both more strenuous and more publicly
visible. Because WEP workers were issued bright orange vests, they were
readily identifiable, and so they wore the stigma of welfare publicly.[38]

In a random-encounter survey of 649 WEP workers conducted between
1999 and 2000, Community Voices Heard (CVH)found that in the agencies that used WEP the most—Parks and Recreation, Citywide Administrative Services, and HRA—WEP workers reported doing thirty-five of thirty-
six tasks in entry-level job descriptions, and on average, they reported
doing 35 percent of the tasks in the job descriptions.[39] CVH's findings
were not surprising. For years, WEP workers and city administrators alike
had been quoted in local newspapers saying that WEP workers were critical to keeping the City running. As early as 1997, the Department of Parks
and Recreation reported, "The biggest contributor to the improved clean-
liness of New York City's parks has been the workfare program, known as
the Work Experience Program (WEP). By the fall of 1997, more than 6,000
able-bodied welfare recipients, men and women, were working approximately 21 hours a week in parks, helping to paint benches, shovel snow,
rake leaves and pick up litter in exchange for their benefits."[40]

Chris and Charles Tilly, in their ambitious *Work under Capitalism*,[41]
suggest one way of classifying labor contracts, based on the pay and
control over time that workers have and on the direction of supervisory
authority. Figure 2.1 reproduces their schema. Pay is denoted more precisely as the "extent of short-term monetization" of labor, and control
over work time is denoted more precisely as "extent of time-discipline."
The boxes and arrows refer to the balance of power between recipients
"R" and producers "P" of the product of the labor.

It makes sense to locate most WEP contracts in the lower right-hand

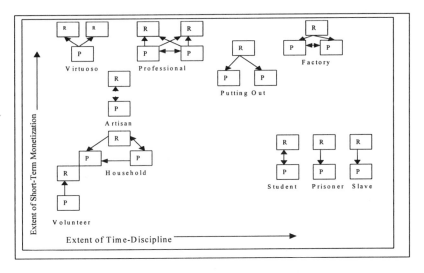

Figure 2.1. Classification of labor contracts by extent of short-term monetization and extent of time-discipline. Reprinted by permission from Chris Tilly and Charles Tilly, *Work under Capitalism* (Boulder, CO: Westview Press, 1998), 167.

quadrant of the figure. Whatever one says about the relative value or harm that WEP has for WEP workers, there is little doubt that supervisory authority over WEP workers is generally high, as are the costs for noncompliance with orders. These costs are, however, subject to the discretion of supervisors. There is also little doubt that the potential for short-term monetization of labor is low: benefits are lower, in general, than minimum wage (with the effects of the income not being treated as "earned" for the purposes of the Earned Income Tax Credit). Moreover, because WEP curtails opportunities for many recipients to supplement their welfare checks with off-the-books work, the net potential for short-term monetization of a given worker's labor is even lower.

Another way of thinking about labor contracts has to do with whether, in fact, there is a market for the labor, and if so, what kind of market exists. Theorists of labor market segmentation[42] persuasively argue that even within firms, jobs are divided between those who enjoy decent pay and benefits and some measure of autonomy and those who enjoy none of these things. The first set of jobs, in the primary labor market, implies a capitalist's investment in the workers. This investment is rewarded by the employee's loyalty. Hence, primary labor markets are characterized by low turnover. Secondary labor markets are turnover pools of low-wage

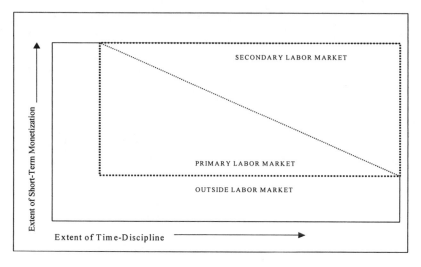

Figure 2.2. Labor market configurations according to extent of short-term monetization and extent of time-discipline. Reprinted by permission from Tilly and Tilly, *Work under Capitalism*, 171.

labor. Again, Tilly and Tilly provide a schema for arraying labor contracts on the coordinates of potential for short-term monetization and extent of time-discipline. Figure 2.2 represents this schema.[43]

Workfare—particularly as instantiated in public-sector assignments—is in an interesting position: Although it forms a large turnover pool, access to the turnover pool itself is, unlike typical labor *market* arrangements for this sector, highly restricted both by barriers to collecting benefits and by the remaining effective protections for public employees. Moreover, unlike many actual recruitment links to turnover pools, it offers little evidence of chain recruitment to welfare. Instead, the bureaucratic barriers to welfare prevent such recruitment (though there are differences, organized around ethnic lines, regarding likelihood to seek public support in similar situations of deprivation).[44]

These properties of workfare produce two important outcomes in labor markets. First, the porous boundaries between welfare receipt and low-wage secondary labor-market work for welfare recipients[45] suggest that the bureaucratic barriers to welfare receipt limit the size of the workfare turnover pool and enforce the presence of a large turnover pool in the private and informal sectors. Second, in setting up a workfare program this way, a government can gain limited advantages over a unionized public-sector workforce and enforce work in the private sector, even if that work is only marginally secure.[46]

It is useful now to address the changes effected by WEP's expansion, with respect to the workfare labor contract. By curtailing education and training options, the City curtailed exit options from exploitative work. But WEP's expansion also meant constricting the ways to insert workers into labor markets and promotion pools. If a worker can work with less supervision (lesser extent of time-discipline) as a result of education and training, that worker's entrance into labor markets, as suggested in figure 2.2, would take place on different terms and be more likely to include primary-sector work. Thus, by cutting back on education and training, WEP appears to be a way of enforcing minimalist labor contracts and regulating the informal sector's ability to supplement services offered in the formal sector, as the economic geographers Jamie Peck and Nik Theodore suggest.[47] WEP thus effects a segmentation of the production of services such as child care or laundry and of retail sales. It segments the consumption of these services as well, because informal arrangements (significantly, in child care) are increasingly the only ones available to poor mothers forced into WEP or into low-level turnover jobs.

In addition, by neither providing significant incentives for nor enforcing job creation in the formal private sector, work-first workfare programs also push workers into the sector over which the state does exert some control, namely, the public sector and its nonprofit contractors. Civil service rules and public-sector unions reach into low-skilled jobs, so what might be thought of as secondary labor markets in the public sector are buffered from high turnover by the higher wages and benefits than would be available elsewhere. For this reason, it is common for workers in low-level public-sector jobs to make an entire career in entry-level positions. The introduction of workfare in these jobs means that public-sector employers have an incentive to break unions and more fully "secondarize" the labor market structure of these positions. Moreover, workfare appears, from the standpoint of public finance, in much the same light as privatization of these same services, that is, as a labor cost-savings.[48] Accordingly, WEP does not likely disturb greatly the functioning of internal labor markets in the public sector because they are not mobile for many without skills, even though there are civil service career ladders. Instead, it simply allows the City to enforce instability, to suggest neoliberal solutions for the bottom rungs of the public workforce, and to break the class solidarity suggested by the joining of skilled and unskilled workers within the same union. Again, WEP's nature as a hybrid form of labor contract increases the flexibility of the City to deploy workers according to various needs for their labor while shedding the public accountability that is forced upon it by public-sector labor contracts.

WEP and Municipal Jobs

As it happens, there was not much public accountability forced upon the City by public-sector unions in the first place. Since its challenge of PWP in the early 1980s—and even earlier—DC 37 had ceased to be the militant public-sector labor union it originally was. Since the fiscal crisis of the 1970s, DC 37 had appeared to contain rather than foster rank-and-file militancy.[49] Stanley Hill, the executive director of the union from 1986 to 1999, was a leader in a 1965 welfare workers' strike that built worker-welfare-recipient solidarity, but by 1995 he had become so complacent—or chastened—that he did not investigate allegations that his closest allies had rigged the contract vote. Moreover, because DC 37's constituent locals vote as proportionally weighted blocs, the two largest locals, whose presidents were Hill allies, controlled the union for most purposes. WEP was already entrenched in one of the two locals—the clerical workers' local, which was a major local in HRA—and Mayor Giuliani secured the support of the other local's president prior to expanding WEP. The clerical workers' local president was one of the leaders most implicated in the rigging of the 1995 contract, which included side agreements that enabled WEP to expand by providing substantial pay differentials to municipal workers charged with overseeing WEP workers.[50]

Displacement and Quasi Displacement

Earlier, I mentioned Community Voices Heard's 1999-2000 survey finding that WEP workers were doing much of the work in regular workers' job descriptions. Beginning in 1999, under new leadership, DC 37 sued the City on the grounds that this situation constituted displacement of regular workers under the State welfare reform law of 1997. The law, on its face, seems unequivocal:

A recipient may be assigned to participate in such work experience program only if . . . (e) such assignment would not result in (iv) the performance, by such participant, of a substantial portion of the work ordinarily and actually performed by regular employees; or (v) the loss of a bargaining unit position as a result of work experience participants performing, in part or in whole, the work normally performed by the employee in such position.[51]

CVH's findings figured into lawsuits after its report was released, but the principal problem underlying efforts to prove displacement was that the conditions of the law were often difficult to meet. First, in many workplaces, the loss of the bargaining position had arguably occurred in 1991, under Mayor David Dinkins. Though attrition and early retirements under Giuliani resulted in thousands of lost bargaining units among nonuniformed, noninstructional municipal employees, including many in positions whose job descriptions were being fulfilled by WEP workers, the bulk of the bargaining unit position loss occurred under layoffs ordered by Dinkins at the behest of the city's bond raters.[52]

Second, and related to the first point, there were many jobs in which the work "normally performed by the employee in such a position" was no longer performed by anyone but WEP workers in many worksites. The experience of Ellera, an interviewee in CVH's 2000 report, is indicative of trends that prevailed, especially in the Department of Parks and Recreation (DPR), but also in the Department of Citywide Administrative Services (DCAS), where she was assigned:

> I worked in the *Museo del Barrio* in East Harlem for about a year. There are between 8–12 workfare workers in the museum doing maintenance and some clerical work. Every day, we would sign in on the timesheet and see our supervisor who would give us our work assignments for the day. *Workfare workers did all the housekeeping work, all the cleaning. There were no paid workers in housecleaning.* We sweep, mop, clean bathrooms, and dispose of garbage, and empty trashcans. Sometimes we would run errands. Every day we did the same job, just like a regular worker, except we didn't get paid; we didn't get a paycheck.[53]

Finally, the Giuliani administration backed away from WEP deployments that would blatantly result in displacement. In 1996, Giuliani blocked a provision in the Transit Authority contract with Local 100 of the Transport Workers Union to replace five hundred subway cleaners with WEP workers, and in 1998, he withdrew one thousand WEP workers from public hospitals in which he had announced nearly the same number of layoffs.[54]

Nevertheless, trends suggested significant displacement of regular workers with WEP workers, even if the direct link between the use of WEP workers and bargaining unit position loss was attenuated.[55]

WEP and Work Reallocation

Why, if the City was bent on replacing regular workers with WEP workers, did it stop putting so many welfare recipients into WEP after 2000 and switch to a more service-intensive three-days-on, two-days-in-service WEP program? The answer is that in spite of the trends just shown, the City was *not* bent on replacing regular workers with WEP workers, and the relationships between changes in the City's workforce and welfare were more complex. The main objective of the City seems to have been, especially under Giuliani, to reduce labor costs and full-time, full-benefit civilian head count in order to save whatever could be saved on benefit payments.

Over a span of eight years, the Giuliani administration reshaped the municipal workforce. In contrast to the earlier pattern of hiring back municipal workers laid off during fiscal crises, Giuliani simply made do with fewer full-time, full-status municipal workers. Though the city's payroll actually increased under Giuliani, it did so only by adding teachers and uniformed personnel (mostly police officers). It cut an equivalent number of full-time jobs—roughly sixteen thousand—in social services and other city agencies. Moreover, Giuliani greatly expanded the use of provisional, seasonal, and per diem workers in city agencies, increasing spending on these employees "from $62.5 million in 1993 to $444.3 million in 2001."[56] These workers are considered employees, and they enjoy union representation. Nevertheless, they do not qualify for pension and other employee benefits, and they do not have to take civil service examinations. They have relatively little job security, and they cost the City less to hire—and less in the long run—than regular, full-time employees do.

It is in the light of workforce restructuring that the City's use of WEP amid larger welfare reduction goals should be understood. This perspective becomes clearer once we locate these two goals within a broader account of neoliberalism in New York City. With it, the more complex relationships between neoliberal governance and its legitimating discourses will become clearer as well. Two preliminary observations are needed. First, throughout the ten-year period spanning 1994 to 2004, the principal priority of welfare reform was to push welfare recipients into the labor market, conceived first in relatively undifferentiated, sector-insensitive terms (i.e., workforce attachment is valued within both the public and the private sector). In this sense, New York City's has been a classic "work-first" program. The City's switch to a system that relies relatively less heavily on WEP therefore reflects both greater opportunities within the private labor market for contingent and low-wage work and, importantly, the imprint of advocacy efforts to delegitimize and to block public-sector placements. As a result, a higher cost structure is now associated with New York City's workfare/welfare-reform program as it has been supplemented by a more service-intensive course of engagement, but this structure is supported by surpluses generated through the dismissal of half a million welfare recipients from the caseload.[57]

Second, the City's labor force issues remain problematic, in part because WEP can no longer easily plug the gaps in the workforce. The city's workforce, though smaller than it was prior to 2001, has begun to grow slowly again, even amid mounting City pension obligations to its previous employees. In fact, most of the growth in the City's nonpedagogical head count is in agencies that lost many employees during the Dinkins layoffs and suffered attrition under Giuliani. Most of these agencies' staffs—like DPR and HRA—were supplemented by thousands of WEP workers. WEP workers' absence now may lead to longer-run pressure on the municipal workforce head count, and in the shorter term, it contributes to the pressure on municipal employees to accept stingy contracts in the face of layoff threats. Again, seen from this perspective, WEP is not the only strategy available to cost-cutting public managers. It is one of several strategies, one that both in its presence and in its absence threatens municipal employees' wages and benefits.

Neoliberalism and the WEP Labor Contract

It is nevertheless still important, from a theoretical and empirical point of view, to understand how WEP fits with larger patterns of urban and welfare-state governance. In particular, because the larger questions in this book deal with the relationship among neoliberal policies, political economy, and the cultural definition of political actors in the context of contention, the ways in which WEP instantiates a broader neoliberal policy repertoire is of central importance. In this section, I consider the WEP contract with respect to three issues: its flexibility and accountability structures, its role in disciplining labor, and its role in creating new distinctions among beneficiaries and victims of state action. I conclude the chapter by considering WEP within the broader context of neoliberalism in New York and the temporal and spatial strategies of neoliberal governance.

Flexibility and Accountability Structures

That WEP workers can be deployed in any city agency and shifted from worksite to worksite as needed; that they lack the same rights as regular workers; and that they are subject to multiple authorities as welfare recipients and as workers; all suggest that the WEP contract is flexible in a number of senses. First, as with secondary labor-market work, there is little short-term monetization of labor (or long-term, in the form of pensions) and no generation of sunk costs or fixed investments in the labor force. Related to this, there is high turnover at worksites. Accordingly, like secondary labor-market work, the WEP assignment puts WEP workers into high-turnover, low-paying pools. Moreover, because of the context of stepped-up administrative procedures to sanction and cut off welfare, *unlike* nonmarket, exploitative forms of labor contract such as slavery, WEP entails little commitment on the part of the recipient of the labor (here, the City) to maintain the labor force when it is idle. Second, however, there is some sense in which WEP workers are *not* formally free. Like slaves and prisoners, they are compelled to work by the state, even if the state defines this compulsion as a simple choice between working in WEP and working in the labor market.[58] Third, the City's own administrative and contracting apparatus, by which HRA sends WEP workers to city agencies and nonprofits with municipal service contracts, spreads out accountability, making blame avoidance for program failures easier.

In all these ways, WEP's flexibility makes WEP a quintessential neoliberal program and appears to justify those social geographers who see the current spread of workfare as an epochal shift from "welfare" to "workfare" states, based on neoliberal reregulation. Neoliberalism promotes reliance on market mechanisms for the allocation of goods and services and hence deregulation and reregulation of allocation decisions toward market mechanisms; devolution of decision making from national states to lower scales of governance, which are closer to place-based market actors; and managerial flexibility at these lower scales of governance in order to allow governments to function according to a rapid decision-making market rationality. Put another way, if the Keynesian welfare state, which applied countercyclical state spending in order to stimulate demand, also functioned to "protect society from the market," neoliberal, workfarist governance is an attempt to "protect markets from society" and its needs. At the same time, as Daniel Cohn shows, this flexibility—which ostensibly subjects policy objectives to the discipline of the market and therefore *depoliticizes* policy—allows policymakers to shift blame to administrators if programs fail; administrators, then, would simply be regarded as people who failed to understand well enough the markets in which they were dealing.[59]

WEP simply concentrates within a single program the main ambiguities of labor contracts under a neoliberal framework. Indeed, contention over who works for whom and over the very definitions of labor contracts is becoming increasingly common. Though WEP workers' lawyers in the *Brukhman* case argued that "an employer- (or employee-) imposed label, such as 'trainee' or 'independent contractor,' is not dispositive of coverage [of the category of "employee"], and nor is the putative employer's intent relevant," there is increasing deference—as there was in *Brukhman*—to precisely these labels or stated intentions. As increasing amounts of litigation attest, there simply is no commonly agreed-upon standard.[60]

Moreover, the introduction of HRA—a social service agency—into the equation confuses things further. For example, in an editorial in 1997, the *New York Times* argued that WEP workers should not be unionized:

> City Hall should figure out a way to insure that workers have the tools and conditions they need to do their *jobs* with self-respect. But it would be a mistake to organize welfare workers into a union, because what they are doing *does not amount to a job.* . . . Instead, in return for receiving welfare, they must show up at a work site, follow instructions and carry out tasks that the city might not even be subsidizing if it did not have to put welfare recipients to work. In addition to their welfare checks, participants also receive vouchers for day care if needed. Many also get Medicaid, food stamps and other benefits that increase their total compensation.[61]

This editorial anticipated the language that the court of appeals used to rule in *Brukhman* three years later:

> Program participants simply are not "in the employ" of anyone—that is the very reason they are receiving public welfare benefits and required to participate in the Program, until they can find or be placed in jobs with the customary array of traditional indicia of employment. . . . Participants are "assigned" to various "work sites" where they provide "valuable service" until they are able to "secure employment in the regular economy." While the agencies providing work assignment opportunities obviously

employ some people, they are not "employing" Program participants. These agencies and entities simply do not pay a salary to the Program participants—one of the fundamental requisites that sparks the prevailing wage entitlement.[62]

And yet, to organizers, it was precisely the social service agency that often appeared as "the boss." Said one CVH organizer, who doubted the possibility of organizing WEP workers *as workers:*

> Because the person that they're directly accountable to is not the supervisor at their job [but rather] their caseworker and HRA. . . . A perfect example is Shelly. Shelly went to Black Vets for Social Justice to work at a particular workfare site. Black Vets for Social Justice said: "You came in late, this is messed up, we're not going to place you, go back to your caseworker." And so she was in conciliation [the process by which recipients must show why they should not be sanctioned]. I mean Black Vets for Social Justice wasn't the employer. They're not the boss. The boss to me is the person who controls your paycheck and controls your time. They don't control your time and they don't control your paycheck. HRA controls your time and your paycheck. HRA is in essence the employer. Not the Parks Department, not the Department of Housing.[63]

This sentiment, of course, echoes commonly voiced concerns among labor advocates about subcontracting and the difficulties of holding both subcontractors and contractors accountable for pay and working conditions. Though this concern is particularly true with respect to the global dispersion of commodity production, for example, with respect to the lack of labor regulation in developing countries' export processing or free-trade zones, it is also true of domestic sweated labor. Here, too, resistance to regulation from producers, contractors, and subcontractors fits in well with the reorientation of legal and social regulation toward protecting market-based allocation.

Discipline

In 1971, Frances Fox Piven and Richard A. Cloward proposed that welfare programs are primarily labor market regulating devices, expanding countercyclically in order to diffuse the potential for popular unrest amid high unemployment and contracting in better times to push more people into the labor market so as to cap wage demands. In good times, a residual welfare program would remain, but recipients would be so badly treated that it would serve as a public warning for those contemplating the benefits of the dole vis-à-vis exploitative labor contracts that paid inadequate wages. For Piven and Cloward, the "dramaturgy" of workfare accomplished just this.[64]

A second strand of neo-Marxist theory, proposed by James O'Connor in 1973, sought to understand the already-emerging tendency of the welfare state to sink into crisis. O'Connor suggested that capitalist states are caught between their reliance on privately accumulated capital for taxes, and hence their need to support capital accumulation, and the need to be seen by their subjects as legitimate, even when supporting capital accumulation that puts the majority at a structural disadvantage. Later analysts argued that capitalist states do not always succeed in regulating labor and accumulation on the one hand and public claims of universality and legitimacy on the other. They find instead that state actors and private capital form coalitions that support broad regulatory projects— which these "regulation theorists" call *regimes of accumulation* and *modes of regulation*—that define the public policy instruments they are willing to use. These theorists, moreover, suggest that modes of regulation may shift when a dominant regime of accumulation such as "Fordist" mass-production, enters a crisis in which alternative modes of organizing accumulation appear more efficient. For the regulation theorist Bob Jessop, the current post-Fordist, post-Keynesian period is consolidating around a "workfare regime" less anchored than Keynesianism in central planning by national state actors and more likely to promote flexibility and contingency in labor market governance. The geographer Jamie Peck even finds that workfare is a mechanism that *specifically* prepares recipients to accept as legitimate their consignment to contingent labor markets.[65]

WEP, like other workfare programs, demonstrates both strands of theory. Well into 2000, WEP workers frequently complained about the indignities they had to suffer in the program. Although Besharov and Germanis correctly note that no systematic research shows how widespread mistreatment of WEP workers was (they believe that it was sporadic), it was at least common enough to generate multiple class-action lawsuits and to attract the notice of several researchers. The indignities ranged from the common practice of issuing WEP workers orange or green vests (which might as well have been scarlet letters, marking them as welfare recipients) to municipal workers' denying them access to workers' restrooms or break rooms. Often, the indignities were worse, even health-threatening: WEP workers in outdoor assignments complained about having no place to urinate, no place to store their lunches, nor access to drinking water; others were not issued protective goggles when working with toxic solvents and cleaners; still others were not issued protective equipment when picking up garbage, including dead animals and feces. For example, in testimony given in a lawsuit for greater workplace protections for WEP workers, one WEP worker related that

> On June 18th . . . we came across two dead cats and two dead dogs. . . . They had been dumped by the side of the road. Because I had no gloves, I had to pick them up with my bare hands. The animals had been run over by automobiles and were oozing blood and entrails. When I picked up the animals to throw them into the garbage truck, the guts splattered on my shoes and pants. My co-worker vomited and the supervisor in the van said nothing.[66]

Piven and Cloward would expect nothing less.

Similarly, the Giuliani administration's early preference for "basic WEP," or the assignment of WEP workers to the maximum number of hours allowable under federal minimum wage guidelines, was expressly pitched *against* job training for welfare recipients. In 1998, the city's welfare commissioner, Jason Turner, put the philosophy succinctly in testimony to the state legislature: "What the employment community means by basic work skills is not a GED . . . but rather coming to work on time, getting along with co-workers, working a full day, being courteous and learning to take direction so that they can improve on the job. . . .Work experience is the best vehicle to provide that kind of training. . . . Once an individual is in employment and is meeting his or her obligations both to her family and to society, that's when additional educational training can be most effective."[67] Like Koch, Giuliani and his appointees claimed that for welfare recipients generally—regardless of the actual patterns of welfare use and work histories—the best preparation for a job was either a job or a "simulated" job, in the quasi-free, secondary-labor contract of WEP.

Distinctions

It is important in this regard, too, to note the ways in which two common distinctions work under workfare. The first is the well-known distinction between the deserving and the undeserving poor. Piven and Cloward date this distinction to the late Middle Ages, as protocapitalism and the first shadows of mass pauperism appeared. The difference is implicit both in Turner's explanation of workfare, cited in the previous section, and more generally within New York City's welfare reform program as it developed, not just in the rhetorical flourishes of politicians and administrators. The State welfare reform act of 1997 contained relatively generous "earned-income disregards" that allow welfare recipients to exempt a portion of their earnings from their reported income and thus continue to receive welfare benefits at a level that provides a financial incentive to stay employed but is still lower than the benefits they had been receiving.[68] In other words, in providing what is essentially a wage subsidy for contingent employment, the State legitimizes contingent labor contracts, even for those who are not on welfare. Moreover, the State funds programs for the working poor from the surplus generated by the TANF block grant. A State Earned-Income Tax Credit—for which WEP workers are ineligible—is paid for by funds generated from reducing the welfare rolls, as is a large portion of the subsidized child-care vouchers jointly paid for by the State and local governments. Indeed, these programs are credited for a net reduction in child poverty in the State since welfare reform. But they come at the cost of the increasing hardship for those who do not benefit, often those left on the welfare rolls.[69]

At the same time, workfare also reinforces a second distinction, that between public- and private-sector workers. In neoliberal discourse, the public sector is generally regarded as a drain on social resources. Since neoliberalism allows for few public goods—most things can be turned into commodities that can be bought and sold, even things like clean air—the public sector is not needed to correct for market failures, as it is under neoclassical theory. Denial of the importance of public action accounts for the preference for privatization in neoliberal governance and for a general hostility to public-sector workers. By putting WEP workers to work in jobs that are substantially similar—even if not identical—to those done by regular workers, the City could devalue public-sector workers, both symbolically by drawing them closer to WEP workers and in fact by exerting pressure on the unions' bargaining power. The same effect does not occur when welfare recipients are pushed into the private labor market.

WEP and the Times and Spaces of Neoliberal Governance

In this chapter, I have placed WEP in the context of neoliberalism to make sense of it. The combination of flexibility, fostering contingent labor contracts, public-sector employment shifts away from social services and infrastructure maintenance, and attacks on both public employment and on countercyclical income-maintenance programs are of a piece. The assemblage is best considered a set of institutional strategies with particular temporal and spatial dimensions that shape subsequent contention around the issue. Moreover, it corresponds to a specific response, developed in the early to mid-1970s, to a global crisis of accumulation, manifest in various ways across nations and localities.

Workfare and Fiscal Crisis

Here, consideration of New York's recent history of fiscal crisis is important in situating WEP more fully. The fiscal crisis that wracked New York City in the 1970s continues to influence city politics thirty years later. As the city lost over half a million manufacturing jobs during the 1960s, its population shrank, and its tax base fell. Nevertheless, its expenditures rose, in part due to State laws mandating that the City pay half of the State's share of expanding federal entitlement programs and in part due to the recent unionization and consequent wage and benefit gains of municipal workers. As a result, New York's revenues fell short of its expenditures for what the historian Joshua Freeman calls its local "social-democracy"—including a large public hospital system, a huge network of public libraries, and a free higher-education system.[70] For years, mayors and the Board of Estimate (then the city's legislature) engaged in fiscal shenanigans by issuing short-term debt, ostensibly for capital projects but actually to meet operating costs. The investment firms that marketed this debt encouraged this behavior, even though they knew it was risky, because they made significant commissions on the bond sales and because "municipal paper paid high interest, entailed low risk, and was exempt from federal income taxes. New York City debt had the additional attraction of being exempt from city and state taxes."[71]

By 1975, the banks' entanglement in increasingly mobile, global capital flows that were subject to crises of profitability following the oil crisis in 1973 and the concomitant threat of default by developing nations led to bankers' skittishness about allowing the City to continue rolling over its short-term debt.[72] Further, declining federal aid to cities under Presidents Nixon and Ford left the City with few untapped sources of revenue. Calculating that New York posed less of a default risk than did some of their other creditors, the banks cut off New York City's access to the capital markets pending a large-scale restructuring—and retrenchment—of the relatively generous local welfare state. The banks insisted on imposing an Emergency Financial Control Board on the City that had veto power over its fiscal decisions; this breach of democracy also disciplined the unions, forcing them—at the risk of their newly won collective bargaining rights—to accept tens of thousands of layoffs and to invest their pension funds in then risky municipal debt. Anything less than this onerous regime would not satisfy the Ford administration, which could provide needed loan guarantees. William Simon, Ford's treasury secretary, was especially vociferous in his opposition to a federal rescue of the City, in spite of his former job as head of municipal lending at Salomon Brothers, a premier Wall Street investment firm. Simon, a neoliberal, was a principal player in the conservative wing of the Republican Party and later helped consolidate conservatives' relationship with the think tanks and foundations that set the tenor of the welfare reform debates of the 1990s, having begun decades earlier by attacking President Johnson's Great Society programs.[73] As the fiscal crisis continued for three more years, conservatives, who had pushed New York over the edge, then held up the city's crumbling infrastructure as a national example of the price of liberal good intentions.[74] The Nixon administration's first proposal of workfare programs represented one of several responses, including a national minimum income, to address the looming crisis of accumulation due to steady deindustrialization in northern cities. And though timid in the face of welfare's actual expansion, the workfare proposal fit better and for longer with the party's "Southern Strategy," by which it used racially coded public policy to solidify its appeal to white voters in the South.

Blame directed at welfare recipients, and particularly to black city-dwellers, was not, however, confined to conservative circles in Washington, D.C. In New York City, too, the dominant explanation for the City's fiscal crisis was that liberals were unable to stand up to the demands of African Americans and Puerto Ricans and city unions, which were unreasonable in light of the City's shrinking fiscal capacity. The newly elected mayor, Edward I. Koch, also accepted this story of blame.[75] In trying to assemble a growth coalition that would direct public investment toward the financial sector in hopes of stimulating the local tax base, Koch took pride in anticipating the wishes of the city's creditor investment banks and the bond raters. His embrace of fiscal austerity in his first two of four terms put the City on better financial footing, though it also exacerbated long-term problems such as homelessness, gentrification, and structural fiscal imbalance, as New York became more dependent than ever on Wall Street.

Accordingly, when Koch's successor, David Dinkins, took office as Wall Street and the country entered a recession, fiscal crisis again ensued. Thus, the crisis, too, was partly due to the city's creditors and bond raters showing a lack of confidence in the liberal Dinkins' ability to demand concessions from his electoral constituency, which included municipal workers and organized African American and Latino interests. In the end, the bond raters forced Dinkins to cut more than twenty thousand municipal jobs, mainly in social and nonuniformed services, wrecking in the process the loyalty of his electoral coalition.[76]

In 1993, after narrowly losing the 1989 mayoral race to Dinkins, Giuliani reassembled the Koch coalition, capitalizing on racial tensions that flared at the end of Dinkins's term. The city's economy was still in recession, with its 8.5 percent unemployment rate three points higher than the nation's rate, infrastructure crumbling from years of deferred maintenance, high levels of homelessness, and demand for welfare at a historical peak. Giuliani pursued an aggressive neoliberal agenda, drawing extensive advice both from former Koch officials and from the Manhattan Institute, a local right-wing think tank. Through tax incentives and tax cuts, he deepened the city's financial dependence on Wall Street and aggressively cut welfare. To avoid outright conflict with the battered municipal unions, he agreed to a no-layoff clause in the negotiations with DC 37 in 1995 over the master contract in return for steady attrition, workfare expansion, and, most important, two years without raises.[77] At the same time, through the use of WEP workers, Giuliani was able to keep City services running at the same or higher levels than they ran before and to burnish the City's image among bond raters. Thus, he managed to hold the line on labor costs, reduce entitlement payouts, cut taxes, and raise the City's bond rating to postcrisis highs. This meant, however, that the City could, and did, borrow enormous amounts of money, even as public employee raises phased in during the out-years of the contract. Accordingly, even before the September 11 attacks of 2001, the City faced a $4.5 billion budget deficit that Giuliani's successor would have to tackle.[78]

Here, then, is another way in which workfare is a flexible program. Taken over the long term, workfare appears as part of a fix for several crises at once, adaptable to national electoral crises for the Republican Party; an aid to implementing and publicly legitimating a neoliberal urban regime; and a major strategic move to consolidate that regime. In all cases, the legitimation of neoliberal austerity depended in part on racial and gender stereotyping but cannot be reduced to it. Instead, the racialized and gendered blame that was leveled at poor urbanites justified austerity and depoliticized a new, segmented labor market regime that by the 1990s resulted in net losses of income for the bottom four quintiles of New York's residents.

Yet despite its apparent durability, the new neoliberal regime—with its geographic basis in the selective devolution of national administrative authority to states and localities, preference for privatization, and institution of marketlike mechanisms throughout government administration— contains its own emerging institutional limits, even as it creates new institutional opportunities for austerity-driven accumulation.

WEP and the Temporal and Spatial Parameters of Neoliberal Urban Strategy

WEP's labor market characteristics and its role in disciplining both public-sector employees and welfare recipients into contingent or secondary labor markets demonstrate its place in neoliberal governance, both at the urban scale and by extension at the national one. In the previous section, I have given some idea of the long-term development of the workfare-related cure for the crisis of the welfare state since the 1970s. But what is particularly important about this long-term story is that, in general, neoliberal policy invites short-term, strategic policy innovation, spread through networks of private and public policymakers.

This emphasis on short-term calculation can be seen in the high turnover at welfare worksites, in the Job Center program's emphasis on diverting people from applying for welfare, in its later performance-based contracts with employment service providers that reward job placement first (though they provide job retention incentives, too), and, principally, in resisting WEP's opponents' calls for mechanisms of recourse comparable to those available to employees.

To be sure, under neoliberal governance, longer-term calculation is not swept away. Instead, it is converted into a hedge against accountability.[79] In the previous chapter's introduction to contention over WEP, the Giuliani administration was shown to have pushed activists to challenge his welfare reforms in court. But courts and Public Employee Safety and Health inspections take far longer than most welfare spells or workfare placements. The Giuliani administration could often, therefore, push the time of crucial decision making beyond its tenure. Similarly, the administration's labor policies that secured back-loaded wage increases for municipal employees allowed the Giuliani administration both to avoid blame and to create a potential long-term debt crisis for his successors.

Giuliani's blame avoidance suggests the spatiotemporal limits of neoliberal strategy as well. For example, though Giuliani was long out of office when a United States Court of Appeals ruled that WEP workers were enough like employees to merit protection from sexual and racial harassment, the court did, eventually, render that decision. Without changing WEP's prospects completely, this decision does suggest potential new limits on its expansion should neoliberal policy developments at the national level require states to intensify their work requirements for welfare recipients. These requirements would issue from proposals drawn in part from New York's model, thanks to Jason Turner's influence in the national policy networks that President Ford's treasury secretary, William Simon, helped establish in the 1970s. If localities are required by federal neoliberal policy to put more people to work; and if these localities' secondary labor markets are depressed in the private sector, creating little demand, local governments may have to push welfare recipients into work experience programs, much as the Giuliani administration did in 1995. If, at the same time, courts require WEP workers to be treated more like employees—and thus open up potential challenges to WEP workers' nonemployee status—the use of the courts as a blame-avoidance tactic will have run its course.

Additionally, neoliberal workfare policy, as it diffuses through national-level policy networks and filters back down to localities through federal policy, makes local labor market conditions important in shaping the form that local programs take, their outcomes, and the form their opposition takes. Jamie Peck indicates that workfare programs, when instantiated in buoyant labor markets, will tend to take the form of aggressive private-sector labor force attachment policies, including wage subsidies to employers, or will rely heavily on benefits terminations. By contrast, where labor markets are depressed, with few private-sector jobs available, the public sector will often absorb workfare. By extension, the latter situation will most often result in mobilizations that attempt to extend unionization to workfare workers, while the difficulties of organizing dispersed, disadvantaged workers will more likely lead to moral protest campaigns and boycotts.[80]

Peck's theoretical insights are acute, but the spaces and times of workfare are complexly enough related that workfare politics is not easily deducible from local labor market conditions. As the discussion of the use of the courts makes clear, labor market institutions, such as unions and worksites, and labor market dynamics, such as changing local job markets, interact with neighborhood groups, local and national media, legal settings, and legislatures, spanning multiple scales of governance to produce distinctive patterns of workfare politics and challenges to neoliberals' public justifications of workfare. The discussion here has highlighted WEP's regulatory history and statutory context and has located them in a larger discussion of neoliberal welfare-state politics, particularly on the urban scale. With an idea of what the actors in this story are shouting about, we move to a discussion of the actors themselves.

CHAPTER THREE

The Formation of a Protest Field

Workfare is both a product of neoliberal governance and a strategy to accomplish it. One important aspect of studying workfare politics, therefore, is tracing the ways in which welfare-work policies are implemented over time, how they fit with other neoliberal policies, and how they generate opposition, when they do. We have already seen the ways in which the workfare contract under New York City's Work Experience Program (WEP) had spillover effects in other areas of policy. I have also given a thumbnail sketch of WEP's connection with attempts by successive municipal governments to impose policy solutions to align policy with the demands of bond raters and federal mandates that imposed increasing austerity on the city's poor.

Here, I extend this analysis but push it in a somewhat different direction. In this chapter, I build the foundation for understanding the relationship between the rise of a network or field of anti-WEP organizations and coalitions and the policy experience that led to the formation of these groupings. As David Meyer and Nancy Whittier remind us, social movements are often influenced in formative ways by other movements, as they share repertoires of action or claim-making, personnel, or organizational styles.[1] Moreover, they claim that social movement spillover is most likely to occur when political opportunities—especially elite alliances—change, so that movements can either openly adopt each other's practices, potentially fusing into a larger movement, or shift goals, so that new movements appear when the institutional avenues for success in previous movements become blocked.

Meyer and Whittier's connection between movement spillover and the spillover of policy arenas is important because it helps make tractable key questions in the study of anti-WEP activity: Why did groups that advocated around housing and homelessness form an important core of anti-WEP struggles? Why did unions, which were possibly threatened most by the public-sector expansion of WEP, play a subordinate role in opposing the program? What kinds of coalitions emerged from the meeting of housing and antipoverty advocates, antipoverty lawyers, and unions?

This chapter moves through three steps. First, it lays out a theoretical framework for understanding the history of the groups that would eventually form the core of WEP's opposition. Then in the second step, drawing on the history of WEP (as discussed in chapter 2), on Meyer and Whittier's ideas about movement spillover, and on the regulation theory introduced in chapter 2, I argue that each institutional actor—housing and homelessness activists, antihunger and antipoverty advocates, legal advocates for the poor, and labor unions—was incorporated differently in the post-fiscal-crisis effort to regulate and manage New York's public services. As the tensions within these arrangements developed, these institutional actors variously strove to retain what power they preserved in them or to find ways to challenge them. By the time WEP expanded in 1995, some groups had emerged as core actors in what could be called—drawing from studies of robotics—*hard-assembled* coalitions, and others rmed *soft-assembled* ones. The former term refers to coalitions that are oriented to a specific object, make public claims together, and share staff and resources. The latter type of coalitions, by contrast, may share rhetorical claims but do not coordinate their work or resources. As a result, hard-assembled coalitions are more costly to maintain but also have more easily measured outcomes. Soft-assembled coalitions are more flexible and may form the substrate out of which hard-assembled coalitions form. The third step in the chapter relies on a combination of concept-metaphors from Gramsci's work and from Bourdieu's to characterize the ways in which movement coalitions relate to one another and to authorities to form "fields" of politics, marked by relative intensities of institutional and rhetorical spillover and by various strategic considerations that follow from them.

An Analytical Framework for Political Fields

In 1994, Meyer and Whittier's seminal article on social movement spillover formalized and abstracted what historical accounts of movements had long known, namely, that movements often share personnel, learn from one another, establish links based on converging ideological preferences, and spin off other movements that bear the stamp of their origins. As chapter 2 shows, policy spillover is also common. What spills over and how, both in movements and in policy, should, however, have something to do with the ways in which movement organizations (or potential movement organizations) and state actors relate to each other.

Bob Jessop has extended regulation theory and regime theory in urban politics to a more general, ideal-typical framework for understanding various coalitional configurations of state and civil-society actors in the wake of Keynesian social policy's eclipse. He contrasts neoliberal coalitions—which are marked by strong efforts to privatize public services, apply marketlike mechanisms to residual public services, devolve costs of social protections to lower levels of government, and "protect the market from society"—from other arrangements, such as neocorporatist, neostatist, and neocommunitarian ones. Neocorporatist coalitions also rely on privatization, but they do so primarily by means of contracting for public services with existing sectors of civil society, while neostatist coalitions opt for more-direct state direction and management of public services, even if they are scaled back. Neocommunitarian coalitions are also heavily devolutionary, but they do not expect that the community organizations charged with maintaining public services will do so according to market principles but will rather be the main conduits for state-led redistribution.[2]

As I will show subsequently, the emergence of the anti-WEP political field took place in the context of movement spillover prompted by similar dynamics of transition between a neocorporatist arrangement that had prevailed in New York since the fiscal crisis and that had been steadily chipped away by neoliberal policies and a more fully neoliberal regime. How did new coalitions emerge from this transition? How do these coalitions structure the field, and vice versa?

Coalitions and Fields

The first task in unpacking these questions is to define and distinguish coalitions and fields. *Coalitions,* as I use the term, refer to assemblages of actors that consciously or unconsciously support common sets of political claims. This is, to be sure, a minimalist definition but one that allows for considerable variation in the extent of explicit collaboration among the actors within it. Another way of thinking about coalitions is that they are essentially network structures that may be more or less densely joined, more or less centralized, and more or less internally clustered. The same is true for fields.

As Raka Ray explains in her adaptation of Bourdieu's concept of a field,

> A field can be thought of as a structured, unequal, and socially constructed environment *within* which organizations are embedded and to which organizations and activists constantly respond. Organizations are not autonomous or free agents, but rather they inherit a field and its accompanying social relations, and when they act, they act in response to it and within it. . . . Within political fields may lie smaller or even more localized political subfields. There may also be critical or oppositional subfields, which I call *protest fields*. Protest fields consist of groups and networks that oppose those who have the power in the formal political arena and may or may not share the logic of politics in the larger political field, although they are constrained by it.[3]

The difference between a coalition and a field, therefore, is that they are different orders of relational structures, with fields containing the organizations that may form coalitions.

Hard Assembly and Soft Assembly

For Meyer and Whittier, the principal components of social movement spillover were shared embeddedness in the policy outcomes and rhetoric of state actors, shared culture, and shared personnel. To these components should be added shared forms of organization and action and shared resource mobilization. It is useful to extend this idea to think about the kinds of coalitions that can emerge when one of these components is shared, as opposed to when several are shared. Figure 3.1 suggests a continuum of overlap among organizations by which we can characterize coalitions as being soft- or hard-assembled.

The concept of hard assembly in robotics refers to such things as robotic arms that are designed for specific tasks, such as moving particular objects from one side of an assembly line to another. Soft assembly refers to objects such as the human foot, which adjusts to shifts in surface texture, shoe tightness, knee or ankle stiffness or soreness, and body weight. Though soft assembly is the "cutting edge" in artificial intelligence and robotics,[4] when thinking about social movement coalitions,

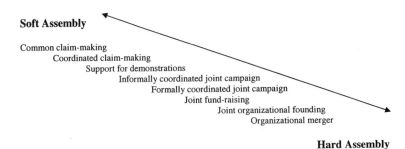

Soft Assembly

Common claim-making
Coordinated claim-making
Support for demonstrations
Informally coordinated joint campaign
Formally coordinated joint campaign
Joint fund-raising
Joint organizational founding
Organizational merger

Hard Assembly

Figure 3.1. Hard- and soft-assembled coalitions

it is important to understand that hard-assembled coalitions, which are more labor intensive to sustain, are also more clearly accountable to their members and better able to coordinate the shows of "worthiness, unity, numbers, and commitment," or "WUNC," that are central features of movement campaigns.[5]

Soft-assembled coalitions may be thought of as loosely joined networks, where personal acquaintance and shared information form the principal ties in the network. Further along the continuum toward hard assembly are coordinated actions, and further still, coordinated campaigns among separate organizations. Hard-assembled coalitions are networks in which formal coordinated action, joint fund-raising, and centralized planning predominate.

Types of Fields

The imagery of hard- and soft-assembled coalitions can be usefully employed in characterizing fields, which are second-order relational structures. Consider Ray's characterization of fields according to concentration of political power and ideological homogeneity (fig. 3.2).

Ray explains that in fragmented fields, "a multiplicity of organizations and ideologies can coexist," whereas in segmented fields, multiple cultures coexist with a concentration of power. In pluralist fields, "organizations of more or less equal power coexist, although all share . . . the same understanding of how politics is to be done."[6] In hegemonic fields, a single organization concentrates power—all organizations are tied to it—and controls the dominant discourse.

Another way of thinking about this is that ideal-typical fragmented fields may not contain coalitions at all; segmented fields can contain hard-

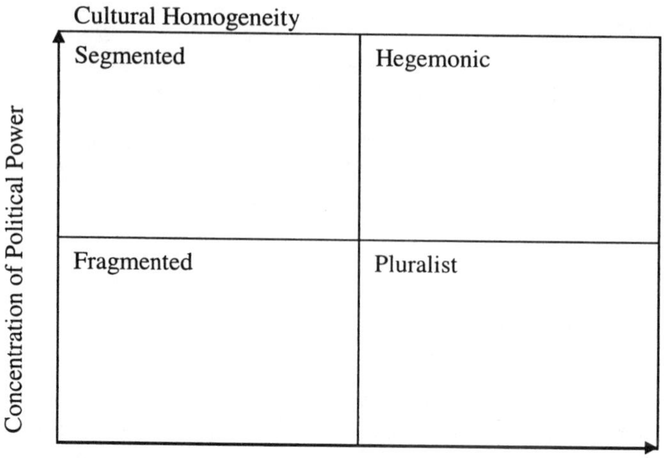

Cultural Homogeneity

Segmented	Hegemonic
Fragmented	Pluralist

Concentration of Political Power

Figure 3.2. Cultural political fields. Reprinted by permission from Raka Ray,
Fields of Protest: Women's Movements in India (Minneapolis: University
of Minnesota Press, 1999), 11.

assembled coalitions but do not necessarily contain soft-assembled ones; pluralist fields can be thought of as large, soft-assembled coalitions in which it is difficult to sustain hard-assembled coalitions (a point central to most accounts of pluralism); and hegemonic fields can be understood as containing a hard-assembled coalition at the core, with multiple hard- and soft-assembled coalitions joining the central structure. Of course, as ideal-types, the various sorts of fields are not seen in their pure forms; rather, sub-fields, and even coalitions, differ with respect to the degree of ideological homogeneity and power concentrations.

In principle, it is possible for the various kinds of regimes outlined by Jessop to live in any of these arrangements. Practically, however, hegemonic fields secure each most efficiently, even though, in the case of neoliberalism, the libertarian ideology professed by its proponents would likely find greatest support in pluralist, or even fragmented, fields.[7] Beyond the formalism implied in this model, however, the concept of a political field requires not just an understanding of the relation of the protest organizations to one another but also an understanding of protest organizations interacting with authorities. This is true both within a protest field and within the political field where protest fields exist. Therefore, it is difficult to understand why the organized opposition to workfare arises where and when it does, and in what coalitional formations, without understanding the dynamics of the field and the influence of a generation's worth of neoliberal initiatives and neocorporatist compromises in the City. It is to these questions to which I will now turn.

The Formation of the Field

Organizational Substrates of the Anti-WEP Field

HOUSING GROUPS. The late 1960s and the 1970s witnessed an efflorescence of community-based organizations dedicated to neighborhood preservation and renewal. Using such programs as the Comprehensive Education and Training Act (CETA) to subsidize job creation in the community-based social services sector and in organizing jobs, they continued to grow into the 1970s as low-income communities were increasingly threatened by abandonment and reductions in municipal services in the wake of the fiscal crisis.[8]

Many neighborhood-based nonprofit organizations began, in the 1980s, to take advantage of City programs to rehabilitate housing previously abandoned by landlords, if not by tenants. Particularly because the CETA funds that allowed community-based groups to maintain staff were cut by President Reagan in the early 1980s, many of these groups began to take advantage of City rehabilitation funds to keep their organizations afloat, along with providing the housing and neighborhood improvement services that were their original raisons d'être. The assumption of the role of landlord, however, led to inevitable tensions, as organizers turned into managers. Groups had to implement rent increases and other management changes and became more professionalized in accordance with the demands of funders and the government agencies that administered housing development programs. As Harold DeRienzo, a veteran of one of the city's best-known community-based housing groups, bitterly wrote in 1994: "Local housing groups have, for the most part, ceased to be agitators and protagonists for change. Instead, the organizations that comprise the so-called community housing movement have become content to merely manage a desperate crisis of dilapidation, abandonment, and homelessness. . . . They became service providers, agencies, landlords."[9] DeRienzo, is, of course, indicating the pitfalls of housing groups' incorporation on an unequal footing with other coalition partners into a neocorporatist regime. With an eye on the long-term response to the

City's fiscal crisis—prompted in part by the loss of over half a million manufacturing jobs from the 1960s to the 1980s, which in turn was fueled, at least in part, by real estate speculation that raised industrial rents past any point of sustainability—DeRienzo pinpointed the legitimizing function played by housing groups for the very dynamics against which they thought they were reacting.

Some groups, cognizant of this challenge, tried to avoid demobilization and co-optation. Two of the groups that became deeply involved in organizing WEP workers emerged from this milieu. The Fifth Avenue Committee (FAC), in particular, fit the profile of community-based housing groups that began as tenant organizers and became increasingly professional housing development outfits. Nevertheless, several factors may have contributed to FAC's ability to maintain strong community support in spite of its expansion and professionalization. FAC expanded its housing and economic development activities slowly and kept its tenant organizing capacity strong. In the housing it developed, FAC formed mutual housing associations and limited-equity cooperatives, two forms of resident- and community-controlled housing that take housing off the speculative market and leave most management decisions in the hands of residents. Accordingly, FAC had to maintain its organizing work after development and to balance organizing with management.[10] Though this balance is hard to strike, FAC's deliberate expansion left it less vulnerable to the kinds of development pressures that led other groups to favor management over resident involvement in their organizations. It is partly through FAC's constant contact with the residents in the housing it organized and developed that it came to provide public benefits advocacy in 1994, as greater obstacles to receiving and keeping welfare benefits became apparent.

The Association of Community Organizations for Reform Now, or ACORN, also came to workfare organizing through housing, though it did so differently from FAC. ACORN began as a membership-building project of the National Welfare Rights Organization (NWRO) in 1970, in Little Rock, Arkansas (the A used to stand for Arkansas). After the demise of its parent organization in 1971, ACORN branched out, eventually starting chapters in fifty-five cities in thirty-eight states. During the early and mid-1980s, ACORN chapters in several cities, including Philadelphia and New York, staged large squatting campaigns in abandoned housing in order both to highlight the severity of the affordable housing crisis then emerging and to gain title to the properties for low-income renters. In New York, in order to resolve a standoff with the Koch administration and to gain control of dozens of housing units in Brooklyn, ACORN agreed to set up a mutual housing association, jointly governed by its members and technical assistance providers from the Brooklyn-based Pratt Institute Center for Community and Environmental Development.[11]

WEP's expansion in 1995 added an element of policy spillover to the already recognized tensions marking FAC's and ACORN's position as low-income housing providers and advocates. The policy spillover, moreover, was palpable: as the combination of increased sanctions, onerous workfare assignments, harassment and maltreatment at worksites, and increased barriers to welfare registration mounted, FAC's and ACORN's low-income constituents began to complain to organizers in the groups, fall behind on rent payments, or both.

ANTIHUNGER AND HOMELESSNESS ADVOCATES. Activism around homelessness and hunger provided a second strand of the organizational substrate of the anti-WEP field. Three quite different groups came from this sector: the Urban Justice Center, Community Voices Heard, and the Community Food Resource Center. The Urban Justice Center (UJC) began in 1984 as the Legal Action Center for the Homeless (LACH) to provide public benefits advocacy to homeless people. LACH held legal clinics at neighborhood soup kitchens and helped homeless New Yorkers get or retain the public benefits they were due. It also did advocacy-oriented research on issues that affected the health and safety of homeless people, especially those living on the street. By 1995, LACH had expanded into several areas, including public benefits advocacy for nonhomeless poor people and advocacy and legal work on domestic violence, exploitation of homeless workers by business improvement districts, and the growing use of prisons to house the poor. Like the housing groups discussed earlier, it sought to balance this expansion—which required the expansion of its professionally trained staff—with greater grassroots input into the organization. In 1995, LACH reorganized as the Urban Justice Center, an administrative core for a half-dozen partly independent projects. Among these was the UJC Organizing Project, which worked mainly with low-income and homeless women in a leadership-development course. In the course, the women came up with a focus for an organizing project that was of immediate concern: the expansion of WEP, working conditions, and the tightening of eligibility for welfare.

At roughly the same time, Community Voices Heard (CVH) was founded as a separate, membership-based organization from within an existing antihunger advocacy group, the Hunger Action Network of

New York State (HANNYS). HANNYS was founded in 1982 to address food security issues in New York City and in Albany, the state capital. By the mid-1980s, the New York City chapter had begun to organize residents of homeless shelters into a Homeless Clients Advisory Committee that could advocate for changes in the shelter system and in system administration. Though the committee had the sporadic organizational life typical of grassroots homeless groups (due mainly to turnover in the organization), HANNYS organizers remained active in recruiting homeless shelter residents to self-advocacy projects. By 1995, the New York City organizer had a cohesive group of activists who were concerned primarily with the looming changes in the City's welfare system. Through 1995 and 1996, CVH separated itself from HANNYS—which also continued to advocate around these issues—and became a membership organization with a board of directors composed almost entirely of welfare recipients.

The third group to emerge from homeless and hunger activism was the Community Food Resource Center (CFRC). CFRC was founded in 1980 by staff from the Community Service Society (CSS), a charity and advocacy organization with roots in nineteenth-century social work and reform movements. At the time, CSS was also promoting awareness of the growing homelessness problem and was a major participant in founding the Coalition for the Homeless, some of whose homeless constituents formed part of CVH's core organizing group. CFRC addressed a growing food emergency in New York City, a crisis only exacerbated by cuts in welfare and federal aid to cities under President Reagan. With several other antihunger organizations, CFRC helped set up an extensive network of soup kitchens, food banks, and food-delivery systems for poor people in New York. It also advocated around hunger-related issues such as President Ronald Reagan's proposal to classify ketchup as a vegetable in school lunches.

CFRC also developed a crack policy advocacy team that was second to none in developing up-to-date analyses of welfare policy changes. Though CFRC, unlike the other groups discussed so far, did not rely on or foster grassroots participation, it was prominent in a number of ways in the development of the antiworkfare network. First, the CFRC policy director, Liz Krueger (now a state senator), was a cochair and co-organizer of the Welfare Reform Network (WRN), a contact group of the City's welfare-, hunger-, and homeless-advocacy groups that convened to issue policy statements and to share information on policy changes. WRN formed in response to the imminent passage of the Family Support Act of 1988 (FSA). This act, written by then Sen. Daniel Patrick Moynihan, Democrat from New York, was pivotal legislation in that it both encumbered federal welfare benefits for mothers with children with work requirements and created the waiver system by which states could—and increasingly did—get federal authorization to design their own, more punitive welfare reform programs. Though WRN lost its fight against the FSA, it kept meeting, and it became an important forum in which groups such as FAC, UJC, CVH, and others could share their on-the-ground experience with others and gain intelligence on new policy developments. CFRC played another role as the organization to which grassroots activists looked for policy analysis and regularly testified in front of city council and other legislative bodies on welfare reform issues.

Unlike the housing groups, the antipoverty and antihunger organizations were mainly left out of the neocorporatist regime. HANNYS and LACH, and certainly CVH and UJC's organizing project, tried to exert pressure from outside official decision-making networks. CFRC, on the other hand, fulfilled much of its hunger relief work, a function that arguably enabled the neocorporatist system to work as smoothly as it did without major unrest. Nevertheless, in its advocacy work, CFRC was also agitating from the outside. Its unparalleled research made it an important resource for critics of neoliberal policies, even among those within the regime. The general outsider status of the antihunger, homelessness, and antipoverty advocates made it difficult for them to gain concessions on their own. For them, the spillover of WEP policy into housing and labor politics provided an opportunity to gain institutional traction not previously available to them.

LEGAL ADVOCATES. Legal advocacy groups formed another essential sector in the development of anti-WEP networks in New York. WEP's expansion and the toughening of Eligibility Verification Reviews (EVRs) mobilized the existing welfare-rights infrastructure to new levels. At the outset of WEP's expansion, the principal groups dealing with welfare rights in New York City were the Legal Aid Society's civil division and the Legal Services Corporation's neighborhood offices.

Legal Aid is a private corporation supported in large part by its contracts with the City for the defense of indigent criminal suspects. It maintains a civil division, too, to represent poor clients in civil cases, and it has done so vigorously in many cases against the City. Over a period of more than twenty years, through class-action litigation, Legal Aid lawyers have, for example, been crucial in establishing and safeguarding a right to shelter for New York's homeless people. The Legal Services Corporation, by contrast, is a federally funded organization whose mission is to provide legal services to the poor. A product of the Johnson-era Great Society, Legal Services built on the model of community-based services for the poor established by Mobilization For Youth, a program that was later funded in the early 1960s by the Office of Economic Opportunity and that was a wellspring of poor people's organizing in New York.[12]

In addition to neighborhood offices, Legal Services maintained several "backup centers" with experts in legal subfields relevant to the lives of poor people. Among these backups were the National Employment Law Project (NELP), the National Housing Law Project, and the Center on Social Welfare Policy and Law. These offices both assisted local offices on matters of the law in cases they were pursuing, including large, class-action cases, and provided advice for advocates and testimony for public officials. Lawyers from the Center on Social Welfare Policy and Law were the main attorneys whose arguments established a right to welfare in the United States Supreme Court's decision on *Goldberg v. Kelly*. In *Goldberg*, the Court held that states could not withdraw welfare benefits from welfare recipients without due process. It established the priority of the administrative fair hearing, by which welfare recipients could contest penalties levied against them, establishing, too, in the process, a property right in welfare.[13]

In 1996, however, Congress nearly defunded Legal Services; as a compromise, legislators limited its activities, making it illegal for the organization to challenge federal welfare reform laws or to pursue class-action suits, among other things.[14] This action effectively would have shut down Legal Services' backup centers and with them the advocacy activities. In response, while several backup centers closed, others spun off as independent nonprofit corporations. Among the latter were the Center for Social Welfare Policy and Law, now renamed the Welfare Law Center (WLC), and the National Employment Law Project. WLC and NELP, though both formerly part of Legal Services, had not worked extensively together. Now, free of the restrictions on their activities and rooted in New York City, they both became central to work with organizers, advocates, and Legal Aid lawyers in challenging WEP. Though the three organizations sometimes disagreed about legal strategy, each approaching the law differently, they formed a core of litigators who worked well with advocates and community groups. They developed a distinctive workfare-related set of hybrid legal claims, combining welfare law and labor law. Several other, smaller legal advocacy groups and pro bono lawyers from large New York City firms also worked on anti-WEP litigation.

NELP, with the services of a lawyer paid by a public-service fellowship run by Skadden, Arps, Slate, Meagher, and Flom, one of the major corporate law firms in the city, developed a particularly good working relationship with CVH. The fellow, a recent law graduate, worked with CVH to start a legal clinic at CVH's East Harlem offices. Quickly, the group turned into a forum for legal help and also into a political consciousness-raising group. In discussions with CVH members, most of whom were on welfare and subject to WEP requirements, the lawyer found that the limits of the law were reached rapidly, and so was legal leverage on behalf of welfare recipients. This finding meant that discussions turned to the ways in which legal strategy and organizing strategy could work together. In many respects, the strong ties between CVH and NELP helped drive forward the major areas of activism around WEP.

Legal advocacy groups, therefore, were part of older corporatist arrangements, organized by federal antipoverty programs to bypass, at least in part, state and local governments that were, at the time, viewed as obstructing, rather than facilitating, the redistributionist politics of the Great Society. These corporatist arrangements were explicitly under attack by neoliberals in Congress, who saw that the federal-community partnership they implied could undermine a differently pitched devolution of welfare under reforms, both legislated and granted under waivers allowable under previous legislation. Certainly, this is less true specifically for the Legal Aid Society. But it, too, was under attack by the City government and saw its City funding cut as well. The main point here is that WEP's expansion came at roughly the same moment as efforts to eviscerate the organizations that would protect welfare recipients and the poor. The Legal Services groups' reorganization at this time focused more of their efforts than before on the unusually extensive workfare program unfolding locally.

A Fourth Piece or a Fifth Column? Municipal Labor and Labor Revitalization

Community housing and homelessness organizations worried about co-optation by the government, but this concern was less evident among the city's public-sector labor unions. First among the unions affected by WEP was District Council 37 of the American Federation of State, County, and Municipal Employees (AFSCME). DC 37 is the city's largest public employees' union and is an umbrella organization of fifty-six independent locals representing nonmanagerial city employees. Though it is the largest local organization of AFSCME, a union at the forefront of the progressive takeover of the AFL–CIO in 1995, and a leader in committing resources to organizing,[15] DC 37 has been lackluster at organizing. It has also become increasingly weaker and conflict-averse since the early 1980s.

Here, too, the pivotal period was the fiscal crisis of the late 1970s. There were three key elements of the workout plan developed to reestablish New York's access to capital markets. The first was the creation of an Emergency Financial Control Board (EFCB) with state, city, and private representatives and the authority to dictate the City's finances. The EFCB brought with it the ability to veto any collective bargaining agreement between the City and its unions. The second key element was forcing the City's public-sector unions to invest pension funds into low-rated municipal bonds, based on the power the EFCB had to unravel more than twenty years of municipal union gains and newly won recognition. The third was the requirement of massive layoffs in municipal agencies, which the unions had to accept as a condition of keeping fiduciary control over their pension funds, given the first two conditions.[16] While the City's financial recovery ended by being relatively good for the unions' pension funds, the important thing here is that the principal municipal unions, and DC 37 chief among them, were seriously weakened.

In addition to these elements was the earlier passage, in 1967, of the Taylor Law, which, in the wake of the 1966 transit strike, banned strikes by public employees and set stiff penalties for striking, including jail time for leaders.[17] Municipal unions had recently won the automatic checkoff of union dues from municipal salary checks. The immediate result was that organizers were free to agitate for change and to attend to member services rather than to chase down members in their role of dues collectors. But as Robert Fitch, a sociologist of urban labor issues, indicates, the downside of the automatic checkoff, especially as the strike was taken away as a weapon in collective bargaining, was that unions began to bureaucratize and leaders to lose contact with the rank and file.[18] The labor historian Mark Maier concludes that during the 1970s and 1980s, municipal unions dampened rather than encouraged rank-and-file militancy.[19]

While Stanley Hill, the executive director of DC 37 in 1995, had been a leader of a social services workers' strike in 1965 that involved demands for higher welfare benefit levels, too, the next quarter century had turned him into a moderate, disinclined to publicly rein in the increasingly corrupt local leaders who formed his base of support. Because DC 37 has a bloc-voting system, the two largest locals controlled the votes for the positions of executive director and members of the executive board. Accordingly, the presidents of these two locals developed a strong stake in the union's stability. Perhaps unsurprisingly, these were the two locals accused of the greatest malfeasance in the wide-ranging corruption scandal that broke in mid-1998.

Apart from rampant embezzlement, the main aspect of corruption lay in the ratification vote of the master contract negotiated between DC 37 and the City in 1995. The contract, which set a pattern for all other municipal unions, according to municipal labor bargaining tradition, was passed by a fraudulent vote over the wishes of the rank and file in early 1996. Still smarting from nearly twenty thousand layoffs forced upon Mayor David Dinkins by bond raters during the fiscal crisis of the early 1990s, DC 37 wanted to do as little as possible to antagonize Mayor Giuliani so as not to display the union's weakness to its membership. The five-year agreement featuring two years of no raises followed by small raises in the next three years was, in the estimation of union leaders, the best deal that could be reached without layoffs. The leaders faced a revolt by the rank and file, especially from hospital workers who were excluded from the contract's no-layoff clause to allow for the possibility of public-hospital privatization. Therefore, certain deputies and local presidents at DC 37 chose to stuff the ballot boxes to ensure a narrow victory.[20]

Only in the light of these events is it possible to understand DC 37's position on WEP. WEP was already a feature of the social welfare landscape in 1995, though it was much smaller than it became. Workfare's last large-scale expansion had been in 1978 with the growth of the Public Works Program (PWP) under Mayor Koch. The PWP turned into the Work Experience Program later but was focused only on Home Relief (HR) program participants; it concentrated clerical jobs in the Human Resources Administration (HRA), the welfare department. Accordingly, the clerical workers' union chief had long adjusted to WEP. In December 1994, the public-school employees' president became the first union leader to embrace the expansion of WEP, by agreeing to set up a program in the local to train WEP workers to fill vacancies.[21] This agreement meant that even before expanding WEP in March 1995, the administration had lined up the most important support for its initiative within DC 37. The 1995 contract, moreover, had side agreements that tacitly, if not explicitly, accepted WEP by giving unionized employees substantial pay differentials if they supervised WEP workers. It is likely for this reason that by the time the scandal in the union broke over embezzlement and vote fraud, WEP had become a symbol of DC 37's selling out.[22]

The Communications Workers of America Local 1180 symbolized the opposite end of New York's public sector labor scene. CWA 1180

represents many white-collar workers and supervisors in City government, typically in the middle-range civil service categories, especially in
the HRA. While Local 1549, the DC 37 union representing many eligibility workers and clerical workers at HRA, had long accommodated to
WEP, CWA 1180 had not. There were certainly local presidents within DC
37 who were unhappy with the contract—and even alleged, years before
it was proven, that it was passed fraudulently—and there was discontent
among an increasingly vocal rank-and-file reform movement, but the District Council's inertia made it hard for these groups to move easily. CWA
1180 was one of the few unions to stand up to Mayor Giuliani in the
1995–96 round of collective bargaining. It paid dearly, losing nearly 15
percent of its membership through layoffs and job reclassifications. Led
by more ideologically uncompromising leaders, CWA 1180 is also part
of a progressive national union. CWA 1180's leaders rejected the terms
offered by the Giuliani administration as part of the pattern established
by its contract with DC 37. But because it, like other public-sector unions,
cannot strike without suffering dire consequences, CWA was forced to
accept the bulk of the deal *and* be excluded from the no-layoff clause.[23]

Unions were in much of the same position as were housing groups.
On the one hand, they were accepted as a legitimate partner in governance and as a legitimate representative of municipal workers in the
neocorporatist regime governing New York since the fiscal crisis. On the
other hand, the terms of their inscription into the neocorporatist regime
slowly but surely cut into their power. Further, unions were critical of any
move to erode their positions in the neocorporatist regime, and so they
tended to be critical of workfare, too. Nevertheless, the steadily increasing distance between unions' leaders and their members meant that rank-
and-file union members often saw WEP workers only as a threat, rather
than as potential allies. This perception combined with internal problems plaguing unions like DC 37 and access problems plaguing unions
like CWA 1180 to make unions uncertain partners in the coalitions that
emerged.

What Kind of Coalitions? What Kind of Field?

Hard Assembly from Soft

The first explicit effort to oppose workfare by mobilizing workfare workers
occurred with the formation of WEP Workers Together (WWT) in 1996,
as activists from FAC, UJC, and CVH (then separating from HANNYS)

agreed to combine their efforts. A soft-assembled network of antipoverty activists existed, both in the context of the Welfare Reform Network and in friendship and acquaintance networks. Paul Getsos, the lead organizer of CVH, and Benjamin Dulchin, FAC's organizing director, knew each other through a common friend at the Food and Hunger Hotline, one of CFRC's principal partners in hunger relief work; at the same time, CVH and UJC's organizing project had an important member in common. From here, in early 1996, the three groups began "informal discussions [addressing such questions as] . . . What would happen if you organized workfare workers? Could you actually organize a union? Could you actually organize? Would people think about their workfare spots as jobs? Is it easier to organize? Because everyone was in agreement that it was really hard to organize welfare recipients."[24]

The formation of WWT in 1996 involved joint fund-raising and joint strategizing. Though the components raised money together, they were never fully coordinated despite the strong informal ties that joined the organizations. There were two reasons for this lack of coordination. First, CVH was then splitting from HANNYS and was therefore simultaneously expanding and finding self-definition as a poor-people's membership organization. The principal difference from HANNYS was that it was led by membership. CVH's organizing director and board took this difference very seriously. Though the executive directors of FAC and UJC were committed to supporting WWT and appear to have given their workfare organizers as much organizational support as needed and free rein in their organizing activities, the membership-led structure of CVH meant that its members' power to steer WWT would be diluted by the coalitional demands of the project. Accordingly, the tasks of building WWT and CVH simultaneously were partially incompatible.

Moreover, UJC's organizing director left the organization late in 1996, and the new organizing director was less invested than her predecessor was in the emerging worksite-based organizing strategy WWT had adopted as a coalition. Disappointed at the lack of labor solidarity, dubious of WWT's ability to build effective, representative, union structures at worksites, and frustrated at the competition between WWT and ACORN in organizing worksites, the new director focused UJC's energy and resources toward alternative ways of protesting WEP (about which more will be said in the next chapter). The UJC Organizing Project activists who were involved in WWT identified more with WWT, the organization that they suggested building, than with UJC itself, which was a decentralized, multipurpose agency focused on legal advocacy. Therefore, internal conflict over defection from the main thrust of WWT's activity was minimal. Nevertheless, in the year in which the hard-assembled WWT coalition was active, it set a clear agenda for opposing WEP. Its constituent parts, even split, continued to work together in more soft-assembled ways for years afterward.

Soft Assembly

WWT's primary focus in 1996 was to push organized labor to commit resources to the fight against WEP by showing that WEP workers could be organized and that their status as welfare recipients did not make them unorganizable. Yet, for reasons suggested earlier, organized labor was split. In contrast to DC 37, CWA 1180's opposition to Mayor Giuliani meant that it had little to lose by giving succor to Mayor Giuliani's enemies. Long represented in liberal and progressive coalitions in the city, CWA's leadership helped coordinate the "WEP Coalition" from 1996 through 1997. The WEP Coalition met regularly, joining staff from WWT, ACORN, CFRC, and legal advocacy groups. This loose coordinating role played by Local 1180's staff was important for developing relationships among some of the NELP, WLC, Legal Aid, and community organizations that were organizing workfare workers. As FAC's organizing director recalled, "CWA 1180 pulled together the WEP Coalition which formed a lot of these initial relationships. . . . Those groups that were interested in the issue got together, and that was a really key role. . . . The relationships that were forged from that coalition were really important."[25] These relationships, in turn, developed into institutionally bounded, campaign-specific coalitions, moments of coalitional "hardening" punctuating the soft-assembled, larger network.

To be sure, there was other labor involvement in the issue of workfare, though much of it probably stemmed at least in part from the legitimacy that CWA 1180's early engagement in the issue lent antiworkfare activists. Personal contacts among WWT and ACORN organizers and progressive DC 37 staff members helped keep communication open while not visibly changing DC 37's essential caution with respect to its dealings with the mayor. DC 37's own halfhearted efforts to organize WEP workers in 1997 also encouraged its participation in the WEP Coalition, thus increasing the degree to which its efforts were exposed to direct criticism.

Apart from CWA 1180's coordination of the WEP Coalition, the most significant early labor involvement in WEP came from the local chapter of Jobs with Justice, an organization whose purpose is to foster soft-assembled local coalitions of labor and community organizations. As mentioned in chapter 1, Jobs with Justice helped coordinate ACORN's mock union election in 1997. But through a tactic nationally disseminated among Jobs with Justice chapters, the group also held two Workers' Rights Board hearings in which labor, religious, and political leaders heard testimony about workers' rights violations. At these events, WEP workers were given a public platform to make their case that WEP was a labor issue. The hearings, one in New York City and one in Albany, deepened WEP worker activists' commitment to frame workfare as a labor issue in 1996.

———

At the beginning of antiworkfare activism, therefore, the subfield of antiworkfare politics was marked by both hard- and soft-assembled coalitions but primarily by a large, soft-assembled one of progressive activists who knew one another or knew of one another from their already overlapping, spilled-over networks.[26] On the one hand, WWT, as the hard-assembled coalition of organizers, and ACORN, as a relatively well-resourced, multi-issue organization, both commanded enough power and enough soft connections to set the political agenda within the protest subfield around the *worker* status of workfare workers. On the other hand, the larger political field was structured by the centrality of the increasingly hostile, soft-assembled neoliberal coalition that was set on undermining the remaining neocorporatist structures that had survived the fiscal crises of the 1970s and early 1990s, and by the coalitional outcomes arising from the combination of a neoliberal president and neoconservative Congress. As a result, one can argue that, where the politics of workfare in New York is concerned, there was initially no common ideological framework among subfields and that the larger field would have been fragmented but for the soft-coalitional subfield of protest and for the instrumental links that joined housing, homelessness, antipoverty, and labor groups to the vestiges of the transitional neocorporatism that characterized the fifteen-year period between the fiscal crises of the mid-1970s and the early 1990s.

Strategic Implications

A caveat is necessary. Rather than saying that there was no "common ideological framework" shared among the actors in the anti-WEP subfield and Mayor Giuliani's neoliberal coalition by the time the latter expanded

WEP, it would be more accurate to say that there was no common political project. The difference lies in the ideological and discursive consequences of even "instrumental links," such as the honoring of contracts, between regime opponents and supporters. Those links help structure what regime critics may say and do not say and in which institutional contexts they can criticize freely. This structuring influence of challenger-regime ties, of course, has consequences for the development of soft-assembled coalitions as much as it does for hard-assembled ones. It also suggests that the task of changing the configuration of a field—that is, effecting large-scale political or policy change—is one that involves specifically institutional as well as broader discursive or ideological work.

A War of Position

From a strategic point of view, anti-WEP forces faced what Antonio Gramsci, using the analogy of trench warfare, called a "war of position," rather than a war of maneuver, which described massed armies facing each other directly on the battlefield. For Gramsci, the shape of the battlefield of class warfare was vastly different in institutionally differentiated societies than it was in societies in which quasi-state and private civil society organizations did not exist in large numbers.[27] In wars of position, opposition to dominant discourses and the state and civil institutions that promulgate and defend them occurs in a dispersed, or distributed, way and in multiple institutional spheres. Although Gramsci clearly argued that challenges across institutional spheres must be coordinated,[28] for our purposes here, the important point is that WWT's challenge to WEP, occurring primarily at the workplace, catalyzed a war of position. In this war, challenges to WEP crystallized from the soft-assembled coalitional substrate in which actors politically involved in contests and cooperation with state authorities in multiple institutional arenas were already joined. The field of workfare politics was, therefore, one in which anti-WEP advocates were limited, from the start, to fighting a war of position; there was no sufficient organizational infrastructure to fight a war of maneuver. Mayor Giuliani's expansion of workfare and contraction of access to welfare were popular, and in a war of maneuver, anti-WEP activists would surely have been too weak to change the policy right away. Moreover, the softness of the coalitions—mainly information-sharing groups—formed of welfare advocates and policy specialists, lawyers, community organizers, and homeless, housing, and antihunger activists promoted the growing anti-WEP movement's ability to open several trenches at once.

The Choice of the First Trench

In this context, soft-assembled coalitions could sometimes agree to harden their ties and to become more explicitly task-oriented. Such was the case in the formation of WEP Workers Together, early in 1996. In beginning to organize WEP workers, moreover, WWT initiated a new challenge to WEP that changed the relations among authorities and the loose network of antipoverty advocates in the field. By challenging WEP on the basis of the claim that WEP workers were *workers*, WWT induced changes in and the initial weakening of the dominant neoliberal discourse as well. As the City defended itself publicly, and as DC 37 tried to deflect charges that it ignored or even deepened the WEP workers' plight; as antipoverty advocates stepped up their rhetoric, emboldened by the grassroots challenge; and as other groups, such as ACORN, began to organize WEP workers later in the year, a battle was joined within the field.

I suggested in the first chapter that Katznelson's extension of Gramsci's metaphor of trenches to the modes of organization, action, and public speech of community and labor organizations is a useful way of understanding the quality of the connections among actors in the network structures making up coalitions and their fields. The key to this extension is that the institutional lives of the various kinds of organization operate according to different rules. As a result, when WWT hit on WEP workers' *worker* identity as the first organizing principle in their protest, they gambled that, relative to other possible claims, workers' rights would be able to build more hard connections within the soft-assembled subfield of regime opponents.

In keeping with the metaphor of trench warfare, the next chapter provides a tour of the institutional arenas within which activists and the Giuliani administration and other authorities engaged WEP. Examination of the campaigns, strategic decisions, and structural problems activists faced within these institutional settings will reveal a clearer picture of the changes in the coalitional structures of the movement.

CHAPTER FOUR

In the Trenches

Antonio Gramsci's metaphor of "wars of position" for counterhegemonic politics in liberal democracies reflected more than the novelty of
that form—and of its awful consequences—in World War I. Gramsci's
analysis of the failure of Europe's revolutionary Left after the war concluded that the Communists' strategy was ill suited to their political-
institutional structures. Instead of fighting a "war of maneuver" in which
they would overcome the forces allied with capital in one glorious act of
revolt, Gramsci counseled that they work through the "trenches" of the
state and civil society and gain control of institutions; by doing so, Communists could sufficiently build support and simultaneously disorganize
the state's defense of capital for a more decisive revolutionary confrontation. A war of maneuver—a massed army rushing into a breach in the
enemy's defenses opened up by advanced artillery strikes (a metaphor for
economic crises)—yields "successes as great as they [are] ephemeral."[1]

The key point in understanding the metaphor—and in understanding its more general usefulness—is that it is related closely to Gramsci's
tendency to blur the distinctions between civil society and the state. As
Gramsci wrote, "The State = political society + civil society, in other
words, hegemony protected by the armor of coercion."[2] In this formulation, Gramsci holds that "the distinction between political society and
civil society is merely methodological . . . in reality, civil society and State
are one."[3] In other words, the institutions of civil society and the government are infused with class power through the power of leadership, per-
suasion, and, finally, coercion.

Ira Katznelson's adaptation of Gramsci's metaphor to describe the
peculiar path of working-class politics in the United States also shares

in the larger idea. Katznelson proposes that the fusion of working-class life with working-class politics in the United States was hampered and marked by "a sharply divided consciousness . . . that finds many Americans acting on the basis of the shared solidarity of class at work, but on that of ethnic and territorial affinities in their residential communities." He continues, "The links between work and community-based conflicts have been unusually tenuous. Each kind of conflict has had its own separate vocabulary and set of institutions: work, class, and trade unions; community, ethnicity, local parties, churches, and voluntary associations." He notes that "each system of trenches . . . defines both the place and the content of conflict."[4] For Gramsci, too, these institutional settings are the sites in which people learn to speak and act politically.[5] Learning what goes on *in* them—what kinds of coalitions are built, what kinds of claims are made and shared, what kinds of actions are carried out—and what goes on *among* them, is critical for our understanding of how public definitions of workfare workers and their rights gained or lost persuasive power over the course of a ten-year span.

Gramsci's analytical metaphor of trench warfare perfectly fits the context of the Work Experience Program (WEP) in New York City. Defining WEP workers politically is caught up in the crosscutting trenches in which contention over workfare unfolded. These are the institutional lives of welfare politics and labor markets; local union politics and national policy networks; child-care placements and health-care assessments; outdoor Parks Department sites and indoor clerical jobs; press conferences, council chambers, and courts. Understanding the ways in which political identities form in the interstices of these institutional contexts is one of the main tasks of a broadly Gramscian analysis. This chapter traces the ways that the groups that challenged workfare organized and talked about the program, and about the prospects for opposing it, in four distinct ways, namely, worksite organizing, church- and nonprofit-based moral protest, legislative advocacy, and litigation. Each of these modes of opposition can best be thought of as "relational settings," in Margaret Somers's terms: "A relational setting is a pattern of relationships among institutions, public narratives, and social practices. As such it is a relational matrix, a social network. Identity-formation takes place within these . . . contested but patterned relationships among narratives, people, and institutions."[6] The analysis of the ways in which political claims converge onto one or several meanings in the context of institutions and organizational actors and of the ways in which these claims' authority is challenged demands a careful theoretical language able to capture the interactions inherent in these patterned relationships and the weight that established patterns exert on the interactions themselves.

Establishing a framework to study the warp and weft of political claims, however, means taking several steps farther into Gramsci's and kindred theories of language, such as those of Mikhail Bakhtin and Valentin Vološinov that were developing in the 1920s and 1930s in the context of a not-yet-ossified Soviet Marxism. In these theories we find an effort to steer between structuralism and pragmatism. Like Bourdieu's concept of "field," encountered in chapter 3, Gramscian and Bakhtininan theories invite us to examine the ways in which existing meanings of political claims limit the ability of authorities and challengers to craft new political claims and new identities within specific arenas of contention, even as each new intervention may shift the structures of meaning. These perspectives prompt investigation both into the conditions under which change within a given institutional setting is likely to be sudden or gradual and into the conditions under which institutional settings and the contention that unfolds within them spills over into other institutional settings in consequential ways.

Like Gramsci, Bakhtin and his collaborators criticized both individualist or expressivist accounts of language, in which the speaker's intent was held to be determinative of meaning, and structuralist accounts, in which meanings are determined by the place of utterances in a larger semiotic system. The task, for Bakhtin, was to understand the relationship between speakers and larger semiotic systems. Bakhtin and Vološinov first focused on the social locations of language as it was instantiated through *dialogue* among actors. Four related concepts from their work are important in framing the analysis of anti-WEP groups' institutional strategies, as it appears in this and the following chapters.

First, Bakhtin and Vološinov insist on the analytical importance of dialogue. Speakers construct their claims through dialogue with others, real or imagined. When speakers anticipate what Vološinov calls "choral support"—not agreement, necessarily, but signs of understanding— from an interlocutor, they craft their claims accordingly, as they do in the absence of expected choral support. Expectations of choral support, moreover, come through experience with particular interlocutors in particular settings.[7]

Second, interlocutors meet regularly within given institutional settings and conduct dialogue more or less according to generic rules. *Genres*, for Bakhtin, are akin to what Charles Tilly, in the study of political sociology, has called "repertoires of contention," that is, relatively stable sets of shared performances that form the basis of improvisation in actual interactions.[8] For example, a mass rally and a march are performances from the "social movement repertoire." They were adapted, historically, from ceremonial processions, but they have become routinized forms of political protest, with marchers often negotiating in advance the route of a march with the police. Similarly, as choral support solidifies, people develop shared genres of talking about things, which in turn affect their interpretation of them. Genres, which are both substantive and stylistic, are institutionalized and historically specific.[9] Novels and short stories are literary genres, while a motion to file for appeal is an example of a legal genre, and a rally or bill a political one. One would scarcely offer a novel in court (though one might offer a narrative in testimony), and a technical legal document would not pass as a novel. Were it not for our ability to recognize genres, we could not count on choral support and would construct others' intended meanings for the first time each time.[10]

Third, genres are defined and demarcated by what Bakhtin calls a *chronotope*, or "the intrinsic connectedness of temporal and spatial relationships."[11] Though Bakhtin addresses chronotopes as a formal property of literary genres contained in their content, the concept can usefully be applied to the institutional meeting points between political contenders and authorities. As will become clearer, the routinized spatial and temporal dimensions of worksites, courts, legislatures, and so forth shape the ways in which dialogues about WEP workers' political identities unfold. To the extent that particular kinds of claims about workfare workers' identities, rights, responsibilities, and the like span multiple institutions, are implicated in multiple genres, and are characterized by multiple chronotopes, we can expect them to exert varying degrees of *centrifugal and centripetal force* on dialogue—the fourth concept from Bakhtin and Vološinov—both within and across institutional settings.[12]

Here is an essential link to the war of position and to the concept of political fields as discussed in the previous chapter: struggles for hegemony within political fields rely on actors' ability to work *within* the constraints of institutions to fashion political claims that resonate *across* institutions with potential allies and opponents. The coalitions that emerge from actors' attempts to do so are contingent institutional products. They are also linguistic in that a key element of these coalitions is the presence or absence of shared political claims centripetal enough to ensure choral support and centrifugal enough to ensure choral support across genres and institutional settings. In New York City, the most enduring trenches were those separating welfare recipients from the *political* language and

institutions of work. As community-based or community-oriented housing, antihunger, and homelessness activists sought to join their struggles
with those of workfare workers, they saw increasingly that, as with regular
workers, they found themselves pushing at and limited by genre boundaries. They experienced the force of genres in varying degrees depending
on the social and linguistic cohesion of the genres themselves.

The First Trench: Navigating Worksites and
the Labor Movement

Knocking on Labor's Door

Recalling his initial forays into workfare organizing in 1996, the organizing director of the Fifth Avenue Committee (FAC) said,

> We went out to Prospect Park, hoping just to . . . find a group of welfare
> recipients and talk to them and see how we can begin. And what we found
> was a group of workers. And we were sort of shocked by that. We were sit-
> ting around in the band shell on their lunch hour, and they were talking
> about how pissed off they were about the way they were being treated. And
> they were talking like workers . . . and we realized this is the strength, this
> is the issue here: these aren't welfare recipients, these are workers.[13]

This realization quickly became the organizing "hook." As the FAC organizing director said in an interview two years earlier (1997), "The strength
of WEP is that it takes welfare recipients and turns them into workers. . . .
Suddenly you've got people with the same interests, with potential you
could ally with labor. Everything you do has to be focused on helping
to forward that potential alliance. Absolutely everything. So working at
worksites is continuing to say, 'They're workers, they're workers, they're
workers, organize them as Parks people, organize them as Sanitation workers, organize them as clerical workers,' and . . . helps to invite in labor."
As early as September 1996, WEP Workers Together (WWT) marched in
New York's Labor Day parade as guests of Communications Workers of
America (CWA) Local 1180. There, they distributed flyers titled "Why We
Are Marching in the Labor Day Parade." The flyers read, in part:

> Why does WEP displace workers and harm *all* working people?
> The mayor is balancing the budget on the backs of WEP workers at the
> expense of paid city workers. In the past two years, the city has downsized

its workforce by 21,000 workers. Many of these full-time jobs with benefits have been filled with un-paid WEP workers.

Although WEP now hurts city workers, as it expands it will hurt working New Yorkers in all sectors of the economy. . . . *When WEP workers are denied the right to work in decent conditions, and are used to displace paid employees, it is an assault on all working people.*[14]

WWT's press release that day claimed further emphasized that the "presence of WEP workers in the march is a challenge to both the City unions, and to Mayor Giuliani."[15]

And yet, support from most corners of organized labor was tepid, at best, and worksite-based organizing itself entailed many challenges. Moreover, WWT faced competition from the Association of Community Organizations for Reform Now (ACORN), which, by the end of 1996, fielded more organizers and had a more-extensive presence at municipal worksites. But ACORN, too, faced similar challenges. Even though WWT and ACORN ultimately chose different paths—with WWT trying to attract unions to WEP workers and ACORN trying to represent them itself—the groups made many of the same political claims about WEP workers' status. They were similarly (though not identically) affected, therefore, by the features of the labor movement and the worksites they had to navigate.

Three initial problems presented themselves. First, organizing at worksites was complicated by the features of the WEP assignment that made WEP work like work in the secondary labor market. Second, especially as new rules for the welfare reform program New York City–Work, Accountability, and You (NYC–WAY) were rolled out, sanction rates were high, and with them, turnover at worksites was rapid. Compounding this problem was a third, namely, that relative to the size of the organizing staffs of ACORN, WWT, and the all-volunteer Work*fairness*, the number of worksites and their dispersal was overwhelming.

These spatial and temporal dimensions of workfare organizing were refracted through ongoing questions about the ability of WWT and ACORN to form organizations based at worksites, as American union organizing demanded. Both groups tried to form worksite-based committees and to encourage WEP workers to sign membership cards affiliating them with their organizations. ACORN went farther than WWT in its mimicking of the union organizing genre: it began by signing up WEP workers at worksites into the WEP Worker Organizing Committee, and then, in July 1997, it presented sixteen thousand signed cards at a demonstration at City Hall. This demonstration mimicked unions' demands for "card-check" recognition, which allows a union to ask an employer to bargain collectively based on a majority of workers in a shop having signed union cards, rather than on a National Labor Relations Board–run election. When this action did not yield recognition by the City (it was hard to imagine that it would), ACORN then organized an election for October. Over the course of three days, in an effort coordinated by ACORN and Jobs with Justice, volunteers from advocacy groups and unions distributed and collected ballots at dozens of welfare offices and worksites around the city. Of slightly more than seventeen thousand votes cast, 98 percent of the WEP workers polled voted to have ACORN represent them.

Even amid evidence that WEP workers overwhelmingly wanted union representation, however, labor movement allies were asking questions about and debating the substance behind the symbolism. Working with Jobs with Justice, ACORN organized a blue-ribbon panel of labor, civic, and religious leaders to oversee the election and certify its results. One member, recounting his concerns, asked,

> What is it about, really. . . . Either they're going to try to set up a real representation structure . . . within this group of people—and I can define what that means . . . it means regular meetings, it means an election . . . just as in any union, area stewards, etc. . . . And the people could . . . develop their own platform, so to speak, in terms of what it is they really need as minimal conditions for this thing. . . . The other thing, of course . . . is, suppose it succeeded, what would it do? Would it entrench a program that is structurally horrible? Would it in fact give the mayor exactly the line he needs to defend it? Which is, "Now they have a representative; I deal with the representative. . . . Shut up already." [16]

Even the head of Jobs with Justice emphasized the problematic connection between the performance of the union genre and the substantive gains that it could produce for WEP workers: "By focusing on the right to collective bargaining . . . we are trying to make the point politically that these folks are workers. . . . But I mean the mayor could smart up tomorrow and say, "Yeah, I'll recognize so-and-so union as the representative." But of course, what will that mean? What will that mean for negotiations over collective bargaining rights? Will they be able to negotiate an increase in benefits?"[17] And yet, as sociologist Jeffrey Olick has indicated, the ability to make a public performance that is recognized by others to be in a specific genre—the ability to generate choral support—depends on memories that at once structure the new performances and lend coherence to the genre itself.[18] The blue ribbon panel member recounted that at a Jobs with Justice meeting,

> I sat next [the] political director for [a major union]. . . . And I said, "A continuing concern of mine [is]: Does this evolve into a bona fide union structure?" Because we were critiquing what we had tried to do with this election. . . . And [he], of all people, said—gave a speech—about, you know, "Look, Local 1199 didn't have so-called bona fide union standing, and the Teachers didn't." And other people said, privately, "Yeah, they got there, but everybody knew there was a goal and that a paraunion type of organization was not the destination."[19]

ACORN activists themselves tried to encourage memories of this type by invoking the struggles of other unions, such as the United Auto Workers and other Congress of Industrial Organizations (CIO) unions and the United Farm Workers, who were using alternative organizational forms and operating without official recognition before finally becoming accepted into the ranks of organized labor.[20] In doing so, moreover, they invoked militant union struggles seen by many observers, both in and out of the labor movement, as lost golden moments of labor progressivism. The very act of having an election to show labor activists and others what labor organizing should be about reinforced these "genre memories."[21] As an ACORN organizer explained, "I think part of what happened was that we created a climate where it would be very difficult for anyone who in some ways either sees themselves as progressive, or sees themselves as prolabor to not support an election of working people wanting to vote on whether they wanted to have a union or not. And for that reason it made it easier for unions like DC 37 and AFSCME to say, 'Sure, we're going to support the union election for workfare workers, and we think that people should come out and vote.'"[22] Nevertheless, whether ACORN's goal was a real union structure or a "paraunion type of organization" run as a subsidiary of ACORN, ACORN's own organizing began to flag. One benefit of the election for ACORN was that the sign-in sheets, ostensibly insuring that people did not vote twice, became the basis for organizers to contact WEP workers over the next few months. For a time it looked as if ACORN's organizing would pick up after the election. But "deal[ing] with the real-life [challenge] of building organization, membership, local campaigns, no longer assuming the media spotlight, and keeping a stable staff" yielded "no major victories [and] some lessons on what doesn't work in workfare organizing."[23] ACORN's WEP Worker Organizing Committee lost many organizers, at one point dwindling to four full-time workers. ACORN's low pay and long hours often prompted staff members to seek comparable but better-paid employment within labor unions or to enter graduate school. With a staff now as small as those of WWT and Work*fairness*, ACORN began to feel the strain of organizing a "large workforce spread out over +300 sites through the City, [and which] is transient due to constant terminations and reassignments . . . mak[ing] building a stable committee at the sites difficult."[24]

In their attempt to attract union support by acting like unions, anti-WEP activists began to learn a difficult lesson about trenches and genres. As Gramsci's trench metaphor suggests, trenches—here, ways of organizing and making claims—are held and guarded by actors. Even allies like the blue-ribbon panel convened by ACORN and Jobs with Justice understood there to be proper union structures and suspect ones. This is not a simply matter of jealousy or competition. Instead, WEP workers' union allies were willing to form labor-community coalitions, but only on the condition that they were the representatives of labor and not the community groups. Though ACORN and even some union officials recalled historical changes in the definition of unionism pushed by farmworkers and the unskilled workers of the CIO, they were not able to overcome the more centripetal aspects of workers' rights discourse as defined by even sympathetic unions.

The (Bad) Taste of Bread and Butter: Worksite Organizing

The question remained about what union or unionlike representation at the worksite would accomplish, or even what it *should* accomplish. As the ACORN organizer noted, organizing at worksites was terribly difficult, combining high turnover, dispersion of authority among agencies, spatial dispersion of actual worksites, supervisor hostility to organizers, and the fear WEP workers had of being sanctioned for self-advocacy.[25]

Turnover—the principal temporal marker of the WEP assignment—greatly complicated WEP organizing. Organizers from WWT and CVH both complained that turnover made organizing stable groups of WEP workers based at worksites all but impossible. Said one, "We . . . knew every worker at 2 Lafayette. We had every list, we had everybody in there, and then, I remember, she went back there one day and everyone was gone. They had moved everyone because it was successfully organized."[26]

Even when WEP workers were not transferred for organizing well, they were frequently shifted among worksites or had their hours changed. Many were also sanctioned or left to join the private labor market.

A second temporal element of WEP that affected the organizing was the time spent at the work assignment itself. CVH's director claimed that it had been easier to organize people before 1997, when WEP placements increased following the passage of State welfare reform. Members and potential members simply had more time to commit to civic activity. When combined with the gendered tendencies that made Home Relief (HR) predominantly a single men's program and Aid to Families with Dependent Children (AFDC) predominantly a women's program, these temporal dimensions of the WEP assignment also changed the composition of the organizing groups.

> It's been this very strange irony . . . the first "poor people organizing" I did was homeless folks . . . single men and single women. . . . And that was really hard, it was really frustrating, and they didn't have any ties to the community. And then . . . we started organizing women and children. And it was great. They were stable and had an investment. . . . And now, ironically . . . women with children are the people most without time, most have other issues on their agenda, so it's hardest to get them. So now, who are the people who are around most in our organization? It's all people . . . not forced to work forty hours a week.[27]

The spatial aspects of WEP also made organizing at worksites difficult. Cumulating and defending victories was especially difficult because getting one district supervisor in the Sanitation Department to issue boots to WEP workers did not necessarily mean that all WEP workers would get the protective gear they needed. And even where department commissioners ordered changes, implementation at the worksite level was erratic.

WEP workers' fear of being sanctioned for organizing activity was both a hindrance and a help to organizing. Though even as late as 2000, a CVH organizer was able to claim that WEP workers were "still very afraid of harassment, of being sanctioned, of being singled out,"[28] and of bearing the sole costs of "step[ping] out on their own, and challeng[ing] the system," CVH's ability to provide organizational resources, such as a legal clinic that could inform WEP workers of their rights, helped get WEP workers over the collective action problem they faced, "know[ing] that they were going to be helped."[29]

Finally—and perhaps most important—union organizing is probably most compelling to the people being organized when the labor contract is generally recognized as voluntary, at least to some extent, when claiming a collective identity as a *worker* is given choral support, and when collective claims are not themselves the object of stigma. Accordingly, as one CVH organizer put it, "Nobody gave a shit about winning gloves. I mean, people gave a shit about winning gloves, but they didn't want *gloves*. They don't want better working conditions. They wanted a job and they wanted . . . to get paid for the work that *they* wanted to do."[30] The organizing director for WWT and FAC,[31] after having said earlier that CVH never "really [fully agreed with] the crucial point of organizing people as workers and keeping the issue focused on workfare workers *as workers*,"[32] later agreed,

> We were fundamentally misunderstanding the way WEP workers understood themselves. On the one hand, WEP workers saw themselves as being workers and wanted to organize as workers because they worked, they were proud of what they did and wanted decent treatment in return for that work. They were workers. On the other hand, they weren't working at jobs, and that's an absolutely key distinction. The lowest-paid service worker is there voluntarily and might want to organize to improve the conditions, to get better pay, to be treated better, or leave voluntarily. So they're working, but if they're not there voluntarily, it's not a job.[33]

Nevertheless, both before worksite organizing became the primary focus of anti-WEP groups and after other strategies eclipsed it, the WEP worksite was a frequent locus of contact between organizers and WEP workers. As one CVH organizer put it, "even though it doesn't produce [members for the organization], we still have to do it. . . . It keeps things real, it keeps us very much aware of . . . what the realities are of the workplace and the WEP program." Citing the apparent imbalance between the numerous WEP workers and the regular employees on maintenance jobs, she continued, "Because the workers tell us, and then we see it. . . . You know, if we hadn't . . . kept going to 2 Lafayette . . . we wouldn't have seen that wall of green WEP [punch] cards and then the five white city employee cards. You know, it's things like that that are definitely the germs of [campaigns]."[34] Organizers found that without full union support, organizing at worksites entailed enormous challenges. Though WEP workers responded to their overtures and were attracted by efforts to ameliorate their working conditions, it became clear to organizers that the repertoire of worksite organizing limited their claim-making in ways that hurt their organizing. The genre of labor organizing presumes the formal freedom of workers and is historically linked to the emancipation of labor from various forms of bondage. WEP workers understood their labor contracts as less than fully free. Thus a temporal orientation focused on present conditions conflicted not only with the temporal dynamics of worksite turnover but also with WEP workers' orientations toward their own exit from WEP or toward the program's abolition. Nevertheless, as long as WEP required work in city agencies, worksite organizing remained important for organizers' efforts to challenge the program.

The Tinny Harmony of Choral Support

Impeding the claims of WEP workers' organizations to represent *workers* was weak union choral support. Union officials and other activists had their own understandings of what a union was—a "bona fide union structure"—and what it was for. Weak support was evident even when, in the summer of 1997, District Council 37 announced that it, too, was going to organize WEP workers. Pressured by the American Federation of State, County, and Municipal Employees (AFSCME), its parent union, DC 37 hired an organizer to supervise the formation of a Workfare Workers Organizing Committee. From both non-DC 37 activists at the time and from the account of the organizer, DC 37's effort was halfhearted, at best, and destructive of WEP workers' claims, at worst.

From the organizer's perspective, the "whole atmosphere [in the union] always was a total lack of interest. . . . 'Who's this guy wanting to . . . find WEP workers?'" The lack of interest extended to the selection of allies. DC 37 hired several Work*fairness* activists to help sign up WEP workers to union cards. Work*fairness*, an organizational affiliate of the Workers World Party, was an unlikely ally to a "Giuliani-friendly union," and "in comparison to ACORN, it had no ability to mobilize anybody."[35] The alliance with Work*fairness*—rather than with ACORN or another organizing group—was taken by many other anti-WEP activists as a sign that DC 37 was not serious about opposing WEP. This impression was reinforced in August 1997 by the "Principles of Agreement" between Stanley Hill, DC 37's executive director, and Mayor Giuliani. One labor leader called the agreement "toothless," while the organizing director for WWT, reacting to language in which the City agreed not to "intentionally displace" union workers with WEP workers, said, "I can't believe a labor leader agreed to that kind of language."[36] Accordingly, DC 37's public act of solidarity with WEP workers actually undercut their political claims by providing them apparent choral support—saying publicly that WEP workers were workers—while neutralizing the substantive force of this claim.

Several major problems led many anti-WEP groups to search for other means of advocating for WEP workers by the summer of 1997. Unions were used to build stable worksite organizations, but WEP worksites were unstable. Most anti-WEP activists, at least early, needed to demonstrate WEP workers' worthiness by demonstrating their "workerness" through the performance of the union genre. But debates among labor activists about the meanings of these performances and worksite organizing's spatiotemporal characteristics' interaction with those of standard union organizing performances and historical stories about winning recognition as workers impeded WEP workers' full occupation of the workers' rights trench in the field of workfare politics.

Moral Protest in Churches and in the Media

Activists also used models of protest other than unionlike performances and worksite organizing to oppose WEP. The Pledge of Resistance campaign was conceived early in 1997, in discussions between Heidi Dorow, who replaced an early proponent of worksite organizing as director of the Urban Justice Center (UJC) Organizing Project, and Rev. Peter Laarman, the new pastor of Judson Memorial Church, a venerable liberal congregation in Greenwich Village. Dorow had been active with ACT-UP—the AIDS Coalition To Unleash Power, the premier AIDS activist organization of the late 1980s and early 1990s—as well as with workers' rights groups. Reverend Laarman, prior to going to divinity school (at Yale, during a contentious organizing drive among the staff), had been a public relations director for the United Auto Workers in Detroit. He was on the Jobs with Justice steering committee in New York and a member of the blue-ribbon panel that oversaw the ACORN election. Dorow and Laarman, along with many others, anticipated an expansion of nonprofit-sector WEP placements. They feared that charities would be co-opted into supporting WEP because they could obtain needed workers from the program. They were also upset at apparent middle- and working-class support for the program. Accordingly, the Pledge of Resistance was designed to change the moral tone of the public debate and to block WEP's expansion.

The pledge was conceived in a mood of pessimism about the potential for worksite organizing and about the strategy of courting union support for it. The UJC organizer concluded that the difficulties of organizing people to improve conditions at worksites to which they otherwise had no commitment were probably insurmountable and politically ineffective, given what she described as DC 37's "cowardice." Her analysis of the difficulties the groups faced was similar to that made by others in WWT. She was also concerned with what might be the results of success. In an interview shortly after ACORN's election, she explained, "Even if they are acknowledged as the representative of WEP workers, [it] is not going to do anything to end WEP. I think it's going to entrench WEP. . . . Does that do anything to create more jobs? I don't think it does. I mean, you're giving WEP roots. You're not uprooting it, and I think that that's problematic."[37] This assessment suggests that the pledge's organizers hoped that the combination of moral disapprobation, organized elite and middle-class opposition, and interference with the program's expansion might be powerful enough to scuttle WEP. As I will show here and in the next chapter, the Pledge of Resistance was able to change the terms of debate over WEP, but it was unable to occupy enough trenches to defeat the program.

An Alternative Strategy

The demand to "uproot" WEP moved the focus of organizing from the worksite to organizing a broader "conscience constituency" against WEP, abandoning the potential leverage that worksite organizing had in mobilizing unions into an anti-WEP coalition. The analytic point was that workfare flourished with broad acceptance as a program that upheld a moral social contract, by which people on welfare should be given the opportunity to compensate society for their support. The Pledge of Resistance sought to build on what the labor historian Michael Hanagan has called the "opportunity for reformers" embedded in "the contradiction between capitalism's claim to reward work and its frequent inability to provide it."[38] In its campaign materials, the Pledge of Resistance claimed that

- WEP forces welfare recipients to work without pay and without hope for full-time employment.
- WEP workers lose their opportunity to pursue higher education and real vocational training.
- WEP displaces a shrinking city workforce and weakens the unions that represent it.[39]

The pledge's claims were further couched in terms of human rights and as a more general moral claim for active labor market policies. Its materials cited the Universal Declaration of Human Rights guarantees of "freedom from poverty . . . right to work, to receive a living wage, to free choice of employment, to just and favourable conditions of work and to protection against unemployment." The pledge further stated that

> we the undersigned morally oppose and reject the existence and con-
> tinuation of WEP in its current form. We will not be party to the City
> Administration's efforts to expand the workfare program. We will not
> allow our organization/congregation to become a WEP site, nor will we
> use WEP workers to perform agency business. Instead, we will make
> every effort to end workfare and fight for the creation of living wage jobs
> for all who need them. Additionally, we will fight for the availability of
> a four-year college education for all, regardless of their economic cir-
> cumstances. We believe that government is responsible for promoting
> job creation and, if necessary, for developing public works programs to
> employ hundreds of thousands of the poor and unemployed across the
> nation.[40]

It is easy to see that the Pledge of Resistance attempted to unite the varied constituencies addressing workfare. It mentioned worksite issues, educational demands (reflecting, too, UJC's cooperation with the Hunter College Welfare Rights Initiative), and allegations of displacement (not then being made by DC 37's leaders). Though the pledge often drew on rhetoric familiar to unions, its target audience was made up of organizations that did not necessarily have much leverage over WEP. At the same time, it appeared as if WEP would expand rapidly into the nonprofit sector. An article in *City Limits*, the newsmagazine of record in the progressive nonprofit community in New York, claimed at the time:

> Thousands of New Yorkers on public assistance are about to get acquainted
> with the nonprofit world—not as volunteers or employees, but through . . .
> WEP. . . . The city is preparing to have 100,000 or more public assistance
> recipients performing work-related activities—though not necessarily
> wage-earning work—by the middle of next year, about 10,000 of them at
> nonprofits. The reason: city agencies are reaching their capacity to absorb
> the thousands of public assistance recipients already working as clerks,
> trash collectors, demolition crews and street sweepers. And the nonprofit

community, with more than $3 billion annually in city contracts, has so far absorbed a little less than 3,000 WEP participants.[41]

By connecting hundreds of organizations with the antiworkfare struggle by having them refuse to cooperate with WEP's expansion, the Pledge of Resistance sought to give these organizations the leverage they did not already have. The organizers imagined an even larger goal: to shift the terms of debate over workfare in the nonprofit sector from one of service to one of solidarity. Said the UJC organizer during the pledge campaign, "It's really to change the moral debate. . . . We're moving people away from a charity model of mobilization and more toward a justice model of mobilization."[42]

In pitching the pledge to the nonprofit sector, however, its organizers left action on public-sector WEP placements substantially to ACORN, CVH, and FAC. In focusing on nonprofit and religious groups, pledge organizers gambled that unions, which could not pledge, would eventually have only a small role in promoting an end to the program. Understandably, therefore, the strategies of worksite organizing and attempts at recruiting union opposition and of the pledge were often seen as contradictory rather than complementary.

In Gramsci's terms, the Pledge of Resistance organizers sought to initiate a "war of maneuver" by uniting several large groups against WEP into a single campaign directed at a potential weak point in the program's implementation strategy. Despite important links to organized labor, however, the pledge dealt most with nonprofit groups and religious congregations (which frequently are not unionized). Accordingly, it respected, rather than challenged, the trenches separating labor activism from community activism and advocacy, even though it based its claim of WEP's immorality primarily on complaints about various aspects of the WEP labor contract and working conditions. It appears that Laarman and Dorow counted on their ties to unions and to anti-WEP organizers to bolster the pledge campaign by bringing activists from the larger soft-assembled coalition into their more hard-assembled effort. This strategy worked to some extent, but for the purposes of the pledge campaign, it was most important to target their organizing efforts to congregations and charitable groups. Just as anti-WEP organizers found that unions were guarded about their support for worksite organizing campaigns, pledge organizers found that religiously based moral discourse was sufficiently multivocal to allow support for as well as opposition to WEP.

Making the Moral Argument

As with organizers using unionlike performances to attract unions in order to ratify their claims for workplace rights, Pledge of Resistance organizers understood that the recruitment of specific types of organizational allies could ratify their claims for workfare's moral shortcomings. As the UJC organizer said, "It's very clear that organizing amongst churches is a way to . . . hammer home the moral . . . framework of the issue."[43]

The term *moral framework* in the sense used by the UJC's pledge organizer signals the generality of the challenge posed by the pledge. The pledge's invocation of a general interest in ending WEP—for example, that WEP exerts general downward pressure on wages—was part of this moral challenge as much as was its invocation of human rights. The Pledge of Resistance sought to recruit churches and nonprofits and conceived of them as peer groups that needed to be educated about WEP if the outrage that the organizers felt about the program were to be disseminated widely:

> The Pledge [of Resistance] . . . brought home for me . . . that . . . our role would be to organize—the easiest way to say it is—nonwelfare constituencies. Meaning, in some cases or many cases, working- and middle-class people. And the pledge provided an opportunity to do that because we could reach working- and middle-class people through religious congregations, through churches, and through nonprofits. In some ways, part of what we were doing was reaching our peers . . . in the advocacy community and saying whatever you're doing, whether it's being a service provider or you're doing counseling, or you're doing a food pantry, whatever it is you're doing . . . there is political content to these issues. Not that people didn't know that. . . . What we were doing is saying, "Here's a mechanism to make a political statement by being a part of the . . . Campaign of Resistance, and hopefully we can come together . . . to make a bolder political statement if there's more of us."[44]

In order for the Pledge of Resistance to get a hearing, the social action committees and the ministers of congregations needed to be won over. The UJC organizer herself had nearly 120 speaking engagements in 1997 and 1998, addressing churches, conferences of social workers, community organizations, law students, homeless women, Head Start programs, university students, academics, soup kitchen staff and clients, and trade unionists.[45] The moral posture taken by the pledge and ratified by the prominence of religious organizations among its supporters was often contested, on both sympathetic and unsympathetic grounds.

Sympathetic critics of the pledge made two kinds of criticisms. Most common was the idea that a posture of noncooperation would not increase the leverage of nonprofit and religious organizations over WEP by forcing it to change but instead would actually decrease this leverage because it removed the possibility for further intervention on behalf of workfare workers. In a widely distributed document called "Some Common Questions and Answers About Non-profits and Religious Congregations Becoming WEP Sites," pledge organizers sought to address the following questions:

1 Won't working for a nonprofit provide the WEP participant with real job training that will lead to employment?
2 By taking WEP workers, can't my non-profit agency save welfare recipients from doing demeaning and unsafe work in WEP assignments with the Parks or Sanitation Departments?
3 With continued cutbacks in private and public funding to non-profits, why not use WEP workers to ensure that badly needed services remain intact?[46]

The pledge's answers regarded the importance of opposing the program as a whole and sought to counter some charities' claims that they could help WEP workers more by treating them more humanely than did the City.

Nevertheless, nonprofits and congregations were sometimes difficult to convince. Public opposition to the mayor was risky from the standpoint of public relations; Mayor Giuliani used his media access to humiliate opponents in the press. But beyond being scared, some organizations appeared to have been uncomfortable with adopting a prophetic stance toward WEP. Even within Judson Memorial Church's ministerial conference, the United Church of Christ, Metropolitan conference, the pledge was contested on these grounds. Wrote one conference member on the Mission Priorities and Stewardship Committee, "While I agree with the concern about WEP, I do not agree with the action that Peter Laarman proposes. I feel we could follow a more positive direction, one that will benefit participants in the work program and set an example which would illustrate how the WEP program might be improved. I would suggest something like the following . . ." The letter went on to list WEP worker preferences, skills, and experience; placement of WEP workers in jobs not normally done by paid workers; safety and health provisions; and resources made available for effective job search and labor market entry.[47]

The other set of sympathetic criticisms leveled against the Pledge of Resistance turned on doubts about its long-term efficacy. Said the lead organizer from the Fifth Avenue Committee (which joined the pledge) in the fall of 1997:

> I don't think it's the best strategy. I mean, it's been successful. They've done a very good job with the Pledge of Resistance. I can't criticize it. . . . It's gotten far more coverage than anybody could have reasonably expected. . . . [But] I wouldn't have phrased it in terms of abstract calls for human rights and morality 'cause I don't think that endures. What endures is: What is your self-interest? Your self-interest is you do not want to have WEP workers displacing people and being put into dead-end jobs. And I wouldn't phrase it in terms of: "This breaks the Geneva Convention" 'cause I think that appeals to a relatively limited group of faith-based organizations that have the luxury of those considerations. But you know, again, it's been very successful.[48]

This criticism emphasizes the extent to which the *moral* and *universalizing* dimensions of the pledge's arguments dominated its reception. And it was on these dimensions that the Pledge of Resistance attracted its most sustained, unsympathetic criticism.

Claiming that "work is moral and so is workfare," Robert A. Sirico, the executive director of the Acton Institute for the Study of Religion and Liberty, a conservative think tank, attacked the Pledge of Resistance in an op-ed in the *New York Times*.[49] Like others who attacked the pledge,[50] Sirico began with the claim by some proponents at the pledge's launching press conference that WEP is tantamount to slavery. He and others ignored the actual pledge that the organizers asked members to take and instead concentrated on the appropriateness of the slavery analogy: "The clergy members and leaders of nonprofit groups who insist that they would be 'slave drivers' if they employ people on workfare obscure the fact that recipients are not actually forced to take the jobs the city assigns them. They have another option: They can stop receiving public assistance and instead enter the labor force on their own."[51] Beyond this assertion, Sirico equated opposition to workfare to opposition to work, employing a common trope of retort against opponents of workfare. In another attack on the pledge, Michel Faulkner, a local Baptist minister and apparent ally of the mayor, opined in the *Daily News*,

Starting with the book of Genesis, religious leaders have recognized work as essential to a life of fulfillment. To call any workfare program immoral is to ignore the teaching of thousands of years and the wisdom of the ages. . . . All religious principles agree that work is good and honorable. All also would agree that it is better to work for assistance than to receive a handout for doing nothing. The Book of Proverbs 18:9 says: "One who is slack in his work is brother to one who destroys." Ecclesiastes 2:24 instructs, "A man can do nothing better than to eat and drink and find satisfaction in his work."[52]

Sirico, too, discussed the dignity conferred by work, but this dignity is socially (and religiously) enforced:

Most everyone remembers his first job. The pay is low, the work is hard, and the frustrations are many. . . . This experience is what prepares us for higher-paying jobs and greater responsibility. . . . When we are productive, we are entitled to self-respect and we elicit respect from others. . . . Work can also be seen, from a theological perspective, as a moral duty to those who can do it. Saint Paul said, "If a man will not work, neither let him eat." Through work a person develops not only physically and mentally, but spiritually as well. . . . Workfare may not accomplish miracles but it offers hope. Its main benefit is that it teaches that there is moral merit to work.[53]

While Sirico's response to the pledge betrayed a nearly complete evasion of the pledge's central claims, his evasion shows that recruiting clergy put workfare's proponents on the defensive when it came to workfare's moral value.

By "bringing the clergy back in" to the debate over workfare, the Pledge of Resistance encouraged a certain amount of scripture slinging in support of and in opposition to WEP. The pledge leaders' response to conservative ministers was first to distance themselves from the claim of slavery and to reinforce their own reading of biblical injunctions: "We dare recover a much stronger, more telling strand of the Biblical tradition than the weak moralizing of notions like: 'Let him who would not work not eat.' The stronger judgment is pronounced against those who prosper by injustice, 'making their countrymen work for nothing, not paying them for their labor' (Jeremiah 22:13). In our eagerness to condemn the poor for their alleged moral defects, we have chosen not to hear the Bible's far more slashing condemnation of the smugly 'successful' who don't care how the poor are treated."[54] The result of this trading of scriptural reference was to force other ministers who were on the fence over their stance on WEP to choose sides or at least to give the pledge activists a hearing. But because the pledge activists were often more familiar with the particularities of New York City's workfare program (and not workfare as an abstraction) than were their antagonists, they were able to target question-and-answer sheets to various constituencies with considerable specificity.[55] Said the UJC organizer, "I think that even if they vote not to go onto the pledge, going through that exercise internally is very helpful because they've got to educate themselves a little about WEP. They've got to understand, for example, that if they were to become a WEP site, they'd have to be involved in sanctions."[56] Four months after the Pledge of Resistance rollout in late July 1997, it had grown from sixty-eight congregations and nonprofits to more than 125, with another fifty to seventy-five pending.

A War of Maneuver in a Positional Field

In spite of its early appearance of success, the Pledge of Resistance failed to expand significantly after the beginning of 1998. A major reason for this lack of expansion is that the City largely abandoned its plans to expand WEP wholesale and to expand the program into the nonprofit sector. There are likely several explanations for the City's abandonment of these plans. First, the pledge probably exerted some pressure on the City and effectively blocked the administration's blanket claims to WEP's benefits. Media outlets, too, began to be more critical of the program, and early reports on what limited research was possible on outcomes of welfare reform in New York State equivocated on whether WEP led to the sort of stable employment that WEP's proponents claimed it did.[57] Second, and perhaps more important, the City appears to have realized that it did not need to significantly expand WEP because reductions in overall caseloads allowed the City to meet federally mandated participation rates in work activities that would, in turn, allow the City and the State to maintain full federal funding for its welfare program.

In spite of their goal to "crush WEP" and to deny it avenues for institutionalization, it appears, however, that pledge organizers miscalculated the ways in which WEP was *already* institutionally inscribed within New York City politics (e.g., within municipal workplaces and in the interface between local government and a pacified municipal union movement) as well as within State politics and welfare politics across several scales of government. Here, Gramsci's comments comparing the war of maneuver with the war of position show the problems with the former and suggest an analogy to the Pledge of Resistance strategy. "It would sometimes happen that a fierce artillery attack seemed to have destroyed the enemy's entire defensive system, whereas in fact it had only destroyed the outer perimeter; and at the moment of their advance and attack the assailants would find themselves confronted by a line of defence which was still effective. . . .Of course, things do not remain exactly as they were; but it is certain that one will not find the element of speed, of accelerated time, of the definitive forward march expected by the strategists of political [wars of maneuver]."[58]

While the "artillery attacks" to which Gramsci refers in this passage are economic crises, the same observation can apply to maneuvers such as the Pledge of Resistance. The pledge strategists saw that the moral arguments for WEP could be shown to be flimsy in comparison to the moral arguments against it. So they attacked there, rather than in the more difficult arena of workplace politics. Gramsci's reference to "accelerated time" is important here as well. The pledge's ability to stymie WEP depended in part on its ability to quickly organize nonprofits and congregations to block the placement of WEP workers, thereby compressing political time and forcing the City into a financial crisis born of its inability to meet federal standards in a timely manner. The City would then be forced to redefine work activities, typically away from the dead-end WEP placements it had created. For its part, the City continued to threaten to expand WEP, but it averted this crisis through a temporal ploy of its own: It reduced the rolls fast enough to meet the federal standards without expanding the program.

This apparent miscalculation raises another, two-part question: Where did the idea for the Pledge of Resistance come from, and why was it believed to be a way to break WEP? My interviews with the two principal organizers of the pledge provide some clues. The organizers drew on their own experiences of activism, citing work with ACT-UP and making analogies to antiapartheid solidarity work. In particular, the UJC organizer cited an ACT-UP petition drive to change the Centers for Disease Control's definition of AIDS.

> We had put together a position paper on what the new definition must include to be inclusive of the opportunistic infections that women and IV users were facing as a part of their HIV infection and we got physicians, we got community health centers, we got academics, we got doctors, we got

nurses, we got community-based organizations, we got them all to sign onto this pledge of sorts . . . and we did things like we ran a full-page ad in the *New York Times* on the opening day of . . . the International AIDS Conference. And . . . in conjunction with the sign-on pledge, we did direct actions and we dogged CDC officials all over the country. . . . We were ultimately, after several years, successful. The CDC definition changed and included . . . everything from our position paper on the issues. So that was the successful model and . . . what I was hoping to duplicate was the idea that we made this through that effort, and hopefully through this WEP pledge, is to make workfare a moral issue [in] which people feel compelled to take a side, and there becomes so much moral indignation about the issue that change has to happen.[59]

The strategy of refusal, however, most likely derives from the analogy to apartheid. In a debate over WEP with Lilliam Barrios-Paoli, then the commissioner of New York City's Human Resources Administration (HRA), in front of social service providers in the fall of 1997, Rev. Peter Laarman of Judson Church made an analogy between nonprofit participation in WEP and "constructive engagement" with apartheid-era South Africa.[60] In a later interview, he expanded on the analogy: "The message is that there are situations which are not subject to amelioration from within but that need to be attacked as systematically wrong. . . . *Apartheid* means "separation" in the Dutch language or Afrikaans language, and WEP in New York is another way of saying *separation*. It's taking a whole group of people and putting them into programs under conditions and standards that nobody else is subjected to, with very few rights and so forth."[61] Just as antiapartheid activists rejected the Reagan administration's claim that corporations could "constructively engage" the apartheid regime and sway it to end its policy of racialism, and instead pushed companies to divest from South Africa, Pledge of Resistance organizers rejected the idea that there could be "constructive engagement" with WEP.[62]

The application of these models to the pledge elided most differences between the temporal and institutional dimensions of AIDS and anti-apartheid activism (themselves vastly different) and those of WEP. In campaigning to get the CDC to shift the definition of AIDS, only one institution had to be moved, whereas state and local governments had to be convinced to shift the definition of countable work activities. In the case of the antiapartheid struggle, corporate divestment was explicitly called for by most activists in South Africa and in exile as a complement to their struggles; it was not an alternative strategy to activism within South Africa itself. Most important, however, pledge activists overestimated the City's reliance on the nonprofit social-service sector in implementing and expanding WEP. Nevertheless, where they appear to have been correct—if even contingently so, given the unusual attention given to the pledge in the *New York Times*—is that the pledge *did* change the debate over WEP, even if it did not crush the program institutionally.

In Bakhtinian terms, the multiple sources of the Pledge of Resistance campaign are an important reminder of the limits exerted on genres by their chronotopes. Just as worksite organizers' attempts to organize like unions were stymied, at least in part, by the incommensurability of the WEP contract with the historical stamp of the emergence of free labor on labor organizing, the application of activist models from ACT-UP and antiapartheid organizing to WEP was fraught with problems. Attempts to change genres and to recombine repertoires, however, always involve the selection of particular performances from genres as instruments of change. The Pledge of Resistance promoted criticism of WEP's working conditions and questioning of WEP's fundamental morality. With an already-organized constituency criticizing working conditions, only the former claims gained currency. A wider moral challenge to WEP never arose again, in spite of sporadic attempts on the part of some activists to forge an explicitly moral, human-rights-based discourse of labor rights.

Syncretism and Localism: Labor Rights Are Human Rights

The Pledge of Resistance foundered less than a year after its initiation, setting it barely apart from worksite organizing strategies in terms of organizers' ability to sustain campaigns. Nevertheless, its short-term dominance of the debate strengthened several different claims within the field of anti-WEP actors. References to human rights and the rights to work and to join unions—under Article 23 of the Universal Declaration of Human Rights—joined the moral discourse of the Pledge of Resistance to organized labor's opposition to WEP (e.g., labor leaders on the blue-ribbon panel, Jobs with Justice). A rally on December 10, 1997, was called by Jobs with Justice and attended by ACORN, WWT, CVH, and union members from a wide variety of unions, but not from DC 37.[63] It was scheduled to coincide with International Human Rights Day. One speaker made explicit the claim that "labor rights are human rights" in his demand that the results of the ACORN election be recognized.[64] Moreover, the right to work—as opposed to the right *not* to work—became a central trope of activists. Chapter 3 dealt with the claim that WEP was a "dead end" in that it did not lead to real jobs. Complaints about displacement now replaced complaints about conditions and administration as the central claims communicated in the press.

Meanwhile, the UJC increased its efforts to define welfare reform as a human rights issue. This interpretation became UJC's niche. Citing competition over resources and strategic differences with other organizations, the UJC organizer began to focus on coalitional work with the nationally known, Philadelphia-based Kensington Welfare Rights Union (KWRU, which also emphasizes human rights violations under welfare reform). UJC began to document various abusive practices at welfare offices. UJC's self-removal from the thick of the field thinned the connections among human rights and right-to-jobs discourses, as the Pledge of Resistance no longer served as an organizational-discursive link between nonprofits and advocates on the one hand and labor activists on the other.

In late 1997 and early 1998, the soft-assembled coalition out of which anti-WEP organizing arose in 1996 had changed into loosely connected clusters of hard-assembled coalitions focused on particular niches in the field. UJC's retreat from the field was symptomatic, rather than causative, of diminishing dialogue among occupants of the various niches or trenches. Although there were still some common forums for dialogue, such as Jobs with Justice, they provided little centripetal pull on the claims activists made. Nevertheless, over the course of 1998, some network ties were repaired as separate but overlapping legislative coalitions led by ACORN, FAC, and CVH promoted cooperation where previously competition among organizations had held sway.

Legislative Strategies

The pursuit of legislation to promote alternatives to workfare was a second response to disillusion with worksite organizing. From mid-1997 onward, legislative campaigns for public job creation and education and training options took center stage in anti-WEP activism, prompted by frustration at worksite organizing and by the sense that WEP's current policy configuration was locked in by the 1997 state welfare reform law. The mayor's sweeping reelection victory and hiring of a hard-line welfare reformer as his new HRA commissioner seemed to require groundwork for alternative policies in a subsequent administration. This shift also had consequences for the kind of identity claims that organizations made on behalf of WEP workers. Claims that workfare workers were just like regular workers and demands for unionization or union recognition began to yield to demands for full employment, job creation, and training. This meant that WEP workers were portrayed as *potential* employees rather than as employees *in fact*. Other factors in the emphasis on job creation were that $100 million in federal funds were announced to implement welfare reform, and various advocacy groups began to publicize research on the persistent job gap facing potential entrants into the formal labor market. Nevertheless, it was clear to all anti-WEP activists that the administration was unlikely to create well-paying jobs for welfare recipients. Besides, the mayor had already gone on record saying that he intended to use the federal aid to expand WEP, and a job creation program would have revealed the shortcomings of one of his favorite programs.

The job creation programs evolved on two levels. First, during the spring of 1997, CVH approached the National Employment Law Project (NELP), a group with which it had run a legal clinic for WEP workers, to draft state legislation for a "community jobs" bill. It envisioned a pilot program to be implemented in several localities, which would undergo a community-needs survey. Jobs designed to meet these needs would then be created in local organizations and would "include on-the-job training [and] classroom-based training and education."[65] Moreover, while the jobs would be limited to eighteen-month cycles (extendable to twenty-four months), they would pay $7.50 per hour in New York City and $6.00 upstate, where the cost of living was lower. Workers would be subject to all employee protections, would have the right to unionize, and would be guaranteed not to replace other workers.

Transitional Jobs in the City

After the stinging legislative defeat of the 1997 state welfare reform bill, FAC approached NELP to draft similar "transitional" job legislation for New York City. In the city bill, as originally proposed, welfare recipients could apply for the transitional jobs, which would last eighteen months and pay $8.50 per hour. Transitional job placements would also build in education and training time and enjoy the full benefits of employee status. Conceived as a pilot project, the Transitional Employment Program (TEP) would create ten thousand positions over a period of five years.

The legislative campaigns also meant that encounters at the worksite focused less on ameliorating worksite conditions and more on getting WEP workers to meetings away from the worksite and on developing organizational leaders[66] among WEP workers who could speak for the organization in front of the press and in legislative testimony. Organizers, in turn, focused somewhat less on increasing the number of WEP workers in their organizations (though they hardly ignored this) and more on political education. They also coached WEP workers to be succinct and stay on message in their encounters with the press and with lawmakers.

Both transitional job efforts also moved beyond organizing workfare workers to organizing broad coalitions to support the legislation. CVH's relationship with the Hunger Action Network of New York State (HANNYS) gave it immediate credibility among Albany-based advocacy groups and ties to such groups as the Fiscal Policy Institute (FPI), a union-backed research and advocacy organization. Both HANNYS and FPI had extensive ties throughout the progressive policy community in Albany. The coalition was able to win support in both houses of the legislature and the governor's signature on a budget bill allocating funds (but no programmatic outlines) for job creation in 1998.

In New York City, FAC and WWT took the lead in building the Ad Hoc Coalition for Real Jobs, which could count on support from anti-poverty activists such as the Community Food Resource Center (CFRC) and the Welfare Reform Network (WRN). Yet, in part because TEP would create jobs in the public and nonprofit sectors, the coalition needed support from unions in the areas in which these jobs might be created, which meant securing DC 37's support. In contrast to challenges to WEP through worksite organizing, TEP won DC 37's support quickly, for a number of reasons. First, WWT worked quickly to secure support from a wide array of unions, including the civil service painters' union, which had earlier sued the City for using WEP workers to displace its members. The president of the painters' union worked hard as a spokesperson within union circles to gather support, even from unions that were less directly involved in worksites threatened by WEP. This was an important relationship, too, because the president of the Central Labor Council (also a Democratic state assembly member) was a union official in the construction trades. The United Auto Workers (who represent a wide array of workers, many far from the automobile industry) and the health-care giant Local 1199 introduced a resolution in the Central Labor Council to support TEP and urged DC 37's executive director to support the bill.[67] Moreover, sympathetic staff within DC 37, including policy directors and attorneys, worked closely with NELP and WWT to craft legislation guaranteeing that TEP participants would not displace regular workers.

At the same time, in trying to attract union support, the WWT organizer, especially, conceived his task as lending choral support for what he understood as a union-based rhetorical genre of engagement.

In so doing, he hoped build more durable relations across the trenches separating community organizing and antipoverty work from bread-and-butter unionism. FAC's pitch to the unions was based primarily on their supposed narrowly defined, organizational self-interest. It required FAC's performative self-transformation based on a model of narrow business unionism, a model apparently confirmed by contemporary events. In the view of the FAC executive director,

> The labor politics of this is interesting actually, because labor unions, with a few notable exceptions . . . are generally suspicious of advocates because advocates talk about principles, what's right, how we're all going to work together because we're going to fight for justice; and labor unions are all about "What the fuck are you going to do for my people? I represent a set of people. These are their interests . . ." So, when an advocate comes to the table, they don't really understand what we're asking them to do. They can see in . . . the long term, WEP workers and union workers fighting together makes a lot of sense . . . but it's not the language that labor unions use. . . . So what we're able to do with . . . focusing around jobs was to go to the unions and say, "Our people want jobs. Your people want jobs. Let's work together." And that [is] the culture and the language that the labor union is much more comfortable with.[68]

It is true that TEP contained minimal threats to organized labor and carried some potential benefits to it, including the easing of displacement pressures on public-sector unions. In addition, TEP gave unions the opportunity to be as confrontational as they saw fit when speaking to the administration in support of the bill. In FAC's testimony to the General Welfare Committee shortly after the bill's introduction, the lead organizer introduced the bill and its supporting coalition in a way that both twisted the knife on WEP and allowed other members of the coalition to choose their battles:

> The Coalition has been led, in part, by WEP workers . . . who have struggled with the abusive conditions in the fatally flawed WEP program. But this hearing, and the bill, is not about WEP, it is about jobs. The Transitional Employment Program is not a referendum on workfare; it is an opportunity to help people move from welfare to work. Although we could speak at length about the numerous problems that make WEP bad public policy, we are instead here to testify about a positive alternative: a program which

uses available resources to create decent jobs with training for ten thousand New Yorkers who desperately want and deserve an opportunity.[69]

Accordingly, unions and other coalition members were invited to support TEP whether or not they supported WEP or had supported the mayor's reelection. While this catholic approach to criticizing WEP probably helped build the coalition and drew in members who were less likely to have joined the Pledge of Resistance (though there was considerable overlap), it is notable that the unions were at least as likely as the other coalition members to testify about WEP's shortcomings. To be sure, the building trades unions were less likely to do so than were the representatives of DC 37 and its constituent locals.[70] The former concentrated on their belief in the in the individual and social importance of work and their conviction that the old welfare system was a failure as a way of leading into the importance of real jobs. The latter emphasized displacement as a lead-in to the same conclusion.

Although firm opposition to WEP was not a prerequisite for support of TEP, TEP was widely viewed as a condemnation of the workfare program in the guise of a demonstration project. The administration's response was to oppose TEP on the basis of its cost, on legal grounds, and on a broad defense of WEP. The administration's cost estimates for TEP were, unsurprisingly, far higher than the council's. It claimed that TEP would cost[71] in excess of tens of millions of dollars more than the council's estimates,[72] in part because the administration included supervisors' salaries in program costs and did not include the bulk of federal and state money that could be applied to the program. It also contested the city council's authority to add head count to the city payroll: "The City Council does not have the authority to institute TEP. The Council is attempting to mandate the requirement of certain services and circumvent state law."[73] Moreover, it complained that the city council would undermine the administration's success in governing: "The administration has worked hard over the past several years to reduce government expenditures, improve the efficiency of government and reduce public employment. At a time when all levels of government are streamlining their operation to reduce their need for tax dollars, this bill would force the city to go against that trend and lead to a much more bloated city government."[74] It further complained that the availability of the TEP workers to civil service unions could make it difficult to ensure that the jobs were temporary, saddling the city with further costs down the road. The administration even warned that "the bill may violate the New York State Constitution as well as provisions of the Civil Service Law. TEP would give its participants an unfair advantage by allowing them to bypass the many people who have taken competitive tests and are waiting to be called from hiring lists."[75] This final claim was a serious concern for public employee unions, one calculated to challenge the resolve of these unions in the coalition. In presenting his testimony to the General Welfare Committee, the administration's point man for WEP-related testimony, Seth Diamond, was continually interrupted by Chairman DiBrienza and roundly scolded and ridiculed for expressing concern over civil service provisions. DiBrienza accused the administration of trying to undermine civil service rules at every turn, and he derided as misleading the deputy HRA commissioner's claims that the agency had documented nearly two hundred thousand job placements since expanding WEP. The deputy commissioner only barely managed to finish his testimony.

Genres, Choral Support, Dialogue, and Chronotope in the Transitional Jobs Fight

Though the city council overwhelmingly passed TEP and overrode a mayoral veto, the program remained mired in court battles for the rest of the Giuliani administration because Giuliani refused to implement the law. Nevertheless, the Giuliani administration didcreate the Parks Opportunity Program (POP) by the end of 2001, using some of the same sources of funding envisioned by TEP advocates and creating real employment for more WEP workers at higher wages than the advocates' program contained, though POP had no education or training component.

The TEP fight and the creation of POP demonstrate in several ways the analytic importance of genre, dialogue, choral support, and chronotope in attempts to build connections between labor and community politics. For WWT and CVH, legislative activism marked a spatiotemporal shift away from the worksite as the focal point of their organizing and from short-term amelioration of working conditions as an orienting focus. At the same time that activists were deferring into the future the tangible goals of their organizing (i.e., funneling their demands through the long-acting milieu of legislative action), they were shifting their rhetorical temporal horizons to accord with established union genres of coalition negotiation. In these union genres, narrow self-interest, rather than justice and doing what's right, takes precedence. Implicitly, self-interest is realized much sooner than is justice.

At the same time, if the WWT organizer is to be taken at his word, though the switch to a legislative transitional jobs strategy accorded more with the way in which WEP workers understood themselves, that is, as not full-status workers, adaptation to the institutional patterns of legislation sapped the militancy of WEP worker organizing. It involved testimony before committees separated by months of behind-the-scenes negotiation and long periods of inaction. Different groups handled this differently; by the end of the TEP campaign, there were clear stylistic differences between WWT and CVH, with the latter more likely to disrupt council proceedings to show internal and external strength.

The Giuliani administration's shift of TEP from the city council to the courts introduced another layer of institutional temporality, deferring TEP's realization even more. The issue at hand was the legality of the council's passage of job creation legislation under the strong-mayor system instituted in New York City.[76] This issue was not one upon which the voices of WEP workers, however well organized, could weigh with any clear relevance. Holding up TEP in court, however, completed the administration's attempt to outrun the city council's attempt to hold it publicly accountable for WEP's failures.

As it instituted POP, the Giuliani administration also had to acknowledge the demand for transitional, non-WEP jobs, as the demand was the subject of the first override of a Giuliani veto. But the administration was able to contextualize this demand in the spatiotemporal matrix of the federal devolution of welfare policy. Accordingly, the administration could save face by coming up with its own program that solved the problem of an imminent cutoff of federal funds for families reaching their five-year time limits as mandated by the Personal Responsibility and Work Opportunity Reconciliation Act of 1996 (PRWORA). To preserve these funds, the City used surplus funds from the Temporary Aid to Needy Families (TANF) program to fund POP in order to maintain that workforce as federally funded.

Running parallel to all of this was a separate piece of legislation, called the *grievance procedure*. Pushed by ACORN, with some initial support from the blue-ribbon panel convened for ACORN's election, the bill called for the creation of a WEP-specific grievance procedure that would, among other things, allow for the filing of group grievances; let organizations assist WEP workers in filing grievances; and exempt WEP workers from returning to the worksite at which they were being aggrieved while the grievance was pending. Here, the legislative strategy corresponded to ACORN's unionization strategy. It kept the focus on WEP worksites and would allow ACORN to represent large numbers of WEP workers in work-site-specific grievances, just as a union might for municipal employees. Again, however, ACORN ran up against initial opposition from DC 37. The union feared that WEP workers would file grievances against its members rather than against nonunion supervisory personnel. Like the TEP bill, the grievance procedure legislation was delayed for nearly two years before it passed.

Two changes led to the passage of the grievance procedure and TEP along with it. First, in the DC 37 corruption scandal, which unfolded from mid-1998 to the following spring, the indictment and banishment of much of the union leadership and the appointment of an administrator by AFSCME meant that the national union leadership—which had tried to nudge DC 37 toward a less-conciliatory stance on WEP—was now in charge. More to the point, among reformers within DC 37, WEP stood as an emblem of ineffectiveness and corruption. The AFSCME administrator, Lee Saunders, quickly reversed the union's opposition to the grievance procedure and began to attack WEP in the press and in court filings contesting displacement. The new, public opposition to WEP was a way of marking time—saying "that was then, this is now"—to secure legitimacy in a field grown skeptical both of DC 37 and of the national union that had let corruption fester locally for so long.

The second, and probably more important, change that pushed the bill to passage was the formation, across city trenches, of the Working Families Party (WFP) as a collaborative effort among several unions, including CWA 1180 and ACORN. New York State's election laws allow for cross-endorsement by parties, so third parties can flourish, at least compared with those in other states. WFP organized after a national third-party effort, called the New Party, spearheaded by some of the same actors, lost a Supreme Court case in 1997, in which the court ruled that states were not required to allow cross-endorsement.[77] In 1999, the city council speaker, who, like all elected city officials, faced term limits following a 1993 ballot measure, decided to continue his political career by running for governor. Eager to attract the WFP's endorsement, he promised to bring up the grievance procedure and TEP for a vote. Thus, the success of the legislative campaigns in actually moving the two bills through the city council depended in good part on dynamics that were not central to the campaigns themselves. Moreover, neither bill was ever implemented. Just as with worksite organizing and the Pledge of Resistance, therefore, it is difficult to say that work within the institutional framework of legislation was successful. Nor did it result in the creation of clear alternatives to WEP. Indeed, WEP continues to exist alongside the Job Training Program, the successor to POP.

Accordingly, the story of the transitional jobs and grievance procedure bills is an example of contentious dialogue at a moment of intense inter-animation,[78] where choral support for claims breaks out of generic and chronotopic boundaries, only to recombine with new ones and set new limits on discourse. The transitional jobs legislation in particular created a new kind of labor contract that overcame some of the limitations of WEP. Transitional jobs were "freer" and better compensated than WEP assignments, and public-sector transitional jobs would be unionized. The education and training component of transitional jobs looked forward to postwelfare labor market participation in a position that was not necessarily in the contingent, secondary labor market. At the same time, the grievance procedure bill tried to change WEP, as it existed. The bills were forced together as the temporal dynamics of electoral politics intersected with the labor-community alliance-building effort represented by the Working Families Party. Together, the bills defined WEP workers as workers *and* as potential workers. In spite of this potential conflict, the bills gained wide support as the new administrators of DC 37 forsook the narrowly protective stance toward WEP that had come to symbolize the union's corruption.

Legislating Away from the Work-Cash Nexus

A partial exception to this judgment can be found, however, in a different set of legislative programs that were introduced into the state legislature and city council supporting the expansion of opportunities for education and training. These programs were championed primarily by the Welfare Rights Initiative (WRI). WRI began in 1996 as a class on welfare policy taught by two professors at Hunter College, part of the City University of New York (CUNY) system. The idea behind the class was to teach welfare recipients about welfare advocacy and to undertake a class project on the issue. At the time, federal welfare reform was being passed, and WEP had recently expanded to AFDC recipients in New York City. As a result, enrollment of welfare recipients in CUNY two- and four-year colleges plummeted by more than seventeen thousand students over the next two years and continued to decline more slowly for five years after that. Pushed by the city into workfare assignments that often involved long travel or conflicted with class schedules, welfare recipients in college had to choose between maintaining their main or sole means of support and gaining the education that could mean an end to their reliance on welfare. Very quickly, WRI turned its attention to this issue and began to organize Hunter students to support several campaigns to enable welfare recipients to stay in school and to count school-related work, such as internships and work-study jobs, toward work requirements.

In contrast to the other organizing groups, however, WRI not only had a more targeted constituency but also had a constituency that was both largely composed of mothers and exposed to feminist welfare-state analysis through the class materials; these materials were originally developed in part by Mimi Abramowitz, a leading feminist welfare-state scholar. Accordingly, WRI did not organize against WEP on the basis that it fundamentally transformed the status of welfare recipients into that of workers. Instead, it claimed that WEP simply piled work on top of work and that mothers who were in school were already working at mothering while attempting to get off welfare by going to school, where they worked both as students and in work-study and internship jobs. In this perspective, WEP was merely punitive and counterproductive even on its own terms.

For its initial legislative activism, WRI targeted the state. First, it gained bipartisan support for a bill, called the Marchi-Ramirez bill, after its sponsors in the state senate and assembly. Marchi-Ramirez required the City to attempt to place WEP worker students at worksites at or near their campuses. As with the other legislation around WEP, the City refused to implement the bill. WRI followed this effort with another in 2000 that enabled work-study jobs and internships to count as work-related activities to satisfy state and federal workfare requirements. This bill, too, won bipartisan support and was signed by Governor Pataki—hardly a friend of welfare recipients—in 2000. The bill was backed by a large coalition, including the presidents of the State Universities of New York (SUNY). WRI obtained their support when a SUNY college president called one of its leaders after a letter from the leader complaining of a lack of educational and training possibilities for welfare recipients was published in the *New York Times*. WRI continued in this vein and began to organize a large citywide coalition—with ACORN, Families United for Racial and Economic Equality (FUREE, WWT's successor organization), CVH, and many other anti-WEP organizations—to increase welfare recipients' ability to obtain education and training. The coalition, called the Coalition for Access to Training and Education (CATE), supported city council legislation making it possible to count secondary education and a wide array of job training activities toward work requirements. Introduced in 2001, the CATE bill foundered for a while after September 11. Taken up by the council again during the Bloomberg administration, the bill faced stern opposition from city hall. Nevertheless, in 2004, the council passed the CATE bill and overrode Mayor Bloomberg's veto. Just as his predecessor did, Bloomberg forced the issue into court, where the court held—as it had earlier in the TEP lawsuit—that the council had overstepped its jurisdictional authority.

Like TEP, the CATE bill defined WEP workers primarily as *potential workers* whose potential was as yet unrealized. Unlike TEP, which would have created an alternative to WEP that could exist alongside it, the CATE bill would have empowered welfare recipients to make WEP their last option, rather than have it be among the first, forced upon them by the City.

Whether focused on transitional jobs or on education and training, the legislative campaigns that focused on WEP workers as *potential* workers were vulnerable to the litigious strategies of the mayor. To be sure, the definition of WEP workers as potential workers helped resolve the ambivalence of WEP workers who saw the fight for improved worksite conditions as akin to rearranging deck chairs on the *Titanic*. Nevertheless, the temporal orientation of this definition made it difficult for advocates to charge that some irreversible harm was being done to WEP workers if the programs were left unimplemented. Without being able to make this claim, WEP workers and their organizations had dubious standing to force Mayors Giuliani and Bloomberg to comply with the law. Ultimately, the strong-mayor system of government shaped the institutional logic that drove the court to overturn the TEP and CATE bills. Here, too, interanimation was at work: An older genre of urban reform measures geared toward rooting out patronage and corruption intersected with the demands of activists to provide opportunities for higher-level labor market participation to welfare recipients. As with older urban reform measures, however, the mayors' jurisdictional claims against the city council's power enabled them to paint the advocates' efforts as wasteful impediments to good government.

Litigation

Litigation was a fourth institutional arena of contention. In this section, I treat law as many legal scholars do, as a contested domain and a site of struggle, even though contention channeled through the courts tends to support hegemonic definitions of social actors and secure conditions in which subordinate groups remain subordinate. Nevertheless, even in a context characterized by the interpretive demands of common-law precedent and formalism—characteristics that might ordinarily be construed as promoting conservatism—and even in a context marked by increasing judicial deference to executive power, courts respond to challenges neither in a unified way nor in a manner that automatically and functionally upholds the status quo. Put another way, law relies on existing, developing genres of interpretation. But in the process of litigation, there is room for dialogue, and judgments rendered are always construed in numerous ways and from various standpoints.

Law does two other things more explicitly than do many other institutions within which contention unfolds. First, in the concept of standing—who can bring a given cause of action to the court—courts delineate who is a qualified speaker. Closely related to this determination is the decision courts make on whether or not to "certify a class" in class-action lawsuits—that is, to decide that members of a given group of plaintiffs have complaints with enough in common to have them considered together and to have the resulting judgment apply to anyone situated similarly to the plaintiffs.

Second, litigation elicits stories from its participants in order to establish the facts of a case. The process of lawyering, therefore, is one of organizing stories so as to suggest the application of one or another category of law or judgment to the protagonist or antagonist. Parties to litigation try to establish classes of similar and different facts, according to the ways in which their narrated facts fit the legal principles. In this process, lawyers and other participants (e.g., parties to the litigation, filers of friend of the court briefs, etc.) on both sides try to connect stories with quite different chronotopic or spatiotemporal profiles by claiming some generic similarities among them. The results of this dialogue are contingent but are nevertheless structured by institutional processes within courts, even specific courts, and by the changing, broader relations among courts, legislatures, and executives. A few illustrations will make this point clearer.

Similarity and Difference

Recall from the previous chapter that two legal advocacy groups that figured prominently in anti-WEP contention, NELP and the Welfare Law Center (WLC), were backup centers for local Legal Services Corporation offices around the country. When before PRWORA, Congress limited Legal Services' ability to bring class-action suits against government agencies, NELP and WLC spun off into independent nonprofit organizations and became more active in fighting WEP in New York City, where both were based. With the Legal Aid Society, the three groups supported much of the litigation around WEP between 1996 and 2000.

NELP and WLC, along with Legal Aid, collaborated on class-action lawsuits beginning in 1996 that challenged the flexible status of WEP workers. Had they succeeded, the suits would have challenged the City's ability to implement the program. *Brukhman v. Giuliani* and *Capers v. Giuliani* challenged the formula by which the City calculated required work hours and the working conditions in the departments of Sanitation and Transportation, respectively.

In *Brukhman*, the legal advocates worked with WWT and Work*fairness* to recruit plaintiffs to challenge the City's practice of using the minimum wage, rather than the prevailing wage for the work done, in calculating WEP workers' hours. At the time, in 1996, both constitutional and statutory law in New York State required that welfare recipients' work hours be calculated using prevailing wages. If successful, the suit would have required that the City determine the work done by each WEP worker and calculate the workers' hours according to the prevailing wage, determined by the city comptroller, for the kind of work they were doing. This would have been a forbidding administrative task.

In *Brukhman*, the lawyers worked with the plaintiffs to craft testimony that would speak to the legal issues involved. This meant that WEP workers' stories needed to be retold not according to the priorities WEP workers themselves placed on elements in their stories but rather in a way that highlighted the issues before the Court. Whether or not a WEP worker's main complaint had to do with working conditions or his or her inability to attend school, the client narratives were crafted to emphasize prevailing-wage issues. For example, the plaintiffs' testimony was all marked by a variant of the sentence, "I have never been told how my hourly WEP assignment was calculated or what a regular worker would make for the work that I was asked to do."[79] But beyond this focus, the stories were told to illustrate many WEP workers' previous work experience and the burdens placed on WEP workers such as having to leave school, being forced to work outside in fear of being found by an abusive ex-boyfriend, having to work in hazardous conditions, and being forced to leave vulnerable or sick family members. The point was to show that WEP was *not* training or anything like it and to dispute the City's claim that "the primary purpose of this program is to provide a supportive environment in which adults can gain work experience and immediately apply the skills they need to become job ready, look for and find work, and keep a job."[80] If they could show that WEP was a program designed primarily to allow the City to take advantage of WEP workers' labor, then the legal advocates had a better chance of winning. Moreover, though the City argued that the plaintiffs were trying to "enjoin WEP"[81] altogether, figuring that these more-radical objectives should be obscured from view, the plaintiffs quoted a case from the late 1970s to claim that "the Intervenors in this case do not 'object to a "work-relief" program, nor do they object to working off their grants [and thus their] complaint is grounded on the argument that their wages are arbitrarily determined at a rate below that required by the New York State Constitution, and statutes, and lower than the rate applied to others in identical employment.'"[82] The advocates' strategy, therefore, was to use WEP workers' stories of hardship to bolster a legal claim that they constructed as narrowly tailored to the law. Just as in the WWT organizer's claim that TEP "was not about WEP," the lawyers' citation of moderating language from a decades-old prevailing-wage case was meant to show the reasonableness of their claims.

The *Capers* suit also generated stories, like those in chapter 2, describing the poor working conditions to which WEP workers were subject. Both *Brukhman* and *Capers* met with mixed success. They enjoyed significant success, however, at the trial level. Both cases were assigned to the same judge in the trial court, and she was broadly sympathetic to WEP workers. In *Brukhman*, she ruled that even if WEP workers need training, they are enough like regular workers to trigger both statutory and constitutional prevailing-wage requirements. Having dispensed with the distinction between regular workers and WEP workers in Parks Department jobs, she wrote, "The City defendants similarly seek to minimize and distinguish the nature of the tasks performed by WEP participants in clerical positions. The City defendants urge that there is a meaningful distinction between someone who performs 'simple' filing and 'complex' filing; between someone who answers 'routine' telephone inquiries and someone who answers more 'complex' inquiries. These purported distinctions are absurd. Moreover, that WEP participants may need training does not necessarily make them different from any other entry level City employee."[83]

But these favorable rulings could not stand. In New York State, governments are entitled to automatic stays of judgment upon appeal. This policy results in a certain amount of impunity on the part of governments because they can delay implementation of a court ruling for years. But it also gives governments a chance to appeal to what are, in New York, more conservative courts and to push for legislation to change adverse statutes. Just months after the *Brukhman* ruling, the state legislature repealed the statutory language in the Social Services Law upon which the judge's opinion was based. This action left only the constitutional basis for the case, namely, a provision from the 1938 New York State Constitution providing that "no laborer, workman or mechanic, in the employ of a contractor or subcontractor engaged in the performance of any public work, shall . . . be paid less than the rate of wages prevailing in the same trade or occupation in the locality within the state where such public work is to be situated, erected or used."[84] In order to argue this case, the attorneys worked with the state AFL–CIO and Service Employees International Union and with DC 37, which together represent roughly two million workers. They wrote an amicus curiae brief outlining the history of the constitutional article as a response to Depression-era threats of using Works Progress Administration (WPA) workers to displace union members. As with community organizers engaging in worksite organizing, the lawyers in the case looked for labor's imprimatur and recruited unions into the now-historical story they had to tell.

The City made a distinction between large public-works projects and other public or public-sector work, and it argued that the constitutional provision applied to the former and not the latter. The appellate division and then the court of appeals agreed. Moreover, they reversed the lower court's judgment that WEP workers were like employees. In March 2000, the New York State Court of Appeals, the state's highest court, ruled:

> Program participants simply are not "in the employ" of anyone—that is the very reason they are receiving public welfare benefits and required to participate in the Program, until they can find or be placed in jobs with the customary array of the traditional indicia of employment. . . . Participants are "assigned" to various "work sites" where they provide "valuable service" until they are able to "secure employment in the regular economy." While the agencies providing work assignment opportunities obviously employ some people, they are not "employing" Program participants. These agencies and entities simply do not pay a salary to the Program participants—one of the fundamental requisites that spark the prevailing wage entitlement.[85]

Accordingly, the courts finally adopted the City's logic and allowed the City to define WEP just as it pleased, creating a catch-22 for WEP workers: if they were not paid a wage, they could not be employees, but if they were not employees, they were not owed prevailing wages.

In *Capers*, the appeals court's solution created a worse catch-22. In *Brukhman*, the court ruled that WEP workers were essentially different from regular workers, but in *Capers*, the court ruled that they were similar in important respects. In *Capers*, the court, rather than requiring the City to upgrade working conditions for WEP workers, ruled that WEP workers were entitled to use the Public Employee Safety and Health (PESH) grievance process to address dangerous conditions at their worksites. Chapter 2 discussed the limitations of the PESH process for WEP workers. PESH inspections often take months to activate, and workers work with their union representatives to file grievances. But turnover at worksites—due to NYC–WAY procedures as well as regular turnover—was frequent enough that WEP workers were unlikely to still be at the worksite by the time a PESH inspector came. Moreover, WEP workers were not entitled to union representation. Yet, in allowing WEP workers to access the PESH process, the courts effectively decertified the class of plaintiffs, since courts require plaintiffs to exhaust existing administrative remedies before bringing suit. This would have to be done individually, just as it would for a regular worker.

The question of whether WEP workers were similar to regular workers animated other lawsuits as well. In 1997, the NOW Legal Defense and Education Fund (NOW–LDEF) and other attorneys represented WEP workers who charged that they were subject to sexual and racial harassment by supervisors at their worksites. They brought a case before the Equal Employment Opportunity Commission (EEOC), which ruled that the City was responsible for protecting its workers from harassment. The case ended in federal court, with the City relying on the *Brukhman* decision to argue that because WEP workers were not "employees," it had no legal responsibility to protect them. After years of litigation, in 2004, the United States Court of Appeals for the Second Circuit ruled in favor of the WEP workers, finding that the work they did was substantially similar to that done by regular workers and that they were equivalent to employees.[86]

The other, and most obvious, area of litigation in which the similarities and differences between WEP workers and regular workers were at issue was in lawsuits brought by DC 37 and other unions charging that WEP workers displaced union members. Though the District Council of Carpenters and the painters' union brought suits as early as 1996 charging displacement, suits that were settled out of court, the main displacement suits were filed by DC 37 after the leadership change in 1999. Here, however, although emerging research documented the attrition of union jobs and expansion of WEP in the most attrition-affected lines, the union was unable to make a clear, causal connection between the two trends.

Moreover, the union did not act immediately against the placement of WEP workers; it had in fact, let the situation go for five years and negotiated raises for its members who supervised WEP workers. The courts agreed to a procedural motion barring the union from litigating any action more than several months old. Accordingly, though *Brukhman* was in many ways a lawsuit contesting displacement of union members, its claim was indirect and made at a time when the DC 37 leadership was uninterested in antagonizing the mayor. Only unions had the standing to bring displacement lawsuits, but by the time DC 37 initiated them, it was too late.

Contention in the legal arena was not limited to efforts to make WEP workers more or less like regular workers in the eyes of the law. Legal advocates also brought cases to ensure that welfare recipients were assessed for their skills before being sent to WEP assignments, although doing so, as with the prevailing wage requirement in *Brukhman*, would have been administratively difficult. Other efforts sought to prevent welfare recipients with disabilities from being assigned to inappropriate worksites and to ensure proper medical screening. Suits tried also to block the expansion of Job Centers until procedures were in place to ensure that applicants for Medicaid and Food Stamps received their applications on the first visit.

The Job Center litigation, known as *Reynolds*, resulted in emergency injunctions and succeeded in changing the administration's practice of denying applications for all public assistance until the second visit. The assessment lawsuit, called *Davila*, was finally settled in 2003, with the City agreeing to inform welfare recipients of their rights to education and training under the law, to provide them with a frequently updated list of preapproved programs, and to consider approval of other programs on an individual basis. These were more straightforward cases than were *Brukhman* or *Capers* or the EEOC case because they could be fought in a single trench or more or less within the genre of welfare law.

In addition to litigation, the main legal advocates in the anti-WEP field engaged in other lawyerly practices, including drafting litigation, holding legal clinics, talking to government officials, and advising organizers. In the process, they became essential participants, but they faced limitations, both in working with each other and in working alongside other, less institutionally enduring forms of contention.

Welfare rights and labor lawyers deal with different kinds of law. Both WLC and NELP and their respective bodies of law have different histories. Accordingly, they are marked by different chronotopes and are different genres, which mark their expert speakers as different from each other. Welfare rights and antipoverty law developed in the context of the civil rights movement and later expanded in the context of the welfare rights movement of the late 1960s and 1970s. In 1970, the United States Supreme Court recognized a property right in welfare: welfare benefits could not be taken away without due process. Other litigation ended the more intrusive practices of welfare administration, such as midnight raids of welfare households in search of hidden breadwinners. The Center for Social Welfare Policy and Law (WLC's previous name) was a key locus of welfare law development and strategy, and it favored "impact litigation," or class-action cases that would expand access to welfare. Hence, in the *Brukhman* case, it is not surprising that a welfare-rights strategy prevailed where the Human Resources Administration's violation of statutory law was so clear.

For its part, NELP dealt mainly in labor law. Even though impact litigation was an important part of NELP's work, historically, it played a somewhat smaller role in the group's formative history and in the slower accretion of labor law. One NELP attorney who worked on *Brukhman* described the difference between the welfare attorneys' modus operandi and those of labor lawyers.

> At the time that we brought *Brukhman*, for instance, the state statute was so clear that we brought it as a class. Because it was on the books, it was right there. But if we had just started with the Article 1, Section 17 [the constitutional provision] or even a labor code violation, I would not have brought it as a class, because it was just too risky. . . . So Article 1, Section 17 survived as the case was appealed, but it wasn't the meat or the main thrust of the case. And for that reason, NELP, and those of us sort of coming from the labor side, the unions, we weren't really taking the lead on the welfare piece of it. We learned it and tried to understand what it was, but we were sort of bowing to the welfare advocates who have done this work for years. And we thought, you know, "This is an overlapping case. Let's work together." But if it had been started in the labor and employment [field], it would have had a much different feel to it. . . . We would have sent a couple of test workers in to the comptroller and . . . they would have won . . . and we would have gotten it established that some workfare workers are doing prevailing-wage work. And that would have been the end of it. I mean . . . it didn't have the magnitude, but that's kind of how you start . . . that's how labor and employment law works.[87]

Accordingly, even within the institutional framework of litigation, there were multiple genres bearing the markings of their institutional histories. That made it difficult to forge a new, stable set of claims that could consistently contest the "flexible" WEP placements. The legal advocates had to construct the legal figure of the "workfare worker," relying on existing case law that rarely contemplated the kind of labor contract embodied in WEP.[88] In organizing stories to do so, lawyers had to construct multiple, and sometimes conflicting, edifices out of precedent, judging whether courts would find cases in other departments (a geographic unit of the court system) or from different periods compelling. Historical differences among labor and welfare lawyers in strategy and style made this a deeper challenge than typically exists within, rather than across, legal genres.

The Forms and Formation of Coalitions within and across Sites of Protest

In their attempts to fight against WEP's expansion, invent alternatives to WEP, and ameliorate the conditions of WEP placements, New York's activists continually found themselves trying to define WEP and WEP workers politically within institutional arenas already structured by legal, moral, and procedural distinctions between work and welfare. Katznelson's observation of enduring differences in the rhetorical styles and organizational forms of labor and community politics in the United States appears to hold well here, too.

Though Katznelson's thesis in *City Trenches* could be summed up by saying that people go to work as workers and come home as ethnics, ethnic and racial divisions did not strongly order the ways in which WEP workers and their organizations operated. Awareness of racial and ethnic inequality was always present, but all the organizations made successful efforts, usually with little difficulty, to overcome whatever barriers ethnic and racial differences created.[89]

Consider the institutional arenas of worksite organizing, institutionally based moral protest, legislative strategies, and litigation as spaces within which relatively stable genres of interaction are played out among state and civil-society actors. These are the trenches defining the debates over workfare. It is clear that even *within* these trenches, the tension between work and welfare prevented activists from arriving at completely unified paradigmatic views on what WEP was, how it should be opposed, the kinds of political claims that were most appropriate to make on behalf of WEP workers, and what activists should expect or hope for from activism. The generation of alternative strategies in alternative trenches reflects defections from an initial, more or less consensual worksite-based strategy.

In keeping with the framework introduced in the previous chapter, focusing on soft- and hard-assembled coalitions and their relation to dimensions of shared claim-making and the ability to build strong inter-organizational ties across a field, we can begin to characterize and compare the various institutional trenches. We can do so in terms of the kinds of coalitions to which they gave rise and their place within the analytic space structured by Ray's "culture" and "power" dimensions.

Characterizing the Trenches

Figure 4.1 schematizes the differences among the institutional arenas and organizational strategies of worksite organizing, moral protest, legislative strategies, and litigation within the context of a structured field. Worksite organizing was characterized by an initial homogeneity of political claims, that is, that WEP workers were *workers* whose labor was unfairly being used to undermine union labor and who deserved the rights of regular workers. By late 1996, however, three groups, including the composite WWT, were organizing at worksites, and they were joined in 1997 by DC 37's halfhearted effort. Taken together, one might call the

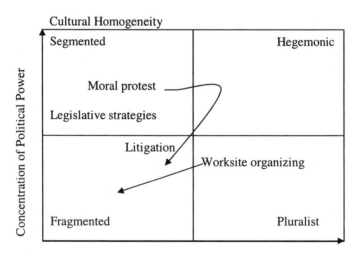

Figure 4.1. Worksite organizing, moral protest, legislative strategies, and litigation within the context of a structured field.

multiple efforts at worksite organizing evidence of a *soft-coalitional effort.* But it would be more accurate, at least at the beginning of the worksite organizing campaigns, to think of the arena as characterized by *pluralist competition.* Only when the contrasts in organizing strategies between ACORN and unionization, on the one hand, and WWT and incremental pressure, on the other hand, became evident both to them and to their supporters did the arena become more fragmented. Clear ideological differences emerged, with a hard-assembled coalition forming around the ACORN election, WWT and CVH's shift of focus into job creation, and UJC's shift into Pledge of Resistance activity.

For its part, the Pledge of Resistance strategy sought the creation of a hard-assembled coalition with a consistent line against WEP's immorality. In this sense, it was a play at organizing hegemony in the field. Like ACORN with its election, the pledge hoped that anyone claiming to be progressive would have to take a public stance against WEP. Yet, this effort to "crush" and "break the back of" WEP was essentially a strategy of a war of maneuver. Behind the initial publicity and success in bringing the issue of WEP's morality to the fore, the pledge found considerable ideological heterogeneity and fragmentation among its target congregations and charities. This fragmentation was reinforced by the City's financial leverage as a contractor for social services and by the City's failure to generalize WEP placements in its service contracts.

The legislative strategies, by contrast, were hard-assembled coalitions with little demand for common claim-making about WEP beyond the demand for transitional jobs, while the litigation strategies were the result of multiple hard-assembled coalitions among legal advocacy groups and the organizing groups who supplied the bulk of the plaintiffs. Both the legislative and litigious arenas lay somewhere between fragmentation and segmentation, as multiple and overlapping hard-assembled coalitions maintained a heterogeneous set of claims. They wanted a grievance procedure cementing the workers' rights of WEP workers within WEP and work-based and education-based alternatives to WEP in legislation, and they wanted multiple objectives with varying definitions of the legal WEP worker in litigation.

The Significance of Differences

Taken a step further, the problems activists encountered in each setting of contention in securing homogeneous, counterhegemonic views of WEP might suggest that they would be too weak to make much of a difference in City policy around WEP. But anti-WEP forces did change both policy and discourse about workfare. They did so although it was difficult to build consistent, enduring political claims for WEP workers. Turnover at worksites, programmatic ambiguities of charity work, the dynamics of bargaining in legislatures, and the changing and contradictory elements of the law in litigation, both within and among these sites of contention, provided both obstacles to and opportunities for these changes.

The differences among these institutional political arenas and their genres of political claim-making lead to different ways in which the struggle advances. The partial sequencing and overlap of strategies and the coalitions that sustained them meant that the temporal and spatial boundaries of claim-making spilled over from one trench to another. These form larger, metafieldwide coalitions that changed the debate in ways not immediately deducible from the difficulties WEP activists encountered in each trench.

Moreover, as the political scientist Michael McCann explains in discussing "legal mobilization," or the ways in which litigation and organizing often work together, the very act of contesting rules creates new expectations of the law and new demands for legislation regardless of outcomes such as the adverse decision in the *Brukhman* case or the perverse one in *Capers;* regardless of the failure of three organizations to organize lasting WEP workers' organizations at worksites; regardless of the Giuliani administration's "running out the clock" on TEP; and regardless of the media's evanescent attention to workfare's morality.

Accordingly, the next task is to step out of the trenches and regard the field from above in order to discover more easily the ways in which the various institutional sites of struggle and the strategies of actors within them articulated with one another to form claim-making coalitions, or *choruses,* across the field. This is the object of the next chapter.

CHAPTER FIVE

Mapping Passages through the Trenches

Hegemony is an outcome—always temporary—of struggles over the configuration of meaning. The trenches of civil society and the state, the institutional settings in which people develop political relations and political language, are themselves at once the locus and the object of political claims. In trench-cut battlefields, what happens within the trenches is obviously important. But what happens *among* the trenches is also important. One cannot understand a battle without understanding their relation to one another.

In this chapter, I want to take advantage of what Pierre Bourdieu called the "privilege of totalization," that is, the ability the researcher has to consider the field from "above" and to "secure the means of apprehending the logic of the system, which a partial or discrete view would miss."[1] By doing so, I hope too to identify the formation and dissolution of harder- and softer-assembled claim-making coalitions and of genres of claim-making that are capable of anchoring the debate as a whole. Finally, I will try to identify moments in which a variety of "mechanisms" of change can be identified and who or what kinds of claims trip them. I do so by means of a formal, network-analytic content analysis of Work Experience Program (WEP) politics in ten years' worth of two newspapers and by going back and forth between this analysis and the record of what events helped drive the reported content.

In spite of the debt I owe to Gramsci, Bakhtin, and Vološinov in developing the schema I use, and in spite of the technical apparatus from network analysis I borrow, I want to avoid the inherent problem of such a view from above, that is, that "there is every likelihood that [the analyst] will overlook the change in status to which he is subjecting practice and its products, and consequently that he will insist on trying to answer questions which are not and cannot be questions for practice."[2]

The questions for practice are these:

1 If one cannot control the meanings of one's claims because they are freighted with connotations they have previously accumulated and with meanings derived from their contemporaneous use in other settings, can we at least map the range of these uses and meanings in a way that makes it possible to see *who* is supporting *what kinds* of discourse among *which kinds* of settings?

2 Can we identify the actors, claims, and settings that are most influential in orienting the debate over WEP at various times in its development? To do so might be useful in casting oppositional discourse more effectively.

3 Can we identify paths or mechanisms through which the choral support for claims is organized or disorganized among actors in a field? To do so would not just clarify "the logic of the system" pace Bourdieu but would also distill descriptions of tactics and strategies as they unfold in particular moments rather than as complete abstractions.

In chapter 4, I addressed these questions, too. But I did so by training my analytic focus on the spatial and temporal dimensions of the relational settings of contentious claim-making. As a result, I was able to uncover some of the reasons that claim-making in these settings took the form it did. Nevertheless, claim-making and the meanings it imparts are not necessarily confined to institutionally defined relational settings that are fully separate from one another. Claim makers, after all, may make claims in multiple settings. By bringing actors, claims, and their multiple settings together in a single analysis, this chapter aims to synthesize the concern with coalitional form and configurations of power in chapter 3 with the concerns of genre and meaning making in chapter 4. By looking at the changing configurations of related actors, claims, and settings as they appeared in the fairly extensive newspaper coverage granted to the issue of workfare politics, I hope to provide a means by which to move up one level of analysis from the institutional-historical and ethnographic levels in the previous two chapters to reveal the ways in which action within particular institutional settings may influence or be influenced by action in others.

Maps and Mechanisms

Theoretical Background

In chapter 3, I drew on Raka Ray's work on protest fields in India to suggest a larger framework into which soft-assembled and hard-assembled coalitions could be understood. Though my definition in that chapter of hard- and soft-assembled coalitions dealt both with claim-making and resource sharing, the larger idea behind the distinction was that hard-assembled coalitions focus discursive and organizational power into special-purpose groups, whereas soft-assembled coalitions are more flexible, able to address multiple issues in multiple settings, but less organizationally intensive. In this chapter, I discuss these types of coalitions in this more general and looser definition rather than specifically in light of resource sharing. In the extremes, Ray's description of pluralist fields describe soft assembly; segmented fields, hard assembly; fragmented fields, the absence of coalitions; and hegemonic fields, the generation of hard-assembled coalitions around a soft-assembled core.

If we return to Gramsci, however, the landscape of possibilities becomes more differentiated and complex. As several writers have indicated, Gramsci uses the term *hegemony* in various ways. Joseph V. Femia recommends that Gramsci be understood to have described *integral, decadent,* and *minimal* levels of hegemony. Integral hegemony is based on the real integration of the rulers and the ruled in a way that generates a common idiom for social and political life that is substantially without contradiction. It is a revolutionary outcome and the product, at least in part, of the integration of organic intellectuals, that is, those who have a key role in shaping relational settings, and traditional intellectuals, that is, those whose function it is to articulate the relations of these settings to one another in public. Decadent hegemony describes the hegemony of a ruling coalition or "bloc" whose leadership no longer serves the interests of those over whom it rules. This description applies to "bourgeois economic dominance, whether or not it faces serious challenge" in "modern capitalist society."[3] If bourgeois dominance was important for representing and carrying the challenge to feudalism, it is nevertheless unable to contain its own contradictions now. As Peter Ives elaborates, "Such a hegemonic class maintains its predominance mostly due to the lack of an effective alternative challenging it."[4] Minimal hegemony depends on the exclusion of nonelite actors from participation in social and political life. "They maintain their rule through *trasformismo,* the practice of incorporating potentially hostile groups into the elite network, the result being 'the formation of an ever broader ruling class.'"[5] Minimal hegemony, therefore, relies on the disorganization and co-optation of challenge and of any other larger meaningful framework within which to cast it.

Understanding hegemony to be a differentiated phenomenon allows for the combination of Ray's ideal-types and Gramsci's. Hegemonic configurations can be consistent with a segmented field (i.e., a minimal hegemony) or even with a pluralistic one (i.e., a decadent hegemony). In the following analysis, I will go a step further and formalize these configurations, even if doing so cuts against some of the grain of Gramsci's larger project.[6]

It is one thing to generate maps of hard and soft coalitions and the meanings that gird them. It is another to explain why the maps change over time. As Chik Collins writes, "Precisely because discourse is produced by the logic of evolving activity, its analysis will tend to reveal traces of that historical evolution and of its twists and turns, moments of reconstitution and realignment. These traces provide vital prompts to the researcher who can begin from there to investigate, to reconstruct, and . . . to grasp, the historical evolution of the . . . activity from within, and out of, which particular uses of language emerged."[7]

I am particularly interested in finding mechanisms of change, moments of dynamism within the dialectic of context and action. On a methodological level, mechanisms are descriptions of regularly observable shifts in the relations of social actors, of them to the material and relational settings in which they interact. A mechanism describes regularly occurring—and thus comparable—processes of social interaction, which, when combined in different ways, lead to regularly identifiable changes in relations among social actors and settings. They are never unilateral and are always relational. The language of mechanisms is contested in social science explanation. Some scholars, such as Jon Elster, rely on the term *mechanism* as a way to move from higher levels of analysis to lower ones and to identify causal processes that are as proximate in time as possible to the events being explained. Others, like Charles Tilly, do not require that mechanisms be described on the lowest level of analysis but rather only that they occur relationally, that is, between readily identifiable social actors or social sites. Though this interpretation can lead to some "ad hockery" in the definition of mechanisms, it has the distinct advantage of neither reifying micro-, macro-, and mesolevels of analysis nor treating any particular level as ultimately causative of social outcomes. Thus, when McAdam, Tarrow, and Tilly write that mechanisms are "delimited sorts of events that alter relations among specified sets of elements in identical or closely similar ways over a variety of situations,"[8] they envision action among discontinuous institutional or relational settings that change relations in the networks that exist in them.[9]

Mechanisms exist, as it were, *between strategy and context* as manipulable, structured, environmental levers of action. As such, mechanisms must be tripped by actors in a network, but they do not have to be done so consciously or by single actors. In addition, they are available in specific ways, depending upon contextual factors. Like repertoires, then, mechanisms depend on relations among actors, a shared medium of relations (in this case, political claims), and settings within which they unfold. Ann Mische, for example, enumerates several conversational mechanisms, such as "multiple targeting" and "identity qualifying." Multiple targeting occurs when a speaker addresses several audiences at once, relying on the multivocality of his or her claims to "target" multiple audiences differently. Identity qualifying is, in a way, the inverse. A speaker with access to numerous possible identities or modes of address, publicly limits them, as in, "As a WEP worker, I believe that . . ."[10] Identity qualifying, like multiple targeting, depends on the presence of an audience able to lend choral support and on a setting within which the mechanisms evoke salient genres. Though one can multiple-target by accident, one cannot do so in the absence of multiple, discontinuous, and weakly joined networks.

In the following analysis, I place particular emphasis on mechanisms that exert centripetal or centrifugal force to build coalitions and genres of claim-making, to join them together, or to dissolve their internal or external connections. These mechanisms help determine how hard- or soft-assembled a coalition will be. Four groups of mechanisms, derived from the literature on social movement organization and framing, geography, and pragmatist cultural sociology, seem especially relevant: (1) *certification* and *decertification*, (2) *amplification*, (3) *institutional spillover*, and (4) *scale and time shifts*. I will briefly outline each.

Certification and Decertification

Doug McAdam, Sidney Tarrow, and Charles Tilly, in their mechanism-enumerating work *Dynamics of Contention*, define *certification* as "validation of actors, their performances, and their claims by external authorities. Decertification is the withdrawal of such validation by certifying authorities."[11] It is clear from the narrative of workfare politics that "external authorities" may be any of a wide array of state actors of various kinds (e.g., the Giuliani administration, the courts, the city council), and social actors, too (e.g., District Council 37 of the American Federation of State, County, and Municipal Employees [DC 37] for the initial anti-WEP organizers' claims to represent workers; the clergy for moral claims; labor leaders and welfare recipients for the Association of Community Organizations for Reform Now [ACORN] election; and bond raters for larger City labor and welfare initiatives). Certification and decertification are, at bottom, "gatekeeping" mechanisms, and thus they are critical to the formation and dissolution of hegemonic blocs of various sorts.[12] Certification tends toward the expansion of participation in a genre. To the extent that the genre is itself hegemonic, certification can enhance either integral or minimal hegemony, depending on the circumstances. Decertification tends to limit integration and promotes either segmentation or fragmentation in a field by withholding the choral support necessary to expand participation in a genre and to expand the genre itself.

A variant of certification and decertification—indeed, a combination of the two—might be called *subject switching*. Here, powerful actors simply start talking about something else or innovate new programs against which their adversaries must respond. Though frequently tied in with institutional spillover (discussed subsequently), subject switching can also change the object of policy by redefining central actors affected by it. For example, when Jason Turner took over as commissioner of the Human Resources Administration (HRA) in New York City, he began to put less emphasis on WEP and more on creating obstacles to welfare application. This change in focus, in turn, helped push advocacy groups back into a language of welfare rights and away from a developing language of labor and workers' rights.

Amplification

David Snow and his colleagues denote "frame amplification" as the sharpening and "clarification" of a frame or set of claims.[13] As in certification, amplification involves the strengthening of a claim's associations with actors and settings, but it differs from certification in two ways. First, amplification does not have to be set into motion by a locally powerful actor; it is not a gatekeeping function. Second, amplification tends to promote the discursive homogeneity of a claim—and often, too, its claimant(s) and settings. The point of amplification is that through it, a claim's or set of claims' multivocality is limited, without needing to be "qualified" in the sense that Mische employs. In the (usual) absence of overwhelming institutional power, amplification appears as a tactic of a war of maneuver. By limiting a claim's multivocality, amplification limits the reach of the claim *across* settings, thus limiting its potential to organize claims in other settings. At the same time, the justification for amplifying a claim lies in the potential that in doing so, political power can be concentrated locally and a foothold established within the debate. As we will see, the use of an explicitly religious and moral condemnation of workfare in the Pledge of Resistance was amplified as a defining feature of the campaign to end nonprofit workfare placements. Its association with that campaign made it highly visible, but it also limited its application in a wider variety of settings.

Institutional Spillover

Recall from chapter 3 that social movement spillover, as defined by David Meyer and Nancy Whittier, relied on and produced shared personnel, culture, rhetorics, and organizations among movements. This spillover creates degrees of hard and soft assembly in coalitions, as described in figure 3.1.

Institutional spillover occurs when events in one institutional setting or subfield alter patterns of communication in another.[14] This mechanism is the principal reason that whole-field analyses are important to do and central both to the dynamics of hegemony and genre change generally and to the politics of WEP in particular. Institutional spillover can combine with scale and time shift (discussed subsequently) to broaden or limit the extent to which institutional settings, actors, or claims coalesce. For example, electoral politics can intrude on policy debates when incumbents running for higher office amplify their claims, or certify and decertify actors according to an electoral logic, and break continuity with past practices. We saw this dynamic clearly in chapter 4, where the council speaker introduced the grievance procedure and transitional jobs bills as a way of securing the endorsement of the Working Families Party (WFP) in his gubernatorial run.

Institutional spillover can induce and enhance actors' and claims' multivocality when actors or claims bridge among genres or clusters of claim-making in a field. In this sense, institutional spillover can serve "consulting" or "liaison" functions by joining together genres that would otherwise be disconnected. In chapter 3's terms, then, institutional spillover can soften the assembly of coalitions, enabling them to operate more flexibly among settings while maintaining some measure of stability and staving off fragmentation. If genres live in the chronotopes of institutional settings—and sometimes among several—institutional spillover can be the result of, or result in, the centrifugal pull away from established genres, resulting in the "interanimation" of dialogue and the establishment of new genres situated across new settings. This is why "hegemonizing is hard work."[15] The tendency for institutional spillover would be toward pluralism but for the agents of this spillover, who can concentrate power in the process. But to do so, they have to accompany spillover with certification or decertification (or both, directed at different actors and claims) or with amplification.

Scale and Time Shifts

Scale shift refers to shifts in the level of governance—whether political or economic—on which claim-making activity takes place.[16] Economic and political geographers have long noted the importance of scale in shaping contention and have insisted that the scalar dimensions of governance and contention are constructed through the action of participants in a field. The geographer Andrew Herod, for example, shows that locked-out workers at an aluminum factory owned by companies with links to the fugitive billionaire Marc Rich rescaled their fight from a local battle with plant managers to an international campaign against Rich's financial dealings. In so doing, they took advantage of the existing scales of governance (e.g., European Union rules on firm acquisition) to exert leverage on their very local situation.[17] In a similar way, the federal system of government in the United States gives pro- and antiworkfare forces multiple scalar levers. The devolution of cost and program administration to state and local levels under the Personal Responsibility and Work Opportunity Reconciliation Act of 1996 (PRWORA) is an important scalar strategy of workfare, just as are the centrally dictated incentives for trimming welfare rolls and enforcing work.[18] By the same token, when legal advocates seek federal help in enforcing antidiscrimination law; when mayors tap national networks of welfare administrators to carry out welfare reforms; and when activists invoke antiapartheid divestment pledges in opposing WEP, they are shifting the scale of the field to varying degrees.

Scale shift, then, is akin to—and sometimes a precondition of—institutional spillover, but it both speaks to larger issues in the organization of governance and contention and cuts even more directly to the chronotopic composition of genres. In looking at the maps of discourse that follow, therefore, it will be important to identify whether and how scale shifts occur in the midst of institutional spillover.

Time shifts, or temporal shifts, are more complex still but, like scale shifts, are both a variant of and a precondition for institutional spillover. Time is a multifaceted metric, and it includes event sequences marked by structural change; calendar and clock time; action horizons of narratives; and the temporality of institutional routines.[19] All are related in some ways but are analytically distinct, as suggested in the previous chapter. Time shifts occur when the temporalities of claims and claim-making align and when they fall out of alignment. For example, a time shift occurred when anti-WEP organizers decided to focus on legislative action around job creation rather than on improving worksite conditions. They were at once left somewhat less vulnerable to the temporality of worksite turnover and less likely to focus their claim-making on short-term change. The mayoral veto of the job creation bill, which pushed many of the decisions about the future shape of workfare beyond Giuliani's final term, is another example of time shift.[20]

Formalizing the Argument

How would we know if any of these mechanisms were tripped? How can we identify the trippers? How can we discern the results of mechanisms on the configuration of claim-making in the field of WEP politics? What might the formalization of the stories in chapter 4—or of other stories—into "mechanisms" add to our analysis?

If mechanisms denote changes in the ways in which networks of actors relate to one another across institutional and relational contexts, then identifying mechanisms can be facilitated by mapping relations across a political field and by noting how the map changes over time. In discerning the changes among the connections among actors, their settings, and their networks of relations with one another, we can identify many of the mechanisms I have proposed and can, conversely, show how these mechanisms concatenate into new relations downstream. Finally, by identifying mechanisms, we can more easily accomplish two fundamental analytic tasks: first, to take the dynamics identified through narrative analysis in chapter 4 out of their singular settings and to show the ways that they trigger change across relational settings; and second, to take these dynamics out of the singular context of WEP politics so that we can explicitly or implicitly compare them to the dynamics of contention against neoliberal regimes in other policy domains and in other localities.

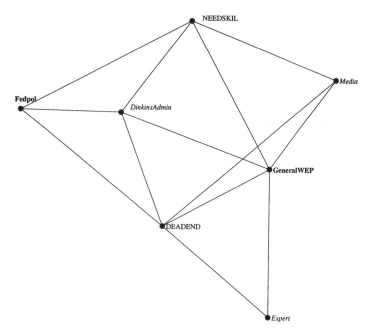

Figure 5.1. The layering of actor-claim-context/object triangles. In this figure, there are three actors (*DinkinsAdmin*, *Expert*, and *Media*), two claims (DEADEND and NEEDSKIL), and two contexts/objects (GeneralWEP and Fedpol). The Dinkins administration makes claims about WEP's being a dead end in the context of general discussion of WEP policy, as do experts and the media. The Dinkins administration also makes this claim with respect to federal welfare reform politics. The media also share with the Dinkins administration a claim that welfare recipients need skills and, like the administration, make it in the context of general discussion of WEP. The Dinkins administration also makes the claim in the context of federal welfare reform politics.

Again, I'll cut against the grain of the theories I use in hopes of making their contributions clearer. Though Bakhtin was no fan of formalization, I find it useful to resort to some formal heuristics in order to get a handle on the development of claim-making around WEP. If we consider, at a bare-bones level, that a debate is composed of actors, the claims they make, and some sort of substantive context or object of these claims, we can understand the field as composed of successive layering of actor-claim-context/object triangles (fig. 5.1).

Genres develop through the association of claims, actors, and contexts/objects with one another, which is crucial for the development of choral support. The three elements might become associated because they appear together frequently. But they might *also* become associated because they are associated with others in similar ways. For example, a union leader might denounce working conditions for WEP workers and call WEP "slavery" in the context of labor politics, while an organizer might denounce working conditions and call for WEP's abolition in the same context. Though they will not be fully equivalent, the label of *slavery* and the call for abolition will become associated with each other.

The logic of hard and soft assembly suggests that hard-assembled coalitions are blocks of relations among actors, claims, and contexts wherein relatively few contexts are present, or where the contexts that are present are structurally equivalent. Thus, where we find blocks of actors or claims with or connected to only one block with contexts, or where we

Blocks are designated as hard (H), soft (S), elaborations (E), or isolates (I) based on the ways in which they unite actors (A), claims (C), and context/objects (c) within blocks and join them with actors, claims, and context/objects in others. Below are the most common combinations.

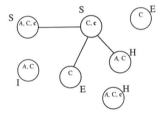

The configuration of the field depends on the patterns of coalitions within it. Six ideal-typical configurations are shown below.

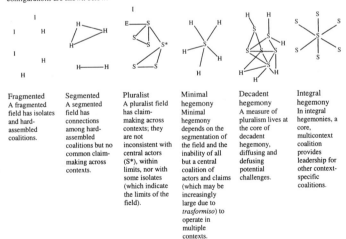

Fragmented	Segmented	Pluralist	Minimal hegemony	Decadent hegemony	Integral hegemony
A fragmented field has isolates and hard-assembled coalitions.	A segmented field has connections among hard-assembled coalitions but no common claim-making across contexts.	A pluralist field has claim-making across contexts; they are not inconsistent with central actors (S*), within limits, nor with some isolates (which indicate the limits of the field).	Minimal hegemony depends on the segmentation of the field and the inability of all but a central coalition of actors and claims (which may be increasingly large due to *trasformiso*) to operate in multiple contexts.	A measure of pluralism lives at the core of decadent hegemony, diffusing and defusing potential challenges.	In integral hegemonies, a core, multicontext coalition provides leadership for other context-specific coalitions.

Figure 5.2. Hard- and soft-assembled coalitions and field characteristics

find especially strong connections between actors and claims and a small set of contexts, we can find hard-assembled coalitions and genres; where there are strong associations among actors or claims and many contexts, we find soft-assembled coalitions and genres. Where claims are just associated with actors or just associated with contexts, they are elaborations on genres but not of them. The relations of actors, claims, and contexts/ objects and of genres and hard- and soft assembled coalitions with one another account for the character of the political field, as outlined in Ray's and Gramsci's terms (fig. 5.2).

Some mechanisms can be discerned by the patterns (and changing patterns) of intersection and layering of actor-claim-context/object triangles. For example, in certification, a prominent actor in a coalition might adopt claims made by an actor outside of it and thus redraw the boundaries of the coalition and the genres it enacts. In amplification, an actor or set of actors might intensify their use of a claim in connection

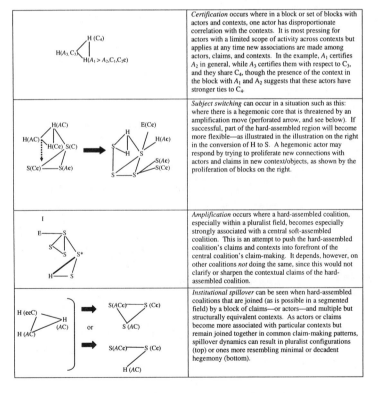

Figure 5.3. Four mechanisms as network dynamics

with a specific group of other claims and toward a specific context/object. Institutional spillover may be identified by the appearance of ties among genres or of the gathering within a genre or the ambit of a claim-making coalition of multiple context/object settings (see fig. 5.3).

Scale and time shifts are more difficult to discern formally, but clues can be found in the introduction of new contexts/objects and new actors. Nevertheless, recourse to knowledge outside of formalized data appears critical here.[21]

A Note about Data

With the idea that the media, while being its own institutional setting, was also a means of disseminating information about action in many other institutional settings, I compiled a catalog of political actors, their claims, and their contexts/objects[22] from two newspapers in New York City over an eleven-year period from mid-1993 through mid-2004. I read each article that fit the LexisNexis search terms *Workfare* and *New York City* in the title and lead paragraphs. For each of the 247 days an article, letter, editorial, or op-ed appeared in the *New York Times* and the *Daily News*, I coded the text according to the organizational type of actor (e.g., Giuliani administration, organizers, advocates, legal advocates, city council, etc.), their claims (e.g., WEP can work if implemented correctly, workers are hurt, WEP workers are workers, WEP does not displace regular workers, etc.), and their contextual settings or objects (e.g., labor politics, federal politics, education and training, disabilities, jobs, etc.). I then partitioned the eleven years into nine overlapping periods, based on the appearance of article-days in which a relatively high proportion of the claims made within a context setting were made. The periods "move diagonally," that is, they contain data from two periods on a moving basis.[23]

For each period, I used the CONCOR algorithm to cluster the actor-claim-context/object triangles based on the similarities in their patterns of overlap. The CONCOR algorithm groups together elements in a matrix (here, a three-way matrix of actors, claims, and contexts/objects) by iteratively measuring the correlation of each element to every other in terms of their patterns of connections to each other element. Because this is an iteration of correlation procedures, eventually the data are split into two groups that are "structurally equivalent" to each other. The process can be repeated, so that the data are split into ever-finer clusters of "structurally equivalent" elements.

The interpretive and theoretical implications of structural equivalence are important: claims and actors are not necessarily grouped into genres or coalitions that seem "natural" to them. Instead, they are clustered in terms of similar patterns of overlap. In structural linguistics, the governing principle is that words do not have any natural relationship to the objects or actions they denote but that they accrete more or less stable meanings based on the neighborhoods of words within which they are located. *Shoe, clog,* and *boot,* therefore, do not have to be spoken at the same time in order to be proximate. As long as they are all used in connection with *put on* and *foot,* they will wind up in the same neighborhood. Of course, this proximity doesn't limit their use, and each can have links with cartoons, drains, and British car trunks, too. But these overlapping meanings are structured by the presence of other contexts. For political claims, their speakers, and their contexts, the same applies. But in contrast to structural linguistics, the method I have outlined here preserves the specificity of context and the importance of specifying in whose mouth claims have recently been. As Collins writes, "Discourse is not to be 'contextualized' after the event, so to speak, because its internal relations to concretely interacting phenomena in the generative process of social existence should not be broken apart in the first place."[24]

By taking the results of CONCOR routines designed to split the data into structurally equivalent clusters, or *blocks,* at a given minimum level of fitness for the data, I then construct maps—or *blockmodels*—of these clusters. The blockmodels show which clusters are connected with each other (or separate) in varying degrees; which are large, which are small; which clusters contain which actors, claims, and contexts; which clusters are strongly tied into the field, which are more peripheral to it, and which are isolated from it; and which clusters and which actors, claims, and contexts form hard-assembled and soft-assembled coalitions.[25]

For more specifics on my use of blockmodeling, I refer the reader to the appendix, which describes the technique in light of other applications to content analysis.

A View of the Field of Workfare Politics "From Above"

Without knowing anything else about the field of WEP politics, important changes can be discerned just by looking at the configuration of the field—without labels—in the nine periods under study. Figure 5.4 shows the maps of the field in succession with the following indicators:

(1) the strength of the association among clusters, or blocks of structurally equivalent sets of actors, claims, and contexts/objects, is denoted by the weight of the lines joining them; (2) no lines connect blocks where the overlap between them is less than the average in the network as a whole; and (3) each block is labeled with an S if it is a soft-assembled coalition, an H if hard-assembled, an I if an isolate, and an E if an elaboration of an existing genre or genres.

With this information, we can reconstruct which kinds of coalitions occur in which kinds of combinations, and thereby characterize the changes in the field as it develops.

Based on the figure, a trend toward increasing complexity is evident. Initially—partly an artifact of little data, which is itself an important indicator of the public visibility of the issue—the field is quite simple. There is a core of the field and a periphery. By the second period, a hegemonic formation begins to take shape, whereby a soft-assembled coalition anchors hard-assembled ones in a core-periphery structure typical of a minimal hegemony; as I will subsequently show, this is an example of *trasformismo* and an illustration of the consequences of DC 37's initial co-optation. The third period shows this hegemony to be increasingly contested and in crisis (in Gramsci's definition, "when the old is dying and the new cannot yet be born"). By the fourth period, it is not clear that anyone controls the debate, and the soft assembly of the field makes it appear almost pluralistic. The strong tie at its center, however, suggests the amplification of a set of claims. As will become clear, this set of claims is linked closely to the Pledge of Resistance.

In the fifth period, the field begins to become a bit more complex. It generates many isolated claims and actors, as the Giuliani administration both meets the pluralist challenge by expanding the field, and as it launches the conversion of welfare centers to Job Centers with the new commissioner of HRA, Jason Turner. The mayor's actions induce subject switching, scale shift, and institutional spillover, this time drawing antipoverty policy advocates into a subordinate position in a claim-making coalition by opening up more trenches. In the sixth, seventh, and eighth periods, this proliferation of new settings of action meets a mobilized anti-WEP constituency but one from which organizing and labor politics, organizers and unions are gradually annealed. The decadent hegemony that stabilizes in this period is characterized by some hard-assembled coalitional challenges but is flexible enough to withstand them. By the ninth period, which, like the first, is bedeviled by sparser data but rep-

Periods	Figure	Description	Field Description
Period 1: mid-1993 until end of 1995		First mention of workfare in nearly a decade; discussion dominated by debate over Westchester County's program and federal welfare reform proposals	Segmented field
Periods 1, 2: mid-1993 until Sept. 1996		First trouble with expanding WEP into unionized sector in 1995, organizing gets started in early 1996 and begins to challenge WEP	Minimal hegemony (with segmentation)
Periods 2, 3: end of 1995 until Aug. 1997		Organizing continues and challenges WEP's expansion, in part through the Pledge of Resistance, which changes the direction of organizing even while highlighting it	Segmented field and crisis
Periods 3, 4: Sept. 1996 until June 1998		After a summer and fall in which Giuliani won reelection but lost momentum on WEP, his administration's counterattack begins and features Jason Turner's arrival to lead HRA and layoffs at hospitals	Pluralist field with increasing fragmentation and with amplification
Periods 4, 5: Aug. 1997 until Sept. 1999		Transitional jobs campaign gets into full swing and DC 37's unraveling begins in mid-1998 and continues through 1999	Minimal hegemony and resegmentation

Figure 5.4. Blockmodels of actor-claim-context/object overlaps, nine periods

resents both the end of the news cycle and the only period in which the Bloomberg administration is without the Giuliani administration, the field fragments and segments again. While this effect is partly an artifact of the data, it is also largely meaningful. The Bloomberg administration has let WEP continue to exist but has neither emphasized it in the way that its predecessor did nor taken all of the same positions on welfare as did Giuliani.

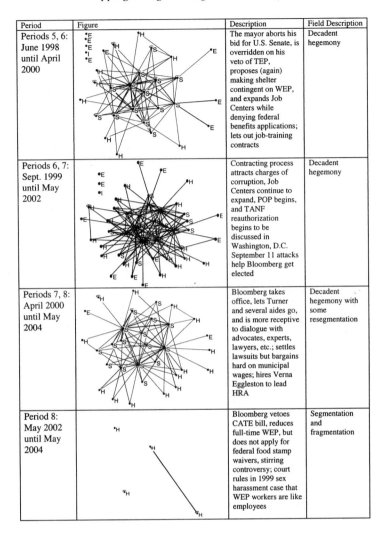

Period	Figure	Description	Field Description
Periods 5, 6: June 1998 until April 2000		The mayor aborts his bid for U.S. Senate, is overridden on his veto of TEP, proposes (again) making shelter contingent on WEP, and expands Job Centers while denying federal benefits applications; lets out job-training contracts	Decadent hegemony
Periods 6, 7: Sept. 1999 until May 2002		Contracting process attracts charges of corruption, Job Centers continue to expand, POP begins, and TANF reauthorization begins to be discussed in Washington, D.C. September 11 attacks help Bloomberg get elected	Decadent hegemony
Periods 7, 8: April 2000 until May 2004		Bloomberg takes office, lets Turner and several aides go, and is more receptive to dialogue with advocates, experts, lawyers, etc.; settles lawsuits but bargains hard on municipal wages; hires Verna Eggleston to lead HRA	Decadent hegemony with some resegmentation
Period 8: May 2002 until May 2004		Bloomberg vetoes CATE bill, reduces full-time WEP, but does not apply for federal food stamp waivers, stirring controversy; court rules in 1999 sex harassment case that WEP workers are like employees	Segmentation and fragmentation

Midway to the Trenches

Having taken a bird's-eye view of the field, it is now important, echoing Collins, to pick up on the "prompts" that its "twists and turns" give and to ask what *particularly* accounted for the shifts in the control over WEP-related political discourse revealed earlier. For this task, a preliminary list of the more prominent codes of actors, claims, and contexts/objects is provided in table A.1 in the appendix.[26]

Prehistory

Bakhtin warns, rather sensibly, that language is irreducibly historical and dialogic and that the search for a word's origins in order to fix its meaning is doomed from the start to be fruitless.[27] Though the origins of the term *workfare* are fairly well known, the story of the field of WEP politics is multiscalar and tied in with the long history of work-testing public aid.[28] A more proximate set of origins is suggested by Jason DeParle's discussion of presidential candidate Bill Clinton's 1991 campaign pledge to "end welfare as we know it."[29] This promise resonated through Democratic and Republican circles in Washington and culminated in the passage of PRWORA in 1996, after the Republicans had retaken Congress in the 1994 midterm elections.

Welfare reform—even WEP's expansion—was well under way by 1996. Nancy Naples notes that then Governor Clinton of Arkansas testified in hearings on the Family Support Act of 1988 in favor of strong work requirements for women on welfare and for strong sanctions for those who refused. Naples points to the emergence of a "new consensus" on the gendered nature of welfare that completely denied the carework and child rearing that fall mainly on the shoulders of women.[30] Ellen Reese goes back even farther, to show the ways in which southern Democrats, concerned with available labor for agriculture, led the initial backlash against Aid to Families with Dependent Children (AFDC) in the 1950s.[31]

The Beginnings of WEP Politics and Contention, 1993–96: Subject Switching and Institutional Spillover

The initial local rumblings about workfare came during the last months of the Dinkins administration in 1993 and 1994 over whether to emulate Westchester County's program. In figure 5.5, which shows a blockmodel of the first two periods shown in figure 5.4, the Dinkins administration is at the core of the field (panel A, block 2), tying together debates over federal welfare policy (in block 4) and Westchester's, which was highly touted in the press in an op-ed and letter by the county executive, Andrew O'Rourke (block 1). The Giuliani administration's first approach to workfare is reflected in the first period by its appearance in the same block (block 3) as unions and labor politics, and a rhetoric of negotiation and program expansion (AGREEMT, GOODPOS, MEANING, PRIVJOBS, TALKING, UNCERTAIN, WKSCARCE, XPANDWEP). This *certifying* rhetoric (which worked in both directions), on the occasion of announcing the agreement with DC 37s'

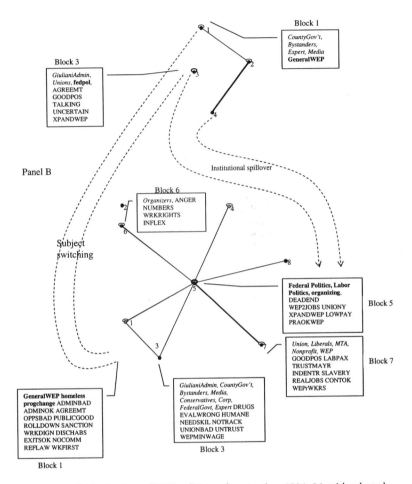

Figure 5.5. The beginnings of WEP politics and contention, 1994–96, with selected actors, claims, and contexts/objects in blocks (periods 1 and 2)

powerful Public School Employees' Local 372 (see chapter 3), helped buy the administration time to implement WEP in earnest.

When it does, the Giuliani administration becomes associated with the more conservative discourse enunciated prior to WEP's expansion (panel B, block 3), with strong links to general discussions of workfare (GeneralWEP), to discussions specifically about programmatic changes (progchange), and to the politics of homelessness, on the one hand (block 1), and to labor politics, federal politics, and organizing, on the other hand (block 5). Put another way, though the clusters of claim-making and claim-makers are distinct, the Giuliani administration acts as the central liaison for *institutional spillover* among the various contexts, so that whatever is said in them, in effect, is part of a conversation or debate with the administration.

The Giuliani administration *switches subjects* from the first period. Though it still has links with labor politics, it quickly becomes unlinked with the union (in block 7), relegating its and its liberal allies' discourse to a hard-assembled coalition linked only to the claims and contexts/objects of block 5, and thus less flexible than the administration's discourse. The unions, the Metropolitan Transportation Authority (MTA), nonprofits, WEP workers, liberals, and state legislators, on the one hand, and city council members, advocates, legal advocates, and judges, on the other hand, all engage with debates over federal politics, organizing, and labor politics with some of the same rhetoric that is closely associated with the administration. They all share in criticism of WEP but temper it with moderating claims. Balancing claims that WEP is like slavery or indentured servitude and that conditions are poor are claims that the mayor is trustworthy, that the contract is good, that labor peace has been preserved, and that block members are in a "good position." This block stays together in part due to the initial support lent to WEP by DC 37 and by the Transit Workers Union Local 100, which at the time accepted a contract with the MTA that would replace five hundred of its members with WEP workers. The Giuliani administration balked at this provision, since it would make explicit the displacement of regular workers by WEP workers and would jeopardize DC 37's already lukewarm support.

The growing opposition to WEP (also among some homeless people in block 2, organizers in block 6, and the members of block 8, which includes advocates and legal advocates) is still fractured.

Organizers have developed their own genre of a kind of militant unionism: along with anger, the organizers talk about workers' rights, the inflexibility of WEP and the legal barriers to realizing workers' rights for WEP workers, the importance of unionizing WEP workers, and the numbers of WEP workers they have organized, and they exhort DC 37 to support WEP workers. This is a discourse in search of certification but one that, as discussed in the previous chapter, did not attract significant union support at first. By contrast, the elements of block 4, with the governor and the former mayor, are not connected to the core, either, which suggests that the Giuliani administration was able to take charge of the field with relative ease.

From Crisis to Pluralism

The effect of the claim-making that is framed by the first signs of union discord over WEP's displacement effects in September 1995 and the two weeks after the Pledge of Resistance's press conference in July 1997 was to unleash a broad-gauged assault on WEP. First, *all* the contexts appear in the same block (fig. 5.6, panel A, block 6), and this block otherwise has strongly pro-WEP claims within it and strong ties to the block containing the Giuliani administration (block 1, which mainly contains moderately pro-WEP claims, e.g., WEP2JOBS, WEPCANOK, WRKDIGN) and a strong presence of conciliatory claims toward unions, such as that DC 37 is "for" WEP workers, that labor peace has been preserved, that WEP does not displace regular workers (DC374WEP, LABPAX, NODISP). On the other hand, block 6

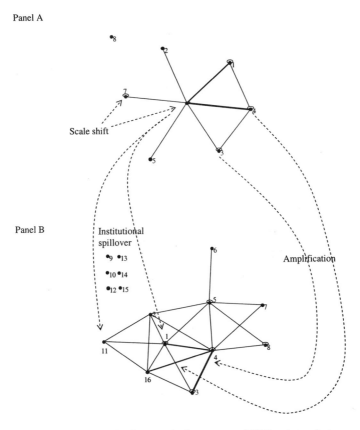

Figure 5.6. Contention heats up in the summer of 1997 and stays hot through June 1998 (periods 3 and 4)

also has even stronger correlations of overlap with block 4, which is both strongly anti-WEP in its claims and contains a relatively cohesive block of actors who compose a hard-assembled coalition against WEP whose members were isolated from each other in the prior period. The concentration of contexts/objects and strong ties to pro- and anti-WEP actors and claims suggests that in this period, a real contest occurred for agenda setting within and across settings between a hard-assembled anti-WEP coalition composed of advocates, legal advocates, liberals, organizers, nonprofit service providers, letter writers,[32] unions, and WEP workers, on the one hand, and the Giuliani administration, which found itself mostly on its own, on the other. At the same time, it also seems clear that insofar as the correlation profiles of anti-WEP claims were more associated with those of *every* institutional context, the Giuliani administration managed to prevail in this contest.

Part of the administration's success had to do, no doubt, with the *scale shift* triggered by federal welfare reform the year before: the Giuliani administration got the state to *certify* nearly all the parts of WEP in the welfare reform bill passed to bring the state into compliance with federal law. A postpassage press release by the governor's office summarized the bill's accomplishments in

> defeat[ing] efforts to water down welfare reform by:
> - Defeating an attempt to unionize workfare participants.
> - Repealing a provision of law that would have required workfare participants to be paid higher, union-level prevailing wages instead of minimum wage.
> - Refusing to grant workfare participants government employee status, which would have given them all the benefits of public employment, including vacation time.
> - Turning back demands for more liberal definitions of disability in the Americans with Disabilities Act, a change that would have expanded exemptions from workfare.
> - Defeating other attempts to expand workfare exemptions.
> - Repealed current law restriction that workfare participants have 20 hours minimum work per week to be eligible for workfare.
> - Repealed current law restriction limiting local DSS districts to 250 workfare workers.[33]

Though this press release itself is not represented in these data, this is the first period in which the state politics of welfare comes into view, and it does so in block 6, which suggests its immediate centrality. A largely justificatory discourse in block 5, similar to that in the press release, appears as an elaboration on the claim-making in block 6. Moreover, given the changes in the state law, reference to legal and legislative barriers in the two principal anti-WEP blocks (3 and 4) is unsurprising.

Tracing the fortunes of the Pledge of Resistance in this and the following period both is interesting in its own right and also demonstrates the strength of this method in revealing clues about the work of mechanisms. Appearing in figure 5.6, panel A, in a block apart from the main opposition to WEP (block 4) is the pledge's principal claim NOCOOP, or noncooperation with WEP. This block (block 3) contains claims most closely associated with the marginalized organizers in the prior period but also other actors, such as conservative commentators. While there remain strong affinities between the most-committed carriers of the Pledge of Resistance (i.e., the religious groups that were the primary target of pledge organizing) and others of WEP's critics (indeed, the other main component of the pledge was its promotion of an explicit protest tactic—i.e., PROTAC, in block 3), in the short term, the pledge was caught up in the theological arguments between progressive and conservative clergy and drew its meaning at least partly from this context. Block 3 also contains some of the more strident claims made by the organizers in the prior period (such as ANGER and INFLEX), while block 4 contains claims for workers' rights (WKRIGHT). This shows that the Pledge of Resistance, though a strategy partly of organizers, was made *apart* from the main organizing claim-making at the time.

In the raw data for this period, the NOCOOP claim appears more frequently than any other. This amplification effect—for it surely was amplified by its coverage on the front page of the *New York Times* and by the publication of the list of its signatories—is clearest in figure 5.6, panel B, block 3. In this block, organizers have joined religious leaders (and conservatives in a clearly subordinate position) with demands to recognize and bargain with WEP workers, not to expand WEP, references to legislative and legal barriers, and others. They also amplify the language and context/object of organizing (block 4, with DIGNITY, RECOURSE, SLAVERY, WEPTWKRS, WRKRIGHT, and SEXHARASS). For their part, nonprofits, which were in a strongly anti-WEP block in the previous period, amplify their view that the program has become too harsh (block 16), but tellingly are no longer as clearly "with the program." This position reflects the ambivalence among many nonprofits about the pledge, suggested in chapter 4.

With the exception of block 5, which contains the context of union politics and both language and ties (to blocks 6 and 7) that suggest its being shaped by the layoff crisis in the public hospitals (about which more, momentarily), and block 13 (an isolate, focused on the context of research), the other contexts/objects in the field are contained in block 11. Block 11 is most strongly tied to block 1, which contains the other actors present in the previous period, including the Giuliani administration. What is important here is that the Giuliani administration is located in a block with a good deal of hostile others and discourse (e.g., that WEP is a sham) clearly critical of WEP. Though blocks 11 and 1 also have ties to block 2, which contains highly pro-WEP claims, this suggests that anti-WEP forces had in some ways gained the upper hand in defining the terms of debate in this period. At the very least, by amplifying the pledge of noncooperation and the context of organizing, they were able to soften the segmentation in the field, prompt institutional spillover, and create a more pluralist environment, where the Giuliani administration might not set the agenda alone.

The Counterattack

The Giuliani administration's counterattack was swift and effective. A two-pronged strategy can be seen in figure 5.7. One prong involves a *scale shift*. Giuliani hired Jason Turner to lead HRA. Along with a shift in claim-making, this strategy involved, over the longer run, a shift in emphasis from public-sector WEP placements to aggressive eligibility restrictions that would push welfare recipients into the labor market, or at least off the dole, which had been the essence of Wisconsin's workfare experiments. This scale shift, in turn, generated a wave of *subject switching*, which can be seen most strongly in the link between blocks 7 and 16. The roots of this link can already be found in the previous period in a proliferation of new contexts/objects in figure 5.6, block 11. In figure 5.7, block 7 contains many of these newer contexts, such as debates about the administration's administrative style (adminstyle) and treatment of the media (mediapol), as well as ones introduced later, including discussion about drugs and—thanks mainly to the declining fortunes of worksite organizing after 1997—jobs. It contains most of the contexts in this period, and mostly proadministration claims relating to them, especially with respect to transitional jobs (opposing them), homelessness (advocating WEP as a condition of shelter and for evicting noncompliers[34]), and sanctions (supporting cutting off aid to whole families for adults'

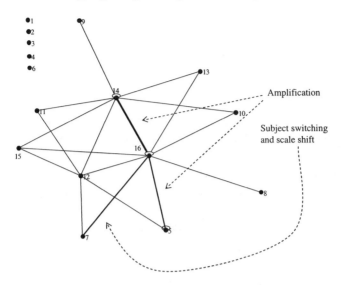

Figure 5.7. Counterattack and finding alternatives, 1998 through
September 1999 (period 5)

infractions). It also contains the terms of a controversy Mayor Giuliani
provoked by opining that methadone use was a harmful addiction and
should disqualify users from receiving welfare. Block 16 is a small block
containing the Giuliani administration, advocates, and three ambivalent
claims that form the basis for a larger debate: that the economy is doing
well (ECONGOOD), that welfare recipients need education (NEEDED), and that
certain proposals are unrealistic (UNREAL). The strong connection the Giuliani administration has with block 7 suggests a core program of subject
switching. The inclusion of the context of program change (progchange)
and references to Turner and to Job Centers in block 7, as well, attest to
the scale shift at its core.

By switching subjects (and after having secured DC 37's support for
his reelection), Mayor Giuliani found that with respect to WEP, his alliance with DC 37 did not matter anymore. In April 1998, Mayor Giuliani
forced a confrontation with DC 37 by announcing nine hundred layoffs in
municipal hospitals (thus violating the spirit, if not actually the letter, of
the no-layoff clause in the DC 37 master contract).[35] Stanley Hill, DC 37's
executive director—who had led the municipal labor movement to back
the mayor's reelection in 1997—cried foul. Because WEP workers were
still working in the hospitals, Hill threatened—and eventually filed—a
lawsuit charging the displacement of union workers, and he called WEP

"slavery" because it did not lead to a "meaningful job."[36] It appears in block 9 with unions, organizers, and liberals, connected to block 14, which contains the context/object of labor politics and many anti-WEP claims associated with the mayor in block 16. In figure 5.6, panel B, the union (in block 8) is tied to the slavery claim and organizing context (in block 4) but is even more associated with its own conflicted but conciliatory discourse, expressing hope, anger, and demands not to displace regular workers, while touting compromise and trust in the mayor. Both the hospital layoffs and the earlier "statement of principles" and union endorsement of the mayor are reflected in figure 5.6. As the hospital crisis unfolded, it seems as if Hill could try but could not credibly talk "like an organizer." In spite of the lawsuit, Hill again tried to mend fences with Mayor Giuliani, whose spokesperson at once patronizingly dismissed the slavery remark and its author. By figure 5.7, the eclipse of the Pledge of Resistance and of other organizing campaigns leads organizers and DC 37 to be structurally equivalent in their opposition to WEP's effects on labor politics.

Related to the fading of the Pledge of Resistance, figure 5.7 shows that campaign to have all but disappeared, and the context of organizing is subsumed in the hospitals crisis. To the extent that the Pledge of Resistance was responsible for making organizing against WEP a focal point of WEP politics, it appears here as a war-of-maneuver tactic in a war-of-position field, yielding some change but ultimately ephemeral.

A minimal hegemony, amid some resegmentation of the field, takes shape here. At its core is a soft-assembled genre linking advocates and the Giuliani administration in a debate about the relative importance of education and labor market slack for moving welfare recipients to work (block 16). Block 5 contains several institutional contexts, among which is education and training. The presence of other institutional contexts, such as General WEP, child care, and research, in this block, as well as a good number of claims, suggest the emergence of a genre of discourse focused strongly around predicting welfare-to-work outcomes but one in which the administration's claims are clearly dominant.

The mayor's counterattack, therefore, was largely to be found in *subject switching*, in creating new contexts and introducing new claims and in *amplification* of labor politics to focus attention on the dysfunctional DC 37, which would soon sink from relational weakness into abject internal disarray (claims about corruption already appear in block 9), beginning with the June 1998 embezzlement indictment of the public-school workers' union chief, Giuliani's erstwhile ally. As Gramsci noted, the successful tactics of a war of maneuver often reveal a new system of trenches that lie beyond the first defenses.

Reestablishing Hegemony by Picking Fights

The main transition that occurred as a result of the administration's reassertion of hegemony was between a minimal hegemony and a changing, quasi-pluralist "decadent" hegemony, where hard-assembled coalitions dealing with the increasing proliferation of welfare-related contexts/objects appeared and dissolved, anchored by a series of soft-assembled coalitions at the core, which were mainly controlled by the Giuliani administration. With organizing and labor politics effectively sidelined, the discourse shifted toward more-elite advocacy and legal advocacy. This transition, too, began a protracted time shift, suggested in chapter 4, in which the Giuliani administration began to run down the clock, pushing challenges to his welfare overhaul and WEP past his term-limited tenure as mayor.

In figure 5.8, the same minimum-fit statistic used in the other models requires a further split of the blocks and yields thirty-two blocks instead of sixteen. This further split and the dispersal of contexts/objects from their relative concentration in the prior period suggest a strong measure of institutional spillover and perhaps, too, of subject switching.

The center of the blockmodel (block 3) is composed of advocates, experts, the media, the governor, and the Giuliani administration, along with claims having mainly to do with the needs of welfare recipients in the context of work (CANWORK, KIDSNEED, NEEDIGNR, DOMABUSE). The actors are largely elite, and while they appear to have greater immediate association with these claims, they do not simply certify the Giuliani administration from a position of power. The amplification of several contexts—education and training, federal politics, homelessness, and pay for WEP workers—comes along with a set of claims that are ambiguous about WEP and appear to refer to renewed efforts to push more welfare recipients into the labor market (blocks 3 to 14). The connection between block 3 and block 20—another of the strong associations—appears as a link to the context settings of transitional jobs and of contracts. Here, the claims are unequivocally defensive and supportive of the administration's positions that the city council would act illegally if it passed TEP, that criticism is politically motivated, that the economy is doing well, and that the transitional jobs bill should be opposed and will be vetoed.

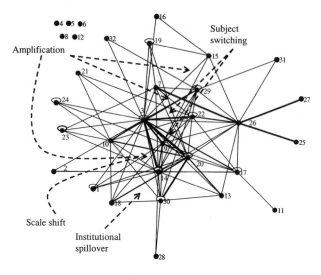

Figure 5.8. Reestablishing hegemony by picking fights, 1999 through
April 2000 (period 6)

The flexibility of block 3 is impressive. It proliferates strong ties to each
of the blocks containing contexts/objects (14, 15, 20, 22, 23, 24 and 29)
and to distinct but combative language in each one. It shows a distinct
pattern of picking fights across the field. The result is a soft-assembled
coalition at the core of the field, due to inevitable institutional spillover,
surrounded by hard-assembled coalitions and genres prompted by amplification and subject switching.

This pattern occurs against the backdrop of Turner's Job Center initiative. Under the combined influence of the continued encumbrance
of welfare with work assignments, a local economy that was beginning
to improve, and increasing obstacles to receiving aid at Job Centers, by
1999, welfare rolls declined precipitously and WEP assignments leveled
off at around thirty-four thousand until they, too, began to decline the
next year.

At this point, much of the action *shifted scale,* expanding from local
contests to ones involving federal authorities and federal courts (blocks 3
and 14, joined to block 1, with justices, legal advocates, nonprofits joined
by frequent plaintiffs, friends and family of workfare workers, homeless
people, and others). The Job Center regime was both compatible with
and hindered by this scale shift. By immediately engaging applicants for
welfare in job search activities (which often involved little else than cold-
calling a required number of "potential employers" from a yellow pages)

and refusing to process applications for any aid until the applicant's second appointment, the City was able to deter many eligible applicants from the rolls. As a result, the rolls were not replenished as quickly as they had been before, which meant, in turn, that New York could take advantage of federal bonuses under PRWORA that lower the proportion of people on welfare required to be in work activities.

The federal-level scale shift worked in other ways, too. When Job Center procedures denied applicants applications for food stamps and Medicaid, advocates sought federal help—both from the federal courts and from the Clinton administration—to force the City to comply with federal laws making them available.

The other context/object that is of central importance in this period is "contracts" (block 20). The administration shifted scales by building on the initial scale shift that brought Turner to New York from Wisconsin and from a national network of conservative activists. In particular, HRA shifted the ways in which welfare-to-work contracts were awarded by defunding community-based organizations that had long done the work and consolidating the contracts into larger ones directed at larger nonprofit and, for the first time, for-profit corporations. Among these organizations was Maximus, a firm that had built a national business in welfare-to-work administration and which was both one of the five major contractors in Milwaukee's high-profile welfare reform program and close to Turner, his family, and several of his aides.

This scale shift was accompanied by considerable institutional spillover into political claim-making about welfare reform and workfare. The city comptroller, Alan Hevesi, who was also positioning himself for a run for the Democratic mayoral nomination in 2001, led the fight against a new contract with Maximus. Hevesi charged that the contracting process had been corrupted and that Maximus had gained unfair access to the bidding process (blocks 18 and 20). Hevesi had previously praised WEP, and there is no reason to believe that he had changed his mind about the fundamental soundness of the program. The Giuliani administration derided Hevesi's objections to the contracting process as solely politically motivated, and it admitted no wrongdoing.[37]

The central claims in this period reflect concern over the contracts, over corruption, about ignoring the many needs of welfare recipients, about the barriers to employment that many welfare recipients have, about transitional jobs, and about the legality and illegality of the Giuliani administration's actions and those of the city council in passing the transitional jobs bill. Further claims about the jobs bill—and the organizers pushing it—are in block 19, which also connects these claims to psychics, consumers, and state legislatures within the block and to contexts of safety and health, administrative style, and discrimination in block 15. This configuration is prompted in part by newspaper reports that WEP workers were being referred to a phone-psychic service as psychic-operators. Organizers who were pushing for transitional jobs protested, as did professional psychics. Organizers also engaged the contexts of health and safety, administrative style, and discrimination, but here, they were fighting far more in the mayor's trenches than in their own. Block 15 joins these contexts with purely justificatory claims for WEP and the Giuliani administration's practices. The amplified connection between blocks 19 and 20, joining organizers and transitional job claims to the jobs context and anti-TEP claims, suggests a failure of amplification due to the larger configuration of the field.

Defense, Tragedy, and Transition

Figure 5.9 depicts the next two periods, in which the decadent hegemony appears to hold. Panel A shows the period from the passage of TEP and override of Giuliani's veto in the fall of 1999 through early 2000 through the protracted fight over the Maximus contract, which lasted throughout 2000; and from the attacks of September 11, 2001, to the beginning of the transition to Michael Bloomberg's first term, when federal job-training money long unspent by the Giuliani administration was threatened with withdrawal. Panel B shows the period from the height of the contract fight until the end of the news cycle, close to the end of Bloomberg's first term.

If anything, the decadent hegemony begun in the last period holds even firmer in this one. The field differentiates further, proliferating more hard-assembled coalitions and only concentrating the dispersal of context/settings slightly (block 19 has the most). What looks like a demobilization among hard-assembled coalitions occurs, however. The principal amplification here is between blocks 45 and 17. Block 45 contains the federal government, the Giuliani administration, the media, and advocates. Block 17 contains the context/setting of homelessness and the claim MAYOROK. If the strongest association of similar patterns of overlap between the block containing the mayor and the general claim that he is doing a good job is the strongest, then this hegemony—which, insofar as it generated dissent, did so mainly from more-elite actors—appears to have disorganized a vigorous opposition. Consider the other strong asso-

Panel A

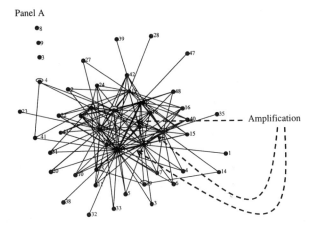

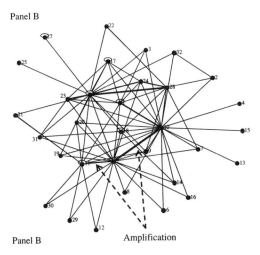

Panel B

Panel B   Amplification

Figure 5.9. Defense, tragedy, and transition, 2000 through April
2002 (periods 7 and 8)

ciation to block 17: it contains friends and families of welfare recipients,
judges, and legal advocates, claims that families are hurt, and a reference
to mental illness. Given that Mayor Giuliani was again touting WEP-for-
shelter plans and a plan to put disabled welfare recipients to work, this is
at least a sign of some vigorous defense, though it operates across several
contexts and is only marginally amplification. The other strong association is between block 19 and block 45, where the former, in addition to
containing a large number of contexts/objects, also contains claims that
tout, in several ways, the benefits of a work-based welfare system.

In panel B, *institutional spillover* is probably the most significant mechanism in this period and one that is not immediately apparent from the map. Electoral politics plays a big role here, not just because of Giuliani and Hevesi's posturing but also because the passage of transitional jobs legislation was secured by the ACORN- and CWA-linked Working Families Party's earlier endorsement of then council speaker Peter Vallone's gubernatorial candidacy. Further, by the time it was clear that the transitional jobs bill would end up in court, anti-WEP activists were beginning to chart strategy for what they felt certain—given Mayor Giuliani's broad unpopularity—would be a Democratic successor administration (the context/object campaign appears in block 10, which has considerable reach across the field).

The terrorist attacks of September 11, 2001, were, to say the least, a huge shock to political claim-making in New York City. A pall of grief, fear, anger, and a sense of violation hung over the city at least as long as the smoke emanating from the long-smoldering ruins of the Twin Towers. An informal period of mourning, as well as a fear of the intolerance with which oppositional political claim-making might be met, dampened activity with respect to workfare and welfare reform for nearly six months. Mayor Giuliani's revived popularity and credibility in the wake of his reassuring messages to the city during the immediate aftermath of September 11 certified him as a hero, perhaps uniquely capable of leading the city. This heroic status, combined with public compassion for the hundreds of thousands of people who lost their jobs in the economic aftermath of the attacks (though the bursting dot-com bubble had already begun to take a separate toll on the city's economy[38]), led to a strained and awkward silence from both sides of the welfare debate. [39] As a result, the field adjusted to Mayor Giuliani's newfound credibility and put the Bloomberg administration in a good position to take office without having to inherit the public relations problems that Giuliani's policies engendered.

Scale shift and institutional spillover once again affected claim-making in this period. First, September 11 was the day of a scheduled runoff election for the Democratic mayoral hopefuls, and the vote had to be rescheduled for the following month. This delay gave the Democrats enough time to implode in racial recriminations stemming from ugly campaign tactics. This disruption suppressed the black and Latino vote for the runoff primary victor, Mark Green, and helped elect the media billionaire Michael Bloomberg. Also helping Bloomberg—apart from the $76 million of his own fortune he spent—was Giuliani's endorsement, secured after Giuliani considered and then declined to challenge New York's term-limit law and run for a third term. Advocates' hopes for more leverage with a Democratic mayor were dashed. References to September 11 appear in block 1 of panel B, with advocates, the Giuliani administration, and a set of claims that express both uncertainty and conflict between the two actors in the block.

Nevertheless, as if to signal more flexibility and openness—and also to unload political liability—Bloomberg did not renew Jason Turner's contract, and the new mayor also let go several of Turner's closest aides (though the deputy commissioner in charge of WEP stayed on). But Bloomberg did vow to stay the course set by Mayor Giuliani on welfare reform. In an administration staffed by many Democrats, Bloomberg chose a staunchly antiwelfare, Republican nonprofit service provider, Verna Eggleston, to run HRA. Under Eggleston, HRA created a client advisory committee to increase communication among advocates, clients, and HRA policy staff, or at least to engage in an attempt at co-optation.[40] Finally, Mayor Bloomberg did not immediately go forward with Mayor Giuliani's parting shot at welfare recipients and poor workers. With only days to go in office, HRA concluded negotiations for a contract with a temporary employment agency, to which it planned to transfer the contracts of Parks Opportunity Program (POP) workers as the first round of POP expired. The workers would have taken a two-dollar-an-hour pay cut and lost union representation.[41]

This period does not yet bear the full stamp of the transition to the Bloomberg administration, but it does suggest some differences. In panel B, the Bloomberg administration appears in a block with academics, the city council, experts, the federal government, the media, nonprofit service providers, the state government, welfare recipients, WEP critics (a generalization in the newspaper record), welfare recipients, and workers (block 5). In this block are also the claims that administering WEP is hard, that individual assessments of welfare recipients should be done, that the poor are hurt, and that they have no skills. In other words, there is a sense in which Bloomberg's claim-making moved from the fight-picking of his predecessor toward a consensus-building strategy among (mainly) elites.

There are three blocks in which contexts/objects cluster: 10, 11, and 26, with block 11 containing only the food stamp issue and the issue of whether to require people with disabilities to work. They are joined by nearly every actor in the field, through the blocks 1, 3, 5, 17, 18, and 28. Block 24, which also joins them, gives a clue to what is occurring in this period: it contains the claims NYCLEGAL and NYCILLEG. In other words, battling legal claims, and the fact the three of the blocks with actors in them contain lawyers of one or another sort, suggest that much of the end of the Giuliani administration and some of the Bloomberg administration were characterized by litigation—another indicator of the Giuliani administration's strategy, toward the end of his term, of *time shifting* and turning policy debates into litigation.

Scaling Down, Fragmenting, and Segmenting

The final period is a residual one and undeveloped relative to the previous periods. Like the first period, it has fewer claims than the others overall. As a "pure" expression of WEP-related contention under Mayor Bloomberg, it helps show the continuities and discontinuities from the Giuliani administration. Unlike its predecessor, the Bloomberg administration has not pioneered new language about welfare reform and workfare. Moreover, because Bloomberg has not engaged in much claim-making about welfare reform, the media has been slow to cover it, even where advocates, legal advocates, and organizers have challenged the administration's policies and practices. As a result, the news cycle—and, in most respects, the protest cycle—over workfare ends in this period.

By 2002, full-time WEP placements had declined significantly. The Bloomberg administration continued an incipient move, begun under Jason Turner, to "engage" many of the remaining welfare recipients in simultaneous treatment and work. As a result, many WEP workers were working "three-plus-two" weeks, in which three days were spent in WEP assignments, and two in treatment, job search, or training of one sort or another. The falloff in the number of WEP workers did not mean that WEP disappeared nor that the opposition to WEP formed in 1996 had ceased working against New York's welfare reform. Instead, its claims have become more segmented, especially in the absence of a strong set of public claims by the Bloomberg administration around which to rally. Nevertheless, invisible to the maps of discourse and to the newspaper reports that are their basis is the organizational basis of a loosely joined, "soft-assembled" coalition whose members readily provide choral support for one another's anti-WEP claims when called upon to do so, as was the case with the broad Coalition for Access to Training and Education (CATE).

WEP's supporters also did not disappear. Jason Turner, for example, took a position at the conservative Heritage Foundation in Washington,

D.C., where he has helped make a further scale shift by touting the "New York Model" of "full engagement" as an essential model for PRWORA's recent reauthorization. His deputy, Andrew Bush, has been responsible for helping to coordinate the Bush administration's work-requirement-enhancing reauthorization proposals, devised under Tommy Thompson, the former Wisconsin governor (and employer of Turner) who was the secretary of Health and Human Services from 2001 to 2004.[42] Richard J. Schwartz, architect of the City's welfare reform program New York City–Work, Accountability, and You (NYC–WAY), sold his welfare-to-work business and became an editor of the *Daily News*, from whose pages he has attempted to decertify any moderating claims by the Bloomberg administration on welfare and has attacked CATE and other advocacy attempts to soften the program as "repugnant" and "shameful" backsliding.[43]

Figure 5.10 shows the field of workfare politics between May 2002 and May 2004. The concentration of contexts/objects in the prior period has given way to resegmentation and "hardening" of coalitions. The vast majority of actors are joined in block 1, and they join with the contexts of GeneralWEP and jobs and a wide variety of claims—both for and against workfare (ranging from WEPOK to SLAVERY and from WKSCARCE to MANYJOBS). These are part of the same genre. That this is so, and that this genre is joined to the institutional contexts of WEP in general and jobs, along with claims that, in effect, cite success in administering the program amid the difficult circumstances welfare recipients present to the state (ADMINIMP and HARD2SERV), means that in spite of some strong disagree-

Figure 5.10. Scaling down,
May 2002 through May 2004
(period 8)

ments (over CATE, for example), WEP politics became relatively more oriented to implementation issues, as the general outlines of criticism of the work-first model in favor of some human-capital interventions became more consensual. Blocks 3 and 4 are hard-assembled coalitions but are not connected strongly to the bulk of the existing field. Block 3 contains the contexts/objects of contracts, disability, and education and training, while block 4 contains that of discrimination. Block 3 is characterized by many claims about the legality of contracts (still) and questions about federal reauthorization of welfare reform, sanctions, and other administrative rules. Block 4 contains claims that appear poorly integrated[44] but that include persistent claims about deepening poverty, recourse, sexual harassment, that WEP is a sham, that WEP workers are workers, as well as others that argue against these claims. Actors include WEP workers and lawyers for the City.

Over the course of the decade of debate over workfare, anti-WEP activists' clearest successes in influencing the general direction of the debate were to be found earlier on, when they were more focused on organizing, or at least partly rooted in that context/object. The disappearance of organizing as an object in the field—and even its partial replacement by the "jobs" context/object—clearly ceded a good deal of rhetorical ground, especially to an administration in the process of shifting subjects to defuse the challenge organizing posed. One indicator of this challenge is the inclusion of the Giuliani administration in a block with hostile claims by the end of the period defined by organizing (September 1996-June 1998). Another is the ferocity of subject switching in the aftermath of the Pledge of Resistance. A hint of the administration's efforts to meet the organizers' challenge can be seen in the raw data, too, as shifts in emphasis in the administration's claim-making. For example, the Giuliani administration effectively stopped claiming that WEP served the public good (PUBLICGOOD) and cut back on claims that WEP promoted good discipline and work habits (DISCHABS) after the fourth period analyzed here, and it deepened its commitment to claims against welfare dependency (DEPEND) and touting the declining welfare rolls (ROLLDOWN).

The larger significance of this finding lies in two areas. First, it suggests the disturbing prospect that the strongest challenge to WEP was manifest in a war-of-maneuver tactic that was not—could not be—robust to a broadening of the field or even to a shift in strategies to allocate WEP labor or to enlist welfare recipients into the WEP labor force. Nevertheless, if considered as one of several important moments in organizing, the Pledge of Resistance's nonresilience may take second place to the larger problem that organizers—and not unions—were consistently more associated with claims for workers' rights and that DC 37's internal and external conflicts shaped the associations around the organizing context more than organizing could shape associations around labor politics. Second, it suggests that state executives—particularly those with access to national policy networks that can enable scale shifting—have tremendous power, if they act shrewdly, to secure hegemony precisely by picking multiple fights rather than by securing simple consent. The switch from PUBLICGOOD and DISCHABS to a focus on DEPEND and ROLLDOWN is evidence of a negative rather than a positive justification for WEP. That a program can withstand as much challenge and as generally low praise for so long is testimony to a larger failure of the Giuliani administration to win over its interlocutors to a key element of its neoliberal urban policy.

Back to the Trenches

Though this is an odd way to read a newspaper, a network-based content analysis yields several interpretive advantages and produces findings different from—if complementary to—those in chapter 4. The formal elements of the analysis help move beyond the ad hoc interpretation of claims in the field by suggesting actor-claim-context/object associations that are better and worse defined and more strongly or less strongly joined together. As these associations are studied over time, they reveal changes in the ways in which political actors, making claims in particular contexts, position themselves with respect to one another in the field. They reveal, in other words, how, through dialogic interaction, political actors of all sorts attempt to dig, hold, and take trenches in a war of position, making their own "structures of opportunity" and one another's obstacles.[45] The changing configuration of these trenches in relation to one another suggests that in a war of position, the nature of power may change, too. Further, by becoming sensitive to mechanisms tripped by dialogue (and constituting it), the analysis indicates ways of identifying the specific interventions in a debate that may cause both gradual and discontinuous shifts.

The analysis here can also aid strategic thinking by raising counterfactuals for intervention. For example, in April 1998, while doing fieldwork with ACORN, I asked an organizer what she thought about Stanley Hill's sudden denunciation of WEP as slavery. She was not very impressed, and she correctly predicted that Hill would come back around and try to make amends with Mayor Giuliani. In the maps of this period, shown earlier, we saw the way in which Hill tried to talk the organizers' talk but could not do so credibly. Yet, the maps then prompt the question: What would have happened if, before Hill could mend fences with the mayor, organizers had amplified the slavery claim anew but in the context of labor politics, with a slew of quickly organized demonstrations and press releases? In the context of the *New York Times* series, which was just then being published, could they have used this approach to gain visibility that the *Times* reporters denied them, even while adopting some of their positions? Or, did the developing strategy of bringing grievance and transitional job legislation before the city council require that they cut loose from the labor politics that had so disappointed them in the past and begin to eschew inflammatory rhetoric that might keep a moderate council speaker with gubernatorial ambitions from entertaining their legislation?

These kinds of questions can be asked independently of formal analysis. In being able to generate maps of overlapping connections, however, the project of generating possible courses of action can be advanced. In contrast to a purely narrative approach, a focus on identifying mechanisms through which the relations among actors, claims, and contexts change helps in the construction of the kind of comparative analogies upon which movements rely to recontextualize their experiences into new strategic possibilities.[46] Moreover, the results in this chapter signal that the difficulties anti-WEP forces encountered in organizing within the institutional contexts described in chapter 4 did not result consistently and evenly in the loss of control over the terms of debate. To understand why action in these contexts unfolded as it did, it is of utmost importance to gain the feel for the contexts and actors that chapters 3 and 4 provide, but neither, on its own, will give a sense of why these dynamics concatenate across contexts with different results in the ability of particular actors to define the terms of debate at different times.

To be sure, there are enormous limitations to this sort of study. The worst kind of error would be to consider what is presented in the data as an authoritative account of "what happened." As Bourdieu indicates, this kind of study changes the "status of practice and its products"—living utterances and dialogues—into coded data points.[47] Moreover, analytic decisions about the level of abstraction at which to code (I have chosen a low level for claims and a slightly higher level for organizational actors), how to deal with temporal cut points in the data, and which algorithms to use to cluster the data all affect the outcomes and interpretation of what occurred. Further, since the data are derived from newspapers searched with LexisNexis, it is beholden both to reportorial and editorial practices and biases and to the text-search capabilities of the indexing software. Nevertheless, even if all these caveats are taken into account, the analysis yields a theoretically informed metareading of mediated public discourse about WEP. In order to produce the newspaper articles from which the data are extracted, reporters and editors had to interact with the claim-makers (who often sought out the media). It is clearly inadequate to rely on the editorial and authorial decisions of even the most balanced of the corporate media for the sum total of observations about the shape and dynamics of contentious claim-making. It is also true, however, that advocacy, activist, and most other groups routinely use their press coverage as evidence of their impact in discussions with potential recruits, funders, allies, and adversaries. Therefore, from the outset, consideration of the mass-mediated, multicontext field is relevant to "questions for practice."

Yet in yielding questions for practice, the investigation in this chapter also shows that there is no inexorable logic to the system of the kind that Bourdieu imagined might be shown by the privilege of totalization. Part of the reason for this is that it matters a good deal how the actor-claim-context networks generate interpretations and of what kinds. In other words, the question of the meaning of discourse cannot simply be left to its objectification but must also be understood in the context of actors' own activity and the problems they confront. The answers to these questions, however, lie not *just* in the mass-mediated field of cross-context contention but also in the interplay between internal and external relations of organized political groups. This means that finer distinctions than appear here among actors and object/contexts must be introduced into the analysis (e.g., between DC 37 and CWA 1180 as "unions" and between targeting the health screener contracted by the City to assess welfare recipients' fitness for WEP and targeted protests over WEP workers' on-the-job deaths as "health and safety"). It also means that divisions of labor within and among groups and the rules and norms by which they are governed must be reintegrated. It is in the meeting of the larger dynamics and these finer distinctions that actors are able to make sense of these questions and act on the object/contexts they target. The cognitive consequence of concentrations of power and ideology, of being located in hard- or soft-assembled coalitions, and in being in a segmented, pluralist, fragmented, or hegemonic field—even in being in different sorts of hegemonic configurations—is not that actors stop thinking or solving problems. It is rather that they are more likely to think and solve problems in particular ways.

CHAPTER SIX

Claims, Cognitions, and Contradictions

In the summer of 1999, as the New York City Council looked as if it would take up the transitional job legislation, Community Voices Heard (CVH) undertook a new campaign. Based on the organizers' experience, noted in chapter 4, of seeing a wall full of green Work Experience Program (WEP) punch cards at a worksite and only a few white punch cards for regular employees, the campaign sought to highlight the difference between WEP and regular employment. Called Count Our Work (COW), it combined organizational development with research and advocacy. By getting members, staff, and volunteers to go to worksites to administer a survey about the jobs WEP workers did at them, CVH hoped to build its visibility and membership. It also hoped to make a larger point about the fundamental unfairness of WEP. Allies on the beleaguered staff of DC 37— District Council 37 of the American Federation of State, County, and Municipal Employees (AFSCME)—provided CVH with job descriptions of entry-level public employees. With the help of a public policy graduate student who had been involved in anti-WEP advocacy since the program's expansion, CVH developed a survey that would document how much work WEP workers did of the tasks normally assigned to entry-level employees in the agencies in which they were placed. The group planned to base an "invoice" for the difference between WEP workers' benefits and public employee pay on the results of the survey and present it to the mayor.

By the next spring, the survey was still unanalyzed, in large part because CVH had gotten distracted from COW by movement on the transitional jobs front. The city council passed the program and overrode the mayor's veto in April 2000. With the program passed, CVH turned, once again, to COW. By that time, the graduate student was out of town, and I (also then a graduate student) offered to help analyze the data and to coordinate the analysis with the graduate student. After we tabulated the data, we drew up some preliminary findings to share with allies.

We presented our findings to a lawyer and organizer from the National Employment Law Project (NELP). Upon looking at them, the lawyer passed around copies of the New York State Social Services law, as amended by the 1997 state welfare reform that was such a stinging defeat for efforts to represent WEP workers as workers. As one of the bargains to ensure the reform's passage, DC 37 gained stronger antidisplacement language in the law, in which partial displacement—that is, workfare workers doing tasks normally assigned to public employees—was not allowed. NELP's lawyer said that the survey provided documentation of what people had been saying for years, namely, that WEP workers *were* displacing regular municipal employees. He said that since even partial displacement was illegal, the angle CVH might think of taking on its research was that WEP should simply be *abolished.*

The organizers were initially taken aback. They were not certain, they said, that the members would be ready to take such a bold position. Upon further consideration, they agreed that the line was a good one and that they should discuss it with their members (their members were, according to their accounts, enthusiastic from the start).

I was taken aback by the organizers' being taken aback. Why should calls for WEP's abolition be surprising, given that CVH routinely called for just that on the placards they brought to demonstrations? Why should there be any doubt that members would be ready, when many spoke openly of WEP as slavery? In some ways, my surprise at the organizers' initial hesitancy about the abolition claim was driven by the collision of my already-objectifying, structuralist stance toward movement discourse and the in-the-moment, pragmatic use of this discourse by some of its primary generators. If I was right about the regularity of the slavery and abolition claims regarding workfare, how could these claims' *meanings* have operated "behind the backs" of CVH's extremely capable, sharp organizers? Or were they operating behind mine?

The Cognitive Environments of Political Claim-Making

If political claims come to life in dialogue, that is, in the interactions of socially situated actors, how do these actors understand what they are saying, what others are saying? What determines their ability to monitor at least part of the field from the trenches they occupy? What leads them to trigger change mechanisms, and when are they conscious of doing so?

This chapter extends the framework introduced in the previous one by means of a *qualitative* investigation of the actor-claim-context/object framework based on Cultural Historical Activity Theory (CHAT), an approach to cognitive psychology rooted in the work of Lev S. Vygotsky, a contemporary of Mikhail Bakhtin and Valentin Vološinov, and developed later by A. N. Leontiev and A. S. Luria in different ways in the 1970s. CHAT has spawned an active research program with applications in linguistic anthropology and the anthropology of human-computer interaction, pedagogy, management, and other fields.[1] Though CHAT and its Vygotskian cousins have been applied in numerous contexts of collaborative learning, they have not yet been applied in contexts in which collaboration meets contention—that is, in contexts such as social movement research.

CHAT begins with Vygotsky's insight that what he called "higher" mental functions—that is, conscious cognition—could not be confined to intracranial processes and competencies. Like Chomsky, Vygotsky understood there to be some innate cognitive capacity. For higher cognitive tasks, however—including language use (and therefore, unlike Chomsky)—cognitive nativism and individual psychology explained little.[2] Like the pragmatist philosophers George Herbert Mead, John Dewey, and Charles Sanders Peirce, Vygotsky understands cognition as the production of meaning and the production of meaning as inseparable from social interaction.

For Vygotsky, lower or basic mental functions cannot be considered conscious cognition. *Higher* cognitive functions depend for their development on "scaffolding" from aspects of the environment. This idea makes intuitive sense for those of us old enough to remember what it was like to compose a letter on a manual typewriter. We think differently, not just different thoughts, when composing in a highly developed word processing or instant messaging program. What is more difficult to accept is that cognitively speaking, we share credit—and blame—for our work with our work environment.

Vygotsky understands cognition and consciousness to be about the activity of subjects toward objects, about human efforts to change the world around them, in large and small ways. This activity is mediated by tools, among which language is the most flexible and versatile. If this is true, then higher mental functions cannot but be *social* from the start and cannot be individually psychological or "mentalist." This view is consistent with the dialogical view of meaning outlined earlier. As Vološinov writes in *Marxism and the Philosophy of Language*, "Signs can only arise on *interindividual territory.* . . . It is essential that the two individuals be *organized socially,* that they compose a group (a social unit); only then can the medium of signs take shape between them. The individual consciousness not only cannot be used to explain anything, but on the contrary, is itself in need of explanation from the vantage point of the social, ideological medium."[3] From the outset, then, *social organization* is a critical element of cognition, and therefore cognition cannot be reduced to what "goes on in people's heads" or the "black box of mental life."[4] Vološinov continues in this anti-individualist vein: "The individual consciousness is a *social-ideological* fact. . . . It has been made the place where all unresolved problems, all objectively irreducible residues are stored away. . . . The logic of consciousness is the logic of ideological communication, of the semiotic interaction of a social group. If we deprive consciousness of its semiotic, ideological content, it would have absolutely nothing left. . . . All that has been said above leads to the following methodological conclusion: *the study of ideologies does not depend on psychology to any extent and need not be grounded in it."*[5] Leontiev is even more explicit: "The individual does not simply 'stand' before a certain window displaying meanings among which he has but to make a choice, that these meanings—representations, concepts, ideas—do not passively wait for his choice but energetically dig themselves into his connections with people forming the real circle of his contacts. If the individual in given life circumstances is forced to make a choice, then that choice is not between meanings but between colliding social positions that are recognized and expressed through these meanings."[6] We are quickly brought to, and then past, the starting point for chapter 5. Cognition depends on actors' orientation to an object, mediated by environmental artifacts they use to make their objects tractable. In political claim-making, these artifact/tools are most often political claims. CHAT adds to the actor-claim-object/context triangle in two ways. First, it specifies the dimensionality of the "social positions" in which actors act upon their objects, by highlighting the importance of discursive and mnemonic communities with determinate divisions of labor and rules. Second, it treats the larger systems of meaning making, or "activity systems," as historical developments and as in the process of development.

Enlarging the Triangle

Though CHAT still highlights human subjectivity, it does not reduce the unit of analysis to the individual. Instead, the unit of analysis for any

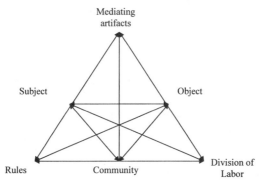

Figure 6.1. Model of an activity system. Reprinted from Yrjö Engeström, "Learning by Expanding: An Activity-Theoretical Approach to Developmental Research," 1987, chap. 4, fig. 4.4, p. 31, http://communication.ucsd.edu/MCA/Paper/Engestrom/expanding/toc.htm.

activity-systematic study of cognition is the *activity system*. The cognitive psychologist Yrjö Engeström has led the recent systematization of CHAT and proposes that an activity system be conceived as a system composed of subjects, objects, and communities of interpretation and of larger rules, mediating artifacts, and a division or divisions of labor (see fig. 6.1).[7]

Engeström's schematization of activity systems is meant to show the ways in which each element is related to and constituted by the other. From the standpoint of most sociological considerations of the subject, this relationship is relatively unproblematic. The idea is that subjects do not stand alone, outside of society, but are constituted in and through social relations. Even individuals, as Georg Simmel pointed out, are "extra-individual" in the sense that their very individuality is composed in the interstices of "intersecting social circles," each of which has its own rules and divisions of labor and the totality of which is created by larger dynamics of social development and differentiation. For Simmel, as for Durkheim and Marx, the analysis of society could not begin with individuals, and the analysis of individuals could not proceed without their social relations. This is the key, after all, to Simmel's understanding that urbanization had cognitive and affective consequences—the blasé attitude—that oriented urban subjects to each other and to their settings in particular ways.[8]

For Engeström, too, subjects are defined collectively, as parts of communities governed by rules and divisions of labor. Communities "certify" their members *as* members in a wide variety of ways, chief among which is through shared adherence to rules. These rules can be thought of as spatiotemporal routines and also generic forms of action (or repertoires) that, with actors, constitute communities. Communities form through divisions of labor oriented to objects; equally, divisions of labor arise in communities confronted with problems or objects of action. Engeström's insistence that Vygotsky's tool-mediated cognition framework needs to be explicitly embedded in social collectivities shows the ways in which this version of cognitive thinking is consistent with many of the governing performative metaphors in studies of culture, contention, and cognition (e.g., Erving Goffman's "front-stage" and "back-stage" behaviors, Charles Tilly's "repertoires" of contention, Jeffrey Alexander's "cultural pragmatics"[9]). Performers (actors) are constituted through community-certified rules (what "counts" as a performance) and divisions of labor (distinguishing, for example, between performer and audience, performer and director, etc.), and act toward their object (e.g., a play, opera, dance piece) by means of artifacts (scripts, libretti, choreography) that are *also* the products of historically accreted activity that are shaped by rules, divisions of labor, communities of interpretation, and so forth. Similarly—and here's the dialogic point—as audiences, we generate choral support for the genre of an "opera" when we see singers perform, most often staged according to a narrative plot (whether or not they can act!) and most often in a formal theater. We do not when we see a mime, covered head-to-toe in silver paint, standing on an inverted bucket on the sidewalk (with another receptacle for thrown coins and bills) and moving slowly to simulate a very deliberate robot.

Now, if the unit of analysis is an activity system, the cogitating subject—as Vološinov's theory outlined earlier would lead us to expect—is an entity of indeterminate scope. To be sure, individuals' cognitions still matter. Nevertheless, when the unit of analysis is no longer the individual subject, then changes in the scaffolding of cognition, that is, changes in the activity system, have cognitive consequences whether or not subjects of a system immediately and consciously apprehend that change has occurred. Like the networks discussed in the previous chapter, then, activity systems exhibit some of the same properties of duality: subjects can be changed by changes in the activity system, even as subjects act within and upon the system.

Perhaps the best way to understand activity systems is not as well-bounded triangles of relations but as crystalline structures built on this foundation (fig. 6.2). As with the actor-claim-context/object triangles in

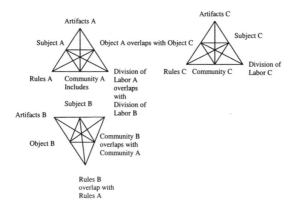

Figure 6.2. Interlocking structure of activity systems

chapter 5, activity systems are best understood as intercalated with each other. In this way, we can better imagine the relative proximities of particular subject-object sets, even while understanding the potential cognitive importance of action at distant points that alter the scaffolding in closer-in subsystems.

Therefore, for example, activity systems can be joined when multiple subjects—even from different communities—act upon the same object. Any change in the object due to the actions of one subject will reverberate through the other subjects' activity systems. Similarly, the object of activity in one subject's system may be the language available for subjects in other activity systems. This effect is precisely what the organizer from the Association of Community Organizations for Reform Now (ACORN) who was quoted in chapter 3 explained as the object of using the symbolic union election. It was a way to "create a climate where it would be very difficult for anyone who in some ways either sees themselves as progressive, or sees themselves as pro-labor to not support an election of working people wanting to vote on whether they wanted to have a union or not."[10]

Nevertheless, there are a couple of sticking points. First, from a qualitative perspective, no clear methodological guidelines exist for determining the scope of an ideological or communicative system or the starting point in an analysis. Second, how can we talk about distributed cognition without talking about the cognitive capacity and communicative activity of the individuals within that system?

On the first point, CHAT defines activity systems first by their subjects, and as such, they are always only partial views of activity, both in the sense that they do not provide a complete picture of interacting subjects and in the sense that they take one subject's point of view. Returning to the word processor example, I begin with my own subjectivity as a writer, rather than with, say, Bill Gates Jr. or with Microsoft as a corporate entity. As a user of Microsoft Word, I have Bill Gates as a member of my "community," even though he plays an indirect role in my activity directed at writing a book.

On the second point, cognition and consciousness are the result of socially distributed processes first and are then internalized by individuals. Forced, again, to work at a typewriter, word processor users will most often be frustrated by the mismatch between the cognitive style they developed with word processors and the technical capacity of the typewriter. We do not develop a Windows-compatible thinking style without first encountering a word processor. Conversely, in the context of interlocking activity systems, if activity in one system begins to induce changes in a genre or a set of tools, then internalized genres or tools may be of less use in making the objects in a second activity system tractable to the subject.

Language is the most flexible and adaptable cognitive tool. Because language is also irreducibly social, we internalize grammatical and generic rules because we can identify, through others' choral support, those moments in which our utterances resonate with others' use of the same tools. It is not, therefore, that the individual subject completely disappears into an activity system. It is rather that the starting point for analysis is with the subject's action in the system, not with the individual's understanding of the system itself or comprehension of its object.

Explaining Discourse Dynamics

The logic of depicting activity systems as nested triangular relations lies in CHAT's understanding of the triggers of change in activity systems. Engeström posits that "contradictions," or mismatches, between or among elements in an activity system create the demand for adjustments to resolve them. When we understand these contradictions and resolutions, we also gain a useful perspective on the production of the change mechanisms described in the previous chapter.

Contradictions

The concept of contradiction employed by Engeström indicates incommensurability between or among parts of a system rather than system failure.[11] Contradictions are "historically accumulating structural tensions within and between activity systems" that "'energise' [them] and therefore . . . can be considered as the motors of development."[12] These mismatches can exist among any of the six corners of an activity system. For example, before the Fifth Avenue Committee (FAC) sent organizers out to Prospect Park in Brooklyn to find WEP workers with whom to speak about welfare rights organizing, the organizer told me, he thought welfare rights organizing had been moribund in the 1990s up until that point.[13] Here, an organizer (the subject) wants to oppose the growth of WEP (the object) and does so by means of a style of organizing (the tool) that is, at the same time, part of a repertoire (the rules) of organizing practices known to a community that includes organizers, welfare advocates, and other allies (the community). Though the advocates and other allies do not employ organizing routines, they engage in other activities directed toward the object of opposing WEP's expansion, such as research, providing testimony, and so on (division of labor). "What we found," said the organizer, speaking of FAC's initial trip to the park, "was a group of workers."[14] In other words, the organizer found that the *object* of activity had to be approached with different language in order to resolve what appeared to be immediate tensions within the activity system.

These tensions included a tension between the expanding WEP program and the repertoire of welfare rights organizing (i.e., between the object and the tools and rules for applying them). Welfare rights appeals had long since failed to prevent the expansion of workfare. A further tension appeared when the organizers conversed with WEP workers: WEP workers themselves were using language more typical of workers. If WEP workers were to be brought into the community of actors opposed to WEP, and if, as part of this community, they were to certify FAC organizers as legitimate actors, then their own languages would have to alter the repertoire of welfare rights discourse. Moreover, WEP workers' invocation of another repertoire (recognizable as "worker talk" by the organizers) suggested the possibility that a work-oriented set of claims (new tools produced by available artifacts) might help activity toward a secondary object, which was getting organized labor to join the community of anti-WEP actors in a more intensive way.

What Engeström calls "expansive learning" has to do with the resolution of contradictions in such a way as to set new problems for the subject. It is not to resolve all contradictions but rather to internalize a given resolution that leads to a greater ability to tackle the next problem. Vygotsky's key concept to describe cognitive development, the "zone of proximal development" (ZPD), relies on the initial condition that cognitive activity is oriented toward a goal. The ZPD is the "idea that adult help, provided at crucial developmental moments, would give the child experience of successful action which the child alone could not produce. Providing support for the first few faltering steps of a near-walker . . . would be [a case] in point."[15] This experience can be internalized in ways that hasten the child's ambulatory facility. The ZPD concept, however, need not necessarily be completely "adult-centric." The main idea is that any environmental elements can scaffold cognition. In fact, as the cognitive scientist Andy Clark has argued, the more scaffolded an environment, the more structured and channeled the actions toward a given goal.[16]

The organizers' realization of the object shift away from simple welfare rights organizing toward labor organizing can be understood as the result of WEP workers' producing a zone of proximal development for them. In the context of the activity system of FAC itself, other WEP workers who were members of FAC or tenants in FAC-managed buildings had already come to staff members to complain about WEP. The further encounter with WEP workers in Prospect Park produced an expansion of FAC's activity and, in so doing, also changed the community's orientation to WEP's expansion.

Again, because activity systems are always understood from partial viewpoints and are more crystalline than separate, contradictions may arise between activity systems that share the same object of activity or between systems in which unmatched corners of the activity system meet, for example, where rules in one system are the object of activity in another (as is frequently the case in litigation) or where the subjects of one system are tools in another (as was the case where the Giuliani administration used a pliant DC 37 to discredit claims that WEP hurt workers).

Contradiction and Pragmatic Resituation

The appearance of contradictions within an activity system does not necessarily result in the creation of zones of proximal development and expansive cycles of learning. The opposite can be true as well. Contradictions can also stymie progress toward an object and result in the demobilization of activity. They can also—and frequently do—lead subjects toward "solutions" that get them no nearer to their object, perhaps even deepening contradictions, in spite of activity. Arguably, in the short term, this is what occurred in the shift into labor organizing: Without a partner in DC 37, WEP Workers Together (WWT) and ACORN deepened the contradiction between the tool of labor-focused claims and their ability to roll back WEP the more they used these claims because without DC 37's choral support, these claims—rather than welfare rights claims—were decertified by a critical part of the community of the claims' speakers. If anyone was going to represent WEP workers *as workers*, it would have to be DC 37, and it would have to be within the existing, or only slightly altered, rule structure of municipal labor relations.

Contradictions' resolution occurs because of changes in the parts of the activity system that are in tension. Because of the crystalline structure of interlocking activity systems, often it is difficult to say whether a change in a part of an activity system was due to the activity of the subject in a focal system (i.e., a system that is the object of most focused study) or due to changes in parts of the system that are shared by other activity systems and caused by action in them. Thus, contradictions and their resolution are much like the mechanisms that appeared in the previous chapter. Indeed, contradictions within activity systems may "trip" relational mechanisms that resituate claims from the mouths of some speakers, or from the company of some claims, to others and thus change the meanings they convey. Conversely, the unfolding of mechanisms will create new contradictions, too.

Mechanisms in the Activity System

Let us revisit the mechanisms introduced in chapter 5 and look at the ways in which they fit into the model of cognition offered by CHAT.

Certification and decertification processes always involve the "community" node in the activity system and frequently entail the application of community-held rules to judge the legitimacy of the tools applied by the subject to the object. In the case of DC 37 and organizers' early efforts to claim that WEP workers were *workers*, certification and decertification struggles involved negotiation over the community's division of labor, too.

We have to be careful about confusing terminology when certification and decertification occur as subject switching. In CHAT, *subject* refers to the actor, or what I'll call an *active subject*. By *subject switching*, as should be apparent from its definition in the previous chapter, I mean only that an actor, in a position to influence the general terms of debate, can change the subject by opening up new institutional arenas for discussion that can overwhelm debate in other arenas. When that occurs, there is, in the activity system, either a contradiction between the *object* and some part of the community's division of labor or a contradiction between its community and another active subject that shares part of its community. Thus, subject switching is about winning the attention of a target audience within a community or attempting to shunt aside a rival active subject and its claims (or linguistic tools) by invoking a different object common to parts of the rival active subject's community but not to others.

If amplification is an attempt to clarify and sharpen a claim, then it is an attempt to resolve contradictions between an object and a set of tools with respect to rules and to a community. The point of amplification is that the subject doing it uses a given claim repeatedly and encourages its use toward the object in the company of a restricted set of other claims. To the extent that rival subjects share communities, amplification succeeds if the shared elements of the community provide choral support to the rival only when the rival uses the same claims as the initial subject. To the extent this does not occur, the initial subject can create a new crisis in the rival's activity system.

As I have described the interlocking and sometimes nested nature of activity systems, institutional spillover is inevitable. Institutional spillover introduces new rules, new communities, new artifacts, and new divisions of labor into a given activity system. In the examples of institutional spillover in the previous chapter, electoral politics played an intermittent but often powerful role in shaping claim-making over WEP and in promoting specific claims about the program (see fig. 6.3).

Like institutional spillover, scale shift and time shift are mechanisms that most directly affect communities, divisions of labor, and rules. There are cognitive consequences to the fact that institutionally based action and action that is defined by its location in a genre or repertoire unfold in specific places and according to specific temporal formats. Among them is that communities and divisions of labor cannot be scaled up indefinitely. Nor can they be subject to significantly changed temporalities (whether these changes involve the temporal horizons of narratives and claims or the expected unfolding of action within institutions) without creating contradictions in an activity system that lead to the certification or decertification of new tools, new subjects, and/or new objects (and therefore the redefinition of the whole system).[17] Scale shift and time shift can also be used to resolve contradictions, however temporarily. Consider the scale shift involved in AFSCME's takeover of DC 37 from the standpoint of a group like Community Voices Heard. If CVH is the subject and opposition to WEP is the object, then DC 37 is part of CVH's community, albeit a particularly troubled part with a small part to play in the division of labor. Since DC 37 is also part of the Giuliani administration's

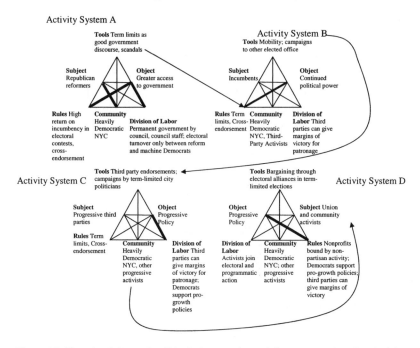

Figure 6.3. The role of electoral politics in intersecting activity systems. Note that Activity System D is a mirror image. Contradictions within the systems are marked by heavy lines. Arrows indicate the appearance of attributes in one activity system as different attributes in another.

community, it plays only a small role in certifying CVH's opposition to WEP. Only when the corruption scandal finally scales up and prompts AFSCME headquarters to send in a trustee for the union, the new leadership changes the union's place as a community member by shifting it institutionally into the courts to challenge the administration's displacement of its members with WEP workers. This shift leads the union to withdraw considerably from the administration's community (and resolves a contradiction in the union's activity system through amplification of a legal genre) and to certify with renewed vigor some of the claims made by CVH and other WEP opponents.

A Tale of Two Claims: Tracing the Fortunes of Abolition and Jobs

We can now return to the story of CVH with which this chapter began. Why is it significant to account for the organizers' surprise and initial hesitancy? The significance of the story is that it marks an isolable point of cognitive development in the long process of anti-WEP claim-making. By applying an activity-theoretical method to understanding the switch from the organizers' initial hesitancy to their tentative embrace of the claim for WEP's abolition, I can show the process by which claims that WEP was slavery and claims for "real jobs" became collectively reinterpreted and resituated in activists' activity systems as the activists and their environments opened, resolved, and opened again, a series of contradictions.

By analytically situating that moment within a far broader historical framework describing the association of the claims that WEP was akin to slavery and claims for jobs, I also show that through dialogic interaction, these claims are not only symbolic artifacts appropriated as tools in anti- and pro-WEP activity but rather, in their appropriation *as* tools, are also at times the very *objects* of activity themselves.

Slavery and Real Jobs: A Developing Association

From nearly the beginning of the struggles against WEP, the language of slavery has coexisted with the demand for real jobs.[18] These paired claims—one descriptive, the other prescriptive—often share billing on placards, in advocacy analyses, in testimony, and in organizing settings as well as in the more contentious comments made by activists. Even before the controversy in the *New York Times* set off by the use of the description of WEP as slavery by some participants in the Pledge of Resistance's press conference in July 1997, the claim that WEP was akin to slavery appeared in concert with demands for real jobs. Moreover, these claims spanned organizational settings. For example, as early as March 1996—even before WEP worker organizing began—James Butler, then the president of the hospital workers' local in DC 37, testified to the General Welfare Committee of the New York City Council that WEP had effected a "massive replacement of city workers by what amounts to slave labor in a program that has become a revolving door, not a pathway to real jobs."[19] Union-provided signs at the WEP Worker Solidarity Day picket organized by WEP Workers Together in early 1997 also denounced the program as slavery and demanded real jobs (fig. 6.4).

Similarly, WEP Workers Together members marched in chains in the 1996 Labor Day parade. Their literature, while making no mention of slavery, nevertheless demanded real jobs and drove home the point that WEP hurts all workers.

Figure 6.4. The paired claims of WEP as slavery and
claims for jobs are represented on a picketer's sign
at WEP Worker Solidarity Day in 1997.

The language of slavery was often used at WEP worksites by organizers
and by WEP workers themselves, though often to describe the conditions
of work and as an expression of outrage at the fact that WEP workers were
not being paid for their work. The language of indentured servitude was
also used frequently, often as a way to invoke a grossly unequal labor
contract without raising the specter of the possibly racialized discourse
of slavery. Doing so, organizers realized, could undermine WEP worker
solidarity as much as it could build it. For example, during the prepara-
tions for their Labor Day march, WWT members had a bitter fight about
certifying the symbolism of slavery as a claim. Reported the organizer:

> There was a huge fight among our members who were writing signs the
> night before, whether to use the word *slavery* in the sign or whether to
> march in chains to symbolize they were slaves. There was a huge fight, and
> I didn't feel I could take part in it. I said, "Slavery's a very laden term, and
> I'm white. You decide. Whatever you want to do is fine with me. This is not
> my decision to make." There was a huge fight between different African
> American members, some of whom were saying, "Yes we should . . . ,"

"Fuck you!" "We *are* the same!" "We're not really slaves!" Sort of threaten-
ing, throwing around "Uncle Tom," "Field hand" . . . It was really nasty. . . .
People ended up marching in chains because they said it is slavery. But it's
a contentious issue among some workers.[20]

The lead pastor in the Pledge of Resistance expressed doubts about the
utility of the analogy of slavery, even as he outlined the way in which he
used it:

> I've chosen not to use it myself, on the grounds that slavery has a very
> concrete meaning in this culture, and as an Anglo, I'm not going to say,
> "This program is slavery." It's not for me to say that. . . . What I say is: "It's
> forced labor." I sometimes say it's indentured servitude, if people ask me. I
> said that here at the church. I would consider this the kind of program that
> was outlawed under the Thirteenth Amendment of our Constitution. . . .
> But sometimes I'll use it in church: Our ancestors were slaves in Egypt,
> right?[21]

Nevertheless, by the time that the Pledge of Resistance announced its formation in July 1997, the language of slavery was already well established
in the opposition. In December 1997, a Jobs with Justice–sponsored rally
calling for WEP workers' rights and union recognition brought nearly
seven hundred demonstrators from all the major anti-WEP organizations
and many unions (though not, significantly, DC 37) to Lower Manhattan.
Signs from this rally, shown here, also attest to the uses of the language
of slavery: as an adjunct to demands for real jobs and as a description
of treatment under the program (fig. 6.5). DC 37's absence was telling,
though. As long as DC 37 did little to oppose WEP's expansion, the claim
that WEP was slavery was also an implicit criticism of the union.

Demands for real jobs were also made by a variety of actors in the
absence of descriptions of WEP as slavery. What exactly was meant by
"real jobs," however, took shape only slowly and did not converge on a
single set of programmatic outlines. The text of the Pledge of Resistance,
quoted in chapter 4, for example, calls for the creation of "living wage
jobs," and affirms that "government is responsible for promoting job creation and, if necessary, for developing public works programs to employ
hundreds of thousands of the poor and unemployed across the nation."
By contrast, at the same hearings at which the union leader James Butler, quoted earlier, described WEP as slave labor, another union president from DC 37 (Charles Hughes, then the leader of the public school

Figure 6.5. Slavery discourse, December 10, 1997. The sign in Spanish at left reads, "Don't Treat Me Like a Slave." The paired claim for "real jobs" is reflected in the wall poster at right from Jobs with Justice (shown in *Spanish as Trabajos con Justicia*).

employees, the largest, and most powerful local) praised the program. Having set up an apprenticeship program in his local through which WEP workers could move into union jobs, he touted the program—and, by extension, WEP—as a way to provide "real jobs."

Moreover, though WEP's proponents did not claim that WEP was a real job—and in fact, insisted that it was not—they used the growing association of the demand for real jobs against their opponents in order to claim that they were averse to *work*. For example, responding to criticism of NYC–WAY's expansion in 1996, Mayor Giuliani told the *Daily News*, "It shows the sickness that we've fallen into that people think it's vindictive to ask people to work. . . . There's no such thing as menial when you're working to support your family."[22]

We can map these conflicts using the activity-theoretical apparatus developed earlier. If we consider WEP's opponents—the soft-assembled coalition that began to develop over the course of 1996—as a collective subject, we can consider the various organizations from which they came as their community. Their use of the slavery and real jobs claims were geared to opposing WEP, and at least insofar as the use of these tools was concerned, there was not a highly differentiated division of labor. Many used the claims together in a variety of settings, from worksites to hearings. At the same time, if we consider DC 37, which was part of the community in the first activity system (fig. 6.6, System A), as a subject, its activity system (System B) includes WEP opponents in its community but also includes the Giuliani administration, with which it had to bargain.

The slavery claim sat poorly with DC 37's leadership, and so did suggestions that WEP be abolished. Though the executive director, Stanley Hill, called for a moratorium on WEP in 1996, he did not call for its abolition. Instead, he made a move to decouple the claim for real jobs from the claim that WEP was slavery and should be abolished. Hence, a contradiction opens up between the tools in System A and the community in System B. Further, if we look at the Giuliani administration's activity system (System C), we see that DC 37 is part of its community. DC 37's use of the claim for real jobs was therefore in direct contradiction with the use to which WEP opponents put it, even though DC 37 was part of the community in System B. Thus, DC 37's position within contradictory communities led it to compound the "historically accumulated tensions" that it inherited at least since the fiscal crisis (see chapter 3). As Langemeyer indicates, however, these tensions and contradictions were not necessarily the source of expansive learning on the part of the union; instead, it made adjustments that deepened the contradictions.[23]

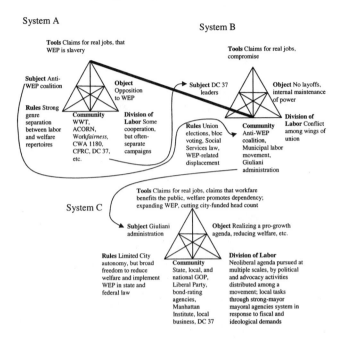

Figure 6.6. Slavery and real jobs in DC 37's activity systems. Arrows indicate attributes of an activity system that become different attributes in another. Thick lines indicate contradictions.

The Institutional Primacy of Jobs and the Ambiguity of Slavery: Summer 1997–99

In the summer of 1997, the worker status of WEP workers at the City level was scale-shifted into the state's welfare reform process. As indicated in chapter 4, this was the moment at which the FAC organizer began to think that his group was "fundamentally misunderstanding the way WEP workers understood themselves," and the lead organizer for CVH realized that "nobody gave a shit about gloves" in the larger picture. WWT cut back its worksite organizing and its focus on worksite conditions. The scale shift and certification of NYC–WAY by the state legislature, which was seen as a serious blow by activists, led them to try to switch subjects and resolve the contradiction between the "unionlike" tools they were using to oppose WEP and the rules governing the union genre. In chapter 4, I argued that the union genre demanded a longer time frame than was available to organizers, and thus, there was a temporal mismatch between the unionlike tools used by WWT and worksite organizing.

For the WWT groups, the shift into a legislative strategy to create transitional jobs was a time-shifting resolution to this contradiction. Engagement with the arena of legislative politics, however, pushed the marriage between the demand for real jobs and the criticism that WEP was slavery toward an amicable divorce.

This decoupling of claims resulted in the amplification of the demand for real jobs through its alignment with a legislative genre.[24] The demand for jobs was clarified and concretized in programmatic terms in a way that the criticism of WEP as slavery was not. Accordingly, the activists transformed the demand for real jobs into a demand for "transitional" jobs carrying the benefits and status of employment, the possibility of union representation, and a statutorily defined living wage. Transitional jobs entailed several temporal properties as well. As a *demand for* a program, the temporality of the transitional jobs bill was wedded to the institutional rules of the city council and to the political considerations and ambitions of its members. As a program, transitional jobs were limited to eighteen-month placements, with a possible extension to two years.

If the demand for real jobs became dominant among anti-WEP organizers after 1997, the slavery claim's temporal ambiguity—already a source of some dissension in its use—led it into contradiction with organizers' newly defined legislative communities and their repertoires of claim-making. As in the courts, the language of slavery, of abolition, or even of an unelaborated objection to workfare in general was off-limits. Recall, for example, that in chapter 4, we saw arguments in *Brukhman v. Giuliani*, the prevailing wage litigation, for example, in which lawyers studiously clarified that the "intervenors in this case do not "object to a 'work-relief' program, nor do they object to working off their grants."[25]

Similarly, in city council testimony, the "extremist" language of slavery and abolition had no place.[26] Moreover, in spite of the actual lack of deference shown to the administration's representatives by council members such as Stephen DiBrienza (who delighted in his periodic public browbeating of welfare officials sent to testify with as little information as possible), on the level of claim-making, the city council's limited power and political moderation under speaker Peter Vallone's leadership left the general outlines of WEP substantially unchallenged. Recall, for example, that in the testimony of FAC's lead organizer in the final hearings leading up to the approval of Intro. 354-A, the transitional jobs bill, he explicitly said, "But this hearing, and the bill, is not about WEP, it is about jobs.

The Transitional Employment Program is not a referendum on workfare, it is an opportunity to help people move from welfare to work."[27]

General Welfare Committee chair DiBrienza echoed this testimony, calling the transitional jobs bill the "next logical step in welfare reform,"[28] as if the program were consistent with WEP. The result was that the slavery claim was decertified.

There was another issue, here, too. In bringing together the Ad Hoc Coalition for Real Jobs to push for the transitional jobs program, FAC was keenly aware of the challenges of holding it together. The city council's rules of propriety were not the only thing leading to moderation in the presentation of the already-moderate transitional jobs proposal. The FAC organizing director also believed that only a focus on jobs, which he saw as in the "self-interest" of both community and labor groups, could keep the hard-assembled legislative coalition together.

CVH chafed against this backdrop of tactical moderation. Several times, it took a more confrontational stance at city council hearings, and its activists were sometimes escorted out of council chambers for interrupting the proceedings. This approach led to disagreements with FAC and ACORN over tactics. As one CVH organizer complained, "With the city stuff it was really like, 'Everyone has to be doing the same thing.' There's this real sense of control and like, you could fuck everything up, if you tried to go alone. I mean maybe trying to go alone is not the most strategic thing to do, but . . . it wasn't even just about that, it was a real hesitation and . . . aversion to action. And to trying to pull numbers out. We never once did a numbers thing. We never once did: Let's try to pull out three hundred low-income people. Which we could have done."[29]

It is important to emphasize that CVH activists were not simply giving in to an infantile refusal to play by the city council's rules or by the rules of coalitional propriety for which FAC advocated. Instead, CVH's activists experienced a contradiction having to do with the way in which they saw their organization. In chapter 3, I mentioned that CVH had difficulty in collaborating within the confines of the hard-assembled WWT coalition because the other members, FAC and the Urban Justice Center, were not led by their members and did not rely on membership building. One can dismiss this as a self-righteousness style on the part of CVH. But a more satisfying explanation is that, having been born in order to resolve a basic contradiction between advocacy and advocating for more power for those unable to be heard in the advocacy process, CVH was always focused on *not* becoming a fully staff-driven organization. Here, too, the

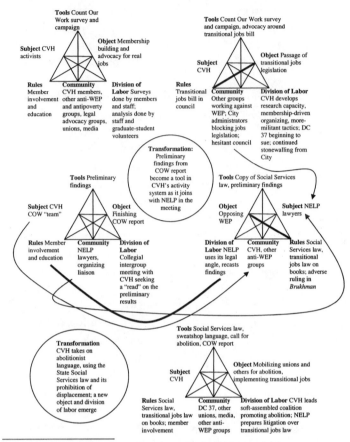

Internal organizational activity system External organizational activity system

[4] Note: Arrows indicate that elements of one attribute of an activity system become different attributes of other activity systems. Heavy lines indicate contradictions. The contraction between CVH's internal rules and NELP's advice based on legal expertise helps to produce both the initial hesitancy of CVH organizers and the resolution toward the new campaign, as members certify organizers' ideas.

Figure 6.7. Transformation in CVH's activity systems. Arrows indicate that elements of one attribute of an activity system become different attributes of other activity systems. Heavy lines indicate contradictions. The contradiction between CVH's internal rules and NELP's advice based on legal expertise helps produce both the initial hesitancy of CVH organizers and the resolution toward the new campaign as members certify organizers' ideas.

activists' concern with "pulling numbers out" has to do with building the group's base and providing the scaffolding internally to the organization to demonstrate to members their own collective power. The strong ethos of member control in CVH combined with the actual turnover in membership (due to many of the factors discussed in chapter 2) makes membership building a constant priority for the organization.

In activity-theoretical terms, therefore, by the end of 1999, there were contradictions between CVH's internally and externally focused activity systems. On one side, there were the rules and tools geared toward membership building and organizational maintenance, which were defined, at least in part, by a community of members and a division of labor heavily weighted toward promoting member control. On the other side were the larger coalitional activity systems geared toward transitional jobs within which CVH was nested. Within these activity systems, the claims for real jobs gained temporal specificity and the claims that WEP was slavery—with their implicit abolitionist claim—were shunted aside (see fig. 6.7).

Contradictions and Resolutions: 1999–2000

The passage of the transitional jobs program was assured as early as September 1999, due to the institutional spillover of city council speaker Peter Vallone's gubernatorial bid and his courting of the ACORN- and CWA-tied Working Families Party (WFP). This was a two-way certification exchange. Though its precise outlines were still the subject of bargaining among advocates and Speaker Vallone, the program's certain passage into law began to shift the terms of debate and the coalitional configurations of the field. In the first place, the promise of mayoral intransigence and a protracted court battle over the program and the actual outlines of the program suggested powerfully that the struggle for "real jobs" was not exhausted by the bill's passage. In fact, its passage became the occasion for a mayoral subject-switch, whereby the essence of the court battle was whether or not the bill was an inappropriate curtailment of mayoral power under the terms of the city charter rather than about the merits of the program itself. Accordingly, in its victory, the claim for real jobs was given more, rather than less, ambiguity than it had achieved in the process of the legislative battle. Moreover, though the Ad Hoc Coalition for Real Jobs persisted, it changed into a softer, less task-oriented coalition called the Alliance for a Working Economy. This meant that the tasks of coordination and certification maintenance among labor allies were less strenuous for FAC, and there was less pressure within the field for allies to "do the same thing." Further, WWT, which had persisted under FAC's aegis, began to change into a membership organization, Families United for Racial and Economic Equality (FUREE) that would eventually spin off from FAC. The name change reflected both the fact that the group wanted to broaden its focus from WEP to other aspects of the welfare and employment systems and the persistent stigma attached to being a WEP worker.[30]

For its part, the National Employment Law Project, which had been the key legal advocate in the fight for transitional jobs and the author of both state and local legislation, anticipated that there would be a legal fight, too. The timing of the transitional jobs bill's passage was welcome, for it was a victory—even if tempered—in the midst of a painful, if mostly expected, loss in New York State's highest court on the *Brukhman* litigation. In *Brukhman*, the court upheld the city's successful earlier appeal of a ruling favorable to WEP workers. In 1997, NELP and other legal advocates scored an initial victory giving WEP workers the right to have their hours calculated by dividing their benefits' value by prevailing, rather than minimum, wages. This ruling was undone by the court of appeals, with additional dicta clarifying the court's position that workfare workers were "not employees" (see chapter 4 for an extended discussion).

It was into this context, shaped by the transitional jobs victory and the coalitional experience associated with it, that the COW research came to completion. I should reinforce that *everyone* in the opposition to WEP had claimed, even before WEP placements mushroomed to thirty-eight thousand in 1999, that WEP workers were displacing city employees. The City, too, had touted WEP's benefits to its overall workforce productivity, even though it implausibly denied displacement. It was not, therefore, that the COW project uncovered a new *idea*; it simply produced documentary evidence for an old one. Nevertheless, for CVH, the reason for holding a meeting with trusted allies like NELP to discuss preliminary findings was that the organizers wanted ideas on what to do with the data, that is, what kind of activity toward the object they should pursue.

Consider, again, the configuration of CVH's activity systems at the time. The internal activity of the COW project was set up to have as few contradictions as possible.[31] As with everything CVH does, however, the rule was that there had to be a good deal of member involvement and control.

The COW findings showed not only displacement but also that WEP workers were denied the training they sought, worked half- to full-time jobs for below-poverty-level compensation, and were a virtually limitless pool of cheap labor for the City. So in spite of the passage of the long sought-after transitional jobs legislation, CVH staff and members were faced with the fact that it was "on the books, we won it . . . but the mayor will never implement it because he doesn't have to because he has all these free workers."[32] There was, therefore, a glaring contradiction between the object of the Ad Hoc Coalition—which had been achieved—and the object of the Giuliani administration in maintaining WEP. Moreover, this stalemate added to the temporal ambiguity of the claim for real jobs that was already growing in the wake of Intro. 354-A's passage.

The illegality of the displacement found by the COW survey, however, struck the strongest chord with the NELP lawyer, who copied the section of the law, distributed it, and—in a small-scale amplification—used it as a tool to scaffold his community's acceptance of his solution, which was to call for WEP's abolition. The organizers' hesitancy can now be explained by two elements. First, the strong rules within CVH that mandate member power in decision making acted as a check on the organizer's immediate embrace of a new interpretation of the abolition claim. The strong ethos of member power had long created contradictions between internal rules and even a soft-coalitional community larger than CVH and made coalition work fraught. Second, we see in the lawyer's presentation of the law the trigger of a time shift. The degree of temporal specificity invested in the often mutually constructing claims for abolition and jobs was reversed. The claim for jobs had been given specificity through the transitional jobs bill, while the claim for abolition had a very vague temporal scope. With jobs now held up indefinitely, abolition took on more immediacy. Signs from a demonstration two years later, on the sixth anniversary of the federal welfare reform law (and on another significant anniversary as well), suggest the ways in which the slavery and abolition claims became wedded to specific programmatic goals.[33]

Other resolutions of the contradictions in CVH's activity systems—and their joint meeting in common activity with NELP—helped resituate the abolition claim from a symbolic tool with no particular temporal horizon to a concrete objective. I have already noted that the appearance of a new leadership group at DC 37 that was newly and openly critical of WEP was due to a scale shift in governance in the union's internal politics. The more-oppositional leadership suggested the availability of a community to support the abolition claim. This was particularly true since the claim was tied to the issue of displacement, and under Lee Saunders's administration, DC 37 had already filed several suits over the issue.[34]

Finding broad support among CVH members for an abolition campaign tied to COW, organizers expanded the campaign. Drawing on

Figure 6.8. Signs from a demonstration, CVH office

institutional spillover dynamics, it further specified the temporal parameters for abolition by linking the claim to electoral politics. Said the lead organizer in a July 2000 interview, "We're going for mayoral candidates; we want the next mayoral candidate to dismantle WEP." It was able to set these parameters in part because of the successful passage of the transitional jobs bill and the experience it gained—sometimes gritting its collective teeth—in working in coalition with other groups, including organized labor and ACORN. Frustrating as it was to be "doing the same thing" as everyone else in the hard-assembled Ad Hoc Coalition for Real Jobs, the experience changed CVH's standing among unions and other organizing groups. The CVH organizer noted that "a year ago, people would have been laughing at us."[35] Instead, by 2000, CVH's range of activity had expanded to the point that it could help set the agenda. In the summer of 2001, CVH and ACORN sponsored a mayoral candidates' forum in which abolition of WEP was among the demands. And well before that, by June 2000, DC 37 was making the same demand.

Broadening the Explanations

Clearly much has occurred with WEP since the summer of 2000. I have discussed some of the developments earlier and will do so again briefly in the next chapter. This chapter, so far, has emphasized that in order to understand the ways in which political actors understand the claims they and others make, it is not necessary to get into—or over—the "black box" of individual cognition (which is, in any case, a dead end). Instead, it is critical to take the actor's point of view and to situate it in the context of the actor's object-oriented, tool-mediated, and socially structured activity. It is then possible to understand the consistencies and contradictions in the systems within which, and toward which, they act. Further, it is necessary to understand these systems as a crystalline structure and not to pretend that the subject's activity occurs in a solipsistic vacuum. Indeed, the inclusion of communities and competing and conflicting activity systems in the model powerfully suggests dialogue and underscores the model's compatibility with the Bakhtinian framework outlined in chapter 4. Nevertheless, the still-unresolved question of the unit of analysis, raised at the beginning of the chapter, remains important to consider.

But Doesn't Individual Cognition Still Count?

The account of cognition I have given here does not negate the individual subject altogether. It simply refuses to make the individual the locus of all cognitive activity. While I have talked about CVH organizers, CVH members, and CVH staff in the plural, it is true that each has his or her activity systems, too. That is precisely the point. In their capacity as CVH staff, CVH staff members had, at least in the situation I have described, remarkably similar reactions. Even larger-scale subjects, like coalitions, may be the subjects in activity systems because collective activity toward an object generates contradictions within activity systems and poses cognitive problems as well. All of this affirms rather than negates subjectivity, for, as Stetsenko argues, "Human subjectivity appears as laden with practical relevance and agency—as existing only through its practical enactments in the sociohistorically developed forms of life and practice. For example, the most vivid creations of social practice (and of human subjectivity), such as language and art, appear as the products and carriers of practice, but only when reenacted (and reconstructed) in new rounds of ever expanding cycles of practice by real people in their real life."[36]

To say that the meaning of claims is a result of their use as tools, appearance as objects, and place in the rules of an activity system does not, of course, mean that claims have the same meaning to everyone or are internalized in the same ways. The point is not that the CVH staffers think the same thoughts; in fact, they may not. But they were acting in concert toward the same object in a fundamentally similar activity system, and they communicated an initial reaction of uncertainty.

Similarly, in a conversation in City Hall Park with two ACORN members in advance of a press conference announcing the introduction of the grievance procedure legislation in the spring of 1998, one member tied the grievance procedure to the taxi workers' strike that was on at the time. He then tied it to Nostradamus-like prophecies regarding the millennium. In our dialogue, the speaker was clearly using artifacts in his immediate surroundings in order to make sense of the grievance procedure. He got choral support when he tied the issue to workers' rights in general and to taxi workers' working conditions, but not when he expounded on the millennial importance of the bill. He also got choral support from his interlocutors when rhapsodizing about the hellfire and damnation that surely awaited Mayor Giuliani on Judgment Day. From a cognitive point of view, ACORN did not depend on complete consonance among all of its members to be a collective subject. Its activity systems could sustain some level of contradiction.

It was also clear that this member was not going to address either the press at the press conference or the crowd at the rally that followed. Accordingly, because collective subjects have activity systems that include communities and rules that certify them as collective subjects, it is important to understand, in general terms, at least, how these communities and rules operate. In the case of antipoverty organizations such as CVH, ACORN, FAC, and FUREE, organizers and other staff members, and occasionally member-leaders with accumulated experience, prepare members who testify in public hearings or give statements to the press in order to ensure that they stay "on message." A well-established and long-recognized practice in the courtroom setting, it is also of central importance in understanding the actual claims that are normally recorded in other venues of contention. There is, then, a strong collective dimension even to individual speech from the grass roots that enters into contentious dialogues.

This collective dimension is equally true of official speech, and perhaps more so. Another episode illustrates this point. In 1997, Reverend Peter Laarman, one of the key organizers of the Pledge of Resistance, and Lilliam Barrios-Paoli, the HRA commissioner at the time, engaged in a debate about WEP and the Pledge of Resistance in front of nonprofit social service providers convened by the Federation of Protestant Welfare Agencies. As the program wound down, the last question from the floor was from a welfare recipient. She began to talk about the difficulties she had in staying in school and raising her child because the caseworker kept insisting on sending her to WEP assignments that conflicted with her class schedule. How, she asked, through growing sobs, could Lilliam Barrios-Paoli defend the program when it was interfering with her plans to get *off* welfare? Barrios-Paoli agreed that this did not seem right and offered to get to the bottom of the problem, personally. Afterward, the commissioner pulled a card out of her purse, handed it to the welfare recipient, and told her to call.

Barrios-Paoli did not give the woman an ideological answer. She did not draw from the repertoire of claims preferred by Mayor Giuliani and his deputies. She confronted the contradiction between the rules of her agency and a member of the community she was trying to persuade by falling back on the practical tools of case advocacy. A social worker and longtime administrator of City programs, Barrios-Paoli ran HRA, but with no apparent zeal for welfare reform and NYC–WAY. Less than six months later, she was replaced by Jason Turner, who was far more capable of representing the administration as a collective subject.

Moving toward Synthesis

The theory and substance of this chapter are important to the larger synthesis I hope to draw in the book: By directly addressing the matter of cognition, I hope to head off the primary objection to studies in both the Marxist and the institutionalist traditions, namely, that their structural analyses crowd out cognition, affect, and acting subjects worth the name. The point is not to concede this objection: understanding the role of cognitive processes in political and social interaction should not begin with the "black box of mental life," as one scholar has called it[37]; nor should it begin with a strong, dualistic theoretical framework. Both require that the researcher come at the object of study freighted down with assumptions. If cognition is an individual process, methodological individualism is completely justified but already completely assumed. If cognition relies on the mapping of data onto a dualistic template, it scarcely matters whether this template is hardwired or culturally constructed. Whether it reproduces a sacred-profane dualism or, in terms proposed by the cognitive linguist George Lakoff to describe contemporary political discourse in the United States, a "nurturing family" or "strict father" morality,[38] the researcher is rather obliged to stuff the objects of cognition into these categories.

By contrast, CHAT allows us to come to the study of cognition without reifying the individual—against all our better sociological advice—as the exclusive locus of cognition. It also facilitates our understanding of the process without requiring that cognition be a one-way mapping of stimuli onto a predetermined framework that eases—or forces—pattern recognition.

This chapter builds on the foundations of the previous ones. After chapter 5, in which actors, claims, and contexts/objects came together and broke apart as genres and blocks, hard-assembled and soft-assembled coalitions, the important question was how to see the ways in which these centripetal and centrifugal dynamics were processed and set off by real actors. Based on actor-claim-context/object triads, the analysis has deep affinities with the Vygotskian approach in this chapter. Chapters 3 and 4 give the organizational history and institutional texture necessary for understanding how these dynamics play out in the activity systems described here. The language of mechanisms from chapter 5 then adds to CHAT a descriptive specificity that enables us to more fully realize CHAT's analytic potential. By bringing in such mechanisms as scale shift, time shift, institutional spillover, amplification, and certification, the investigations in this chapter enable a fuller description of the creation and resolution of contradictions *within* and *among* activity systems.

CHAT's approach, when embedded in larger network dynamics and institutional histories, reminds us that political cognition is neither a fully internal nor fully external process to the cogitating subject. The Vygotskian language of "internalization" does not deny that changes in internal mental states occur; it suggests, however, that they are not capricious and that when learning occurs, it does so in a scaffolded way, directed toward an object, and that both object and scaffold are constructed historically in ways that set limits around what can be learned.

At the same time, the structures that provide the scaffolding of cognition gain relevance for explaining the twists and turns of workfare politics only when they are related to its various actors' activity. There is no overarching structural logic that made FAC shift its claim-making to emphasize the potential-worker identity of WEP workers. Instead, it was FAC organizers and constituents' efforts to solve organizational problems that led to the change in emphasis as the settings within which they acted changed around them. Actors' activity also includes that of elite actors. Indeed, the institutional problems and contradictions that are endemic to states in general and to welfare states in particular—no matter the particular form they take—demand a turn back to political economy. To understand the general contradictions that produce workfare programs in their particular forms helps to locate the finer-grained decisions in the context of more-encompassing dynamics of governance. In order to complete the multilevel analytic synthesis that the preceding chapters have begun, I turn to these larger dynamics in the concluding chapter.

CHAPTER SEVEN

The Contested Language of Neoliberalism

A More Systematic Synthesis

In the 1970s and early 1980s, academic interest in Marxism spawned research programs across the social sciences that resulted in synthetic accounts of protest, class formation, and urban politics and set an ambitious agenda for further research. Part of the motivation for these works—Ira Katznelson's *City Trenches* is one good example—lay in their authors' hopes to understand the dynamics that made the radical challenges of the 1960s so vulnerable to counterattack in the 1970s. In the 1920s and 1930s, too, the work of Marxist-influenced writers both inside and outside the Soviet Union grappled both with the failure of revolutions outside Russia, even in ostensibly more "advanced" countries such as Germany, and with the onset of what would become the Soviet Union's defining sclerotic Stalinism. What both eras have in common is the meeting of Marxist ideas with other ambient analytic traditions: for the twenties and thirties, pragmatism, linguistic structuralism, Freudianism, and the idealist philosophies of G. W. F. Hegel, Benedetto Croce, and the neo-Kantians; for the seventies and eighties, broadly Durkheimian views of culture and Weberian and Michelsian analyses of the differentiation of state institutions and of organizational logics.

The 1990s and 2000s do not offer as clear a set of revolutionary impulses and reactions to frame an analysis of disappointments. By contrast, the emergence of anticorporate globalization protests from the middle of the 1990s through 2001 (and, to a lesser degree, beyond), vibrant antiwar mobilizations, however ineffective in the short term, both in the United States and abroad, and recent immigrant rights organizing, including a strong contingent based in worker centers, have been bright spots in an otherwise bleak period. Nevertheless, the 1990s and 2000s display the consolidation of the neoliberal program that was just beginning to come into being in the mid-1970s. The national welfare reforms of 1988 and 1996 showed the extent to which "the collapse of neo-Keynesian nostrums for managing the economy" identified by Katznelson at the end of *City Trenches* had become the negative basis for the foundation of new hegemonic repertoires of governance.[1]

Nevertheless, new hegemonic repertoires of governance have not been as easy to establish, as the old ones were vulnerable. The full withdrawal of government regulation and the use of executive power as a means of future accumulation—the neoliberal dream of "accumulation by dispossession"—have proven fairly difficult to implement without a fight. The fact that the collapses of corporate giants Enron and WorldCom in the wake of financial trickery were widely perceived as scandals that called out for stronger regulation and criminal punishment; the emergence of a large mobilization of immigrant workers; and the still-muted but increasing calls to protect civil liberties even amid the "war on terror" are all instances that suggest friction in the imposition of unaccountable executive power that is coterminous with the "flexibility" of neoliberal accumulation and legitimation strategies.

Workfare, especially its manifestation in New York City under a strong-mayor system and a bullheaded mayor, exemplifies the trends of neoliberal governance. The study of opposition to New York City's principal workfare program, the Work Experience Program (WEP), therefore, can shed light on the nascent dynamics of opposition to neoliberal hegemonies in other settings. It also provides the occasion for reworking our theories and methods for understanding these challenges in light of the consolidation of neoliberalism and in light of the strengths and limitations of recent scholarship.

In this reworking, both the insights of the 1970s and 1980s and those of the 1920s and 1930s are useful. Both eras occurred in the wake of transitions in both national and global modes of capitalist governance (at the eclipse and birth, respectively, of Fordist-Keynesian regulation). The theories and trajectories of investigation they produced combine into a powerful set of analytic tools to help us understand the current development of and challenges faced by opponents of neoliberal regulation today. Like the scholars of protest in the late 1970s and early 1980s, the series of investigations I have undertaken here emphasize the ways in which particular types of economic regulation and change help shape the options for welfare-state governance and for state actors' efforts to strike a balance—or at least an imbalance whose consequences they can outrun—between legitimation and accumulation. I have also stressed the importance of institutional legacies on the formation of protest. Katznelson's admonition against "an unreflective community politics in the 1980s" now appears as a prescient commentary on the frustration many neighborhood, antipoverty, and housing activists felt by the early 1990s as they realized the extent of their co-optation as junior managers of the ongoing social crises of the poor. This frustration, I have argued, led to efforts among some activists to look for new organizing "hooks" and new coalitions. In WEP, they found the potential for both.

Building on Earlier Syntheses

Yet while Katznelson's book, which initially inspired this one's attention to Gramsci's trench warfare analogy, aims "to marry a structural account of the urban crisis to the cultural inheritance of . . . American working class [formation]," it could not take advantage of more recent work on culture, cognition, and their constitution in and through institutionally situated social networks. His is an account that clearly shows that "the terms of [urban] movements . . . in different societies, whose working classes possess different selective traditions of class . . . cannot be derived directly from events" and that "such cognitive and motivating systems" are the products of longer-standing "*constitutive* element[s] of the relationship between structure, practice, and effect . . . [that] shape the making of history by providing guides to the recognition, interpretation, and categorization of experiences."[2] Yet, even as we can discern an incomplete reversion to separate politics of work and politics of welfare in New York City since 2001, we cannot understand the degrees, extent, or significance of the challenge to WEP on local governance unless we pay closer attention to what William Sewell has called the "eventfulness" of political interaction and to the claims that undergird attempts to legitimize or delegitimize the program. It is true that class formation and urban crises do not follow the same trajectories in different places, as if each were produced by a spatially indifferent capitalism. But to understand each case, it is important to track the shifts in claim-making alliances across the institutional contexts within them.

The earlier work of Gramsci, the Bakhtin circle, and Vygotsky and the work of their more recent interpreters provide tools for tracking these changes. Some tools can also be found in methods of analysis that share a deep kinship with their focus on coalitions and talk-mediated social relations among a variety of social and political actors. The difficulty here lies in two contradictory spots. In one lurks the danger of a mechanistic view of ideology in which workfare workers' expressed faith in the value of work, for example, is taken as evidence for their complete subordination to a logic of exploitation that is cleverly masked in the promise—increasingly unlikely—of upward mobility. In the other spot lives a pluralist vision of the polity in which workfare workers have a shot at influencing policy if only they can compromise and form coalitions with enough other actors and amass enough power. In this version, structural constraints on interaction virtually melt away.

The strengths of Gramscian, Bakhtinian, and Vygotskian understandings of the coalitional, object-oriented constitution of meaning is that coalitions and objects are at once situated in social times and spaces, which means, in turn, in historical relationships. Moreover, by understanding the ways in which each institutional setting and the history of the actors within them shape contentious interaction, the effects of the *results* of the increasingly neoliberal regulation of New York City's welfare state can be more easily discerned. Thus, the regulation and the institutional effects of WEP in chapter 2 *combine with* the formation of the "organizational substrates" of WEP politics in the crucible of the decade between the Great Society and the fiscal crisis, discussed in chapter 3, to shape the content of interaction within the institutional settings, or trenches, examined in chapter 4.

The Bakhtinian passage between pragmatism and structuralism—its insistence on the spatiotemporal shape of genre, formed through dialogue, and bolstered by choral support—contains the elements necessary to trace why, for example, organizing WEP workers around a "worker" identity was so difficult. It is not that WEP workers necessarily felt a greater allegiance to their ethnic or racial identities when addressing demands to the state. It is rather that the spatial dispersion of worksites, the frequent turnover and instability of WEP placements, and the business-unionism of DC 37, that is, District Council 37 of the American Federation of State, County, and Municipal Employees (AFSCME), made it difficult for WEP workers to sustain the unionlike organizations and gain the symbolic certification—the choral support—for their claims of "workerness." The very fact that community groups such as the Association of Community Organizations for Reform Now (ACORN), the Fifth Avenue Committee (FAC), and Community Voices Heard (CVH) identified commonalities across the trenches dividing welfare recipients and municipal employees as significant suggests that the trenches upon which the post-crisis neocorporatism relied had begun to crumble under the weight of a renewed neoliberal assault. Moreover, in spite of the difficulties, some success *was* evident in casting WEP workers as the equivalent of regular workers. The problem was that these successes did not occur across institutional contexts at anything like the same time.

Chapter 5 deepens the analysis of coalition formation across settings by bringing action in the settings into contact with one another and characterizing the interactions that ensue. Though cultural sociologists interested in applying network techniques to symbolic action may find elements of methodological interest, the key element in the chapter lies in the analytic sensibility behind the *blockmodels* I construct. There is a not-altogether-coincidental similarity in the language between blocks and "blocs" in this chapter. For Gramsci, the key to establishing hegemony was the formation of effective political blocs across institutional settings that could steer interactions in specific ways. Here, too, hard- and soft-assembled coalitions, constructed across institutional contexts, shape the centrality and strength of various claims at specific points in the debate over WEP. The mechanisms I describe characterize the action in light of the analyses presented earlier: *certification and decertification* provide or withdraw choral support from more-powerful actors to less-powerful actors' claims and are thus a key to the establishment and shaping of hegemony; *amplification* also lends choral support to claims but does so in ways that reduce its multivocality; *institutional spillover* increases the multivocality of actors and claims by drawing them—through *scale shifts* and *time shifts*—into contact with one another, interanimating them and thereby adding spatial and temporal dimensions to previously better-bounded claims.

The mechanisms-based approach, which emphasizes relational processes and is combined with the actor-claim-context/object triad as the basic unit of analysis in chapter 5, is given further elaboration in chapter 6. Here, the Gramsci-Bakhtin-Vygotsky connections become clearer *and* more analytically focused. Specifically, chapter 6 shows the ways in which coalitions, institutional contexts, and genres or repertoires both shape and are shaped through the object-oriented activity of political actors. It argues against framing theory's propensity to treat cognition in a decontextualized manner and suggests answers to questions both about why strategic and symbolic changes take place in contentious politics when they do and about how consciousness and cognition matter in political struggles.

What Is Gained?

During the 1980s and 1990s, the urgency of the synthetic Marxian projects of the 1970s subsided, and Marxism, with its attendant concerns for the intertwining of political economy, working-class formation, ideology, and political struggle, was gradually eclipsed in disciplinary sociology and political science in the United States by specialized research programs in welfare-state development, social movements, urban politics, and cultural studies. The result has been mixed. On the one hand, in all these fields, we have developed significant new perspectives and important applications of theory. For example, urban political economy and geography have developed a fruitful dialogue around regulation theory that elucidates the spatial consequences of emerging forms of neoliberal governance. Similarly, in social movement studies, Doug McAdam's early insistence on the importance of ideological factors in explaining movement emergence fed research programs in framing dynamics. These, in turn, have developed into more-nuanced considerations of the role played by symbolic action, such as in Francesca Polletta's more recent work on narratives' work in creating ambiguities that fostered solidarity in the civil rights movement, and in Marc Steinberg's systematic application of Bakhtinian theory to the genre-limited and genre-innovating dynamics of claim-making among English textile workers in the nineteenth century. McAdam, Tarrow, and Tilly's approach to identifying environmental, relational, and cognitive mechanisms, discussed in chapter 5, is also a reworking of longer-standing traditions in the subfield that identify political opportunities and shifting elite alliances, mobilizing networks, and framing dynamics as critical aspects in the explanation of movement emergence, effects, and decline.

On the other hand, fields that might otherwise appear ripe for mutual development frequently talk past each other. One easily can find studies, for example, on framing in social movements that attempt to gauge the success or failure of particular frames to produce a specific policy outcome that convey nothing about the complexity of the policy process as outlined in policy studies. One can find writing on urban political economy that says little to nothing about resistance to the imposition of new governance repertoires—even where such resistance exists—and thereby conveys the idea that the process is fairly automatic. Studies in cultural sociology still frequently treat subjects as if they were cultural dopes, without objectives and simply reacting to or assimilating cultural symbols that are arranged according to a fundamentally dualistic cognitive logic. Again, some of these studies can still yield valuable insights, but they are deeply limited by the disciplinary restriction of their field of vision.

In this study, I hope to have shown the utility of some of the more recent abstract formalizing projects in contentious politics, that is, those dealing with networks and mechanisms, in helping to think through the dialectics of structure and activity in the formation of claims, coalitions, and consciousness. I have sought to distinguish the nature of coalitions and their larger patterns across institutional settings. Doing so helps inform a perspective on political opportunities and strategy that redresses shortcomings in the usual mode of analysis. I emphasize the active elements in political opportunities and the structured elements in strategy, including the activity of dominant actors in the process of trying to establish hegemony. Doing this helps to provide crucial links between studies of movements and studies of policy domains and political regimes, the latter of which inform the study of public policy and urban politics, where studies of regime variation are common.[3]

Marrying the recent relational and configurational analyses of social movement culture—and culture more generally—with the study of coalitions and the temporal and spatial dimensions of settings yields a way of understanding the mechanisms-based approach to contentious politics to be relevant to culture and cognition and to the very understandings that activists bring to their work. In moving stepwise from the political economy of workfare and the effects of welfare reform policy on a variety of institutionally shaped problems such as child care, housing, and work thorough the historical development of the organization of anti-WEP politics, the problems of organizing within institutional trenches, the configuration of coalitions among the trenches, and the cognitive consequences on and recursive causes of strategic change, I hope to have constructed a synthetic research program that explains the mediations between the structures of political economy and the relations of contentious claim-making.

In the balance of the chapter, I want to address five issues that have important consequences for the strength of this synthesis. I will begin by addressing a pair of related questions of the soundness of the subtitular conceit, namely, that WEP workers "contested the language of neoliberalism." First, to what extent did anti-WEP politics contest neoliberalism? Second, what does it mean to contest its language?

Third, I will explore whether there is a relation between neoliberalism and the mechanisms of time shift, scale shift, institutional spillover, amplification, and certification to which I hitched a good deal of the analysis in chapters 5 and 6. Why *these* mechanisms and not others I could conceivably have thought up? The relationship between the mechanisms and neoliberalism is important for sewing together the loose threads in the approach I've taken here.

Fourth, I will outline some of the political developments around workfare in New York City since the period 1996–2001 most carefully scrutinized in the preceding chapters. Doing so will help shed light on the extent of the residue of reform left by anti-WEP politics since 1996.

Fifth, I will suggest a range of applications beyond WEP politics in which the kinds of joined analyses presented here might provide new and useful insights about the progress and challenges faced by movements for political and social change.

What's Neoliberalism Got to Do with It?

The reader who wants to know about the "contested language of neoliberalism" may have gotten to this point and wondered, "What's neoliberalism really got to do with this?" Neoliberalism, after all, is never the focus of any claims in the field of WEP. Rarely has anyone involved in the field mentioned the term in recorded public claims or in interviews. Unlike activists in the anticorporate globalization movement, most of WEP's opponents do not refer to neoliberal globalization, to neoliberalism, or even to the depredations of capitalism.

Neoliberalism as a Set of Genres, Not a Unified Ideology

Nevertheless, neoliberalism is not the elephant in the room that nobody talks about. Though anti-WEP activists rarely speak its name, it is not that it is a cleverly self-dissembling ideology that insidiously works its way into a baseline level of acceptance among those it is meant to subordinate. This is a cruder version of ideology and ideological domination than that which I hope to have conveyed here, even though some grains of truth may be found in it.[4] Instead, as I argued in chapter 2, neoliberalism is best understood as a *repertoire of governance*, characterized by a range of performances that form its core and a range of peripheral performances with which it is widely associated. In this sense, Abercrombie, Hill, and Turner's objection to many Marxist versions of ideological dominance makes some sense. They argued that the extent to which ideologies became dominant were an empirical rather than a theoretical matter and that in any case, dominant ideologies were often held in greater esteem by the *ruling* classes than by the subordinates supposedly in their thrall. Though the very concept of ideologies, rather than repertoires or sets of linked organizational and discursive genres, makes their critique less powerful,[5] their point that rulers instead of the ruled are more invested in them is on the mark. Moreover, drawing from Marx, they claim that much of what appears to be ideological domination is merely "the dull compulsion of the economic relations of everyday life."[6] Certainly, part of the difficulty in mobilizing a large movement of WEP workers—there was never a strike, and only rare job actions over relatively small points, in spite of fairly frequent talk about what a mass strike of WEP workers would look like—was that WEP workers were faced with the "brutal need" that required welfare benefits to continue to come into their household budgets. At the same time, neither this brutal need nor the dull compulsion of economic relations fully determined what kinds of claims could be made against workfare when they were. And it did not turn workfare workers into doltish automatons.

Another way of putting this is that far from being "dull," the economic relations of everyday life set important spatiotemporal parameters around organization, and in so doing, they help favor some kinds of claims over others, even while being susceptible to change. Though Abercrombie, Hill, and Turner were correct in pointing to the material determinants of ideological subordination, they misspecify their significance.

The larger point, however, is that it is a mistake to see neoliberalism as an imposed ideology, in the sense of a well-worked-out system of ideas. There is a degree, of course, in which this is the case; neoliberalism has a strong philosophical-economic grounding in the works of Milton Friedman, Friedrich von Hayek, Joseph Schumpeter, and lesser economists, such as Emmanuel Savas, long a guru of privatization. Yet, it would be a stretch to point to these writers' influence as having determined the spread of neoliberal policies from their initial experiments in Chile and New York to the International Monetary Fund, World Bank, and thence to domestic policies around the world. Instead, at best, these writers provided some intellectual justification for elites looking to reregulate the relations of capital and states in order both to reassert their class power, as David Harvey has argued,[7] and to give them more flexibility to preserve it in light of the rapidly changing spatiotemporal organization of production, consumption, and trade.[8] Enacted policies, narrated as models for diffusion and directed at regulating subordinate groups' ability to influence relations at the workplace and in politics (and often excluding them), became the essential core—the centripetally organized elements—of the genres of neoliberalism.

To be sure, many members of subordinate groups believe in the basic individualist tenets of neoliberalism, and they publicly moralize in ways consistent with neoliberalism's particular national and local manifestations. But many don't. Moreover, welfare reform, including workfare, can be seen to generate moral discourses and have regulatory effects far beyond the workplace and the narrow dimensions of the cash-assistance functions of the welfare state—for example, in racial and gender subordination and ethnic exclusion.[9] Further, these regulatory aspects often become transposed onto very different situations (prompting comparisons between excluded groups in different countries with very different histories and conditions of exclusion, where, for example, British Pakistanis and West Indians become the rhetorical stand-ins for African Americans). Yet the question remains whether these aspects are integral or peripheral to neoliberalism now and whether they will retain their status over the longer term.[10] Neoliberalism can coexist with tutelary and paternalistic welfare reforms as well as with libertarian criticism of those reforms; with education and training programs and rapid labor-market attachment programs; such coexistence suggests the extent to which it is a genre supported by, and held in place by, a coalition that is most concerned with the accumulation and distribution of social surplus, largely through the regulation of labor contracts and public finance.[11]

Neoliberalism and Urban Politics

If neoliberalism is not a single set of *ideas* but a genre of governance, the essential question is how it "treads down" in different settings. Since one part of the neoliberal genre is the scalar devolution of governance (however contradictory and complex this can be), the question is still more acute. Many scholars have observed that cities play an important role in this rescaling of capital and labor relations, particular cities (and their regions) like New York, which play both coordinating roles in serving the global economy and innovator roles in urban and social policy that are related to their global roles. In chapter 2, I made the case that workfare should be understood in the context of the reregulation of New York City's economy during its fiscal crisis in the early and mid-1970s. William Tabb's indictment of the regime of public austerity and investment in the finance, insurance, and real estate (FIRE) sector as "iatrogenic" presaged a local political economy that was, in many respects, in permanent crisis, essentially a monoculture vulnerable to exogenous shocks. A generation later, William Sites would understand the "disembedding of social relations" in the fiscal crisis as a precursor to gentrification that deepened this dynamic while generating both high rates of housing precariousness and exclusion, on the one hand, and deeply segmented service labor markets, on the other. Against this background, WEP *and* its opposition can be better understood.

As a spatially variegated phenomenon, however, neoliberalism does not produce the same results everywhere and for everyone. As Ness indicates, the growing presence of agribusiness and wage-based agriculture as a neoliberal development strategy in Central and South America, for example, feeds migration patterns to its cities and to cities in North America, where former agricultural laborers often seek employment as casual day laborers, or contingent service workers.[12] The presence of immigrant niches in contingent service work—for example, in New York, Francophone Africans in grocery delivery, Mexicans and Ecuadorans (replacing Dominicans) in kitchen staffs, West Indians and Filipinas in domestic work—may provide these workers with some greater ability for mobility among employers and to avoid the worst employment conditions on a long-term basis, as well as organizational ties away from the workplace that may facilitate joint labor-community activism. The larger point, however, is that in spite of its spatial variegation, neoliberalism as a governance genre that operates on multiple geographic scales relates places to one another, and it does so in ways that often create contradictions for the integral realization of hegemonic projects, which requires ruling coalitions to seek suboptimal, and less-stable hegemonies.

Nevertheless, as a genre—that is, as a set of practical *relationships* among actors, claims, and their settings of activity—and a hegemonic project operating at multiple geographic scales, neoliberalism can support policies and claims that are generated in places and times that bear only a superficial relationship to the problems they are meant to address in any *particular* place. The ability of neoliberal policymakers to "jump scale" from, for example, an increasingly unpopular program in New York to think tanks in Washington, D.C., from which they tout New York's successes as a model for national policy, and the global industry of welfare program consulting that has emerged in the context of U.S. welfare reform, reinforce what Schram called the increasing prevalence of "facts from nowhere" in welfare policy discourse.[13] It is precisely these "facts from nowhere," however, that feed contradictions in neoliberal policy, as when governors and mayors, who stand to lose a good deal of policy flexibility and money under the new round of welfare reform but who otherwise support neoliberal social policy, lobbied against the new work-enforcement mechanisms in the new law.

Workfare and New York City's Neoliberal Urban Politics

John Mollenkopf has claimed that New York City has often played the role of policy innovator, even when this role has belied its public image as politically liberal. From machine politics to the sometimes-regressive Progressive backlash against it, to the New Deal and Great Society programs, and finally, the neoliberal backlash against them, New York City has often been the battleground on which coalitions and projects later reproduced elsewhere have taken shape. Were it not for this role—and for its emblematic clarion call in the 1975 *Daily News* headline, "Ford to City: Drop Dead"—a focus on New York City might not be justifiable. Certainly, some might object that I have fallen into the trap parodied by Saul Steinberg's famous *New Yorker* cartoon from the same era, which shows the detailed world ending at Eleventh Avenue and the rest of the world fading into increasing vagueness across the Hudson River. Nevertheless, three things argue for this focus. First, there is the connection between workfare as a performance of *urban* policy that has repercussions for public finance, which, in turn, is clearly connected with the "primitive globalization" and reregulation of New York City's social democracy. Second, there is the persistence of a neoliberal coalition or, in terms familiar to urban political scientists, "urban regime" that has exerted strong governing and policy influence across mayoral administrations and which has largely supported the growth of workfare. Third, the focus on New York City's workfare politics, *especially* in light of its connections to national politics, trains a clearer lens on the ways in which welfare reform varies across urban sites. For example, Jason Turner was recruited from Wisconsin, where neoconservative claims for "family values" were far stronger than they were in New York as an adjunct to welfare reform.[14] Turner's charge, however, was not to promote marriage or responsible fatherhood but to enforce work discipline in a neoliberal way. Similarly, the genre of neoliberalism, and particularly the performance of for-profit privatization, ran into far greater contention in New York City than it did in Milwaukee. The ease with which it was achieved in Milwaukee stemmed in part from the Wisconsin legislature's anticipation of resistance from Milwaukee politicians. It deprived Milwaukee County—uniquely among Wisconsin counties—the ability to administer its own welfare and welfare-to-work program, keeping these decisions in the hands of the suburban and rural politicians who dominated the state legislature and occupied the governor's mansion.

In this sense, it is interesting, too, to consider contention over workfare politics as a test of the hold of neoliberalism on New York's urban regime. After all, through WEP, we can see the coalition's attempt to create a "Guantánamo of the labor force," a "state of exception" in which only those rights granted through administrative fiat—that is, no *rights* at all—would be granted to welfare recipients and by which the rights of all public employees would be eroded.[15] For when public officials propose to run government like a business, public-sector employment ceases to be seen as a vehicle for patronage (and the opportunities patronage provides) and becomes an object of discipline and public humiliation. To the extent that public workers can be shown to be no better than welfare recipients (by the simple fact that the latter are doing public workers' jobs), the impression can be given that public-sector workers are all, in some sense, on the dole. The resistance to WEP and the resilience of the neocorporatist arrangements that formed during the tendentially neoliberalizing transition between the fiscal crises of the 1970s and the late 1990s have dismantled neither WEP nor neoliberalism. They have, however, gone some distance in delegitimizing overt government hostility toward the poor and the promotion of austerity. This resistance and resilience can be seen both in increased pressure on the Bloomberg administration to invest in affordable housing and to change its policy on food stamps and in the increasing coordination among municipal workers' unions in presenting bargaining positions to the City.

Contesting the Language of Neoliberalism

What does it mean, then, to *contest the language of neoliberalism* through contesting local welfare policy? The key to the answer lies in the conception of language and meaning for which I have argued here. If language is understood as dialogic activity limited and shaped by genres and their relational settings, a collective enterprise linking organization, cognition, and signification in coalitions of meaning making and "choral support," *contesting* the language of neoliberalism is not a project of ideological debunking, whether from "traditional" or "organic" intellectuals, that is, from the ivory tower or the grass roots. Instead, contesting the language of neoliberalism is a practice of claim-making and coalition building that is organized on multiple geographic scales and across institutional settings. In this trench warfare—fought necessarily in and across settings—the terms within which objects of neoliberalism are defined are shaped and reshaped in the midst of contending and shifting hegemonic projects.

Workfare as a Context and an Object of Activity amid Neoliberal Governance

The distinctiveness of understanding neoliberalism as a genre or repertoire of governance rather than an imposed ideology lies in its calling analytic attention to neoliberal policy in practice and in understanding neoliberal politics as both a context for and object of contentious claim-making. As an emblematic and integral performance of the neoliberal governance repertoire, workfare also constitutes a context/object or field of political activity within which other contexts/objects of activity are nested.

Again, we can draw a link between the basic dialectics of regulation theory, in which each new mode of regulation generates contradictions that lead to new crises of accumulation or legitimation, and the dialectics of Cultural Historical Activity Theory (CHAT), in which contradictions open possibilities for cognitive expansion, but neither determine the precise outcomes or mechanisms of this expansion nor are necessarily resolved in the first place. The key to both is that they are driven by subjective activity toward objects. Neoliberal governing coalitions act toward and on the object of state and social institutions, including welfare programs, social services, and labor markets. They do so in ways that seek to maintain their flexibility and to limit the ability of probable opponents to respond effectively.

That workfare policy is a tool in this larger picture of a neoliberal system does not negate its appearance as both a context and an object of other activity. As I argued in chapter 6, workfare is as much a context as an object of claim-makers' activity. Within the context of workfare, however, are numerous other contexts that are both larger and smaller in scope, including education and training policy, job creation policy, childcare policy, labor relations, and so on. In addition, there are the relational settings defined by particular institutional contexts and objects, such as worksite organizing, moral protest and media politics, litigation, and legislative strategies. Accordingly, it is important to understand that as a key performance in a repertoire of governance, and as a context/object of claim-making, workfare does not simply get imposed but is constantly reshaped through contention and compromise in the activities of the collective subjects it engages.

In the Trenches

Workfare is not contested on a level field. The very properties of the workfare assignment, as I argued in chapter 2, make difficult the organization of workfare workers into groups that would conform to central tendencies in the organizational and discursive genres of labor organizing. High turnover, fear of arbitrary discipline, and perceived risks of sanction make workfare a clear training ground for much contingent, secondary labor-market work but also reproduce those features of these labor markets—and of non-labor-market, compelled work—that impede workers' power.

The moral protest against WEP—exemplified by the Pledge of Resistance campaign—exposed the diversity of moral opinion about the program and the degree to which shallow justifications of the mere compulsion to work held only tenuous sway, appealing primarily to the "revanchist" politics characterizing a part of Mayor Giuliani's coalition. Nevertheless, it also exposed, and ran aground on, the programmatic flexibility that federal welfare reform afforded to governments that reduced their welfare rolls rapidly.

Legislative action in the New York City Council did not fare well against elements of the welfare reform program New York City–Work, Accountability, and You (NYC–WAY). The Transitional Employment Program (TEP) and the Coalition for Access to Training and Education (CATE) bills collided with the division of powers under the city charter, a division that makes for a very strong mayor and a weak council, a partial legacy of Progressive Era thinking about redistribution and patronage but also a way of limiting public input into the policy process enacted in 1989 in the wake of a court-mandated charter revision process. Nevertheless, the deliberate pace of legislative activity enabled anti-WEP groups—organizers and advocates alike—to develop long-standing working relationships, which "softened" over time. Moreover, both campaigns pressured the Giuliani and Bloomberg administrations to take the issues more seriously, resulting in the Parks Opportunity Program (POP) under Giuliani and the *Davila* settlement and loosening of education restrictions for single welfare-reliant adults under Bloomberg.[16]

Litigation related to WEP confronted the essential lawlessness at the core of the program but was only partially successful in reining it in.

Though only in dissent, a federal appeals court judge who ruled on the sexual harassment case complained bitterly that the only result of the majority's ruling that workfare workers were enough like employees to merit protection would be a reduction in the flexibility needed to run a welfare work program. In general, the jurisprudence on workfare remains highly contradictory, with workfare workers having gained some rights as, but not the full status of, employees. Thus, as in the *Capers* decision, the granting of rights to a grievance process designed for municipal employees made it impossible for WEP workers—who were not defined as employees and could not join public employee unions—to gain *actual* grievance rights or relief. Moreover, on a practical level, the temporal rules of the legal setting, combined with the strong executive powers in the New York City charter and state law, mean that judgments, even when in favor of WEP workers, could take years to appeal, settle, and implement.

Among the Trenches

One of the important conclusions of the analysis of the press on workfare in chapter 5 is that the Giuliani administration *never* enjoyed an integral hegemony. In other words, in spite of the general popularity of workfare, there was never a situation in which the program enjoyed unanimity of support or when the administration could set the entire terms of debate over the issue. There are other ways of thinking about this conclusion that give the flavor, though not the analytic depth, of what it means in practice. One way is to consider a "man in the street" who hears about workfare and whose first reaction is, "Isn't it good that they're working instead of sitting at home?" Or, "Why shouldn't they work if I'm working and paying taxes?" In an integral hegemony, it would be nearly impossible to counter this initial positive response. Under decadent or minimal hegemonic conditions, it would be possible to counter these responses by indicating that WEP workers' placement in city agencies hurt "regular" workers' bargaining power for decent jobs and benefits; that these workers are the core of what's left of New York's middle class; and that welfare recipients who go through workfare are no better off—and frequently materially worse off—than they were before; and that the "hassle" through which they are put can plausibly be said to have increased hunger and homelessness and the corresponding governmental and social costs. In a decadent or minimal hegemony, however, the WEP critic does not have a good answer to "So, what's the solution?"

Another way of thinking about the Giuliani administration's failure to establish an integral hegemony is to recognize that the disorganization of opposition, both to WEP and to neoliberalism, is not, and perhaps cannot be, complete. This is true even if some of the opposition is in some senses conservative. For example, an argument can be made that the emphasis that activists ranging from CVH to the Welfare Rights Initiative (WRI) put on education and training was essentially a recapitulation of a human capital argument, one fully consistent with neoliberalism's emphasis on individual value in the labor market. It might be an example of a cruder version of hegemony's view that *even opposition* has to be framed in terms consistent with the dominant ideology.

I think that adopting a less-nuanced version of hegemony would miss two important things about the debates over WEP in particular and about the contested language of neoliberalism in general. First, whatever else it does, neoliberal urban policy enforces austerity on the poor and on workers. The segmentation of labor markets in general and the role of workfare in training welfare recipients for contingent work mean that social "investment in human capital" is unlikely. This should be especially true in a city like New York, where the leading sectors of the economy can recruit from a regional, national, and even global labor pool for skilled, primary labor-market work. Second, in this light, the discourse of human capital can be a critique of neoliberalism and the politics of exclusion. By arguing for education and training against a recalcitrant administration, antipoverty advocates and activists highlighted the tension between the official line that decries dependency and praises competitiveness and the policies that redefine education and training activities as shirking and abet the segmentation of labor markets and the erosion of wages and job security.[17] Similarly, campaigns for decent working conditions at WEP worksites highlighted the contradiction between the Giuliani administration's claims that work promoted dignity and the degraded conditions under which many WEP workers had to toil. People cared about gloves, but the claims were not *about* gloves.

The issue, then, is not whether a particular claim or set of claims is consistent with the overall philosophical underpinnings of neoliberalism—anti-WEP activists no more need to be Marx than bond raters need to be von Hayek—but instead whether or not the claim or claims help form soft- or hard-assembled coalitions in and across settings in a field and do so in a way that advances the possibilities for action. In this light, the Welfare Rights Initiative's claims for education and training were *not* fully individualizing but were also made alongside claims about the importance of carework, gender inequality, and maintaining families. It was not *simply* speaking in the language of human capital theory but interanimating it with other claims. The question for analysis, therefore, is whether this interanimation drew WRI and its claims any closer to the core of the field or whether these other inflections remained fragmented, with other claims underpinning the coalitions most associated with the context/object or setting of education and training.[18]

The Giuliani administration found its hegemony over the workfare debate challenged at several junctures but was able to recover some form of dominance. One key to this outcome is that the administration could take advantage of neoliberal networks organized across institutions and geographical scales. Furthermore, Giuliani's position as a strong executive gave his administration the ability to switch subjects almost at will. This flexibility allowed the administration to maintain a minimal hegemony, in effect, by digging new trenches anytime it was threatened. In this regard, it bears a deep affinity with the flexible accumulation strategies to which the neoliberal mode of regulation is joined. Flexible accumulation is more than flexible production, that is, the post-Fordist arrangement of production in short product runs and with the corresponding ability of capital and labor to retool. It is, instead, the ability of capitalists to switch between relative and absolute strategies of accumulation. The former refers to strategies that reduce the cost of reproducing labor, while the latter refers to strategies of driving labor to produce more, faster, or to work longer hours. Neoliberal globalization has produced this flexibility by giving capitalists and states the ability to import cheap labor, export production, and raise consumption levels in industrialized countries such as the United States in spite of falling real wages.

Through the Trenches: Neoliberalism and Mechanisms of Change

The affinity between flexible accumulation and flexible hegemonizing strategies suggests a further effect of neoliberalism on the unfolding mechanisms in the field of workfare among the institutional and relational settings and contexts/objects of policy. Time shift and scale shift, institutional spillover, amplification, and certification and decertification are also made available in ways specific to neoliberal regulation and are enacted as part of this regulation. Recall that regulation theorists explicitly consider modes of regulation to be governance repertoires by which state and private actors seek to fix crises of accumulation and of legitimation. The neoliberal solution effectively counts on being able to solve accumulation crises by becoming decreasingly accountable to organized constituencies other than organized business interests.[19] This decrease in accountability, however, leads to problems for neoliberalism too, as its base of support is weakened by its inability to integrally incorporate organized constituencies, such as organized labor, as Keynesian regulation did in the post–World War II period through the 1970s. Instead, neoliberal governance involves significant time and scale shifting, resulting in the fracture and disorganization of the organized constituencies for the Keynesian welfare state. Some of the dominance of neoliberalism also has been accomplished through an alliance with conservative religious organizations and political forces with little use for the principles of neoliberal governance itself.[20] As a result, though a conservative, moralistic discourse underwrites much of neoliberal social welfare policy, as the Pledge of Resistance showed, this discourse is relatively easily challenged depending on the extent to which the moralistic element is part of a local hegemonic bloc.

Time Shift

The time-shifting attack on collectivities that neoliberal governance promotes can be seen in the expansion of contingent, turnover-pool jobs, as well as increased turnover in public services. People who cycle through an endless string of jobs cannot develop long-term commitments to the workplace, but neither can they develop long-term, common claims on their employers. Similarly, New York City's governance of its prison and homeless-shelter systems under Mayor Giuliani was geared toward shortening lengths of stays. While such a shortening might seem counterintuitive with respect to the prison system, the idea was that in the criminal justice system, generally, the cost of incarceration increases with length of stay, while short prison stays—even as short as two days—can be used to punish misdemeanant arrestees *before* trial and therefore to intimidate would-be criminals and cut crime on the front end of the system. In homeless shelters, cutting length of stay and increasing turnover does not necessarily mean finding or creating housing for homeless people faster. It means increasing eligibility restrictions that decrease the legal pressure on the city to confront its chronic low-income housing crisis.[21] Finally, another example of neoliberal time shifting can be seen in the practice of paying for raises for current employees by lowering the salary levels of entry-level workers in collective bargaining agreements. This practice, which exacerbates internal salary tiers within a workforce, also undermines the union leaders who succumb to pressure to accept these terms, a fact that is lost neither on the leaders nor on the employers.

Scale Shift

The scale shifting that is an essential feature of neoliberal governance tends toward devolution and decentralization, but it does so as a matter of strategy rather than of principle. By pushing program administration to the state and local levels (to the extent that they are not deeply shaped by federal incentive structures), neoliberals claim that they can make programs more responsive to local needs. As with welfare reform, devolution also brings with it several attractive by-products from a neoliberal standpoint. First, devolution of federal programs invites collective action problems, as each state and/or locality tries to save money in order to produce a "better business climate" free of taxes and social burdens. Thus, devolution promotes a race to the bottom in social assistance. Second, devolution of program administration in welfare exacerbates the problems with a system that had already produced fifty separate welfare policies (and more, if one takes local administration into account). This means that collective action around welfare policy takes on different institutionally inflected demands, which, in turn, makes the coordination of hard-assembled, national coalitions around welfare policy very difficult. Third, deepening the differences among the various welfare programs makes program evaluation and comparison difficult, since apples are always being compared with oranges, grapes, bananas, and durians. Thus, it becomes increasingly difficult to hold any and all programs accountable for reaching their goals (or the goal of poverty reduction). This scenario empowers the shrewdest policy entrepreneurs in search of national reputations and consultancies, rather than the front-line staff and clients.

Devolution and decentralization also create hidden vulnerabilities for neoliberal governance. The problem lies in that the policy networks that push neoliberal solutions are centered in several conservative policy institutes and foundations. At the local level, however, there remain enough competing electoral demands and demands for social redistribution—however inchoate they may be—that centrally promulgated or disseminated neoliberal programs do not maintain their constituencies if they do not have ample time to leave a secure policy network supporting them in place. Changes during the Bloomberg administration in the governance of workfare suggest that such is the case. When Mayor Bloomberg declined to hire the scandal-tainted Jason Turner as his commissioner of the Human Resources Administration (HRA), Turner and several of his assistants sought employment elsewhere. Turner installed himself at the conservative Heritage Foundation in Washington, D.C., where he promoted the "New York Model" as a prototype for national reform. In particular, he promoted the work-first credo and the idea that all welfare recipients should be engaged in some form of work activity or compulsory treatment. Though New York City's welfare and workfare policies retain many features of the Turner-era programs, the Bloomberg administration has allowed—and has been pushed by advocates and the courts—to provide more opportunities for education and training. It also advocated *against* requiring more hours of work-activity participation from welfare recipients, a centerpiece of the Turner-endorsed model, ostensibly based on New York's "successes." Like other state and local officials, the Bloomberg administration has noted that these requirements increase the cost to and administrative burden on state and local governments. Thus—as with Medicaid reform and other programs whose cost is shared between federal and state governments—the shifting of burdens to state and local officials, based on their supposed superior responsiveness to local needs, threatens to undermine neoliberal policy coalitions' scalar strategies.[22]

Institutional Spillover

Like any other governance repertoire, the neoliberal mode of regulation is applied in multiple institutions. Because of this, institutional spillover is a given; the question is only *how* it manifests itself and *when*. The application or imitation of market mechanisms and privatization, for example, is applied widely as a principal feature of neoliberal governance. As suggested by the discussion in chapter 6 of the crystalline structure of activity systems, the use of common tools among activity systems may induce institutional spillover. Consider another case: There is a strong argument to be made that the spread of term limits among state and local politicians in the early 1990s (implemented for the mayor and city council in 1993, the year of Mayor Giuliani's election) is an extension of the time-shifting short termism of neoliberal governance. One result was that the city council speaker, Peter Vallone Sr., sought to continue his political career in the governor's mansion in Albany. As noted in chapter 5, Vallone's gubernatorial bid provided ACORN the lever it needed (in conjunction with the Working Families Party, or WFP) to get the full city council to consider the languishing transitional jobs and grievance procedure bills.

Institutional spillover associated with neoliberal regulation also affects the recombination of constituencies, both for government programs and for nongovernmental organizations. As such, institutional spillover is both an effect of and a potential threat to neoliberal regulation. Again, consider the neocorporatist privatization of New York City's social welfare apparatus in the wake of the fiscal crisis. Recall, from chapter 3, that tenants' rights groups and other housing activists became increasingly involved in housing management and development, particularly during the Koch administration's housing initiative beginning in the mid-1980s and principally through the disposition of tax-repossessed property. Through this work, community-based organizations gained income and access to policymaking and succeeded in alleviating some of the worst of the housing crisis. Nevertheless, these groups also faced an increasing crisis of legitimacy among their constituents. Accordingly, some groups sought to regain (or retain) legitimacy through more-oppositional organizing, particularly as the Giuliani administration threatened the compromises they had reached with previous administrations. In anti-WEP organizing, we see the ways in which institutional spillover induced by neoliberal reregulation helped organize a constituency to fight against other aspects of the regulatory program.

Amplification

Amplification is the process of reducing the multivocality of a claim while giving it greater institutional impact. The relational nature of mechanisms suggests that in order for a claim A to be amplified—that is, clarified—it has to be more distinct with respect to other claims, B, C, and D. In other words, if all claims are amplified at the same rate at once, there is no relative amplification for claim A. The combination of this property of amplification and the spatial and temporal strategies of neoliberal governance create a selection process that privileges claims made by actors with stable access to central institutions. Consider the way in which the Pledge of Resistance amplified labor rights claims, even as it relocated them into a more moralistic discourse about WEP. The labor rights claims had already gained some measure of multivocality, as public discussions of labor politics were prominent during the initial phases of NYC–WAY. Nevertheless, criticism of WEP was pulled in multiple directions because DC 37 had little political commitment to fight WEP and because of the difficulties in worksite organizing facing the activist groups (not the least of which was DC 37's reluctance to fight city hall). Though it faced difficulties in recruiting some of the major charities in New York City, such as Catholic Charities, the Pledge of Resistance campaign amplified labor rights claims because it had the time, resources, and space to organize advocacy and religious organizations. Religious organizations, in particular, are relatively insulated from the organizational difficulties neoliberal governance imposes on poor people's organizing groups and unions. The major expansion of WEP into the nonprofit sector had not yet occurred, and therefore, the pledge campaign had some time to enter into extended deliberations with nonprofits and religious organizations to clarify their position and to wed their moral objections to existing criticisms of WEP. That the pledge campaign—and the moralistic objections to WEP it pushed—fell out of the news and substantially out of positions of prominence in the debate is partly a result of its success. In focusing labor rights claims on the issue of WEP's nonprofit expansion, however, the pledge concentrated oppositional energy on a single "trench" while the mayor's office opened up new fronts, particularly in the area of applications for benefits, well away from labor issues.

Certification

The account of amplification relates easily to the ways in which certification works within the context of neoliberalism. Some claims, and some actors, are certified as authoritative within given institutional settings, whereas some are not. As a result, there are also claims that become certified across settings and those that are confined within one or several. If hegemonic claims are, by definition, claims that are certified across many institutional settings, then fragmented and pluralist claims are ones tending to have little institutional traction. Good examples of fragmented claims would be those most associated with the feminist critique of workfare, that is, that it does not recognize the work done inside the home, caring for family or other dependents as *work*, and that this work usually falls to women. By counting only work outside the home or for explicitly exchanged remuneration as work, workfare doubly burdens women who have the fewest resources with which to manage their time. Hence, a broader hegemonic certification process unfolded even amid the most pointed opposition to WEP, in which worksite organizing that sought to portray WEP workers as *workers*, and so to ally with unions, elided the carework in which most welfare recipients are engaged. Thus, in engaging the claim that WEP workers were "unfree" labor, organizers relied on a model of free labor beholden to a model of labor markets that also elides carework.

To be sure, several groups made claims consistent with the feminist critique. The Welfare Rights Initiative at Hunter College was the group most clearly making this claim, likely because the group was based in an academic institution, rooted in a program of study, and advised by a feminist historian of the welfare state. Nevertheless, it won little choral support outside of the academy.[23] WRI won its main victories and gained its greatest power when fighting for changes in state welfare laws to allow for education-based and training-based exceptions to WEP requirements, such as allowing college students to fulfill their WEP requirements on campus; to have WEP assignments adjusted to fit class schedules; and finally, to enable work-study and internship jobs to count toward work requirements. To be sure, the last of these changes challenges the dominant definition of the "work-cash nexus" by acknowledging the time constraints on mothers in school and the idea that work-study and internships should not count toward work requirements because they are part of an already-existing exchange (i.e., work for financial aid, work for training). As successful as both campaigns were, however, they did not challenge the greater market-based idea of work. Moreover, as noted earlier, they fed this idea in other ways by focusing on the enhancement of "human capital" that education provides, arguing that education ultimately reduces government expenditure by keeping welfare recipients off the rolls and in the labor market, providing a higher value return to employers than an uneducated worker.[24]

There is therefore no single selection process typical of neoliberal governance that certifies contentious political claims of one sort and not another. "Contesting the language of neoliberalism" depends on the ways in which governing and oppositional coalitions are configured and how these configurations work dialectically with coalitional action within and upon settings to secure more or less stable sets of claims. Gramsci argued that the bourgeoisie's hegemony could not be an integral one because "no longer is it capable of representing, or furthering, everyone's economic interest. Neither is it capable of commanding unequivocal allegiance from the non-elite: 'as soon as the dominant group has exhausted its function, the ideological bloc tends to decay.'"[25] Even if we step back from the functionalist aspects of Gramsci's formulation, the observations in chapter 5 suggest the same. The ways in which neoliberal governance works with and through mechanisms, with organizational, cultural, and cognitive consequences, however, reinforce this but also help create decadent hegemonies (through *trasformismo* or co-optation) and minimal hegemonies (through a fevered flexibility). The conclusion, then, reinforces a larger point by students of neoliberal governance who understand the repertoire as having integrated the crisis of legitimation and accumulation of the 1970s and put the state in a long-term crisis, in which the gutting of the redistributive functions of the Keynesian welfare state is used as proof of their general obsolescence.

Political Transitions and Their Significance

The Difference a Mayor Makes

The transition from the Giuliani administration to the Bloomberg administration in New York City resulted in changes in but not in a redirection of larger policy styles. The total simplification of the graph in the last period in chapter 5's analysis suggests as much, even if the graph is partly an artifact of few data points. Thought of in another way, the paucity of articles on workfare under Bloomberg shows the extent to which others of Bloomberg's projects eclipsed it in the public eye.

There were substantive differences, too. Mayor Bloomberg worked far harder than his predecessor did to broaden his base of political support, in part because it was clear that only the combination of Democratic Party squabbling, Bloomberg's personal fortune, and Giuliani's endorsement in the wake of his own political rebirth following September 11 allowed Bloomberg to eke out an electoral victory in 2001. Moreover, Bloomberg only ran as a Republican because he had no political history with the Democratic Party and could not rise to the top of a crowded field of candidates. The weakness of the city's Republican Party, however, allowed Bloomberg to be its candidate with little opposition, although he has many political differences with Republicans.

Bloomberg's greater nonpartisan stance shows results in welfare policy by a greater openness to education and training and to dialogue with advocacy groups. CVH and ACORN, for example, had two representatives on a client advisory committee set up by Commissioner Verna Eggleston of HRA. Although Bloomberg vetoed the city council's Access to Training and Education bill, which would have allowed welfare recipients to count education and training activities toward work requirements, he settled the long-standing *Davila* litigation (initiated in 1996), which requires case-workers to inform welfare recipients of education and training options open to them. Further, WEP has been scaled back significantly under Bloomberg, and most people on welfare work for City agencies for fewer hours than they did under Giuliani. Most are on a so-called three-plus-two schedule, in which they work for three days a week and are engaged in education, treatment, training, or job search programs for two.

The Difference a Mayor Doesn't Make

This new program configuration cannot be credited solely to Mayor Bloomberg's gentler and more ecumenical approach to city government. Instead, several important factors figure into this change. First, as New York's welfare rolls declined, so did the supply of potential WEP workers. Therefore, the City had to figure out new ways to supplement the workforce in departments such as Parks and Recreation that had become reliant on WEP workers' labor.[26] The city's need to seek out alternative sources of labor was exacerbated by union- and advocate-initiated lawsuits on displacement, sexual harassment, and education and training. These suits resulted in obstacles to implementing WEP as it had been in the past. DC 37's lawsuits claiming displacement were unsuccessful on procedural grounds because the City argued successfully that the union had agreed to let WEP workers do the work they were doing years earlier, and procedurally, the court could not let the union sue over a procedure that had been in place for years. There was a strong implication, however, that any expansion of WEP in municipal worksites might have to be approved by a now reluctant union. The lawsuit brought by the federal Equal Employment Opportunities Commission (EEOC) and initiated in 1999 by NOW–LDEF (an offshoot of the National Organization of Women founded in 1970 as the NOW Legal Defense and Education Fund; now called Legal Momentum) claimed that the City was obliged to protect WEP workers from sexual harassment. The federal appeals court's rejection of the City's argument that equal employment law did not apply to WEP workers because they were not "employed" reduced the flexibility with which the WEP labor contract could be implemented across the board. In addition, the settlement in the *Davila* lawsuit impeded the City from using the thirty-five-hour WEP model without regard to the education and training needs of welfare recipients.

Nevertheless, even as Mayor Bloomberg has worked to increase his own legitimacy as a state actor (even going so far as to distribute his private fortune strategically to nonprofit organizations),[27] he has adopted a tough stance in collective bargaining and has cited the City's chronic fiscal problems and inability to raise taxes without State approval as part of the reason for his austere posture vis-à-vis the City workforce.[28] The Bloomberg administration once again took advantage of the disarray in DC 37 to negotiate a contract that, though widely—and honestly— ratified by the union rank and file, was decried both within the union and across the city's labor movement as a disastrous one for workers. A second negotiated settlement in 2006 was more generous, but it did not make up for the concessions given by the union in the earlier deal. In an earlier round of negotiations, Bloomberg simply discontinued union representation of workers in the Parks Opportunity Program (POP)—the transitional, seasonal job program implemented by Giuliani in 2001 in the wake of the city council's override of his veto of the transitional jobs bill—rather than agree to lower-than-demanded wage concessions.[29] The fundamental framework of WEP, therefore, remains in place. It is just less widely applied than it was under Giuliani.

WEP remains as a viable, though degraded, labor contract in the armamentarium of municipal governance. Should welfare rolls rise, or should the changes in the work requirements of those remaining on welfare under the welfare reform bill passed by Congress in early 2006 mandate changes in the City's welfare program, one might expect the numbers in WEP to expand once again. For Mayor Bloomberg, unlike for Mayor Giuliani, workfare has been a peripheral concern. Mayor Bloomberg has sought to make his mark upon the city with high-profile development projects and alliances with real estate concerns, rather than with social-policy initiatives. In spite of this difference, however, the preservation of the fundamentals of the Giuliani-era status quo with respect to WEP, and especially Bloomberg's hard-bargaining, anti-Keynesian stance toward municipal labor, suggest a deep—if more emotionally forgiving— embrace of neoliberal governance.

Beyond Workfare

This book's close focus on New York City's workfare politics should not subtract from the larger project at its core. In search of a more systematic synthesis of the environmental, relational, and cognitive mechanisms through which political contention occurs, it reaches into recent work on social movements, culture, urban political economy, and cognition and back to this work's bases in the works of Gramsci, Bakhtin, Vološinov, and Vygotsky. The point is to reproduce a mode of social analysis that, though driven by an explicit political project, yields analytic insights that can apply more widely than to the politics of the case at hand. More than one author has been frustrated at what can sometimes be a desiccated formalism at the heart of this subdiscipline. Nevertheless, I hope to have shown the utility of some of the more recent abstract formalizing projects in contentious politics, that is, those dealing with networks and mechanisms, in helping to think through the dialectics of structure and activity in the formation of claims, coalitions, and consciousness. Distinguishing the nature of coalitions and their larger patterns across institutional settings helps inform a perspective on political opportunities and strategy that redresses shortcomings in the usual mode of analysis. It emphasizes the active elements in political opportunities and the structured elements in strategy, including the activity of dominant actors in the process of trying to establish hegemony. At the same time, it provides crucial links between studies of movements and studies of policy domains and political regimes, in the study of both public policy and urban politics, where studies of regime variation are common.[30] Moreover, marrying the recent relational and configurational analyses of social movement culture—and culture more generally—with the study of coalitions and the temporal and spatial dimensions of settings yields a way of understanding the mechanisms-based approach to contentious politics to be relevant to culture and cognition and to the very understandings that activists bring to their work.

The genesis of the subfield of social movement studies lies in the dissatisfaction of academics with experience in and sympathy with the civil rights, student, and antiwar movements of the 1960s with then reigning explanations of mass action from below as irrational and dangerous. This dissatisfaction was fed, too, by a conviction that the study of social movements would yield insights into the dynamics of political inequality. The partisanship of this raison d'être is worth recapturing. As the study of WEP-related politics shows, however, it cannot be done without identifying the larger political agendas out of which WEP grew and without explaining neoliberalism's local manifestations.

For students of urban movements—a subfield mainly identified with European scholarship—the recent move toward understanding movements of the "excluded" is a welcome step in this direction. The larger significance of evidence of institutional spillover—where, for example, neighborhood-based housing groups turned into labor organizers— suggests that the lines between labor and community, between "spaces" of capital accumulation and "places" of urban life, are blurred by the very flexibility of neoliberal governance.

A kindred point is made by students of labor-community coalitions, as where Ruth Needleman writes, "Because of the contexts of their lives, there is no way to remedy the needs of low-wage women as workers without also addressing their needs as mothers, heads of households, wives, or children."[31] Moreover, the burgeoning work on organizing immigrant workers within this larger literature makes explicit the ties between neoliberal strategies of accumulation at multiple scales and the prospects for organizing within and across these scales. The methods and theoretical perspectives I have applied to anti-WEP politics in New York City might usefully be applied in this area, too. With the recent efflorescence of immigrant activism and its presence on multiple scales of governance and in multiple institutions, it is important to understand the ways in which activists are fighting—or could fight—the wars of position that are taking shape.

Applications of the framework I have outlined in this book need not be limited to the questions of urban class formation and movements. Clearly, I cannot suggest all the possibilities for the synthesis I propose here, and most applications are far, far beyond my areas of expertise. Given the reach of neoliberal governance repertoires, with their boundary-blurring claims and temporal and scalar shifting away from accountability, the framework should be able to shed light on subject-defining claim-making in contexts as vastly different as homelessness, terrorism and resistance, domestic work, and the "employee" status of middle managers. In the final section, I turn again, however, to workfare, and summarize the lessons that may be gleaned from the substantive analyses presented in this book.

Workfare and the War of Position

The fight against workfare that unfolded in New York City during the administration of Mayor Rudolph Giuliani made for poor drama. Though there were a few dramatic moments, the fight subsided without a clear climax or denouement, and it always had multiple, crisscrossing story lines. With an only weakened workfare program still on the books ten years later, it is difficult to take any clear lessons from the fight against workfare that can be identified as models taken from victory or admonitions gleaned from defeat. What can be learned, then, that might be of use to future challenges to urban neoliberalism? What, if anything, is the broader significance of ten years of contention and debate over the program?

The most important lessons activists can draw from the study of WEP politics lie in the dynamics of claim-making. From the outset, Gramsci's metaphor of a war of position is a useful one for understanding the ways in which political claim-making about workfare occurs in multiple, intersecting, but also quite distinct institutional settings. As a result, the ambiguous status of the WEP labor contract is kept subject to multiple institutionally rooted interpretations and therefore remains ambiguous, giving City administrators precisely the kind of flexible labor contract and contingent labor force that many private employers enjoy.

The trick in a war of position is to reduce the opponent's flexibility and increase one's own. This is done by holding the positions one has gained or by strategically abandoning ones that are no longer useful, joining with allied forces in other trenches. In the terms used throughout this book, it means maintaining soft-assembled coalitions while forming hard-assembled ones for specific tasks or, alternatively, forming hard-assembled coalitions around specific campaigns, and in so doing, maintaining and building on the connections these coalitions provide in order to construct larger, softer-assembled coalitions capable of focusing on new, larger campaigns. Maintaining flexibility involves an explicit strategy on the part of community groups, antipoverty policy advocates, legal advocates, and unions of building claim-making alliances within specific institutions, and coming up with targeted campaigns at multiple levels of governance.

The essential challenge that welfare and workfare pose for the formation of stable soft-assembled coalitions and effective hard-assembled ones is that short-term tenure in workfare assignments and on welfare makes it difficult to develop solid relationships with a group of workers whose needs and demands can drive a program forward. Moreover, though welfare policy has been devolved to state and local governments in such a way as to be able to be integrated with urban policy more generally, the problem remains that this devolution makes larger-scale campaigns and larger-scale coalitions more difficult to assemble. Nevertheless, four critical strategic lessons can be drawn from the analysis this book gives that can make these problems more tractable.

Organize in Maximally Stable Settings

First, it is important to organize in the institutional settings that provide the most relative temporal stability and to organize to secure that stability. For example, the worksite organizing strategy provided little temporal stability, owing to high turnover among WEP workers and relatively easily made adjustments in worksite administration, such as the provision of gloves and other protective clothing. By contrast, the Pledge of Resistance, by targeting a more stable set of institutions (and often a middle-class audience less subject to the short termism of neoliberal governance) could operate relatively unimpeded until it saw fit to "go public." The organizational commitment among Pledge of Resistance members to resisting WEP, however, became largely moot, given the reduction in the program's numbers that made the massive expansion of nonprofit placements less pressing for the Giuliani administration. Had the Pledge of Resistance had a *range* of claims for anti-WEP activity from the nonprofits and congregations among its signatories beyond refusal to become a WEP worksite, it might have been able to tie into anti-WEP organizing in a way that sustained the pressure it created around work-related exploitation well into Giuliani's second term. Instead, the "trench" was lost, and the Urban Justice Center (UJC) moved with the flow of the battle to attack Jason Turner's Job Centers and worksite organizers moved to their legislative campaigns. If the object of the Pledge of Resistance was to prevent WEP's expansion, it succeeded, at least partially. But if it was to promote a "moral discourse" on WEP, it needed to build stronger links between its constituents and the organizing groups.

Choose among Scales of Governance

Second, it is important to build coalitions at all scales of governance but to target hard-assembled coalitional campaigns at scales at which commitment to neoliberalism is weakest and then "jump scale" from there.[32] For example, multiple national-level campaigns have brought together advocacy and activist groups to fight against further attacks on welfare and particularly to target Democratic Party lawmakers who parrot studies that show the "success" of previous rounds of reform. These coalitions tend to be most active when the topic of reauthorizing the Personal Responsibility and Work Opportunity Reconciliation Act of 1996 (PRWORA) comes up in Congress. It is absolutely clear that these coalitions do not have the clout on these issues with Washington policy networks enjoyed by conservative think tanks such as the Heritage Foundation, the American Enterprise Institute, and others.[33] There is no point in welfare rights advocates' trying to emulate them. Instead, mechanisms of time and scale shifting, institutional spillover, amplification, and certification described in the latter portion of this book suggest the possibility of subverting local neoliberal policies and spoiling them as models for future incorporation in federal law, and perhaps strengthening them as antimodels for future policymakers hoping to make their mark as innovators. Though the chance for this was missed in the process leading up to the deepening of work requirements in the Deficit Reduction Act of 2005, targeted campaigns disseminated through national coalition networks (used as soft-assembled coalitions rather than the hard-assembled ones they were made to be) demonstrating the failures of particular local models would put neoliberals on the defensive for a change. That this can be done becomes clearer if the larger trajectory of small victories by anti-WEP groups is considered together. With claims that WEP workers are essentially *workers*, or employees entitled to workplace protections, if not all the benefits of employment, anti-WEP advocates have at last won certification from some courts, including, significantly, a federal appeals court. With moral claims against workfare, based on the Pledge of Resistance, they managed to get the Giuliani administration to tone down its public moralizing about the program. With claims protecting *welfare rights*, they have rolled back some of the Giuliani administration initiatives to limit access to public benefits. And even with an unimplemented transitional jobs program, they focused the policy network on the role of welfare recipients as *potential workers* and pushed the Giuliani administration to create a different but substantially similar jobs program. Though this last move, in itself, is arguably a conservative one—and a compromise position from outright claims for WEP's abolition—it now puts anti-WEP activists in the position of amplifying a more-encompassing abolitionist claim. Specifically, they can point to the sharply reduced use of "pure" WEP in New York City. They can thus demonstrate to national audiences that the New York model that was rooted in WEP is, in principle, bankrupt and barely even supported by the current administration. For its part, it is unlikely that the current administration, which would incur budgetary costs from a punishing "New York-style" national welfare reauthorization, would disagree too loudly. Here, the Giuliani administration's assault on the older policy networks around welfare in New York City helped create a movement that now—thanks to time shifts, spillover, scale shift, and multiscale certification attempts—may make a play for local hegemony. The older networks, in spite of steady retrenchment, still supported a relatively lenient welfare state. The Giuliani administration's efforts to replace them with closed, neoliberal networks that privatized provision, rewarded allies, and shed the fiscal load of caring for the poor prompted pieces of the old networks to resist and to create new local institutions and coalitions. As former local officials become national policy entrepreneurs by touting their former cities' programs as national models, the changes in policy networks at the local level can publicly decertify the entrepreneurs' products.[34]

Broaden Discursive Strategies

Third, in order to sustain soft-assembled coalitions, it is important that individual activist groups begin to broaden their discursive strategies as soon as possible within settings they control. Ten years of anti-WEP activism in New York City built on and significantly reinforced a soft-assembled coalition of community and labor rights organizations that has launched advocacy efforts on a variety of fronts to help poor workers in many sectors of the local economy, from welfare recipient students to immigrant applicants for city services, and from immigrant factory workers in Brooklyn to domestic workers and home day-care providers across the city. The specific campaigns, moreover, have been built on diverse organizational foundations, but all have drawn on a growing set of claims for higher wages, formalization of employee-employer relations, and public certification of the demands of contingent workers and of assistance seekers whose most recent flowering occurred most strongly and visibly within and among anti-WEP activism in the mid-1990s. Accordingly, the layering of hard-assembled campaigns on a soft-assembled coalitional background makes it possible for each campaign to share languages that increase the chances of solidaristic action—and common claim-making—in the future. The model of community organizing that insists on small, "winnable" victories, has restricted political vision, and is suspicious of alliances with other groups is untenable in contexts characterized by a rich associational environment of similarly—though not identically—oriented groups.

Identify Contradictions

Finally, thinking in the framework provided by CHAT can help anti-WEP and other groups seeking antineoliberal urban solutions identify contradictions in their own coalitional activity systems and in the activity systems of their opponents. This framework is, again, quite different from a process of ideological purification of one's own position or demystification of one's opponents' positions. It is also far more important than identifying a correct set of claims that has ideological resonance with the broadest possible target audience. As a framework for reflexive analysis, the identification of contradictions among subjects, communities, divisions of labor, tools, objects, and rules allows political actors to search for mechanisms that will enable them to learn how to broaden the institutional depth and breadth of a changing set of political claims and to defend against further incursions of neoliberal governance. A framework to identify contradictions can allow a kind of planning around claim-making and even inform explicit dialogues within coalitions that too rarely take place, even now. What kind of challenges in the temporal coordination of action can we expect if we combine a campaign for better working conditions with litigation that depends on our certification as employees by the courts? What kinds of campaigns might we have to anticipate five years hence, should a court certify WEP workers as workers? How can we derail the neoliberal strategy of imposing new work requirements from the federal level by building on the ostensible successes of local policies? How can we increase the pressure on a recalcitrant union to support the demands of workers it might otherwise represent if the workers were accorded collective bargaining rights? These are fundamental questions about strategic dynamics that cannot be addressed without answers drawn in equal measure from organizational, cultural, and political-economic explanations but which I hope the analysis in this book have synthesized. In particular, I hope to have moved well beyond the idea that contention over the proper definitions of classes of workers—or any other classification of citizen—can be analyzed by looking at symbols alone. Instead, by forcing policy changes; by inducing shifts in the spatial, temporal, supervisory, and claim-making routines within institutional settings; and by altering the configuration of alliances and divisions of labor within and among communities, social actors can alter the meanings of claims just as surely as—and I wager, a good deal more than—they can if they propose novel ways of understanding or talking about policy and its objects.

When Gramsci proposed the metaphor of a war of position, he did so with the full knowledge that trench warfare was bloody, was confusing, and lasted a long, long time. The forces that will challenge the ascendant regulatory mode of neoliberalism will not, and cannot, organize "all at once." Nor can they find the right kind of discourse with which to discredit neoliberalism, as if they were discovering a silver bullet. The languages within which struggles around workfare were conducted are contested languages as well as languages of contention. Thus the meanings of language are never fully open nor fully closed. Ten years on, workfare workers are *still* neither definitively "workers" nor "welfare recipients." Both categories have changed as well through the contentious dialogues around workfare. Claims live and adapt to their speakers and audiences. Speakers and audiences, through their claim-making and choral support, both adapt to and shape the configuration of alliances and fault lines in the field. For scholars of regulation, this means that greater attention to the institutional dynamics of claim-making will yield greater insights on the contingent policy outcomes across settings. For scholars of social movements and for progressive political strategists, it means that ideas about how unions, community groups, parties, and movement organizations frame issues—and how they should frame issues—will need to attend to the activity systems within which claims appear in order to judge their efficacy. And for those who organize, advocate for, and represent the targets of neoliberal urban austerity, the dynamics of claim-making described here suggest that once the common element of neoliberal attempts to disorganize opposition is recognized, it is possible to identify a range of strategies to bridge among incremental victories in setting the terms of debate, even within the structures of segmentation, fragmentation, and exclusion.

I have used various methods to gather and analyze data among the chapters in this book in order to enrich the views of the dynamics of claim-making I analyze. The bulk of the data for the book come from documentary analysis and interviews. Following Sabatier's advice,[1] I conducted research on workfare for nearly a decade and tracked developments within local policy for a period of roughly eleven years, from late 1993 through early 2004. Sabatier suggests that a decade is the minimum period necessary for studying policy development. Though much of the story I tell in this book begins far earlier than 1993—dating at least back to New York's fiscal crisis in the 1970s—the principal innovation, the expansion of workfare, can be understood as having had a decade-long cycle. This is the case in two senses. First, the expansion of the Work Experience Program (WEP) and the decline in welfare rolls grew and peaked in 1997–99 and begun to fall off gradually in the years following. Much the same can be said of the news cycle. Figure A.1. plots the number of articles per year meeting the LexisNexis search terms *Workfare* and *New York City* in their lead paragraphs and/or titles, and a point-in-time count of WEP workers in those years as well (if multiple numbers are available for a year, due to seasonal fluctuation, the mean is given). It clearly shows a cresting wave of activity that lasts about a decade.

Recall, however, that figure 5.1 showed that there were three cycles within the larger one, in which lasting claim-making innovations were made. There is now the distinct possibility that the contending actors who debated workfare have now moved their debates into other nearby fields. Thus, continuing to study policy development in the field of workfare politics may involve tracing the life and cohesion of the soft-assembled

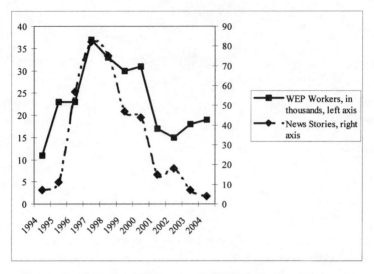

Figure A.1. WEP workers and news stories, 1994–2004. WEP worker numbers are estimates based on March numbers for each year. See Douglas J. Besharov and Peter Germanis, "Full Engagement Welfare Reform in New York City: Lessons for TANF's Participation Requirements," University of Maryland School of Public Policy Welfare Reform Academy, College Park, August 2004, http://www .welfareacademy.org/pubs/welfare/nyc_hra.pdf; "Mayor's Management Report, Supplementary Indicator Tables" (2003), 20; "Mayor's Management Report, Supplementary Indicator Tables" (2004), 20. Note that WEP numbers are for a changed program, as nearly all WEP workers now engage in activities other than WEP to fulfill part of their work requirements.

coalition that developed around workfare but that has turned its attention back to pressing issues of access to public benefits systems and to well-paying jobs.

Data

I conducted formal, semistructured interviews with thirty-one activists between 1996 and 2004. Interviewees were selected on the basis of their importance to the field of anti-WEP politics and on the basis of their response to my inquiries. I was unable to interview several potential candidates, and, during the Giuliani administration, I was unable to interview important administration officials. In addition, some respondents preferred to go on record only after they left the organization in which they had been involved in WEP politics. Accordingly, some of the interviews were retrospective, though most involved commentary on current events as well as on past ones.

In the spring of 1998, I also carried out four months of observation of organizing activity carried out by the Association of Community Organizations for Reform Now (ACORN), mainly by trailing two organizers on their rounds. I include these organizers in my list of interviewees because I was able to interview them nearly constantly during the course of my fieldwork. I was able to record their reactions in field notes but not on audiotape, as I did the other interviews.

During, before, and after the fieldwork with ACORN, I regularly attended rallies, meetings of advocates (including several meetings of the WEP Coalition, convened by Communications Workers of America Local 1180), marches, city council hearings, and occasionally, meetings of groups themselves. I also conducted research in an action-research project[2] with Community Voices Heard (CVH), experiences from which inform some of the narrative in chapter 6.

Many of my interviewees furnished me with documentary sources, including reports, meeting notes, correspondence, flyers, and the like. Some generously opened their files and copiers to me.

In addition to these sources, I regularly tracked reports in the media about WEP, particularly in the *New York Times* and *Daily News* (discussed subsequently); the *Public Employee Press*, the paper of DC 37, that is, District Council 37 of the American Federation of State, County, and Municipal Employees (AFSCME); the *Chief/Civil Service Leader*, a newspaper for civil servants in New York; and *City Limits* and *City Limits Weekly*, a newsmagazine for New York's nonprofit and advocacy community.

The quantitative analysis in chapter 5 draws exclusively on *New York Times* and *Daily News* articles accessed through LexisNexis. The selection criterion was that the articles should have the words *workfare* and *New York City* in the title or first paragraphs. This strategy yielded fewer articles than would a search on *welfare reform* and *New York City* and missed several relevant pieces (including a letter to the editor I wrote!) that turned up in a search of *welfare* and *Giuliani*. There are many permutations that could have yielded a wider sample, but since this is a book focused on workfare and on the difficulties in defining it, I thought it best to keep the term itself as a search criterion. As it is, the search turned up an average, over an eleven-year span, of nearly one article, letter, or opinion piece per week, though overall, they were distributed by year according to the pattern in figure A.1.

Moving from Words to Numbers

Roberto Franzosi correctly casts doubt on content analysis's pretensions to scientific objectivity in unearthing the meanings political texts produce.[3] By turns likening the urge to quantify meaning to Gematria and criticizing its lack of reflexivity, especially with regard to the newspaper sources upon which much of it relies, Franzosi gives reason to doubt the value of the enterprise. Yet, Franzosi also makes a good case that theoretically driven database construction, informed by linguistic theory; greater attention to the limitations and structuring capacities of source material and its own institutional production; and a lower level of abstraction in collecting and coding data can help rescue efforts to measure meanings.[4]

The approach I take here is computationally and programmatically simpler than that taken by Franzosi. Nevertheless, I scale back the ambitions of the quantitative project. The maps in chapter 5 are based on the *interpretive* work of coding texts, but at a low level of aggregation (hence, the large number of codes). With them, we can discover positions that power claims can occupy based on their use by actors in institutional contexts. But we cannot immediately use the maps to discern the dynamics of the field. Rather, we can only use them as an interpretive tool.

Nevertheless, the measures I use (as will be described shortly) are theoretically motivated and move far beyond frequency counts of the data. The theoretical parameters of the study are introduced in chapter 3 and developed in a somewhat different way in chapter 4.

Cautions

Many cautions have been published about using newspaper data to study political contention. These cautions fall into three rough sets.

Newspapers—particularly national ones—tend to underreport protest events. A wealth of studies indicate that well-indexed newspapers, which tend to have national circulation, also do a poor job in reporting on local protest events.[5] They underreport them, and in so doing, they also often misrepresent the actual distribution of activity and claim-making in local social movement fields. As Oliver and Maney argue, however, news analysis does not just *produce* sampling bias with respect to protest events but rather is the result of "triadic relations" among news routines, protest activity, and institutional political processes.[6] Whether protest activity makes the news depends in large part on whether or not it competes with or fits into institutional political temporality, such as election cycles.

The procedures of newsgathering and the conventions of reporting "frame" the news in a manner biased toward government incumbents. Gitlin's classic study of the media and the New Left[7] finds that the institutional structure of news gathering, such as the assignment of "beats" to reporters and the existence of pressrooms in key government offices, makes it much more likely that government officials will be the principal source of reported speech and that reporters will work to maintain access to these officials. Justin Lewis argues that the media's "downplaying of economic issues in defining political difference" and forced political conflict (i.e., playing "Left"—usually moderately liberal—commentators and Right commentators against each other in news analysis shows) create the illusion of openness in a far more closed system of ideas and interests.[8] Representation of movements and movement leadership, moreover, will portray them as isomorphic with the representative and leadership structures of dominant political groups, regardless of the actual structure of the groups, because of the narrative conventions of the news article.

Different newspapers cover protest events quite differently, making source selection crucial. Davenport and Litras, for example, show that coverage of the Black Panthers differed considerably among newspapers in Oakland, creating a "Rashomon effect" in which quite distinct stories are generated about the same events.[9]

To these, I will add a fourth set of cautions. For the particular theoretical concerns I have here, newspaper data represent a problematic choice on three related accounts. First, Bakhtinian theoretical constructs are intended to describe *dialogue,* which consists of *utterances,* or complete statements that are joined in the moment of speech. In newspaper data, reported speech is most often deracinated from its dialogic context and put in a dialogue constructed by the reporter, and it reaches the page through a third-order dialogic process with editorial staff. The problem is compounded in that my coding scheme *further* chops up dialogic utterances into multiple, separate "claims."

Second, *reported* speech has its own generic forms—in which the voice of the reporter, the context of speech, and the reported speech itself are given greater or lesser authority—according to Vološinov, "whose methods of differentiation are dictated by the social and economic prerequisites of a given period. These changing sociolingual conditions are what, in fact, determines . . . changes in the forms of reported speech."[10] Though there may be no reason to believe that changes of this sort, which are, according to Bakhtin and Vološinov, changes of the long term, should unfold in the course of the debates over workfare, there is also no reason to rule out different conditions, such as the relations of the media with the administration, that could affect the methods of speech reporting. Indeed, Davenport and Litras's findings, cited previously, suggest that current genres of reported speech may differ considerably among sources or in relatively short periods of time.

Finally, our inability to access the *reception* of newspaper articles denies us access to the key dialogic moment of newspaper writing; indeed, treating newspaper reports as I do could strip the data of its dialogism on a metalevel.

Defense of Newspaper Data in Analysis

Nevertheless, the use of newspaper data for the kind of project I pursue here is defensible on several grounds. First, newspapers and the media generally constitute a key forum of politics and a virtual arena—as well as record—of debate. Activists hope that they will propel debate into the newspapers, and to the extent that they do, public debate is made more visible and given greater impact. That authorities and challengers spend a good deal of time and effort writing and sending press releases on issues is testimony to this fact. Indeed, beyond organization building—which is not trivial—protests that do not get media coverage may be proverbial falling trees in a deserted forest.

Media outlets such as newspapers also *create* particular dialogues, both through reporters' news gathering and solicitation of comment from trusted sources and through their construction of stories. In this sense, newspapers are like any other textual data source on public claim-making. Examination of legal papers, including legal memos and depositions, in workfare-related lawsuits also involves the examination of speech constructed according to particular institutional rules. While recognition of these rules is crucial to any theory of the data, selection of a single set of institutionally determined speech reports mitigates problems of cross-institutional commensurability and simplifies the analysis. This does not mean that cross-institutional comparison is to be avoided; it simply means that it is possible to treat these sources separately.

At the same time, newspapers' institutional form suggests that while they may privilege the authority of official authorities, they also reach into multiple institutions and create multilayered and hence multivocal stories by drawing in sources and claims from multiple, institutionally based actors. Hence, though in my database, the "types of occasions" are determined by an invisible third-order process (i.e., editorial and staff-allocation decisions), these occasions provide a rich vein for political claim-makers, researchers, and claim-makers alike.

In the present case, the newspaper with a national audience (the *New York Times*) had by far the most complete local coverage of the issue, in part because it also has an extensive local reporting capacity. The coverage of workfare in the *Times* was nearly six times as frequent as that in the *Daily News*. Moreover, because the *Times* has a labor beat as well as several metropolitan beats apart from the city hall beat, its coverage of the issue was varied and drew upon more than two hundred organizational actors. While reporters failed to get comment from one of the most active anti-workfare organizing groups in the period, they did get extensive comment from others working on the same or similar campaigns.

Moreover, in the analysis, I include newspapers as an actor (coded as MEDIA) when reporters or editors speak in their own voices (as opposed to reporting the speech of others, which is, of course, inflected with the reporter's voice). So while the entire analysis is, in a sense, an analysis of media coverage of the issue, we can mitigate some of the layering problems, though not eliminate them, by inserting reporters and editors in the analysis. Indeed, doing so allows us to understand effects of the growing frustration of the media at the Giuliani administration when facing official stonewalling on the release of welfare data. Including the media among the actors, in turn, sheds light on the dynamics that may make *appearance* in the media not synonymous with success outside the media or with media portrayal of the one's cause. For example, while the addition of new claims and new areas in which it could dominate its potential opponents helped the Giuliani administration keep some control in a debate that was rapidly turning against it, its failure to recognize the media as an ally—or a beneficial neutral party—on this issue actually turned the reporters and editors against the program.

Finally, the triadic interactions Oliver and Maney found so important are therefore partly modeled in my approach. At the same time, since the temporal unit of analysis is the news article-day rather than the protest event, I find that WEP's detractors are less limited by the temporal cycles of institutional politics than they would be if only protests were reported. By sampling *all* articles principally about workfare and New York City, I am able to capture political contention as it moves between more and less institutionalized political forms.

Coding for Chapter 5

To code the data, I followed an "open-coding" system, following Koopmans and Statham.[11] In this system, coding is done iteratively on articles, and new codes are devised as needed. A second round of coding reconciles different codes applied to substantially similar claims, and so forth. I repeated this iteration for every thirty article-days. A research assistant coded some of the data (roughly the last eighty article-days) according to the scheme, and I then recoded the entire data set to incorporate the new codes. A total of 594 codes for claims were recorded in the data for 5,778 claims made overall. The distribution of claims was highly skewed toward a low number of claim-making instances, as figure A.2. shows.

In the analyses, I reduce the complexity of the data by omitting claims that appear fewer than four times in the data set (i.e., fewer than roughly 0.5 percent of the time). In doing so, I am left with 261 codes for 5,280 total claims, which provides more density in the table and better-fitting statistics.

Actors were first coded by named speaker, organization, and organizational type (e.g., union, administration, legal advocacy group, etc.). In the analysis in chapter 5, the claims are grouped by organizational type. The organizational types are essentially realist categories, easily recognizable, and often mentioned by my interview respondents.

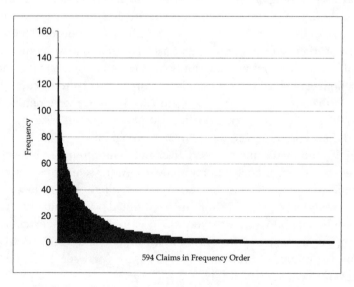

Figure A.2. Distribution of claims in data set

I also coded the *contexts/objects* for each article by coding its principal topic within the debates around WEP. Again, I followed an iterative procedure and invented new codes where appropriate. I took the appearance of the article in the data set to mean that workfare and New York City were important elements in the article, but I coded the article as "Childcare," "Federal Politics," "Labor Politics," and so on, according to the main topic discussed. A list of the most common claims, contexts/objects, and actors appears at the end of this appendix. The concept of a context/object is akin to the concept of a policy domain. A *policy domain* is defined by "inherent substantive or functional criteria, organizational participants, and cultural constructs" shared among instances of interaction.[12] The conventions of journalistic reporting allow such domains to be relatively easily identified among articles.

Quantitative Methods

Time Series

Cutting up time-series data is a notoriously difficult undertaking, particularly when a driving assumption in the research is that the dynamics under study are not stochastic events but path-dependent ones.[13] Since it is a core assumption of dialogic theory and, in its very name, Cultural Historical Activity Theory (CHAT), that meaning making is a nonstochastic, developmental process, the question of how to periodize it is crucial.

Vedres and Csigó's study of newspaper statements about debates over economic transition in Hungary includes a sophisticated model of decay functions and periods for claims in a four-month period in 1997.[14] I have taken a far simpler and intuitive approach here, confronted with a more-complex data structure. Instead of modeling decay functions, I took the nine context/settings that accounted for 75 percent of the claims and then charted the volume of claims made in each context over time, arranged by article-day, as a percentage of the total number of claims made in the context. I periodize the article-days according to three rules: (1) the article-day must contain at least 5 percent of the claims made for a given occasion type; (2) a cut point is made for each *first* time that at least 5 percent of an occasion type's claims are made on a given article-day; unless (3) this occurs for multiple occasion types in close succession, in which case, the article-day with the greatest percentage of claims is selected. In this way, I hope to tap significant changes in a broad selection of contexts. See figure A.3.

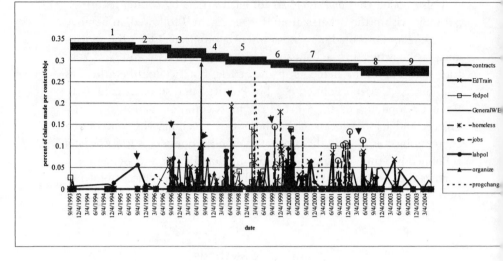

Figure A.3. Periods in workfare debate, New York City, 1993–2004

In the maps I generate in chapter 5, I consider each period and the one immediately preceding it together. Though not arranged as a "moving window" of a set number of time-units (as one standard methodology suggests),[15] it preserves the specificity of each period's influence on the data and embeds it in the larger dynamics of change in the field.

Clustering and Blockmodeling

Numerous scholars have applied network measures to relations between actors and claims and to other aspects of language-mediated action. Of particular interest here are Mohr's blockmodeling of "discourse roles in the 1907 New York City charity directory" and Mische and Pattison's application of Galois lattice analysis to three modes of data—actors, projects, and events—in a study of the impeachment movement against Brazilian president Fernando Collor de Mello.[16]

Mohr builds on Harrison White's quasi-ethnomethodological grounding of social networks as being based on shared stories that concatenate into story sets and thence into roles defined by "types of tie" by extending White's idea to affiliation networks of various identities (e.g., soldiers, tramps, mothers, unwed mothers, widows, etc.) and the charitable treatments described as appropriate to them in an authoritative directory of charities in Progressive Era New York. The principle behind White's and Mohr's classification of identities is *structural equivalence,* that is, similarity in the "pattern of relations to all other individuals within the social structure"[17] defined by the assignment of treatments to identities. The basic idea behind this is that culture exhibits a dual structure: the meanings of identities depend on the treatments they receive, and the meanings of treatments depend on the identities to which they are applied.[18] I adopt this perspective in the analysis in chapter 5 in the following sense: it matters who says what. If the former DC 37 executive director, Stanley Hill, calls workfare "slavery," it carries very different connotations than if, say, a former mayor, David Dinkins, were to have made the same claim, based on the different profiles each had of claim-making and on their closeness to or distance from other speakers based on these profiles.

In chapter 5, I go a step further. In constructing actor-claim-context/object triads, I argue that meaning goes beyond duality, in the sense that institutional contexts/objects have a relevant existence beyond their immediate construction in the interstices of actor-claim networks. In other words, even if contexts/objects are created by the meeting, over time, of actors and claims, they should be understood as exerting influence over actors' use of claims in and toward them. (Again, this squares with the theoretical position I take in chapter 6 as well). Using similar justification, Mische and Pattison develop "three-mode" lattices to analyze the basic shape of a field of protest based on the copresence of actors, "projects," and events over three periods.[19] In order to do so, they construct three mode, actor-project-event matrices, projected into two dimensions, whereby no actors are directly connected to other actors but only through projects and claims; the same rule applies to the other modes of data.

I adopt this approach with respect to the raw matrices of actors, claims, and context/settings in each period. Then, using UCINET 6,[20] I extract cliques from the matrix. The result is a list of all the claims in a given period arranged as an actor-claim-context triad. This routine also yields a matrix of clique overlap, which is a three-mode affiliation matrix, wherein connections within modes (i.e., within categories of actor, claim, and context/object) are established based on the number of times they overlap.[21]

From the overlap matrix of actor-claim-context/object combinations, I created a matrix of correlations, whereby each cell represents the correlation of each actor, claim, or context's/objects overlaps with the claim-making overlaps of each other actor, claim, or context/object. On this table, I ran the CONCOR algorithm[22] in order to generate structurally

Table A.1 List of most common coding elements

Claims

Claim	Count	Definition
ADMINBAD	151	The administration of WEP is bad
ROLLDOWN	126	Reference to falling welfare rolls
REFLAW	111	Reference to the law
DEADEND	97	Assertion that WEP is a dead end
NEEDTRN	91	Training is needed
KIDSNEED	90	Reference to children's needs
UNCERTAIN	90	Expresses uncertainty
NYCILLEG	83	The City is acting illegally
DEPEND	79	Welfare recipients are dependent
NOCOOP	75	Refusal of cooperation
NUMBERS	72	Reference to numbers
PAYBAD	72	Pay in WEP is low
CONDBAD	70	Conditions are poor
WEP2JOBS	69	WEP leads to jobs
WEPCANOK	67	WEP can work if implemented properly
WKHURT	67	Workers' interests are hurt
LITIGATE	65	Reference to litigation
MUSTWORK	60	Welfare recipients must work
NEWSIT	59	This is a new situation
NEEDED	57	Education is needed
SANCTION	55	Reference to sanctions
STUDY	55	More study is needed
CORRUPT	54	Reference to corruption
NOCOMM	54	No comment
POLMOTIV	53	Attribution of political motives
PUBLICGOOD	51	WEP benefits the public
DISPLACE	48	WEP displaces workers
ADMINOK	46	WEP is administered well
DISABLED	46	Reference to disabled welfare recipients
NYCLEGAL	46	The City is acting within the law
APPPROC	44	Reference to the application process
ALARMED	43	Expresses alarm
DEEPOV	43	Poverty is deepened
INFLEX	43	Attribution of inflexibility
REALJOBS	43	Claim for job expansion
GOODPOS	42	Self-evaluation as being in a good position politically
NEEDIGNR	42	Needs are ignored
BIDUNFAIR	41	The contracting process is unfair
NODISP	37	Displacement does not occur
TIMELIMIT	37	Reference to time limits
WKSCARCE	37	Work is scarce
EVALWRONG	36	Evaluations of WEP are wrong
LEGLBAR	34	Reference to legal impediments to policy
WEPrWKRS	34	WEP workers are workers
WEPSHAM	34	WEP is a sham
HMLSHURT	33	Homeless people's interests are hurt
ADMINHARD	32	WEP is difficult to administer

Claim	Count	Definition
COST	32	Reference to cost
DIGNITY	32	Claim for dignified treatment
DRUGS	32	Reference to drug abuse
WEPIMP	32	WEP has improved
BADECON	31	The economy is bad
BENEFITS	31	Reference to benefits tied to employment
XPANDWEP	31	Expand WEP
FEDBENS	30	Reference to federal benefits like Medicaid and Food Stamps
CONTBAD	28	Contract is bad
BIDFAIR	27	Contract process is fair
BURBAR	27	Reference to bureaucratic obstacles to welfare and WEP
UNTRUST	27	Attribution of untrustworthiness
WRKDIGN	27	Work imparts dignity
TALKING	26	Reference to ongoing negotiations
WEPrNOTWORK	26	WEP workers are not workers
DISCHABS	25	WEP imparts discipline and good work habits
MEANING	25	Reference to "meaningful" jobs
PROTAC	25	Reference to protest tactics
TRADVALS	25	Reference to traditional values and symbols (e.g., the flag, religion)
HARD2SERV	24	Reference to welfare recipients with multiple barriers to employment
JOBCENTER	24	Reference to Job Centers
PAYBACK	24	WEP gives the opportunity for welfare recipients to pay society back
HELPING	23	A given action was helpful
PRAOKWEP	22	WEP is certified by federal policy
PREVEXP	22	Reference to previous experience
RECOURSE	22	Claim for recourse for WEP workers
UNREAL	22	A proposal is unrealistic
AUTHBAD	21	The authorities are bad
DEMVOX	21	The people have spoken
ECONGOOD	21	The economy is good
MISTAKE	21	Assertion of a mistake
OPPSBAD	21	Opponents are bad
TRAINOK	21	Training is adequate
WEPOK	21	WEP is well run
DC37CPLT	20	DC 37 is complicit in WEP
DIVERT1ST	20	Diversion is first priority
HMLSWYES	20	Require WEP as a condition of shelter
SEXHARASS	20	Reference to sexual harassment
SLAVERY	20	WEP is like slavery
WKFIRST	20	Work first is a priority
ANGER	19	Expression of anger
CONTOK	19	Contract is good
JUSTICE	19	Claim for justice
AGREEMT	18	Reference to an agreement

(*continued*)

Claim	Count	Definition
LAYOFFS	18	Reference to layoffs
NEWTERM	18	Reference to new terminology
SUSPICION	18	Expression of suspicion
UNIONY	18	Unionize WEP
WEPDEATHS	18	Reference to deaths of WEP workers
INVESTIGATE	17	This must be investigated
TIMEOUT	17	Call for temporary moratorium
EVICTION	16	Reference to evictions
FALLTHRU	16	A case fell through the cracks of a well-run program
NEEDSKIL	16	WEP workers need skills
POLPRESS	16	Reference to political pressure
POORHURT	16	The interests of the poor are hurt
PRABAD	16	PRWORA is a bad law
HMLSWNO	15	Don't require WEP from the homeless
PRACTICL	15	This is a practical solution
FLEXIBLE	14	Attribution of flexibility or need to be flexible
SKILLNO	14	WEP workers are unskilled
WEP4SHELTER	14	Reference to the WEP-for-shelter issue
CHANGE	13	Demand for change
LABPAX	13	Reference to labor peace
LANGBARS	13	Reference to language barriers
LEGISBAR	13	Reference to legislative barriers to policy
MORECCARE	13	Demand for more child care
NOTRAIN	13	There is inadequate training
NYCHURT	13	New York City's interests are hurt
WORTHY	13	WEP workers are worthy
DISCRIM	12	Allegation of discrimination
DOMABUSE	12	Reference to domestic violence
EXITSOK	12	Welfare leavers are doing well
FOSTERCARE	12	Reference to foster care
INFOREQ	12	Request for information
WRKRIGHT	12	Demand to enforce workers' rights
CORPLEG	11	Corporations are acting legally
DC374WEP	11	DC 37 is on WEP workers' side
IMMIGRANT	11	Reference to immigrants
JURISDICTION	11	Reference to jurisdictional questions
MAYOROK	11	Mayor is good
MEDBAD	11	Medical exams are inadequate
NOPOLITC	11	Rejection of attribution of political motive
PAYOK	11	Pay for WEP workers is appropriate

Actors

Actor	Count	Description
Giuliani Administration	1,326	The mayor and the commissioners and aides of mayoral agencies
Media	740	Editorials, columnists, and reporters where they add claims not previously in the article

Actor	Count	Description
Union	437	Unions
Advocates	391	Antipoverty advocates
Judges	246	Judges
WEP	224	WEP workers
Legal Advocates	206	Legal advocacy groups, such as NELP, WLC, Legal Aid
Nonprofit service providers	180	Service providers
NYS Government	176	The governor and commissioners, aides, and employees of gubernatorial agencies
Bloomberg Admin	146	The mayor and the commissioners and aides of mayoral agencies
Federal Government	143	The president and secretaries and aides of executive agencies
City Council	130	City council members
Academics	124	Academics
Comptroller	118	The New York City comptroller
Experts	116	Policy experts
Corporate actors	113	Private firms
Bystanders	92	Bystanders with no political affiliation or tendency implied
Organizers	92	Organizing groups such as FAC, CVH, ACORN
Welfare	69	Welfare recipients not cited as being WEP workers
Worker	59	Workers not cited as being WEP workers
County Government	48	Government executives of suburban counties
Liberals	48	Bystanders or letter writers with evident or attributed liberal politics
FriendFamily	47	WEP workers' friends and family
Applicants	46	Applicants for welfare
Conservatives	41	Bystanders or letter writers with evident or attributed conservative politics
Religious	40	Religious leaders
State Officials	40	Officials of state governments outside of New York State
Homeless	29	Homeless people
NY State Legislators	29	New York State legislators and their aides
Researcher	29	Researchers
WEP Critics	26	Critics of WEP, called as such
Lawyer	25	Private lawyers
Professional Associations	25	Professional associations
MTA	24	Metropolitan Transportation Authority
Congress	22	Members of Congress and their staffs
Dinkins Administration	18	The former mayor and the commissioners and aides of mayoral agencies

(*continued*)

Table A.1 (*continued*)

Contexts/objects

Context/object	Count	Description
labpol	863	Labor politics
GeneralWEP	806	General WEP
Contracts	528	Contracting and privatization
Fedpol	483	Federal politics
Homeless	473	Homelessness
Organize	431	Organizing
EdTrain	331	Education and training
Progchange	283	Program changes
Jobs	226	Jobs and employment
Health&Safety	168	Health and safety issues
Research	167	Research
Discrim	144	Discrimination and harassment
cc	139	Child care
Statepol	130	State politics
Disability	122	Disability issues
Pay	110	Pay and compensation
Drugs	97	Drugs
Adminstyle	80	Administrative style
Elections	63	Electoral campaigns
Mediapol	32	Media politics
ChildAbuse	31	Child abuse
Unemploy	29	Unemployment
Fostercare	15	Foster care
CityServices	14	City services
FoodStamps	14	Food stamps

equivalent blocks of actors, claims, and/or contexts/objects. Doing so results in blocks composed of actors, claims, and/or contexts/objects that are similarly tied to actors, claims, and contexts/objects that share similar patterns of ties to other actors, claims, and contexts/objects. Of several procedures for clustering data based on similarity and structural equivalence, this yielded the best-fitting models and the most easily interpretable results.

In the blockmodels in chapter 5, mapped in *NetDraw*,[23] I follow convention by showing links among blocks only if the density of their overlap exceeds the mean density for the blocked or clustered network as a whole.[24]

NOTES

CHAPTER ONE

1. "'Workfare' Workers Form Union and March in the Labor Day Parade to Protest Conditions,'" press release, WEP Workers Together, 1996.
2. Ira Katznelson, *City Trenches: Urban Politics and the Patterning of Class in the United States* (Chicago: University of Chicago Press, 1981), 4.
3. Ibid., 19, chap. 2.
4. See *Deficit Reduction Act of 2005*, Public Law 109–171.
5. Chad Alan Goldberg, "Welfare Recipients or Workers? Contesting the Workfare State in New York City," *Sociological Theory* 19, no. 2 (2001): 187–218.
6. Vanessa Tait, *Poor Workers' Unions* (Boston: South End Press, 2005).
7. Jane Jacobs, *The Death and Life of Great American Cities* (1961; repr., New York: Random House Modern Library, 1993), 564–65.
8. See Neil Brenner and Nik Theodore, "Cities and the Geographies of 'Actually Existing Neoliberalism,'" in *Spaces of Neoliberalism: Urban Restructuring in North America and Western Europe* (Maldon, MA: Blackwell, 2002), 2–32; see also, in the same volume, Jamie Peck and Adam Tickell, "Neoliberalizing Space," 42–43.
9. See, e.g., Steven H. Lopez, "Overcoming Legacies of Business Unionism: Why Grassroots Organizing Tactics Succeed," in *Rebuilding Labor: Organizing and Organizers in the New Union Movement*, ed. Ruth Milkman and Kim Voss, 114–32 (Ithaca, NY: Cornell University Press, ILR Press, 2004); Dan Cornfield, *The Next Upsurge: Labor and the New Social Movements* (Ithaca, NY: Cornell University Press, ILR Press, 2003); Paul Johnston, "Citizenship Movement Unionism: For the Defense of Local Communities in the Global Age," in *Unions in a Globalized Environment: Changing Borders, Organizational Boundaries, and Social Roles*, ed. Bruce Nissen, 236–63 (Armonk: M. E. Sharpe, 2002);Bruce Nissen, "The Effectiveness and Limits of Labor-Community Coalitions: Evidence from South Florida," *Labor Studies Journal* 29, no. 1 (Spring 2004): 67–89; see also Jeremy Brecher and Tim Costello, *Building Bridges: The Emerging Grassroots Coalition of Labor and Community* (New York: Monthly Review Press, 1989).
10. A good review of recent literature appears in Nissen, "Effectiveness and Limits of Coalitions," 67–73.
11. Carola Frege, Edmund Heery, and Lowell Turner, "The New Solidarity? Coalition Building in Five Countries," in *Varieties of Unionism: Strategies for Labor Movement*

Renewal in the Global North, ed. Carola Frege and John Kelly, 137–58 (Oxford: Oxford University Press).

12. Margaret R. Somers, "The Narrative Construction of Identity: A Relational and Network Approach," *Theory and Society* 23, no. 5 (October 1994): 625–27.

13. See, e.g., Roland Roth, "New Social Movements, Poor People's Movements and the Struggle for Citizenship," in *Urban Movements in a Globalising World,* ed. Pierre Hamel, Henri Lustiger-Thaler, and Margit Mayer, 25–44 (London: Routledge, 2000); see also Immanuel Ness, *Immigrants, Unions, and the New U.S. Labor Market* (Philadelphia: Temple University Press, 2005).

14. Bakhtin quoted in V. N. Vološinov, *Freudianism: A Marxist Critique,* ed. Neal H. Bruss, trans. I. R. Titunik (New York: Academic Press, 1976), 93–106.

15. A paradigmatic case is Jeffrey C. Alexander, "Culture and Political Crisis: 'Watergate' and Durkheimian Sociology," in *Durkheimian Sociology: Cultural Studies,* ed. Jeffrey C. Alexander (Cambridge: Cambridge University Press, 1988); see also Goldberg, "Welfare Recipients or Workers?"

16. See, e.g., Hank Johnston, "A Methodology for Frame Analysis: From Discourse to Cognitive Schemata" in *Social Movements and Culture,* ed. Hank Johnston and Bert Klandermans, 217–46 (Minneapolis: University of Minnesota Press, 1995); George Lakoff, *Moral Politics: How Liberals and Conservatives Think,* 2nd ed. (Chicago: University of Chicago Press, 2002); David A. Snow and Robert D. Benford, "Ideology, Frame Resonance, and Participant Mobilization" in *From Structure to Action: Comparing Social Movement Research across Cultures* (Greenwich, CT: JAI Press, 1988): 197–218.

17. See, e.g., Yrjö Engeström, *Learning by Expanding: An Activity-Theoretical Approach to Developmental Research,* 1987. http://communication.ucsd.edu/MCA/Paper/ Engestrom/expanding/toc.htm.

18. *Personal Responsibility and Work Opportunity Reconciliation Act of 1996,* Public Law 104–193; Gwendolyn Mink, *Welfare's End* (Ithaca, NY: Cornell University Press, 1998); Jamie Peck, *Workfare States* (New York: Guilford Press, 2001).

19. Jason A. Turner, "'Universal Engagement' of TANF Recipients: The Lessons of New York City." *Heritage Foundation Backgrounder* 1561 (Washington, DC: Heritage Foundation, 2003), http://www.heritage.org/Research/Welfare/bg1651.cfm; Jason A. Turner, "Hearing on TANF Reauthorization: Testimony, 2002," in *Welfare: A Documentary History of U.S. Policy and Politics,* ed. G. Mink and R. Solinger (New York: New York University Press, 2003), 767–74.

20. Opposition to PWP was also mobilized by PWP workers through an association organized by welfare rights organizers. They hoped to join DC 37 as a bargaining unit of PWP workers, while DC 37 wanted them to join as members of the locals already present at their worksites. The former solution would have preserved distinct power and identity for PWP workers, but it would have threatened the power of incumbent labor leaders due to a bloc-voting system within the district council. See Tait, *Poor Workers' Unions,* chap. 2. See also Michael Goodwin, "Thousands on 'Workfare' Get Half-Pay for Doing City Jobs," *New York Times,* August 20, 1984.

21. William Sites, *Remaking New York: Primitive Globalization and the Politics of Urban Community.* (Minneapolis: University of Minnesota Press, 2003), 52–56; William Sites, "The Limits of Urban Regime Theory: New York City under Koch, Dinkins, and Giuliani," *Urban Affairs Review* 32, no. 4 (March 1997): 547–48; see also Josh Barbanel, "Dinkins Efforts Set Back by Cut in Bond Rating," *New York Times,* Feb-

ruary 12, 1991; James C. McKinley Jr., "Dinkins Shifts on Fiscal Plan Under Pressure," *New York Times*, November 13, 1991.

22. Celia Dugger, "Fish Story Ends in 'Workfare' and Sweet Smell of Success," *New York Times*, October 8,1994; Andrew O'Rourke, letter to the editor, *New York Times*, September 28, 1993.

23. During the 1990s, only the top quintile gained real income while the bottom four lost income. See James Parrott, "Bolstering and Diversifying New York City's Economy," in *Rethinking the Urban Agenda*, ed. John Mollenkopf and Ken Emerson, 46-53 (New York: Century Foundation Press, 2001). The increasingly skewed income inequality is due to the combination of the loss of middle-income jobs, mainly in manufacturing, and the bifurcation of the service economy into high-wage executive and professional positions and low-wage retail service work. During the 1990s, New York City's gross income growth was directly linked to Wall Street. See also Carl H. McCall, "New York City's Economic and Fiscal Dependence on Wall Street" (report, Office of the State Comptroller, August 13, 1998).

24. Jonathan Hicks, "First Accord by New York with a Union on Workfare," *New York Times*, December 15, 1994; see also Bill Schleichler, "Making Workfare Work," *Public Employee Press* 37, no. 1 (January 26, 1996): 10-11; Charles Hughes, testimony before New York City Council General Welfare Committee, March 26, 1996.

25. Liz Krueger, Laura Wernick, and Liz Accles, *Workfare: The Real Deal*, vol. 2 (New York: Community Food Resource Center, 1997), 5.

26. Benjamin Dulchin (organizing director, Fifth Avenue Committee), interview with the author, April 1997, Brooklyn, NY.

27. Gary Delgado, *Organizing the Movement: The Roots and Growth of ACORN* (Philadelphia: Temple University Press, 1986); John Krinsky, "ACORN," in *Poverty in the United States: An Encyclopedia of History, Politics, and Policy*, ed.Gwendolyn Mink and Alice O'Connor (Santa Barbara, CA: ABC-CLIO, 2004), 107.

28. Larry Holmes and Shelley Ettinger, *"We Won't Be Slaves": Workfare Workers Organize, Workfairness and the Struggle for Jobs, Justice, and Equality* (New York: International Action Center, 1997).

29. Richard Perez-Pena, "Transit Union Agrees to Allow Workfare Plan," *New York Times*, September 19, 1996; Steven Greenhouse, "Giuliani Attacks Transit Workfare Accord and Threatens to Scuttle Union Deal," *New York Times*, September 20, 1996.

30. District Council 37, AFSCME, AFL-CIO, "Federal Welfare Reform and Governor Pataki's Proposed New York State Implementation Plan: A Brief Overview and the Union's Position" (green paper, 1997); New York State Social Services Law, Consolidated Laws Service (CLS), sec. 336-c (2), (3).

31. This was especially true of the practice of calculating WEP workers' hours using minimum wages as the divisor of the value of welfare benefits.

32. For sympathetic portrayals of the reforms, see Lawrence Mead, *Government Matters: Welfare Reform in Wisconsin* (Princeton, NJ: Princeton University Press, 2004); Tommy G. Thompson, *Power to the People: An American State at Work* (New York: HarperCollins, 1996), chap. 3.

33. Carl Vogel and Neil DeMause, "Jason's Brain Trust," *City Limits*, December 1998, http://www.citylimits.org/content/articles/articleView.cfm?articlenumber=508.

34. See e.g., Welfare Law Center, "Welfare Law Center Claims That NYC Job Centers

Deter Food Stamps, Medicaid and Cash Assistance Applicants: Court Grants TRO," *Welfare News*, December 1998, http://www.nclej.org/contents/jobctr.htm; Welfare Law Center, "New York City Admits Monitoring Insufficient to Establish Proper Processing of Applications for Food Stamps, Medicaid, and Cash Assistance: Court Bars Opening of More Job Centers," *Welfare News*, September 1999, http://www.nclej.org/contents/monitoring.htm; Welfare Law Center, "Another Court Victory in *Reynolds v. Giuliani*," *Welfare News*, December 2000, http://www.nclej.org/contents/reynolds_another_victory.htm.

35. Richard Steier, "DC 37 Sues on WEP's Growth in Parks Dept.," *Chief/Civil Service Leader*, February 12, 1999; Andrew Jacobs, "Union Again Files Lawsuit Seeking End to Workfare," *New York Times*, April 15, 1999; see also Steven Greenhouse, "Vowing to Go from Scandal to Strength, City Union Looks for a Fight," *New York Times*, July 12, 1999.

36. Nina Bernstein, "City Fires 3,500 Former Welfare Recipients," *New York Times*, January 5, 2002; Matt Pacenza, "Bloomie: May Tempforce Not Be With You?" *City Limits Weekly*, January 21, 2002; see also Deidre McFayden and Mark Daly, "DC 37 Urges Jobs Program Reprieve," *Chief/Civil Service Leader*, January 25, 2002, 1.

37. Anne Schwartz, "Parks Opportunity Program," *Gotham Gazette*, April 2004, http://gothamgazette.com/article/parks/20040420/14/956. It is possible that the split between Roberts and Rosenthal—already present over other union issues—exacerbated their inability to come to an agreement on POP. In Roberts's reelection campaign for executive director, she singled out Rosenthal (who ran for treasurer on a slate headed by Roberts's rival, Local 371 president Charles Ensley) for criticism, charging that he was willing to "sell out the job-training workers just to increase his dues collection." See Richard Steier, "Roberts Wins, DC 37 Loses," *Chief/Civil Service Leader*, February 6, 2004, 4–6. Roberts, however, was not alone in driving a hard bargain. Community Voices Heard, which was organizing among POP workers—and which thought they were relatively neglected by Rosenthal's local—also wanted to avert a large pay cut for its members in POP. CVH, however, had no direct part in the bargaining process.

38. Turner, "Hearing on TANF Reauthorization." See also Tracie McMillan, "Ending Workfare as We Know It?" *City Limits*, July–August 2005, http://www.citylimits.orgcontent/articles/articleView.cfm?articlenumber=1263. McMillan reports that Turner's deputy, Andrew Bush (no relation to George W.), was an important formulator of the Bush administration's proposals to increase work requirements in subsequent rounds of welfare reform.

39. McMillan, "Ending Workfare"; Robert Pear, "Study by Governors Calls Bush Welfare Plan Unworkable," *New York Times*, April 4, 2002. See also Sharon Parrott, Wendell Primus, and Shawn Fremstadt, "Administration's TANF Proposals Would Limit—Not Increase—State Flexibility," Center for Budget and Policy Priorities, Washington, DC, 2002, http://www.cbpp.org/2-26-02tanf.htm; LaDonna Pavetti, "The Challenge of Achieving High Work Participation Rates in Welfare Programs," WR&B Brief 31 (Washington, DC: Brookings Institution, 2004).

40. See Craig Calhoun, "The Rise and Domestication of Historical Sociology," in *The Historic Turn in the Human Sciences*, ed. Terrance McDonald (Ann Arbor: University of Michigan Press, 1996), 305–38.

41. Frances Fox Piven and Richard A. Cloward, *Regulating the Poor: The Functions of Social Welfare*, 2nd ed. (1971; repr., New York: Vintage, 1993). Jamie Peck makes a similar point more explicitly in *Workfare States* (New York: Guilford Press, 2001)

and in *Work-Place: The Social Regulation of Labor Markets* (New York: Guilford Press, 1996).

42. Antonio Gramsci, "Americanism and Fordism," in *Selections from the Prison Notebooks*, ed. and trans. Quintin Hoare and Geoffrey Nowell Smith, 277–318 (New York: International Publishers, 1971.

43. See, e.g., James O'Connor, *The Fiscal Crisis of the State*, 2nd ed. (1973; repr., New York: St. Martin's Press, 2002).

44. Bob Jessop, "What Follows Fordism? On the Periodization of Capitalism and Its Regulation," in *Phases of Capitalist Development: Booms, Crises, and Globalization*, ed. Robert Albritton, Makoto Itoh, Richard Westra, and Robert Zuege, 282–99 (New York: St. Martin's Press, 2001); Bob Jessop, "The Transition to Post-Fordism and the Schumpeterian Workfare State," in *Towards a Post-Fordist Welfare State?* ed. Roger Burrows and Brian Loader (London: Routledge, 1994); Bob Jessop, "Liberalism, Neoliberalism, and Urban Governance: A State-Theoretical Perspective," in *Spaces of Neoliberalism: Urban Restructuring in North America and Western Europe*, ed. Neil Brenner and Nik Theodore (Oxford: Blackwell, 2002),106–25; Bob Jessop, "A Neo-Gramscian Approach to the Regulation of Urban Regimes," in *Reconstructing Urban Regime Theory: Regulating Urban Politics in a Global Economy*, ed. Mickey Lauria (Thousand Oaks, CA: Sage Publications, 1997), 51–73.

45. Peck, *Workfare States*, 365; See also Peck, "New Labourers? Making a New Deal for the 'Workless Class,'" *Environment and Planning C-Government and Policy* 17, no. 3 (1999): 345–72.

46. Bob Jessop and Jamie Peck, "Fast Policy/Local Discipline: The Politics of Time and Scale in the Neo-Liberal Workfare Offensive" (paper presented at the quadrennial meeting of the International Sociological Association, Montreal, July 1998).

47. Roberto M. Fernandez and Doug McAdam, "Social Networks and Social Movements: Multiorganizational Fields and Recruitment to Mississippi Freedom Summer," *Sociological Forum* 3, no. 3 (1988): 357–82; Bert Klandermans, "The Social Construction of Protest and Multiorganizational Fields," in *Frontiers in Social Movement Theory*, ed. Aldon D. Morris and Carol McClurg Mueller (New Haven, CT: Yale University Press, 1992), 77–103.

48. David S. Meyer, "Social Movements and Public Policy: Eggs, Chicken, and Theory," Center for the Study of Democracy Paper 03-02, January 15, 2003, 6, http://repositories.cdlib.org/csd/03-02.

49. See, e.g., David A. Snow, E. Burke Rochford Jr., Steven K. Worden, and Robert D. Benford, "Frame Alignment Processes, Micromobilization, and Movement Participation," *American Sociological Review* 51, no. 4 (1986): 464–81; Snow and Benford, "Ideology, Frame Resonance"; William A. Gamson, "Political Discourse and Collective Action," *International Social Movement Research* 1 (1988): 219–44.

50. Francesca Polletta, "'It was like a fever . . .' Narrative and Identity in Social Protest," *Social Problems* 45 (1998): 137–59.

51. See, e.g., Marc W. Steinberg, "The Talk and Back Talk of Collective Action: A Dialogic Analysis of Repertoires of Discourse among Nineteenth-Century English Cotton Spinners," *American Journal of Sociology* 105, no. 3 (1999): 736–80; Marc W. Steinberg, *Fighting Words: Working-Class Formation, Collective Action, and Discourse in Early Nineteenth Century England* (Ithaca, NY: Cornell University Press, 1999); Colin Barker, "A Modern Moral Economy? Edward Thompson and Valentin Volosinov Meet in North Manchester" (paper presented to the conference

on Making Social Movements: The British Marxist Historians and the Study of Social Movements, Edge Hill College of Higher Education, London, June 26–28, 2002); Chik Collins, *Language, Ideology and Social Consciousness: Developing a Socio-historical Approach* (Aldershot, UK: Ashgate, 1999).

52. Mikhail Mikhailovich Bakhtin, "The Problem of Speech Genres," in *Speech Genres and Other Late Essays*, by Bakhtin, ed. Caryl Emerson and Michael Holquist, trans. Vern W. McGee (Austin: University of Texas Press, 1986), 84–95.

53. Somers, "Narrative Construction of Identity."

54. See, e.g., Ronald L. Breiger, "A Toolkit for Practice Theory," *Poetics* 27 (2000): 91–115; John W. Mohr, "Soldiers, Mothers, Tramps and Others: Discourse Roles in the 1907 New York City Charity Directory," *Poetics: Journal of Empirical Research on Literature, the Media, and the Arts* 22 (1994): 327–57; Ann Mische, "Crosstalk in Social Movements: Reconceiving the Culture-Network Link," in *Social Movements and Networks: Relational Approaches to Collective Action*, ed. Mario Diani and Doug McAdam (Oxford: Oxford University Press, 2003), 258–80.

55. Katznelson, *City Trenches*.

56. Marc W. Steinberg, "Tilting the Frame: Considerations on Collective Action Framing from a Discursive Turn." *Theory and Society* 27, no. 6 (1998): 845–72, citing Mikhail Bakhtin, *Problems of Dostoevsky's Poetics*, ed. and trans. Caryl Emerson, introd. Wayne C. Booth (Minneapolis: University of Minnesota Press, 1984), 183.

57. M. M. Bakhtin, "Forms of Time and of the Chronotope in the Novel: Notes toward a Historical Poetics," in *The Dialogic Imagination: Four Essays*, by Bakhtin, ed. Michael Holquist, trans. Caryl Emerson and Michael Holquist (Austin: University of Texas Press, 1981), 52.

58. See, e.g., Charles Tilly, "Parliamentarization of Popular Contention in Great Britain, 1758–1834," in *Roads from Past to Future* (Lanham, MD: Rowman and Littlefield, 1997), 217–244; Ann Mische and Philippa Pattison, "Composing a Civic Arena: Publics, Projects, and Social Settings," *Poetics: Journal of Empirical Research on Culture, the Media and the Arts*, special issue, ed. John Mohr, 27, nos. 2, 3 (March 2000):163–94.

59. Paul J. DiMaggio, "Why Cognitive (and Cultural) Sociology Needs Cognitive Psychology," in *Culture in Mind: Toward a Sociology of Culture and Cognition*, ed. Karen A. Cerulo (New York: Routledge, 2002), 274–81; see also other contributions to the volume. For a now-dated critical overview of scholarship in this field, see Paul J. DiMaggio, "Culture and Cognition," *Annual Review of Sociology* 23 (1997): 263–87.

60. See Engeström, *Learning by Expanding.*

61. David Firestone, "He Fights, Patiently, for Workfare Laborers," *New York Times*, January 16,1998.

CHAPTER TWO

1. Peck, *Workfare States*. The book compares programs among states within the United States and among countries as well.

2. Modest work requirements were passed by Congress in 1967 out of frustration with rising costs. This legislation was known as Work Incentives Now (WIN), and it formed the legal basis of Nixon's Work Incentive Program reforms four years later. The name changed, but the WIN acronym stuck.

3. Lawrence M. Mead, *The New Politics of Poverty* (New York: Basic Books, 1992);

Lawrence M. Mead, *The New Paternalism: Supervisory Approaches to Poverty* (Washington, DC: Brookings Institution Press, 1997); Mickey Kaus, *The End of Equality* (New York: Basic Books, 1992).

4. WREP was discontinued in 1976 during the fiscal crisis because of its greater cost relative to regular welfare. At the same time, at a point before the enforced austerity of the fiscal crisis, it enabled the City to save on labor costs. Nevertheless, as a time-limited, wage-substitution program, it served as one model for transitional job programs in the late 1990s. See Douglas J. Besharov and Peter Germanis, "Full Engagement Welfare in New York City: Lessons for TANF's Participation Requirements," University of Maryland School of Public Policy and Welfare Reform Academy, College Park, August 2004, http://www.welfareacademy.org/pubs/welfare/nyc_hra.pdf, 53–54; Tait, *Poor Workers' Unions*, 92.

5. Goodwin, "Thousands on 'Workfare' Get Half-Pay."

6. Ibid.

7. For example, in 1991, William Grinker, Koch's HRA commissioner, in letter to the *City Journal*, expressed regret that workfare programs tended to have poor enforcement mechanisms. The *City Journal* is the magazine issued by the Manhattan Institute, a right-wing think tank focused on urban affairs generally and on New York's profligate, liberal ways in particular. See William J. Grinker, letter to the editor, *City Journal*, Autumn 1997, http://www.city-journal.org/html/1_5_letters.html.

8. Besharov and Germanis, "Full Engagement," 174–75; also see Demetra Smith Nightingale, Nancy Pindus, Fredrica D. Kramer, John Trutko, Kelly S. Mikelson, and Michael Egner, "Work and Welfare Reform in New York City during the Giuliani Administration: A Study of Program Implementation," Urban Institute, Washington, DC, 2002, http://www.urban.org/url.cfm?ID=410542. This report gives a detailed account of changes in the workfare program's administration under Giuliani.

9. Krueger, Wernick, and Accles, "The Real Deal," report that between October 1995 and September 1996, 40 percent of the WEP caseload was sanctioned. The point-in-time estimate is much lower, but the sanction rate increased from 8 percent in 1996 (when AFDC parents were called into WEP) to 14 percent in 1999 and then declined to 9 percent, with an additional 13 percent in the sanctioning process, by 2001. See Nightingale et al., "Work and Welfare Reform," iv. Important in this regard is that New York State does not have a "full-family sanction" for families in the Temporary Aid to Needy Families (TANF) program. Accordingly, there are some "happily sanctioned" cases, in which the parent's share of the welfare benefits are cut off—often for noncompliance with work requirements—but the children's are not.

10. Nightingale et al., "Work and Welfare Reform."

11. This is known as the "three-plus-two" model. See ibid., 37, for a more detailed picture.

12. New York City Independent Budget Office, "Use of Work Experience Program participants at the Department of Parks and Recreation," *Inside the Budget News-Fax*, November 1, 2000, 1–3; New York City Independent Budget Office, "Governor Wants Remaining Welfare Surplus to Help Close Budget Gap," *Inside the Budget NewsFax*, February 25, 2002, 1; Heather MacDonald, "Wimping Out on Welfare," *City Journal*, Autumn 2003, http://www.city-journal.org/html/13_4_sndgs01.html.

13. New York City Independent Budget Office, "Use of Work Experience Program participants," 3; and Besharov and Germanis, "Full Engagement," 113–25 have a detailed cost-benefit analysis that suggests a wide range of estimated cost savings on WEP depending on how the value of WEP workers' work is calculated and whether one extends the analysis to the savings achieved through sanctions.

14. Mercedes Padilla, "Estudiantes de Hostos Protestan Medidas," *El Diario/La Prensa*, September 11, 1998; Dillona C. Lewis, "School's Out for Welfare Recipients: College Students Forced to Abandon Studies by Welfare Reform," National Association of Social Workers, New York Chapter, 1999, http://www.naswnyc.org/w11.html; Felecia Kornbluh, "Class Dismissed: Welfare Recipients Fight to Stay in College," *In These Times*, October 5, 1997, 18–20.

15. Kornbluh, "School's Out"; Maureen Lane, letter to the editor, *New York Times*, January 4, 1998. Besharov and Germanis suggest that the causal relation between declining welfare recipient enrollment in CUNY and workfare may be less straightforward and that fewer CUNY students were on welfare because fewer people were on welfare altogether ("Full Engagement," 98). Nevertheless, for people within the CUNY system, both students and faculty, the relationship was immediate and clear. The Giuliani administration also began to assign high school students who were over age eighteen to workfare assignments, but the courts stopped it from continuing this practice. See Pete Bowles, "Victory for Workfare Students," *Newsday*, June 9, 1998; Welfare Law Center, Summary of *Matthews v. Paoli*, http://www.nclej.org/contents/docket/docket2001.htm.

16. New York State Consolidated Laws Service, chap. 534, sec. 1, 5.

17. See summary of settlement in *Davila v. Eggleston* (index number 407163196, New York County Supreme Court) at www.urbanjustice.org/pdf/litigation/Davila Summary.pdf.

18. Rachel Swarns, "Mothers Poised for Acute Lack of Daycare," *New York Times*, April 14, 1998.

19. Child Care Inc., "Welfare to Work and Child Care: Pathways to Success (Helping Families on Public Assistance to Make Good Child Care Arrangements)" (report, Year I Preliminary Findings, August 1997), 3.

20. This is an aspect of "flexible accumulation" noted by David Harvey: "Sweatshops and the informal provision of services began to emerge as vital aspects of the New York and Los Angeles economies in the 1970s and by now have become important throughout the US urban system. These have been paralleled by an increasing commodification of traditional mutual aid systems within low-income communities. Baby-sitting, laundering, cleaning, fixing-up, and odd jobs, which used to be swapped more as favors are now bought and sold, sometimes on an entrepreneurial basis." David Harvey, "Flexible Accumulation through Urbanization," in *The Urban Experience* (Baltimore: Johns Hopkins University Press, 1989), 268.

21. Swarns, "Mothers Poised."

22. David Lewis, "Poor Squeezed Out of Day Care," *Daily News*, March 1, 1998; Somini Sengupta, "City Hall to Use $54 Million to Add Day Care Subsidies," *New York Times*, April 18, 2000.

23. Roslyn Powell and Mia Cahill, "Nowhere to Turn: New York City's Failure to Inform Parents on Public Assistance about their Child Care Rights," *Georgetown Journal on Poverty Law and Policy* 7, no. 2 (Summer 2000): 370–71. Similarly, a study by the Public Advocate's Office in 1997 found that of seventy-three welfare recipients interviewed, forty-six were threatened with sanctions if they could not

find adequate child care. See Public Advocate for the City of New York, "Welfare and Child Care: What About the Children?" (report, June 1997). See also Brooke Richie and Robin Epstein, "Day Carelessness," *City Limits* 22, no. 7 (August–September 1997): 12–13.

24. See New York City Independent Budget Office, "New York's Increasing Dependence on the Welfare Surplus" (fiscal brief, IBO, New York, 2001); New York City Independent Budget Office, "With Welfare Surplus Shrinking, City Could Face $80 Million Aid Loss" (fiscal brief, IBO, New York, April 2004).

25. See, for example, the comments of Marcia Meyers, "Next Steps: New York City Welfare Policy After Giuliani," Milano Graduate School, New School University, April 25, 2001, http://www.newschool.edu/milano/nycaffairs/welfare/session1. htm. She finds that in New York City, "among the leavers and the recipients, post-welfare reform reports of hunger in the family due to insufficient income were actually up . . . in all cases we see an increase in overcrowding. Not surprising, given that doubling up is a very common survival strategy for families who are on the edge economically."

26. The discrepant percentages are easy enough to reconcile: food pantries are giving out less food per visitor.

27. The numbers around demand for food, met and unmet, are slightly inconsistent, but all point to an increasing problem. In many cases, as will be discussed briefly, the increased incidence of hunger has to do with a corollary problem to toughened Eligibility Verification Reviews, namely, the inappropriate and illegal denial of federal food stamp benefits to applicants for welfare at the new "Job Centers." See esp. New York City Welfare Reform and Human Rights Documentation Project, "Hunger is No Accident: New York and Federal Welfare Policies Violate the Human Right to Food" (report, New York City Welfare Reform and Human Rights Documentation Project, July 2000); New York City Coalition Against Hunger, "Breadlines in Boomtown" (report, NYCCAH, June 1997); Alyssa Katz, "Second Helping," *City Limits* 24, no. 4 (1999): 24–29.

28. Nina Bernstein, "New Welfare Director Defends Stance on Food Stamp Waiver," *New York Times*, March 15, 2002; K. Wright, "Food Stamp Hurdles," *City Limits Weekly*, September 23, 2003, http://www.citylimits.org/content/articles/weekly View.cfm?articlenumber=1313; T. McMillan, "Stamping Out Hunger," *City Limits Weekly*, May 2, 2005, http://www.citylimits.org/content/articles/weeklyView .cfm?articlenumber=1715; T. McMillan, "Bloomberg Balks on Bills," *City Limits Weekly*, July 25, 2005, http://www.citylimits.org/content/articles/weeklyView .cfm?articlenumber=1755.

29. Alyssa Katz, "Losing Home Run," *City Limits* 27, no. 3 (2002), http://www.citylim-its.org. The extent to which this occurs can be difficult to untangle. Jiggetts does pay back rent when a welfare case has been closed and subsequently reopened, as with a sanction; see Alyssa Danigelis, "No More Jiggetts? State Launches Rent Subsidy," *City Limits Weekly*, May 16, 2005, http://www.citylimits.org/content/ articles/weeklyView.cfm?articlenumber=1719. On the issue of Jiggetts, in 2001, the City instituted a job transition incentive pilot program in two Job Centers that provided extended Jiggetts relief for welfare recipients who were employed for at least four continuous months and at least part-time. Community Service Society of New York, "Public Assistance: New Shelter Allowances" (newsletter, Advocacy, Counseling, and Entitlement Services Project, Retired Senior Volunteer Program, Community Service Society, New York, 2003).

30. Peter H. Rossi, *Down and Out in America: The Origins of Homelessness* (Chicago: University of Chicago Press, 1989), 189;Coalition for the Homeless, "Charts Detailing the New York City Homeless Shelter Population," Chart 1, http://www .coalitionforthehomeless.org/advocacy/basic_facts.html#factsheets.

31. Administration for Children and Families, "Personal Responsibility and Work Opportunity Reconciliation Act of 1996," Fact Sheet, August 8, 1996, http:// www.acf.dhhs.gov/programs/ofa/prwora96.htm.

32. WEP assignments regularly exceeded the thirty-hour minimum and were usually thirty-five hours per week in an effort to simulate a regular workweek. HR recipients were required to work twenty-six hours per week.

33. I am indebted to Ricky Blum for explaining these issues to me.

34. *Brukhman v. Giuliani,* 1997 N.Y. Misc. LEXIS 412, May 19, 1997.

35. *Brukhman v. Giuliani,* 2000 N.Y. LEXIS 77, February 22, 2000.

36. The case, *Butler v. Perry,* involved a challenge to Florida's compulsory labor law, which pressed people into service in road-building projects for a week per year, in lieu of a tax payment. Those who could pay the tax were exempt. The U.S. Supreme Court found that compulsory road-building work had sufficient precedent in common law to exempt it from the Thirteenth and Fourteenth Amendments and that a property right in labor was not absolute; see James W. Ely Jr. and David J. Bodenhamer, "Regionalism and American Legal History: The Southern Experience," *Vanderbilt Law Review* 39 (April 1986): 539ff. Because the legal representatives of WEP did not press a Thirteenth Amendment case, nor did they contest the City's interpretation of the *Butler* precedent, we do not have a way of knowing how that claim might have been treated by the Court, though WEP workers' lawyers were probably right in thinking that it would not be entertained. I thank Richard Blum of the Legal Aid Society, a lawyer in the *Brukhman* litigation, for drawing my attention to this issue. See *Butler v. Perry* 1916 U.S. LEXIS 1455.

37. J. Jacobs, Dissent in *United States v. City of New York* 2004 U.S. App. LEXIS 2439 at 53.

38. For a discussion of this and other "Goffmanian" elements of WEP, see Goldberg, "Welfare Recipients or Workers?" Sometimes the concern about public visibility was less symbolic and more immediate, as outdoor work could leave WEP workers vulnerable to attack by abusive, estranged boyfriends or spouses.

39. The study sample appears to be broadly representative. Compared to WEP agency deployments at the end of June 1999 (taken as a baseline because of the seasonal deployment of WEP workers in Parks and because most of the sample was generated during warm-weather months) it oversampled DCAS-assigned WEP workers, slightly undersampled HRA-assigned WEP workers, and almost perfectly corresponded to the proportion of DPR workers in the overall WEP pool.

40. City of New York Department of Parks and Recreation, "Eight Seasons Report, 1996–1997: A Report to the People" (report, City of New York, 1997).

41. Chris Tilly and Charles Tilly, *Work under Capitalism* (Boulder: Westview Press, 1998), 167.

42. David M. Gordon, Richard Edwards, and Michael Reich, *Segmented Work, Divided Workers: The Historical Transformations of Labor in the United States* (Cambridge: Cambridge University Press, 1982); see also Peck, *Work-Place.*

43. Tilly and Tilly, *Work under Capitalism,* 171.

44. There is also increasing evidence from national studies to suggest that work-first welfare reform, in pushing welfare recipients to accept any job that comes their

way, has pushed white women into the labor market with greater success, due to racialized employer preferences for service workers. For an indication of these trends, see Steve Savner, "Welfare Reform and Racial/Ethnic Minorities: The Questions to Ask," *Poverty and Race* 9 (July–August, 2000): 3, http://www.prrac .org; Shiela R. Zedelewski and Donald W. Alderson, "Before and After Reform: How Have Welfare Families Changed?" Urban Institute, Washington, DC, 2001, http://newfederalism.urban.org/html/series_b/b32/b32.html. These tendencies have compound effects when combined with racial residential segregation. Where, for example, in Milwaukee, jobs are plentiful in the close-in suburbs but scarce in the inner city, time-to-work and attendant obstacles (e.g., finding the requisite child-care arrangements) increase, too.

45. See Kathryn Edin and Laura Lein, *Making Ends Meet: How Single Mothers Survive Welfare and Low-Wage Work* (New York: Russell Sage Foundation, 1997).

46. There are several reasons that a government might want to do so. Among adherents of the so-called New Public Management, which include Mayor Giuliani, there is an assumption that municipal government "should be run as a business and is based on a set of interrelated principles applied to reduce the cost of government by encouraging privatization and managed competition of government services"; see Lynn A. Weikart, "The New Public Management and the Giuliani Administration in New York City," *Urban Affairs Review* 36, no. 3 (2001): 359–81. By favoring the private sector over the public sector in this way, administrators can divert resources from the latter to the former and make possible the greater exploitation of labor (see Sites, *Remaking New York*). Daniel Cohn argues that neoconservative governments actively tried to "undermine the capabilities of the state, turning the macrocrisis of Western society into a crisis of the Western state, the solution of which required a broad reordering of governance. . . . The goal is no longer to protect society from the market's demands but to protect the market from society's demands." Daniel Cohn, "Creating Crises and Avoiding Blame: The Politics of Public Service Reform and the New Public Management in Great Britain and the United States," *Administration and Society* 29, no. 5 (1997): 584–85. A still more cynical but defensible view might take note of the profits that can be reaped by officials who leave government to form or join companies that administer welfare-to-work contracts. Mayoral adviser Richard J. Schwartz left city government in 1996 to found Opportunity America, which later was part of a group that was awarded a welfare-to-work contract by the Giuliani administration. Opportunity America was a subcontractor in the bid with Maximus, a nationwide firm that administers welfare-to-work and welfare programs. Maximus, which played a key role in Wisconsin's welfare reform, was favored by Jason Turner, who had administered Wisconsin's welfare program prior to coming to New York. Former Giuliani spokesperson Colleen Roche became a spokesperson for Maximus, and Jason Turner's father got a job with the company as well. See Kathleen McGowan, "The Welfare Estate," *City Limits*, June 1999, http://www .citylimits.org; Kathleen McGowan and Jarrett Murphy, "Contractus Maximus," *City Limits*, January 2000, http://www.citylimits.org.

47. Jamie Peck and Nik Theodore, "Commentary, 'Work First': Workfare and the Regulation of Contingent Labour Markets," *Cambridge Journal of Economics* 24 (2000): 119–38; Jamie Peck and Nik Theodore, "Beyond 'Employability,'" *Cambridge Journal of Economics* 24 (2000): 729–49; see also Peck, *Work-Place*; Peck, *Workfare States*.

48. As with privatization, though, workfare only affords some chance that public entities will "get what they pay for"; see Elliot Sclar, *You Don't Always Get What You Pay For: The Economics of Privatization* (Ithaca, NY: Cornell University Press, 2000). There are costs to turnover pools and to contracting out for services that can be substantial, even in comparison to more-stable, more-remunerative work.

49. Mark Maier, *City Unions: Managing Discontent in New York City* (New Brunswick, NJ: Rutgers University Press, 1987), 90–91, 183–90.

50. Deidre McFadyen, "At 1549, Members Call Fraud Typical," *Chief/Civil Service Leader*, December 4, 1998, 1, 6).

51. New York State Consolidated Laws Service, sec. 336.

52. See, e.g., Sites, *Remaking New York*, 52–56; Sites, "Limits of Urban Regime Theory," 547–48.

53. Emphasis added; cited in Laura Wernick, John Krinsky, Paul Getsos, and Community Voices Heard, *WEP: New York City's Public Sector Sweatshop* (New York: Community Voices Heard, June 2000).

54. An agreement with the MTA was reached three years later. See Mark Daly, "City, MTA in Deal on Subway WEPs," *Chief/Civil Service Leader*, April 30, 1999, 5; on the hospitals story, see Richard Steier, "Dispute on HHC Deal Leads to Layoff of 585," *Chief/Civil Service Leader*, May 22, 1998, 1,7.

55. Besharov and Germanis, "Full Engagement," 74–80. The authors mainly concur with administration officials that large-scale displacement did not occur other than through attrition. Accordingly, they worry about calling it *displacement* if the work was not otherwise going to get done. This seems like splitting hairs, since once work was redistributed, it would no longer be counted in displaced work.

56. New York City Independent Budget Office, "The Municipal Workforce: Big a Decade Ago, but Composition Has Changed." *Inside the Budget NewsFax 92*, December 11, 2001, 1–2.

57. Besharov and Germanis, "Full Engagement."

58. This position is echoed by conservative commentators, e.g., MacDonald; this, of course, cuts directly to the "liberal" assumptions in neoliberalism.

59. Cohn, "Creating Crises," 584.

60. Robert B. Reich, "Working But Not 'Employed,'" *New York Times*, January 9, 2001.

61. Editorial, *New York Times*, February 21, 1997.

62. *Brukhman v. Giuliani*, 2000.

63. Paul Getsos (lead organizer, Community Voices Heard), interview with the author, June 2000.

64. Piven and Cloward, *Regulating the Poor*, chap. 11, esp. 395–97.

65. Jessop, "What Follows Fordism?"; Peck and Theodore, "Commentary, 'Work First'"; Peck and Theodore, "Beyond 'Employability'"; Peck, *Workfare States*.

66. The testimony is from *Capers v. Giuliani* 253 AD.2d 630 (1st Dept. 1998), reproduced in "Welfare as They Know It," *Harper's*, November 1, 1997, 24–29.

67. Quoted in David Lewis, "Welfare Boss: Work Is the Way," Daily News, March 11, 1998, 20.

68. Governor Pataki proposed to cut the earned-income disregard in 1994, but the provision was defeated in the budget process. See Anne Erikson, "The Governor's Welfare Proposals," *Legal Services Journal*, February 2004, http://www.gulpny.org/Public%20Benefits/Cash%20Assistance/governorwelfareproposals.htm.

69. Tracie McMillan, "The Big Idea: TANF Taketh Away," *City Limits*, January–

February 2005, http://www.citylimits.org/content/articles/articleView.cfm?article number=1220.

70. Joshua Freeman, *Working Class New York: Life and Labor since World War II* (New York: New Press, 2000), 272.

71. Ibid., 257.

72. William K. Tabb, "The New York City Fiscal Crisis," in *Marxism and the Metropolis: New Perspectives in Urban Political Economy*, 2nd ed., ed. William K. Tabb and Larry Sawers, 328 (New York: Oxford University Press); Freeman, *Working Class New York*, 257.

73. Felix Rohatyn, a banker who became the head of the Municipal Assistance Corporation, a body created to rescue New York City from bankruptcy, recalled, "The political crisis was of a different nature. New York City was the liberal capital of the U.S. and the media capital. A presidential election was coming up in 1976 and the Ford Administration was making hay of the New York crisis as a symbol of the bankruptcy of liberalism and of the Democratic Party. Bill Simon, Treasury Secretary in the Ford Administration, never tired of this argument. President Ford's spokesman, Ron Nessen, had compared New York to 'a wayward daughter hooked on heroin. You don't give her $100 a day to support her habit. You make her go cold turkey to break the habit.' And President Ford and his advisors had found what they thought was a platform on which they could run: 'New York City must pay for its sins, and the rest of the country must learn from the City's mistakes, or be doomed by them.' The bankruptcy of New York would be the excuse needed to reverse progressive social thinking from FDR's New Deal through Johnson's Great Society." See Felix Rohatyn, "New York's Fiscal Crises, 1975–2002" (M. Moran Weston II Distinguished Lecture in Urban and Public Policy, Columbia University School of International and Public Affairs, New York, February 26, 2002). William Simon became the president of the conservative Olin Foundation after Jimmy Carter's election in 1976. He was a cofounder of the Manhattan Institute in 1978 and a major player in New Right politics.

74. In 1975, Simon testified, "Any federal aid to New York . . . should be on terms 'so punitive, the overall experience made so painful, that no city, no political subdivision would ever be tempted to go down the same road.'" Quoted in Freeman, *Working Class New York*, 259; see also 272. See also Tabb, "New York City Fiscal Crisis," 330. For a contemporary example of this perspective, see E. J. McMahon and Fred Siegel, "Gotham's Fiscal Crisis: Lessons Unlearned," *Public Interest* 158 (Winter 2005): 96–110. See also Sites, *Remaking New York*, 42–44.

75. See Freeman, *Working Class New York*, 284–85.

76. On the growing importance of bond-rating agencies in municipal politics and governance, see Jason Hackworth, "Local Autonomy, Bond-Rating Agencies and Neoliberal Urbanism in the United States," *International Journal of Urban and Regional Research* 26, no. 4 (December 2002): 707–25.

77. The no-layoff clause did not apply to the Hospital Workers' local because the Giuliani administration was pursuing privatization plans for public hospitals.

78. Robert Fitch, "The Mayor's Greatest Legacy," *Five Borough Report* 8 (February 2002): 1–4. For clues to the relation of workfare to New York City's bond rating, see Daniel Kruger, "Moody's Upgrades NYC GOs to A3, Citing Fiscal Prudence," *Bond Buyer*, February 25,1998; Robin Prunty, "New York City; General Obligation, Local GO" (report, Standard and Poor's, 1999), http://www.standardandpoors.com/ratings/publicfinance/. See also "Mayor Giuliani Addresses Public Finance Professionals at

the Bond Buyer 3rd Annual New York Public Finance Conference," (press release 707-97, December 2, 1997), http://www.nyc.gov/html/om/html/97/sp707-97.html. In it, the mayor makes a clear connection between fiscal viability and labor and welfare.

79. See Cohn, "Creating Crises."
80. Peck, "New Labourers?"; Peck, *Workfare States*, 365; see also John Krinsky and Ellen Reese, "Forging and Sustaining Labor-Community Coalitions: The Workfare Justice Movement in Three Cities," *Sociological Forum* 21, no. 4 (December 2006): 623–58.

CHAPTER THREE

1. David S. Meyer and Nancy Whittier, "Social Movement Spillover," *Social Problems* 41, no. 2 (May 1994): 277–98.
2. See Jessop, "Liberalism, Neoliberalism, and Urban Governance."
3. Raka Ray, *Fields of Protest: Women's Movements in India* (Minneapolis: University of Minnesota Press, 1999), 6–8.
4. See, e.g., Andy Clark, *Being There: Putting Brain, Body, and World Back Together* (Cambridge, MA: MIT Press, 1997), 42–43.
5. Charles Tilly, "Parliamentarization of Popular Contention" Charles Tilly, *Stories, Identities and Political Change* (Lanham, MD: Rowman and Littlefield, 2002).
6. Ray, *Fields of Protest*, 11.
7. This is simply to say that the neoliberal ideal bears little relation to the actual demands of politics and governance. Neoliberalism is a state project requiring the coordination of coercion and legitimacy; it cannot do without either.
8. Neither these reductions nor the threats were accidental. Mayor Koch's commissioner of housing, Roger Starr, advocated a strategy of "planned shrinkage," or the withdrawal of city services from economically marginal areas, in order to encourage the economically superfluous to move from the city. Though Starr was chased from office after these comments (and into a job as a columnist for the *New York Times*), his vision was partially implemented, as firehouses closed, and other services were withdrawn from poor areas of the city that were losing population. See Roger Starr, "Making New York Smaller," *New York Times Magazine*, November 14, 1976, 32–33, 99–106.
9. Harold DeRienzo, "Managing the Crisis," *City Limits*, December 1994, 25. See also Doug Turetsky, "'We Are the Landlords Now . . .' A Report on Community-Based Housing Management" (report, Community Service Society, New York, 1993); Ronald Lawson, with the assistance of Rueben Johnson III, "Tenant Responses to the Urban Housing Crisis, 1970–1984," in *The Tenant Movement in New York City*, ed. Ronald Lawson, with the assistance of Marc Naison (Philadelphia: Temple University Press, 1986), chap. 5; and James DeFillipis, *Unmaking Goliath: Community Control in the Face of Global Capital* (New York: Routledge, 2004).
10. For an account of FAC's efforts in setting up a mutual housing association—community- and resident-controlled nonprofit rental housing—see John Krinsky and Sarah Hovde, *Balancing Acts: The Experience of Mutual Housing Associations and Community Land Trusts in Urban Neighborhoods* (New York: Community Service Society, 1996). See also DeFillipis, *Unmaking Goliath*.
11. Krinsky and Hovde, *Balancing Acts*; Steven Erlanger, "New York Turns Squatters into Homeowners," *New York Times*, October 12, 1987; see also Seth Borgos, "Low-Income Homeownership and the ACORN Squatters Campaign," in *Critical Perspectives on Housing*, ed. Rachel G. Bratt, Chester Hartman, and Ann Meyerson

(Philadelphia: Temple University Press, 1986): 428–46. On ACORN generally, see Delgado, *Organizing the Movement*; Krinsky, "ACORN."

12. See Piven and Cloward, *Regulating the Poor*, chap. 10; Martha F. Davis, *Brutal Need: Lawyers and the Welfare Rights Movement, 1960–1973* (New Haven, CT: Yale University Press, 1993).

13. See Davis, *Brutal Need*.

14. These rules have been challenged by legal advocates in suits called *Velazquez v. Legal Services Corp.* and *Dobbins v. Legal Services Corp.* The U.S. Supreme Court struck down the provision barring Legal Services from challenging welfare reform laws as a violation of the First Amendment. Other aspects of the cases were still in litigation as of early 2007. See materials at http://www.brennancenter.org/programs/stack_detail.asp?key=1028.subkey=8313.

15. Rick Fantasia and Kim Voss, *Hard Work: Remaking the American Labor Movement* (Berkeley and Los Angeles: University of California Press, 2004).

16. Freeman, *Working Class New York*, chap. 15; Rohatyn, "New York's Fiscal Crises," 8.

17. The Taylor Law was more recently invoked in the jailing of Roger Toussaint, the leader of Transport Workers Union Local 100, as a result of that local's strike in December 2005.

18. Robert Fitch, "Our Labor Leaders Need French Lessons," *New Politics* 6, no. 1 (1996), http://www.wpunj.edu/newpol/issue21/cont21.htm.

19. Maier, *City Unions*.

20. See, e.g., Richard Steier, "National Union Outs Hill as DC 37 Head," *Chief/Civil Service Leader*, December 4: 1998, 1,7.

21. See, e.g., Schleichler, "Making Workfare Work." The Public School Employees' president was a key figure in DC 37's embezzlement scandal. See Richard Steier, "Say Breakdown by Hughes Led to Wrongdoing," *Chief/Civil Service Leader*, December 4, 1998, 1, 7.

22. This symbolism was reinforced by the fact that Mayor Giuliani's allies in DC 37 were those most implicated in the corruption. See Richard Steier, "Targets: 'Friends of Rudy,'" *Chief/Civil Service Leader*, October 30, 1998, 4. Importantly, the new administration of DC 37 imposed by the national union in late 1998 was quick to denounce workfare, in part to symbolize the break from the previous *modus operandi* the union had reached with the mayor. See Lee Saunders, "Fighting for Our Future Means Returning to Basics," *Public Employee Press*, February 12, 1999, 2.

23. Fitch estimates that CWA lost roughly 15 percent of its members as a consequence of its recalcitrance at the bargaining table (Fitch, "Leaders Need French Lessons"). City unions cannot strike under the terms of the Taylor Law. See, e.g., Kristin Guild, "The New York State Taylor Law: Negotiating to Avoid Strikes in the Public Sector," Restructuring Local Government Series (Ithaca, NY: Cornell University Department of City and Regional Planning, May 1998).

24. Paul Getsos (lead organizer, Community Voices Heard), interview with the author, June 2000.

25. Benjamin Dulchin, interview with the author, October 1999.

26. Another influence on these overlapping networks may also have been overlap from ACT-UP, the AIDS activist group that defined spirited, direct-action tactics for many in the late 1980s and early 1990s. Some important actors in these networks, including CVH and UJC organizers, had experience within ACT-UP itself. Through networks such as WRN—which featured several nonprofit

health-care and housing advocacy groups employing ACT-UP members in more political roles—some antipoverty advocacy groups absorbed a more-militant activist ethos focused on confrontation and on promoting and publicizing the voices of those most affected by policy.

27. Antonio Gramsci, *Selections from the Prison Notebooks*, ed. and trans. Quintin Hoare and Geoffrey Nowell Smith (New York: International Publishers, 1971), 238–39.

28. For Gramsci, this is the role of the party. See, e.g., Anne Showstack Sassoon, *Gramsci's Politics* (Minneapolis: University of Minnesota Press, 1987), 193–204.

CHAPTER FOUR

1. Gramsci, *Selections*, 234.

2. Ibid., 263. Much of this discussion is indebted to Joseph Buttigieg, "The Contemporary Discourse on Civil Society: A Gramscian Critique," *Boundary* 2 (Spring 2005): 33–52.

3. Cited in Buttigieg, 40.

4. Katznelson, *City Trenches*.

5. Gramsci writes, in this vein, "The truth is that one cannot choose the form of war one wants, unless from the start one has a crushing superiority over the enemy." Gramsci, *Selections*, 234.

6. Somers, "Narrative Constitution of Identity," 626.

7. See Vološinov, *Freudianism*, 99ff. Also V. N. Vološinov, *Marxism and the Philosophy of Language*, trans. Ladislav Matejka and I. R. Titunik (Cambridge, MA: Harvard University Press, 1973), 68–70.

8. See Charles Tilly, *The Contentious French* (Cambridge, MA: Harvard University Press, 1986), 10. Here, Tilly explicitly links the development of repertoires with the material circumstances of people's lives. He points out that grain seizures, for example, were directly linked to the existence of regular markets and to a growing system of agriculture that generated surplus grain and material privation at the same time.

9. This is true of repertoires and indicates their dialogic construction. See Charles Tilly, "Contentious Conversation," *Social Research* 65, no. 3 (1998): 491–510.

10. See, e.g., Marc W. Steinberg, "Toward a More Dialogic Analysis of Social Movement Culture," in *Social Movements: Identity, Culture, and the State*, ed. David S. Meyer, Nancy Whittier, and Belinda Robnett (Oxford: Oxford University Press, 2002), 208–25.

11. Bakhtin, "Forms of Time," 84.

12. M. M. Bakhtin, "Discourse in the Novel," in *The Dialogic Imagination: Four Essays*, ed. Michael Holquist, trans. Caryl Emerson and Michael Holquist (Austin: University of Texas Press, 1981), 272–73.

13. Benjamin Dulchin (organizing director, Fifth Avenue Committee), interview with the author, October 1999.

14. WEP Workers Together, "Why We Are Marching in the Labor Day Parade" (flyer, September 6, 1996). WWT is citing the research of Chris Tilly, "Workfare's Impact on the New York City Labor Market: Lower Wages and Worker Displacement" (Russell Sage Working Paper 92, Russell Sage Foundation, New York, March 1996).

15. WWT, "Why We Are Marching" flyer; WEP Workers Together, "'Workfare' Workers Form Union and March in the Labor Day Parade" (press release, September 6, 1996).

16. Rev. Peter Laarman (senior minister, Judson Memorial Church), interview with the author, November 1997.

17. Dominic Chan (executive director, Jobs with Justice), interview with the author, October 1997.

18. Jeffrey K. Olick, "Genre Memories and Memory Genres: A Dialogical Analysis of May 8th, 1945 Commemorations in the Federal Republic of Germany," *American Sociological Review* 64 (June 1999): 381–402. See also David Bakhurst, "Social Memory in Soviet Thought," in *An Introduction to Vygotsky,* ed. Harry Daniels (London: Routledge, 1996), 196–218.

19. Laarman, interview.

20. Speech by Jon Kest to Worker's Defense League, December 1997. From author's notes.

21. See Olick, "Genre Memories and Memory Genres."

22. ACORN did just this. See Stanley Hill, letter to DC 37 Workfare Worker Organizing Committee, October 1, 1997, in author's possession. The quotation is from Milagros Silva (lead organizer, ACORN/WEP Workers Organizing Committee), interview with the author, November 1997.

23. ACORN WEP Worker Organizing Committee, "Year End/Year Beginning" (report, January 1998).

24. Ibid.

25. I have never been able to uncover proof that WEP workers were sanctioned for being active with one of the organizing groups. The threat of sanctions, however, was potent.

26. Getsos, interview.

27. Ibid.

28. Another CVH organizer mentioned this fear of sanction, too, saying in a 2000 interview that "people get scared and they're like: 'Why am I not allowed to talk to you? Are you from ACORN?'" A FUREE activist confirmed it as late as 2003, though she indicated—as others had, too—that she had never actually seen someone be sanctioned for organizing activity. Elaine Kim (organizer, Community Voices Heard), interview with the author, June 2000; Brenda Stewart, (organizer, FUREE), interview with the author, June 2003.

29. Gail Aska (public relations director, Community Voices Heard), interview with the author, April 2000.

30. Getsos, interview.

31. Dulchin, interview, October 1999. The interview was conducted when WWT was under the sole organizational auspices of FAC and shared with FAC an organizing director.

32. Benjamin Dulchin, interview with the author, November 1997.

33. Dulchin, interview, October 1999.

34. Kim, interview, June 2000.

35. Quotations are from Daniel Esakoff (former DC 37/WWOC organizer), interview with the author, September 2004.

36. Dulchin, interview, November 1997.

37. Heidi Dorow (lead organizer, Urban Justice Center Organizing Project), interview with the author, May 1997.

38. Michael Hanagan, "The Right to Work and the Struggle against Unemployment: Britain, 1884–1914," in *Extending Citizenship, Reconfiguring States,* ed. Michael Hanagan and Charles Tilly (Lanham, MD: Rowman and Littlefield, 1999), 123.

39. Workfare Campaign of Resistance, Pledge of Resistance petition, 1997, Pledge of Resistance Files, Urban Justice Center, in the author's possession.
40. Ibid.
41. James Bradley, "Good Works—Without Pay," *City Limits*, July–August 1997, http://www.citylimits.org.
42. Dorow, interview.
43. Ibid.
44. Ibid.
45. "Speaking Engagements 1997" and "Workfare Campaign of Resistance Speaking Engagements, 1998," from Heidi Dorow's files, Urban Justice Center, 1999.
46. Workfare Campaign of Resistance, Pledge of Resistance petition.
47. "Memorandum," United Church of Christ, Metropolitan New York Chapter, Pledge of Resistance Files, Urban Justice Center, 1999, in the author's possession. See also Gramsci, *Selections*, 235.
48. Dulchin, interview, November 1997.
49. Robert Sirico, "Work Is Moral and So Is Welfare," *New York Times*, July 27, 1997.
50. See William Raspberry, "Protesting Up the Wrong Tree," *Washington Post*, July 28, 1997.
51. Sirico, "Work Is Moral."
52. Michel J. Faulkner, "Is Workfare Immoral? It's Assistance with Dignity," *Daily News*, July 27, 1997.
53. Sirico, "Work Is Moral."
54. Peter Laarman, letter to the editor, *Washington Post*, August 9, 1997.
55. See Mimi Abramowitz, "Workfare and Nonprofits, Ten Myths" (pamphlet, Workfare Campaign of Resistance, New York, 1997).
56. Dorow, interview.
57. See, e.g., Terrence Maxwell, "After Welfare: A Study of Work and Benefit Use after Case Closing" (Albany: Nelson A. Rockefeller Institute of Government, 1999). See also National Employment Law Project, "New York City's Workfare Program Fails to Move Welfare Recipients to Work: The Facts behind the Rockefeller Institute Report" (report, September 23, 1999).
58. Gramsci, *Selections*, 235.
59. Dorow, interview.
60. See also the draft of a letter from Rev. Peter Laarman to Rev. John Blackwell: "Churches and non-for-profits [*sic*] should look at WEP the way they looked at *apartheid* and other systemic evils; these are systems of oppression which should be condemned and resisted altogether; talking about humanizing from within, or about 'structural engagement' in the case of South Africa, only validates the system." Peter Laarman to John Blackwell, 4 December 1997, Pledge of Resistance Files, Urban Justice Center, New York, in the author's possession.
61. Laarman, interview.
62. An early meeting of the WEP Coalition, convened by CWA 1180, featured a proposal to promulgate "Sullivan Principles" for WEP worksites. See CWA 1180, "Agenda: WEP Strategy Meeting" (meeting materials, October 1997, from WWT files, in the author's possession). The Sullivan Principles were a list of demands, drawn up by a Philadelphia minister who was a member of the General Motors board of directors, of corporations regarding doing business in South Africa. They were often cited by opponents of divestment as a way that corporations could continue to do business in South Africa, though they were, in fact, rather strin-

gent. The minister, Leon Sullivan, ultimately claimed that this list was receiving more lip service than compliance, and he joined the call for divestment.

63. DC 37's WEP Worker organizer attended the rally, but in the crowd, rather than on the podium.

64. Comments of Nick Unger at rally, December 10, 1997. From author's notes.

65. Community Voices Heard, "Community Jobs Concept Paper" typescript, 1997, CVH files, New York.

66. *Leaders*, in this sense, most often means "indigenous spokespeople" rather than organizers and decision makers. In the model of community organizing common to (though adapted by) CVH, ACORN, and, to a different degree, post–1997 WWT, there is a distinction made among organizers, leaders, and members. *Organizers* are usually paid staff members who are charged with recruiting people into the organization and working with leaders to develop strategy; *leaders* are members of the organization whom organizers identify as being able to communicate the organizations' goals well, both to external audiences and to other members; *members* are the rank and file who have greater or lesser degrees of strategic input but have some loyalty to the organization for any number of reasons. See also Francesca Polletta, *Freedom Is an Endless Meeting: Democracy in American Social Movements* (Chicago: University of Chicago Press, 2002), chap. 7.

67. See, e.g., Dennis Rivera to Lee Saunders, Trustee of District Council 37, AFSCME, 28 December 1998, WEP Workers Together files, New York. As early as 1996, WWT entered into talks with the United Auto Workers and several lawyers to investigate the possibility of organizing WEP workers in nonprofits. "WEPs in non-profits," memorandum, 1997, WWT files.

68. Dulchin, interview, October 1999.

69. Benjamin Dulchin, testimony before New York City Council General Welfare Committee, October 20, 1998.

70. See Rebecca Laurie, testimony before New York City Council General Welfare Committee, October 20, 1998; Brian McLaughlin, testimony before New York City Council General Welfare Committee, April 22, 1999; Michael Power, testimony before New York City Council General Welfare Committee, October 20, 1998; Lee Saunders, testimony before New York City Council Welfare Committee, September 28, 1999.

71. In DiBrienza's notes on the margins of Seth Diamond's testimony before the New York City Council General Welfare Committee (September 28, 1999), next to cost estimates is written "Yankee Stadium," in reference to the cost that the administration proposed that the taxpayers should shoulder to build a new baseball stadium on the west side of Manhattan (a proposal that the Yankees' owner, George Steinbrenner, favored, allegedly because he blamed flagging attendance on the stadium's location in the South Bronx). General Welfare Committee files, photocopy in author's possession.

72. The council estimated an additional $6 million in costs to the City, much of which could be borne by existing funding streams. In addition, it cited the combined availability of $40 million from other sources, out of a total of $900 million in combined Welfare-to-Work funds and TANF surplus money. Steven DiBrienza, n.d. [1999], "How Much Would the Transitional Jobs Program Cost?" typescript, City Council General Welfare Committee files, New York. The administration claimed that the funding streams relied upon by the council's estimates were uncertain. Seth Diamond, testimony before New York City Council General

Welfare Committee, September 29, 1999. Indeed, because New York State was slow to allocate its TANF surplus money, advocates feared that its federal block grant would be slashed and the money lost in the negotiations around federal reauthorization of the welfare law.

73. City of New York Office of the Mayor, "Mayor Giuliani Calls on City Council Not to Undermine Welfare Reform" (Press Release 380-99, September 28, 1999).

74. Diamond, testimony, 3–4.

75. City of New York Office of the Mayor, "Giuliani Calls on Council."

76. In strong-mayor systems, municipal agencies report to and are led by mayors rather than by city councils. Accordingly, city councils have little power to create programs but rather have some oversight and budgetary power.

77. *Timmons v. Twin Cities Area New Party*, 520 US 351 (1997).

78. On interanimation, see Mische, "Crosstalk in Social Movements"; Mische and Pattison, "Composing a Civic Arena."

79. From affidavit of William Mason, *Brukhman v. Giuliani*. Mason was a WEP worker and a key organizer of Work*fairness*.

80. From affidavit of Seth Diamond, *Brukhman v. Giuliani*. Diamond was the deputy commissioner of HRA in charge of the WEP program.

81. Frangiose affirmation, *Brukhman v. Giuliani*, par. 1.

82. "Plaintiff's Memorandum of Law," *Brukhman v. Giuliani*, par. 31, citing *Young v. Toia*, 403 N.Y.S.2d at 394.

83. *Brukhman v. Giuliani*, 1997 at sec. i, par. 3–4.

84. N.Y. Const. art. 1, sec. 17.

85. *Brukhman v. Giuliani*, 2000.

86. *U.S. v. City of New York.*

87. Catherine Ruckelshaus (staff attorney, National Employment Law Project), interview with the author, May 2000.

88. Matthew Diller, "Working without a Job: The Social Messages of the New Workfare," *Stanford Law and Policy Review* 9 (Winter 1998): 19–43.

89. Katznelson, however, located the divide between workplace and community politics in the timing of the defeat of radical labor politics and the ascent of the ethnically based political machine in the nineteenth century. In the case of WEP politics, though there is a labor-community divide, it is one that mirrors far more the basic ideological division of production from social reproduction. See Katznelson, *City Trenches*.

CHAPTER FIVE

1. Pierre Bourdieu, *An Outline of a Theory of Practice*, trans. Richard Nice (Cambridge: Cambridge University Press, 1977), 206.

2. Ibid.

3. Joseph V. Femia, *Gramsci's Political Thought: Hegemony, Consciousness, and the Revolutionary Process* (Oxford: Clarendon Press, 1981), 47.

4. Peter Ives, *Language and Hegemony in Gramsci* (London: Pluto Press, 2004), 70.

5. Femia, *Gramsci's Political Thought*, 47, quoting Antonio Gramsci, *Il Risorgimento*, vol. 4, *Opere di Antonio Gramsci* (Turin: Einaudi, 1949), 100.

6. Gramsci, of course, had a far broader lens, and though he was interested in particular debates (e.g., language policy), he developed his theories of hegemony against the background of larger struggles over the establishment of class rule. I have argued earlier that the debates over workfare capture something important

about the neoliberal phase of capitalism in general, but it obviously does not encapsulate the sum of capitalist relations in toto.

7. Chik Collins, "Discourse in Cultural-Historical Perspective: Critical Discourse Analysis, CHAT, and the Study of Social Change" (typescript, May 2006), 7.

8. Doug McAdam, Sidney Tarrow, and Charles Tilly, *Dynamics of Contention* (Cambridge: Cambridge University Press, 2001), 24–27. Their definition highlights the narrative or "eventful" element of mechanisms; see William H. Sewell Jr., "Three Temporalities," in *The Historic Turn in the Human Sciences*, ed. Terrance McDonald (Ann Arbor: University of Michigan Press, 1996), 245–80). Elster's definition, by contrast, is that "mechanisms are frequently occurring and easily recognizable causal patterns that are triggered under generally unknown conditions or with indeterminate consequences." See Jon Elster, "A Plea for Mechanisms," in *Social Mechanisms: An Analytical Approach to Social Theory*, ed. Peter Hedstrøm and Richard Swedberg (Cambridge: Cambridge University Press, 1998), 45. I prefer McAdam, Tarrow, and Tilly's definition for its potential to bridge the study of structure and strategy. This position is also inconsistent with an idiographic approach to narrative. See, e.g., Zenonas Norkus, "Mechanisms as Miracle Makers? The Rise and Inconsistencies of the 'Mechanismic Approach' in Social Science and History," *History and Theory* 44, no. 3 (October 2005): 348–72. Norkus especially disapproves of the narrative definition of mechanisms because it abstracts too much from the potential richness of narrative analysis. For a good overview of the literature, see James Mahoney, "Tentative Answers to Questions about Causal Mechanisms" (paper presented at the annual meeting of the American Political Science Association, Philadelphia, August 28, 2003).

9. See Ann Mische and Harrison White, "Between Conversation and Situation: Public Switching Dynamics across Network-Domains," *Social Research* 65, no. 3 (Fall 1998): 701–14.

10. See Mische, "Crosstalk in Social Movements," 269–70.

11. McAdam, Tarrow, and Tilly, *Dynamics of Contention*, 121.

12. See Roger V. Gould and Roberto M. Fernandez, "Structures of Mediation: A Formal Approach to Brokerage in Transaction Networks," *Sociological Methodology* 19 (1989): 89–126.

13. Snow et al., "Frame Alignment Processes."

14. See also Lowell Turner, "Globalization and the Logic of Participation: Unions and the Politics of Coalition Building," *Journal of Industrial Relations* 48, no. 1 (2006): 83–97. Note that this definition differs from Elster's in that Elster highlights the ways in which behavior in one setting is carried over and repeated in another. See Elster, "A Plea for Mechanisms," 54.

15. Stuart Hall, cited in George Lipsitz, "The Struggle for Hegemony," *Journal of American History* 75, no. 1 (June 1998): 146.

16. Note that I use this term somewhat differently than do McAdam, Tarrow, and Tilly (*Dynamics of Contention*, 332). In their work, scale shift refers to "a change in the number and level of coordinated contentious actions leading to broader contention and a wider range of actors." See also Lesley J. Wood, "Breaking the Bank and Taking It to the Streets: How Protesters Target Neoliberalism," *Journal of World Systems Research* 10, no. 1 (2004): 69–89, esp. 73. Accordingly, it has less to do with transitions among institutions organized at different geographic scales than with combined qualitative and quantitative transformation of action to larger (or smaller) groups of people. Clearly, the two are related concepts, but as

I use it here, the concept of scale is tied to the concepts of genre and chronotope. Scale, or the geographic reach of activity, is at once an attribution of the jurisdictional boundaries of an institution and a reconstruction of them. See, e.g., Erik Swyngedouw, "Neither Global nor Local: 'Glocalization' and the Politics of Scale," in *Spaces of Globalization: Reasserting the Power of the Local*, ed. Kevin R. Cox, 137–66 (New York: Guilford Press, 1997). William H. Sewell Jr., "Space in Contentious Politics," 52–88.

17. Andrew Herod, *Labor Geographies: Workers and the Landscapes of Capitalism* (New York: Guilford Press, 2001), 200–217.

18. See, e.g., Juliet F. Gainsborough, "To Devolve or Not to Devolve: Welfare Reform in the States," *Policy Studies Journal* 31, no. 4 (2003): 603–23; Robert C. Lieberman and Gregory M. Shaw, "Looking Inward, Looking Outward: The Politics of State Welfare Innovation under Devolution," *Political Research Quarterly* 53, no. 2 (June 2000): 215–40; Joe Soss et al., "Setting the Terms of Relief: Explaining State Policy Choices in the Devolution Revolution," *American Journal of Political Science* 45, no. 2 (April 2001): 378–95.

19. See, e.g., Robin Wagner-Pacifici, *Theorizing the Standoff: Contingency in Action* (Cambridge: Cambridge University Press, 2000), chap. 2; Ann Mische, "Crosstalk in Social Movements," 270–71; Charles Tilly, "The Time of States," *Social Research* 61, no. 2 (1994): 269–95; Colin Hay, "Political Time and the Temporality of Crisis," *Contemporary Political Studies* (proceedings of the Political Studies Association meeting, Jordantown University, Ulster, 1997, http://www.psa.ac.uk/cps/1997%5Chay2.pdf).

20. This is certainly institutional spillover, too, as the politics of term limits bears little direct relation, otherwise, to workfare politics.

21. Duncan Watts, "The 'New' Science of Networks," *Annual Review of Sociology* 30 (2004): 243–70. Watts writes that network analytic operations should be used with circumspection when dealing with social phenomena. In a lot of networks, because "interactions themselves are underspecified, the network alone cannot be said to reveal much about actual social processes." (254).

22. For the purposes of this analysis, I have abstracted the principal topic of the articles in which claim-making over WEP took place and called it the *context/object* of claim-making actors. It is somewhat different from a relational setting—the concept employed in chapter 4—but similar as well. Like relational settings, a context/object is both an institutional context and an object of claims and activity. Moreover, in this analysis, contexts/objects are understood as elements in a network, similar to relational settings. Nevertheless, the concepts differ in that *topics* are different from settings, such as the law, or worksites. They have no particular spatial dimensions.

23. This is a compromise. Bakhtin's view is that the word always bears the evidence of its multiple uses; there is no question of a mathematical decay function. On the other hand, simply counting every claim in every period as if everything that was said two years before had equal bearing on the meanings made in new circumstances does not make a lot of sense.

24. Collins, "Discourse in Cultural-Historical Perspective," 7.

25. All CONCOR blockmodels have minimum R-squared values of 0.6. Blocks are connected with each other if they exceed the average (mean) density. All calculations were made in UCINET for Windows. See the appendix for further explanation of the method.

26. Collins, "Discourse in Cultural-Historical Perspective," 7. A full codebook is available from the author.

27. Bakhtin, "Problem of Speech Genres."

28. See, e.g., Piven and Cloward, *Regulating the Poor;* Michael B. Katz, *In the Shadow of the Poorhouse: A Social History of Welfare in America* (New York: Basic Books, 1986); David Wagner, *The Poorhouse: America's Forgotten Institution* (Lanham, MD: Rowman and Littlefield, 2005).

29. Jason DeParle, *American Dream: Three Women, Ten Kids, and a Nation's Drive to End Welfare* (New York: Viking, 2004), 3–4; see also R. Kent Weaver, *Ending Welfare as We Know It: Context and Choice in Policy Toward Low-Income Families* (Washington, DC: Brookings Institution, 2000).

30. Nancy A. Naples, "The 'New Consensus' on the Gendered Nature of the Welfare State," *Signs* 22, no. 4 (Summer): 907–45.

31. Ellen Reese, *Backlash against Welfare Mothers, Past and Present* (Berkeley and Los Angeles: University of California Press, 2005), chaps. 3–5. Reese indicates, however, that the backlash was not limited to the South and took hold—albeit in different ways—in New York and California, too (see chap. 6); see also Jill Quadagno, *The Color of Welfare: How Racism Undermined the War on Poverty* (New York: Oxford University Press, 1994); Piven and Cloward, *Regulating the Poor,* chap. 4.

32. Letter writing is not, of course, innocent. Having once cited in an article a letter to the *New York Times* from this period, I got an e-mail from its author, who—though the paper gave no clue about this—was a welfare-rights organizer in the early 1980s who had somehow gotten wind of this unpublished article's existence.

33. New York State Office of the Governor, "Governor Pataki Announces Historic Welfare Reforms" (press release, June 29, 1997, http://www.state.ny.us/).

34. Jason Turner even told a gathering of service providers, "We need to make a crisis in [homeless] people's lives" in order to get them to be responsible for themselves.

35. Hospital workers were exempt from the contract because the mayor was planning to privatize at least two of the city's public hospitals. Harlem hospital was not among the two, and the layoffs were not made in the context of privatization.

36. See Robert D. McFadden, "Union Chief Calls Workfare 'Slavery,'" *New York Times,* April 19, 1998.

37. The trial court judge found that the contracting process had been corrupted, but a court of appeals judge did not. See Christopher Drew and Eric Lipton, "2 with Ties to Chief of Welfare Got Jobs with Major Contractor," *New York Times,* April 21, 2000; Eric Lipton, "Rejecting Favoritism Claim, Court Upholds a City Welfare Contract," *New York Times,* October 25, 2000.

38. A telling indicator: Exactly a week before the attacks, an article appeared in the *New York Times* chronicling the disappearance of luxury items from fancy New York restaurants in the wake of falling revenues. Marian Burros, "Waiter, Hold the Foie Gras: Slump Hits New York Dining," *New York Times,* September 4, 2001.

39. Nevertheless, the disorder that ensued after 9/11 for welfare recipients was significant. The HRA computers generated sanction notices for thousands of missed appointments that were impossible, under the circumstances of that week—and sometimes longer—to meet. Advocates learned then that the computers were set to sanction automatically and that *not* sanctioning a recipient had to be done manually. Under these circumstances, the sanctions were revoked and benefits continued.

40. During Bloomberg's first term, I frequently heard advocates say that the difference between Giuliani and Bloomberg was that the former slammed the door in your face, while the latter invited you in to talk but didn't listen.

41. See, e.g., Matt Pacenza, "Bloomie"; Nina Bernstein, "City Fires 3,500."

42. McMillan, "Ending Workfare."

43. Editorial, *Daily News*, April 11, 2003.

44. An indication of better and worse integrated blocks is the presence of a "self-loop" indicating that the density of its internal ties exceeds the mean density of the blocks in the blockmodel as a whole. Block 4 lacks a self-tie.

45. Sidney Tarrow, *Power in Movement*, 2nd ed. (Cambridge: Cambridge University Press, 1998), chap. 3. In his study of the American labor movement, Steven Henry Lopez found that the language of "opportunity" for protest rang hollow; he was struck by "how *difficult* mobilization was, how great the obstacles to it, how complex the problems actors struggled with." The point here, however, is that these perspectives are not at all incompatible. See Steven Henry Lopez, *Reorganizing the Rust Belt: An Inside Study of the American Labor Movement* (Berkeley and Los Angeles: University of California Press, 2004), 216–18.

46. See Marshall Louis Ganz, "Resources and Resourcefulness: Strategic Capacity in the Unionization of California Agriculture, 1959–1966," *American Journal of Sociology* 104, no. 5 (January 2000): 1003–62.

47. Bourdieu, *Outline of a Theory*, 206.

CHAPTER SIX

1. See, e.g., Edwin Hutchins, *Cognition in the Wild* (Cambridge, MA: MIT Press, 1995); Jean Lave and Etienne Wenger, *Situated Learning: Legitimate Peripheral Participation* (Cambridge: Cambridge University Press, 1991); Bonnie A. Nardi, *Context and Consciousness: Activity Theory and Human-Computer Interaction* (Cambridge, MA: MIT Press, 1996); Carol D. Lee and Peter Smagorinsky, eds., *Vygotskian Perspectives on Literacy Research: Constructing Meaning through Collaborative Inquiry* (Cambridge: Cambridge University Press, 2000); Gavriel Solomon, ed., *Distributed Cognitions: Psychological and Educational Considerations* (Cambridge: Cambridge University Press, 1993.

2. A separate critique of the culturalist position on mind can be found in Bergesen's recent "Chomskyan" critique of Meadean interactionism: Albert J. Bergesen, "Chomsky Versus Mead," *Sociological Theory* 22 (September 2004): 357–70. Citing the literature on the innateness of syntactic ability (e.g., Noam Chomsky, *Language and Mind* [New York: Harcourt Brace and World, 1968]; Steven Pinker, *The Language Instinct: How the Mind Creates Language* [Cambridge, MA: MIT Press, 1994]); Bergesen suggests that symbolic interaction may be less of a Meadean and more of a Chomskyan process. Nevertheless, Bergesen's critique neglects the fact that the earlier strong program of linguistic and cognitive nativism advanced in Chomsky's work has been considerably toned down and covers only basic abilities of pattern recognition; see Christopher D. Green and John Vervaeke, "But What Have You Done for Us Lately? Some Recent Perspectives on Linguistic Nativism," in *The Future of the Cognitive Revolution*, ed. David Martel Johnson and Christina E. Erneling (Oxford: Oxford University Press), 149–63. See also Michael Tomasello, *The Cultural Origins of Human Cognition* (Cambridge, MA: Harvard University Press, 1999), 203–6.

3. Vološinov, *Marxism and the Philosophy of Language*, 12.

4. H. Johnston, "Methodology for Frame Analysis."
5. Vološinov, *Marxism and the Philosophy of Language* 12–13. Italics in original.
6. A. N. Leontiev, *Activity, Consciousness, and Personality* (Moscow: Progress Publishers, 1978), 94, http://www.marxists.org/archive/leontev/works/1978/.
7. This is a controversial element of Engeström's work, even for those sympathetic to CHAT.
8. Georg Simmel, "The Web of Group Affiliations" in *Conflict and the Web of Group Affiliations*, ed. Kurt Wolff (Glencoe, IL: Free Press, 1951); see also Georg Simmel, "The Metropolis and Mental Life," in *The Sociology of Georg Simmel*, ed. Kurt Wolff (Glencoe, IL: Free Press, 1950): 409–24. Also see Ronald Breiger, "The Duality of Persons and Groups," *Social Forces* 53 (1974): 81–90. Breiger points out that this is a fundamental precept—though usually only implicit—of modern social theory.
9. Erving Goffman, *The Preservation of Self in Everyday Life* (Garden City, NY: Anchor Press, 1959); Tilly, *Contentious French*; Jeffrey C. Alexander, "Cultural Pragmatics: Social Performance between Ritual and Strategy," *Sociological Theory* 22, no. 4 (2004): 527–73.
10. Silva, interview.
11. See Engeström, *Learning by Expanding*.
12. Yrjö Engeström, "Expansive Learning at Work: Toward an Activity Theoretical Reconceptualization," *Journal of Education and Work* 14, no. 1 (2001): 137, 140, quoted in Ines Langemeyer, "Contradictions in Expansive Learning: Towards a Critical Analysis of Self-Dependent Forms of Learning in Relation to Contemporary Socio-Technical Change," *Forum: Qualitative Social Research/Qualitative Sozialforschung* 7, no. 1, art. 12 (2006): 5; Langemeyer criticizes Engeström for "underestimat[ing] the probability that [people] only comply with and accommodate themselves to [contradictions] in order to avoid any conflict" (6).
13. Dulchin, interview, October 1999.
14. See chapter 4 for a longer version of the quotation.
15. As described in Clark, *Being There*, 45–46.
16. Andy Clark, "Economic Reason: The Interplay of Individual Learning and External Structure," in *The Frontiers of the New Institutional Economics*, ed. John N. Drobak and John V. C. Nye (San Diego: Academic Press, 1997), 269–90.
17. Mische taps this aspect of chronotopically rooted dialogue with her conversational mechanism of "temporal cuing," which she defines as "keying into a particular temporal dimension of the 'projective narratives' of a potential interactive partner." See Mische, "Crosstalk in Social Movements," 270.
18. By June 2000, the two claims had appeared in the same block or in directly and strongly tied blocks in three of the four periods in which the claims appeared at all in the previous chapters' maps.
19. Quoted in "Union Hits Abuse of Workfare," *Public Employee Press*, April 19, 1996, 9.
20. Dulchin, interview, November 1997.
21. Laarman, interview, 1997.
22. Quoted in Bob Liff and Russ Buettner, "City Expanding Workfare for Single Parents," *Daily News*, March 19, 1996.
23. Ines Langemeyer, "Contradictions in Expansive Learning: Towards a Critical Analysis of Self-Dependent Forms of Learning in Relation to Contemporary Socio-technological Change," *Forum: Qualitative Social Research/Qualitative Sozialforschung* 7, no 1 (2006): 6, http://www.qualitative-research.net/fqs-texte/1-06/06-1-12-e.htm.

24. Again, this realignment can be seen in the strong linkage between the blocks containing REALJOBS (30) and the TRANSJOBS claim and **jobs** context (20) in figure 5.8.

25. *Brukhman v. Giuliani,* "Plaintiff's Memorandum of Law," 31, citing *Young v. Toia,* 403 N.Y.S. 2nd at 394.

26. Another confirmation: In the blockmodel of periods 5–6 (fig. 5.8) in the previous chapter, the SLAVERY claim does not appear.

27. Dulchin, testimony before New York City Council General Welfare Committee.

28. Comments of Stephen DiBrienza, chair, New York City General Council Welfare Committee, September 28, 1999, from author's notes of the meeting.

29. Kim, interview, June 2000.

30. Brenda Stewart (cofounder and organizer, FUREE, and member, WEP Workers Together), interview with the author, June 2004.

31. The principal contradiction, based on my involvement with the project, was a tool-community contradiction that became evident during a rehearsal for the press conference announcing the report. Thinking that as the "academic," I had to give details about the sample and methodology, I proceeded do so. With detailed questions and criticisms, the dozen or so CVH members present decided that my presentation was too technical, too boring, and would subtract from the presentation's impact. In no uncertain terms, they told me that I had to go back and rewrite my presentation from scratch. So I did.

32. Getsos, interview.

33. Similarly, an ACORN flyer from 1999, urging WEP workers to come to a WEP Worker Organizing Committee meeting, ties the slavery claim to poor working conditions and the grievance procedure bill.

34. Even before the collapse of the old leadership, DC 37 filed a displacement suit with the hospital workers' union whose members were laid off in 1998. It was in this episode that Stanley Hill charged that WEP was slavery because it did not lead to "meaningful jobs." Quoted in McFadden, "Union Chief Calls Workfare 'Slavery.'"

35. Getsos, interview.

36. Anna Stetsenko, "Activity as Object-Related: Resolving the Dichotomy of Individual and Collective Planes of Agency," *Mind, Culture, and Activity* 12, no. 1 (2005): 83.

37. H. Johnston, "Methodology for Frame Analysis," 218.

38. Lakoff, *Moral Politics.*

CHAPTER SEVEN

1. Katznelson, *City Trenches,* 214.

2. Ibid., 213; emphasis in the original.

3. See, e.g., Charles Tilly, "Regimes and Contention" (working paper, Lazarsfeld Center at Columbia University, May 6, 1998), http://www.ciaonet.org/wps/tic09/; see also Michael Howlett and M. Ramesh, *Studying Public Policy: Policy Cycles and Policy Subsystems* (Don Mills, ON: Oxford University Press Canada, 1995), 103; R. A. W. Rhodes and David Marsh, "New Directions in the Study of Policy Networks," *European Journal of Political Science* 21 (1992): 181–205.

4. This version—which finds mention in some of Gramsci's writing, as well as Leontiev's and that of many other Marxists—calls to mind Marx's praise of an article written by his friend Joseph Weydemeyer (who had hoped to publish Marx's *Eighteenth Brumaire* but ran out of money to publish his radical newspaper) as "both

coarse and *fine*—a combination which should be found in any polemic worthy of the name." See Karl Marx, "Marx to J. Weydemeyer," in *The Eighteenth Brumaire of Louis Bonaparte* (New York: International Publishers, 1963), 136. In this light, teasing out polemical from analytic constructs in Marx's and in Marxist writing in general is shown to be a difficult task, given the close relation between the two in a theory bound inexorably to political practice and that abjures (or ought to) pure academicism.

5. Nicholas Abercrombie, Stephen Hill, and Bryan S. Turner, *The Dominant Ideology Thesis* (London: George Allen Unwin, 1980). Cf. Gramsci, *Selections*, 376–77. Gramsci writes that ideologies " 'organize' human masses, and create the terrain on which men move, acquire consciousness of their position, struggle, etc."

6. See Stephen Hill, "Britain: The Dominant Ideology Thesis after a Decade," in *Dominant Ideologies*, ed. Nicholas Abercrombie, Stephen Hill, and Bryan S. Turner (London: Unwin Hyman, 1990), 3. See also Karl Marx, *Capital*, vol. 1 (London: Penguin Classics), 899.

7. David Harvey, *A Brief History of Neoliberalism* (Oxford: Oxford University Press, 2005).

8. I see no essential contradiction, therefore, between Harvey's assertion in *A Brief History of Neoliberalism* that neoliberalism is a program of reasserting class power and regulationists' view that neoliberalism is a way of regulating capital-state relations in the wake of the late 1960s crisis of legitimation and the crisis of accumulation that erupted in the early 1970s.

9. A wide range of work has treated the issue of welfare reform and racism, much of it quite good. See, e.g., Richard Fording, Sanford F. Schram, and Joe Soss, "The Color of Devolution: The Politics of Local Punishment in the New World of Welfare" (paper presented at the annual meeting of the American Political Science Association, Washington, DC, September 1–4); also Sanford F. Schram, *Praxis for the Poor: Piven and Cloward and the Future of Social Science in Social Welfare* (New York: New York University Press, 2005). On the gender dynamics and consequences of welfare reform, see e.g., Mink, *Welfare's End*.

10. Agnieszka Kajrukszto, in as-yet-unpublished work, argues that feminists in Poland are faced with the difficulty of relying on European Union standards in order to secure a broader gender rights regime in a country dominated by conservative Catholics, even while Poland's accession to the EU depends in part on its adoption of mainly neoliberal economic policies. The contradiction here is that an expanded gender rights regime might be purchased, as it were, at the cost of women's economic well-being. The point here is that there is considerably more variability in the gender and racial regimes wedded to neoliberalism than there is in the class regimes at its core.

11. That there is variation in the enactment of neoliberalism suggests that regulatory projects, even if they have central tendencies, do not look the same everywhere and vary in part according to the strength and composition of hegemonic coalitions. See, e.g., Jane Jenson, " 'Different' but not 'Exceptional': Canada's Permeable Fordism," *Canadian Review of Sociology and Anthropology* 26, no. 1 (February 1989): 69–94. The degree to which these coalitions are suffused with and shape political claims is suggested in Jane Jenson, "Representations in Crisis: The Roots of Canada's Permeable Fordism," *Canadian Journal of Political Science* 23, no. 4 (December 1990): 653–83; see also Gordon MacLeod and Martin Jones, "Reregulating a Regional Rustbelt: Institutional Fixes, Entrepreneurial Discourse,

and the 'Politics of Representation,'" *Environment and Planning D: Society and Space* 17 (October 1999): 575–605.

12. See, e.g., Ness, *Immigrants*, 2–5. See also Saskia Sassen, "Introduction: Whose City Is It? Globalization and the Formation of New Claims," in *Globalization and Its Discontents: Essays on the New Mobility of People and Money* (New York: New Press, 1998), xix–xxxvi.

13. See Sanford F. Schram, *Words of Welfare: The Poverty of Social Science and the Social Science of Poverty* (Minneapolis: University of Minnesota Press, 1995), 17; see also Peck, *Workfare States*, 88–95, for an extended discussion.

14. Vogel and DeMause, "Jason's Brain Trust," recounts Mayor Giuliani's cancellation of a speech in which, at the advice of several of the Wisconsin recruits, he spoke about the importance of responsible fatherhood and parenting. Here, I slightly misrepresent Mead. Mead cites Wisconsin as a place dominated by a "moralistic political culture," which is something different than simply a dominant mode of discourse. In spite of widespread—and largely unmentioned—evidence of patronage, fraud, and dishonest administration of that state's welfare and workfare programs, Mead believes that Wisconsin's experience with welfare reform was a success attributable to a strong culture of "good government." See Mead, *Government Matters*. See also DeParle, *American Dream*, 331–32.

15. The analogy to Guantánamo was made by my research assistant, Dan Skinner, as soon as I explained to him the problem this book project confronted. The "state of exception" refers to a more general theory about the lawlessness at the center of democratic politics advanced by, among others, Giorgio Agamben. See Giorgio Agamben, *State of Exception*, trans. Kevin Attell (Chicago: University of Chicago Press, 2005).

16. See Tracie McMillan, "Welfare 101: More Education Allowed," *City Limits Weekly*, April 25, 2005.

17. The irony is that in the absence of job creation and local economic development policies that include strong labor market regulation, job training becomes a sentimental dodge: that is, a way for liberals and conservatives to demonstrate their concern for the poor and workers without actually altering or desegmenting labor markets. See Gordon Lafer, *The Job Training Charade* (Ithaca, NY: Cornell University Press, 2004).

18. This line of thinking can be carried too far, however. Gramsci's comments on pragmatism illustrate the central conundrum. Though he finds that the pragmatist view of language is "not far off the mark," he finds that the "pragmatist . . . wishes to tie himself immediately to practice" without judging practice from any point outside "the immediacy of . . . philosophical politicism." The result, for Gramsci, is that "the pragmatists, at the most, have contributed to the creation of the Rotary Club movement and to the justification of conservative and reactionary movements" in a way that might be akin to a neo-Tocquevillian celebration of all and any civic associationism without making distinctions among actual civic associations and their political consequences. See Gramsci, *Selections*, 349, 373.

19. Parrott, "Bolstering and Diversifying," paints a picture of aggregate results of these shifts in accountability an urban scale.

20. The neoliberal-neoconservative alliance is subject, of course, to periodic factional tensions. But this is precisely the point of the Gramscian idea that regu-

latory projects are borne by political "blocs" or coalitions that seek to achieve hegemony, even as they must attend to internal cohesion.

21. See, e.g., Michael Jacobson, "From the 'Back' to the 'Front': The Changing Character of Punishment in New York City," in *Rethinking the Urban Agenda: Reinvigorating the Liberal Tradition in New York City and Urban America*, ed. John H. Mollenkopf and Ken Emerson, 171–86 (New York: Century Foundation Books, 2001); Anna Lou Dehavenon, *From Bad to Worse at the Emergency Assistance Unit: How New York City Tried to Stop Sheltering Homeless Families in 1990* (New York: Action Research Project on Hunger, Homelessness, and Family Health, December 1996); Marybeth Shinn, Jim Baumohl, and Kim Hopper, "The Prevention of Homelessness Revisited," *Analyses of Social Issues and Public Policy* 1, no. 1 (December 2001): 95–128. For churning in health care, see Emily Biuso, "Careless Cutoffs," *City Limits*, September–October 2003, http://www.citylimits.org/content/articles/articleView.cfm?articlenumber=1036.

22. See, e.g., McMillan, "Ending Workfare"; Parrott, Primus, and Fremstadt, "Administration's TANF Proposals." See also Robert Pear, "Governors Unite to Fight Medicaid Cuts," *New York Times*, February 27, 2005. Of course, the subsequent path taken by governors, to call for cuts in the program, is the design of neoliberal devolution, but it puts the onus of cutting popular programs on politicians who may be more vulnerable because they rely on fewer voters and spread their electoral risk less than do national candidates.

23. There is a long history of debate over the feminist critique of welfare and workfare in which some argue that the "work-cash nexus" of the free labor market is an important hook on which to hang oppositional politics, if only because capitalism so often fails to live up to its promises to compensate workers fairly. Breaking the work-cash nexus, so the argument goes, takes this contradiction too far out of the spotlight. Moreover, if one were to demand, as some feminists have, "wages for housework," one opens the door to the paternalistic supervisory practices that currently mark and justify workfare and other neoliberal bromides for alleviating poverty. A good summary of these arguments can be found in Jocelyn Pixley, *Citizenship and Employment: Investigating Post-Industrial Options* (Cambridge: Cambridge University Press, 1993).

24. See, e.g., "Strategies for College Access and Human Capital Development," *WRI Update* 4, no. 1 (Spring 1999): 1–6. This article even casts training as an activist in terms of human capital development.

25. Femia, *Gramsci's Political Thought*, 47, quoting Gramsci, *Il Risorgimento*, 72; emphasis in original. Bourdieu's contention that the "essence of neoliberalism" lies in "*a programme of the methodical destruction of collectives*" leads to a substantially similar conclusion, that is, that neoliberal hegemony cannot be integral and is more likely to be minimal or decadent.

26. It has not been successful. It appears that the state of the parks is poorer now than it was under Giuliani. See Timothy Williams, "Report Assails Poor Upkeep in City Parks," *New York Times*, June 16, 2006.

27. See, e.g., Glenn Thrush, "In a Giving Mood," *Newsday*, July 6, 2005.

28. At the same time, the Bloomberg administration has been more measured in its support of privatization. Rather than embrace contracting in an aggressive way, as did Mayor Giuliani, Bloomberg's approach to privatization focuses on licensing and fund-raising from corporations to fund City services. See Gail Robinson, "Private Money for Public Needs," *Gotham Gazette*, February 15, 2003, http://

www.gothamgazette.com/article/20030922/200/524; also see Richard Steier, "Bloomberg Lands a Big One," *Chief/Civil Service Leader*, July 22, 2005.

29. Continuing factionalism within DC 37 likely fed into this arrangement and has continued to spill over into splits in the union over the new contract and endorsement of Mayor Bloomberg's reelection bid. See Gina Salamone, "DC 37 Votes for Bloomberg," *Chief/Civil Service Leader*, July 22, 2005; Steier, "Bloomberg Lands a Big One."

30. See, e.g., Charles Tilly, "Regimes and Contention." See also Howlett and Ramesh, *Studying Public Policy*; Rhodes and Marsh, "New Directions."

31. Ruth Needleman, "Building Relationships for the Long Haul: Unions and Community-Based Groups Working Together to Organize Low-Wage Workers," in *Organizing to Win: New Research on Union Strategies*, ed. Kate Bronfenbrenner et al., 71 (Ithaca, NY: Cornell University Press, 1998).

32. See, e.g., Neil Smith, "Homeless/Global: Scaling Places," in *Mapping the Futures: Local Cultures, Global Change*, ed. J. Bird et al., 87–119 (London: Routledge).

33. Andrew Rich, *Think Tanks, Public Policy, and the Politics of Expertise* (Cambridge: Cambridge University Press, 2004), 18–25.

34. See McMillan, "Ending Workfare."

APPENDIX

1. Paul A. Sabatier, "The Need for Better Theories," in *Theories of the Policy Process*, ed. Paul A. Sabatier (Boulder, CO: Westview, 1999), 3–18.

2. The project was partly funded by the American Sociological Association's Spivack Community Action Research Initiative in 2000.

3. Roberto Franzosi, *From Words to Numbers: Narrative, Data, and Social Science* (Cambridge: Cambridge University Press, 2004).

4. See also John W. Mohr, "Measuring Meaning," *Annual Review of Sociology* 24 (1998): 345–70.

5. John McCarthy, Clark McPhail, and Jackie Smith, "Images of Protest: Dimensions of Selection Bias in Media Coverage of Washington Demonstrations, 1982 and 1991," *American Sociological Review* 61 (1996): 478–99; Carol Mueller, "Media Measurement Models of Protest Event Data," *Mobilization* 2, no. 2 (1997): 165–84; Pamela E. Oliver, and Gregory M. Maney, "Political Processes and Local Newspaper Coverage of Protest Events: From Selection Bias to Triadic Interactions," *American Journal of Sociology* 106, no. 2 (2000): 463–505.

6. Oliver and Maney, "Political Process."

7. Todd Gitlin, *The Whole World Is Watching: The Mass Media and the Making and Unmaking of the New Left* (Berkeley and Los Angeles: University of California Press, 1980); see also Gaye Tuchman, *Making News: A Study in the Construction of Reality* (New York: Free Press, 1978); Gans, *Deciding What's News*; Gamson, "Constructing Social Protest"; Pamela E. Oliver and Daniel J. Myers, "How Events Enter the Public Sphere: Conflict, Location, and Sponsorship in Local Newspaper Coverage of Public Events," *American Journal of Sociology* 105, no. 1 (1999): 38–87.

8. Justin Lewis, "Reproducing Political Hegemony in the United States," *Critical Studies in Mass Communication* 16, no. 3 (1999): 251–67.

9. Christian Davenport and Marika F. X. Litras, "Rashomon and Repression of the Black Panther Party: A Multi-Source Analysis of the Truth(s) Within Our Data" (paper presented at the annual meeting of the American Sociological Association, Washington, DC, August 2000).

10. Vološinov, *Marxism and the Philosophy of Language*, 115–23.
11. Ruud Koopmans and Paul Statham, "Political Claims Analysis: Integrating Protest Event and Political Discourse Approaches." *Mobilization* 4, no. 2 (1999): 203–21.
12. Paul Burstein, "Policy Domains: Organization, Culture, and Policy Outcomes," *Annual Review of Sociology* 17 (1991): 327–50; David Knoke, "The Sociopolitical Construction of National Policy Domains," in *Interdisziplinare Sozialforschung: Theorie und Empirische Andewendungen*, ed. C. H. A. Henning and C. Melbeck, 3 (Frankfurt: Campus Verlag, 2004). In English at http://www.soc.umn.edu/~knoke/pages/Knoke_Constructing_National_Policy_Domains.pdf.
13. See Larry Isaac and Larry Griffin, "Ahistoricism in Time-Series Analyses of Historical Process: Critique, Redirection, and Illustrations from U.S. Labor History," *American Sociological Review* 54, no. 6 (1989): 873–90.
14. Balázs Vedres and Péter Csigó, "Negotiating the End of Transition: A Network Approach to Local Action in Political Discourse Dynamics, Hungary 1997" (working paper, Columbia University, Institute of Social and Economic Research and Policy, 2002).
15. Isaac and Griffin, "Ahistoricism."
16. Mohr, "Soldiers, Mothers, Tramps"; Mische and Pattison, "Composing a Civic Arena."
17. See Mohr, "Soldiers, Mothers, Tramps."
18. See Breiger, "Toolkit for Practice Theory." On the property of duality generally, see Breiger, "Duality of Persons and Groups"; also see John Mohr and Vincent Duquenne, "The Duality of Culture and Practice: Poverty Relief in New York City, 1888–1917," *Theory and Society* 26, no. 2–3 (1997): 305–56.
19. Mische and Pattison, "Composing a Civic Arena."
20. Stephen P. Borgatti, Martin G. Everett, and Linton C. Freeman, *Ucinet for Windows: Software for Social Network Analysis*, version 6.96 (Harvard, MA: Analytic Technologies, 2002).
21. See Martin G. Everett and Stephen P. Borgatti, "Analyzing Clique Overlap," *Connections* 21, no. 1 (1998): 49–61.
22. CONCOR is the "convergence of iterated correlations." It refers to the fact that if a correlation matrix is subjected to a correlation routine and then the resultant matrix is similarly processed, it "will eventually result in a correlation matrix consisting only of +1's and −1's . . . in a pattern such that the items that are being correlated may be partitioned into two subsets where all correlations between items in different subsets will be equal to −1." Once a first division of two subsets is made, the procedure can be repeated on the subsets to produce finer distinctions of structural equivalence among the items. See Stanley Wasserman and Katherine Faust, *Social Network Analysis: Methods and Applications* (Cambridge: Cambridge University Press, 1994): 376–81; also see Ronald L. Breiger, Scott A. Boorman, and Phipps Arabie, "An Algorithm for Clustering Relational Data with Applications to Social Network Analysis and Comparisons with Multidimensional Scaling," *Journal of Mathematical Psychology* 12 (1975): 328–83.
23. Stephen P. Borgatti, *NetDraw: Graph Visualization Software* (Harvard, MA: Analytic Technologies, 2002).
24. Along with a codebook, a full list of blocks and block membership among the actors, claims, and contexts/objects is available on request from the author.

SELECTED BIBLIOGRAPHY

BOOKS, PERIODICALS, AND ONLINE PUBLICATIONS

Abbott, Andrew. *Time Matters: On Theory and Method*. Chicago: University of Chicago Press, 2001.

Administration for Children and Families. "Personal Responsibility and Work Opportunity Reconciliation Act of 1996." Fact sheet, August 8, 1996. http://www.acf .dhhs.gov/programs/ofa/prwora96.htm.

Agamben, Giorgio. *State of Exception*. Translated by Kevin Attell. Chicago: University of Chicago Press, 2005.

Aglietta, Michel. *A Theory of Capitalist Regulation: The U.S. Experience*. Translated by David Fernbach. New York: New Left Books, 1979.

Alexander, Jeffrey C. "Culture and Political Crisis: 'Watergate' and Durkheimian Sociology." In *Durkheimian Sociology: Cultural Studies*, edited by Jeffrey C. Alexander. Cambridge: Cambridge University Press, 1988.

———. "Cultural Pragmatics: Social Performance between Ritual and Strategy." *Sociological Theory* 22, no. 4 (2004): 527–73.

Bakhtin, Mikhail Mikhailovich. "Discourse in the Novel." In *The Dialogic Imagination: Four Essays*, edited by Michael Holquist, translated by Caryl Emerson and Michael Holquist, 272–73. Austin: University of Texas Press, 1981.

———. "Forms of Time and of the Chronotope in the Novel: Notes toward a Historical Poetics." In *The Dialogic Imagination: Four Essays*, by M. M. Bakhtin, edited by Michael Holquist, translated by Caryl Emerson and Michael Holquist. Austin: University of Texas Press, 1981.

———. "The Problem of Speech Genres." In *Speech Genres and Other Late Essays*, by M. M. Bakhtin, edited by Caryl Emerson and Michael Holquist, translated by Vern W. McGee, 84–95. Austin: University of Texas Press, 1986.

———. *Problems of Dostoevsky's Poetics*. Edited and translated by Caryl Emerson, introduction by Wayne C. Booth. Minneapolis: University of Minnesota Press, 1984.

Bakhurst, David. "Social Memory in Soviet Thought." In *An Introduction to Vygotsky*, edited by Harry Daniels, 196–218. London: Routledge, 1996

Barbanel, Josh. "Dinkins Efforts Set Back by Cut in Bond Rating." *New York Times*, February 12, 1991.

Barker, Colin. "Fear, Laughter and Collective Power: The Making of Solidarity at the Lenin Shipyard in Gdansk, Poland, August 1980." In *Passionate Politics: Emotions and Social Movements,* edited by Jeff Goodwin, James M. Jasper, and Francesca Polletta, 175–94. Chicago: University of Chicago Press, 2002.

Bergesen, Albert J. "Chomsky versus Mead." *Sociological Theory* 22 (September 2004): 357–70.

Bernstein, Nina. "City Fires 3,500 Former Welfare Recipients." *New York Times,* January 5, 2002.

———. "New Welfare Director Defends Stance on Food Stamp Waiver." *New York Times,* March 15, 2002.

Besharov, Douglas J., and Peter Germanis. "Full Engagement Welfare Reform in New York City: Lessons for TANF's Participation Requirements." University of Maryland School of Public Policy Welfare Reform Academy, College Park, August 2004. http://www.welfareacademy.org/pubs/welfare/nyc_hra.pdf.

Borgatti, Stephen P., Martin G. Everett, and Linton C. Freeman. *Ucinet for Windows: Software for Social Network Analysis,* version 6.96. Harvard, MA: Analytic Technologies, 2002.

Borgos, Seth. "Low-Income Homeownership and the ACORN Squatters Campaign." In *Critical Perspectives on Housing,* edited by Rachel G. Bratt, Chester Hartman, and Ann Meyerson, 428–46. Philadelphia: Temple University Press, 1986.

Bourdieu, Pierre. "The Essence of Neoliberalism." In *Le Monde Diplomatique,* English edition, December 1998. http://mondediplo.com/1998/12/08bourdieu.

———. *An Outline of a Theory of Practice.* Translated by Richard Nice. Cambridge: Cambridge University Press, 1977.

Bowles, Pete. "Victory for Workfare Students." *Newsday,* June 9, 1998.

Bradley, James. "Good Works-Without Pay." *City Limits,* July–August 1997. http://www.citylimits.org.

Brandist, Craig. "Gramsci, Bakhtin, and the Semiotics of Hegemony." *New Left Review* 216 (1996): 94–109.

Brecher, Jeremy, and Tim Costello. *Building Bridges: The Emerging Grassroots Coalition of Labor and Community.* New York: Monthly Review Press, 1989.

Breiger, Ronald L. "The Duality of Persons and Groups." *Social Forces* 53 (1974): 81–90.

———. "A Toolkit for Practice Theory." *Poetics* 27 (2000): 91–115.

Breiger, Ronald L., Scott A. Boorman, and Phipps Arabie. "An Algorithm for Clustering Relational Data with Applications to Social Network Analysis and Comparisons with Multidimensional Scaling." *Journal of Mathematical Psychology* 12 (1975): 328–83.

Brenner, Neil, and Nik Theodore. "Cities and the Geographies of 'Actually Existing Neoliberalism.'" In *Spaces of Neoliberalism: Urban Restructuring in North America and Western Europe,* edited by Neil Brenner and Nik Theodore, 2–32. Oxford: Blackwell, 2002.

Burstein, Paul. "Policy Domains: Organization, Culture, and Policy Outcomes." *Annual Review of Sociology* 17 (1991): 327–50.

Buttigieg, Joseph A. "The Contemporary Discourse on Civil Society: A Gramscian Critique." *Boundary 2* 32, no. 1 (2005): 33–52.

Calhoun, Craig. "The Rise and Domestication of Historical Sociology." In *The Historic Turn in the Human Sciences,* edited by Terrance McDonald, 305–38. Ann Arbor: University of Michigan Press, 1996.

Chen, David W. "Study Urges City to Require Building of Low-Cost Housing." *New York Times,* February 15, 2005.

Chomsky, Noam. *Language and Mind*. New York: Harcourt, Brace.

Clark, Andy. *Being There: Putting Brain, Body, and World Back Together*. Cambridge, MA: MIT Press, 1997.

———. "Economic Reason: The Interplay of Individual Learning and External Structure." In *The Frontiers of the New Institutional Economics*, edited by John N. Drobak and John V. C. Nye, 269–90. San Diego: Academic Press, 1997.

Coalition for the Homeless. "Charts Detailing the New York City Homeless Shelter Population," Chart 1. http://www.coalitionforthehomeless.org/advocacy/basic_facts .html#factsheets.

Cohn, Daniel. "Creating Crises and Avoiding Blame: The Politics of Public Service Reform and the New Public Management in Great Britain and the United States." *Administration and Society* 29, no. 5 (1997): 584–85.

Cole, Michael. *Cultural Psychology: A Once and Future Discipline*. Cambridge, MA: Harvard University Press, Belknap Press, 1996.

Collins, Chik. *Language, Ideology and Social Consciousness: Developing a Sociohistorical Approach*. Aldershot, Hampshire, UK: Ashgate, 1999.

———. "Vygotsky on Language and Social Consciousness: Underpinning the Use of Voloshinov in the Study of Popular Protest." *Historical Materialism* 7, no. 1 (2000): 41–69.

Cornfield, Dan. *The Next Upsurge: Labor and the New Social Movements*. Ithaca, NY: Cornell University Press, ILR Press, 2003.

Daly, Mark. "City, MTA in Deal on Subway WEPs." *Chief/Civil Service Leader*, April 30, 1999.

Daniels, Harry, ed. *An Introduction to Vygotsky*. London: Routledge, 1996.

Danigelis, Alyssa. "No More Jiggetts? State Launches Rent Subsidy." *City Limits Weekly*, May 16, 2005. http://www.citylimits.org/content/articles/weeklyView.cfm?article number=1719.

Davis, Martha F. *Brutal Need: Lawyers and the Welfare Rights Movement, 1960–1973*. New Haven, CT: Yale University Press, 1993.

DeFilippis, James. *Unmaking Goliath: Community Control in the Face of Global Capital*. New York: Routledge, 2004.

Delgado, Gary. *Organizing the Movement: The Roots and Growth of ACORN*. Philadelphia: Temple University Press, 1986.

DeParle, Jason. *American Dream: Three Women, Ten Kids, and a Nation's Drive to End Welfare*. New York: Viking, 2004.

DeRienzo, Harold. "Managing the Crisis." *City Limits*, December 1994.

Diller, Matthew. "Working without a Job: The Social Messages of the New Workfare." *Stanford Law and Policy Review* 9 (Winter 1998): 19–43.

DiMaggio, Paul J. "Culture and Cognition." *Annual Review of Sociology* 23 (1997): 263–87.

———. "Why Cognitive (and Cultural) Sociology Needs Cognitive Psychology." In *Culture In Mind: Toward a Sociology of Culture and Cognition*, edited by Karen A. Cerulo, 274–81. New York: Routledge, 2002.

Drew, Christopher, and Eric Lipton. "2 with Ties to Chief of Welfare Got Jobs with Major Contractor." *New York Times*, April 21, 2000.

Dugger, Celia. "Fish Story Ends in 'Workfare' and Sweet Smell of Success." *New York Times*, October 8, 1994.

Edin, Kathryn, and Laura Lein. *Making Ends Meet: How Single Mothers Survive Welfare and Low-Wage Work*. New York: Russell Sage Foundation, 1997.

Elster, Jon, "A Plea for Mechanisms." In *Social Mechanisms: An Analytical Approach to Social Theory*, edited by Peter Hedstrøm and Richard Swedberg, 45. Cambridge: Cambridge University Press, 1998.

Ely, James W. Jr., and David J. Bodenhamer. "Regionalism and American Legal History: The Southern Experience." *Vanderbilt Law Review* 39 (April 1986): 539–67.

Emerson, Caryl. *The First Hundred Years of Mikhail Bakhtin.* Princeton, NJ: Princeton University Press, 1997.

———. "The Outer Word and Inner Speech: Bakhtin, Vygotsky, and the Internalization of Language." In *An Introduction to Vygotsky*, edited by Harry Daniels, 121–42. London: Routledge, 1996.

Engeström, Yrjö. "Learning by Expanding: An Activity-Theoretical Approach to Developmental Research." 1987. http://communication.ucsd.edu/MCA/Paper/Engestrom/expanding/toc.htm.

Engeström, Yrjö, Reijo Miettenen, and Raija-Leena Punamäki, eds. *Perspectives on Activity Theory.* Cambridge: Cambridge University Press, 1999.

Erikson, Anne. "The Governor's Welfare Proposals." *Legal Services Journal*, February 2004. http://www.gulpny.org/Public%20Benefits/Cash%20Assistance/governorwelfareproposals.htm.

Erlanger, Steven. "New York Turns Squatters into Homeowners." *New York Times*, October 12, 1987.

Everett, Martin G., and Stephen P. Borgatti. "Analyzing Clique Overlap." *Connections* 21, no. 1 (1998): 49–61.

Fantasia, Rick, and Kim Voss. *Hard Work: Remaking the American Labor Movement.* Berkeley and Los Angeles: University of California Press, 2004.

Faulkner, Michel J. "Is Workfare Immoral? It's Assistance with Dignity." *Daily News*, July 27, 1997.

Femia, Joseph V. *Gramsci's Political Thought: Hegemony, Consciousness, and the Revolutionary Process.* Oxford: Clarendon Press, 1981.

Fernandez, Roberto M., and Doug McAdam. "Social Movements and Social Networks: Multiorganizational Fields and Recruitment to Mississippi Freedom Summer." *Sociological Forum* 3, no. 3 (1988): 357–82.

Firestone, David. "He Fights, Patiently, for Workfare Laborers." *New York Times*, January 16, 1998.

Fitch, Robert. "The Mayor's Greatest Legacy." *Five Borough Report* 8 (February 2002): 1–4.

———. "Our Labor Leaders Need French Lessons." *New Politics* 6, no 1 (1996). http://www.wpunj.edu/newpol/issue21/cont21.htm.

Franzosi, Roberto. *From Words to Numbers: Narrative, Data, and Social Science.* Cambridge: Cambridge University Press, 2004.

Freeman, Joshua. *Working Class New York: Life and Labor Since World War II.* New York: New Press, 2000.

Frege, Carola, Edmund Heery, and Lowell Turner. "The New Solidarity? Coalition Building in Five Countries." In *Varieties of Unionism: Strategies for Labor Movement Renewal in the Global North*, edited by Carola Frege and John Kelly, 137–58. Oxford: Oxford University Press, 2004.

Gainsborough, Juliet F. "To Devolve or Not to Devolve: Welfare Reform in the States." *Policy Studies Journal* 31, no. 4 (2003): 603–23.

Gamson, William A. "Constructing Social Protest." In *Social Movements and Culture*, edited by Hank Johnston and Bert Klandermans, 86–103. Minneapolis: University of Minnesota Press, 1995.

———. "Political Discourse and Collective Action." *International Social Movement Research* 1 (1988): 219–44.

Gans, Herbert J. *Deciding What's News: A Study of CBS Evening News, NBC Nightly News, Newsweek, and Time.* New York: Pantheon, 1979.

Ganz, Marshall Louis. "Resources and Resourcefulness: Strategic Capacity in the Unionization of California Agriculture, 1959–1966." *American Journal of Sociology* 104, no. 5 (January 2000): 1003–62.

Gitlin, Todd. *The Whole World Is Watching: The Mass Media and the Making and Unmaking of the New Left.* Berkeley and Los Angeles: University of California Press, 1980.

Goffman, Erving. *The Preservation of Self in Everyday Life.* Garden City, NY: Anchor Press, 1959.

Goldberg, Chad Alan. "Welfare Recipients or Workers? Contesting the Workfare State in New York City." *Sociological Theory* 19, no. 2 (2001): 187–218.

Goodwin, Michael. "Thousands on 'Workfare' Get Half-Pay for Doing City Jobs." *New York Times,* August 20, 1984.

Gordon, David M., Richard Edwards, and Michael Reich. *Segmented Work, Divided Workers: The Historical Transformations of Labor in the United States.* Cambridge: Cambridge University Press, 1982.

Gould, Roger V., and Roberto M. Fernandez. "Structures of Mediation: A Formal Approach to Brokerage in Transaction Networks." *Sociological Methodology* 19 (1989): 89–126.

Gramsci, Antonio. *Selections from the Prison Notebooks.* Edited and translated by Quintin Hoare and Geoffrey Nowell Smith. New York: International Publishers, 1971.

Green, Christopher D., and John Vervaeke. "But What Have You Done for Us Lately? Some Recent Perspectives on Linguistic Nativism." In *The Future of the Cognitive Revolution,* edited by David Martel Johnson and Christina E. Erneling, 149–63. Oxford: Oxford University Press, 1997.

Greenhouse, Steven. "Giuliani Attacks Transit Workfare Accord and Threatens to Scuttle Union Deal." *New York Times,* September 20, 1996.

———. "Vowing to Go from Scandal to Strength, City Union Looks for a Fight." *New York Times,* July 12, 1999.

Grinker, William J. Letter to the editor. *City Journal,* Autumn 1997. http://www.city-journal.org/html/1_5_letters.html.

Hackworth, Jason. "Local Autonomy, Bond-Rating Agencies and Neoliberal Urbanism in the United States." *International Journal of Urban and Regional Research* 26, no. 4 (December 2002): 707–25.

Hanagan, Michael. "The Right to Work and the Struggle against Unemployment: Britain, 1884–1914." In *Extending Citizenship, Reconfiguring States,* edited by Michael Hanagan and Charles Tilly. Lanham, MD: Rowman and Littlefield, 1999.

Harvey, David. *A Brief History of Neoliberalism.* Oxford: Oxford University Press, 2005.

———. *The Urban Experience.* Baltimore: Johns Hopkins University Press, 1989.

Hay, Colin. "Political Time and the Temporality of Crisis." *Contemporary Political Studies.* Proceedings of the 1997 Political Studies Association meetings, Jordantown University, Ulster. http://www.psa.ac.uk/cps/1997%5Chay2.pdf.

Herod, Andrew. *Labor Geographies: Workers and the Landscapes of Capitalism.* New York: Guilford Press, 2001.

Herod, Andrew, ed. *Organizing the Landscape: Geographical Perspectives on Labor Unionism.* Minneapolis: University of Minnesota Press, 1998.

Hicks, Jonathan. "First Accord by New York with a Union on Workfare." *New York Times,* December 15, 1994.

Holmes, Larry, and Shelley Ettinger. *"We Won't Be Slaves"*: *Workfare Workers Organize, Workfairness and the Struggle for Jobs, Justice, and Equality.* New York: International Action Center, 1997.

Holtzman, Lois Hood. "Pragmatism and Dialectical Materialism in Language Development." In *An Introduction to Vygotsky,* edited by Harry Daniels, 75–98. London: Routledge, 1996.

Howlett, Michael, and M. Ramesh. *Studying Public Policy: Policy Cycles and Policy Subsystems.* Don Mills, ON: Oxford University Press Canada, 1995.

Hutchins, Edwin. *Cognition in the Wild.* Cambridge, MA: MIT Press, 1995.

Isaac, Larry, and Larry Griffin. "Ahistoricism in Time-Series Analyses of Historical Process: Critique, Redirection, and Illustrations from U.S. Labor History." *American Sociological Review* 54, no. 6 (1989): 873–90.

Ives, Peter. *Gramsci's Politics of Language: Engaging the Bakhtin Circle and the Frankfurt School.* Toronto: University of Toronto Press, 2003.

———. *Language and Hegemony in Gramsci.* London: Pluto Press, 2004.

Jacobs, Andrew. "Union Again Files Lawsuit Seeking End to Workfare." *New York Times,* April 15, 1999.

Jacobs, Jane. *The Death and Life of Great American Cities.* 1961. Reprint, New York: Random House Modern Library, 1993.

Jacobson, Michael. "From the 'Back' to the 'Front': The Changing Character of Punishment in New York City." In *Rethinking the Urban Agenda: Reinvigorating the Liberal Tradition in New York City and Urban America,* edited by John H. Mollenkopf and Ken Emerson, 171–86. New York: Century Foundation Books, 2001.

Jenson, Jane. "'Different' but not 'Exceptional': Canada's Permeable Fordism." *Canadian Review of Sociology and Anthropology* 26, no. 1 (February 1989): 69–94.

———. "Representations in Crisis: The Roots of Canada's Permeable Fordism." *Canadian Journal of Political Science* 23, no. 4 (December 1990): 653–83.

Jessop, Bob. "Liberalism, Neoliberalism, and Urban Governance: A State-Theoretical Perspective." In *Spaces of Neoliberalism: Urban Restructuring in North America and Western Europe,* edited by Neil Brenner and Nik Theodore, 106–25. Oxford: Blackwell, 2002.

———. "A Neo-Gramscian Approach to the Regulation of Urban Regimes." In *Reconstructing Urban Regime Theory: Regulating Urban Politics in a Global Economy,* edited by Mickey Lauria, 51–73. Thousand Oaks, CA: Sage, 1997.

———. "The Transition to Post-Fordism and the Schumpeterian Workfare State." In *Towards a Post-Fordist Welfare State?* edited by Roger Burrows and Brian Loader. London: Routledge, 1994.

———. "What Follows Fordism? On the Periodization of Capitalism and its Regulation." In *Phases of Capitalist Development: Booms, Crises, and Globalization,* edited by Robert Albritton, Makoto Itoh, Richard Westra, and Robert Zuege, 282–99. New York: St. Martin's Press, 2001.

Johnston, Hank. "A Methodology for Frame Analysis: From Discourse to Cognitive Schemata." In *Social Movements and Culture,* edited by Hank Johnston and Bert Klandermans, 217–46. Minneapolis: University of Minnesota Press, 1995.

Johnston, Paul. "Citizenship Movement Unionism: For the Defense of Local Communities in the Global Age." In *Unions in a Globalized Environment: Changing Borders, Organizational Boundaries, and Social Roles,* edited by Bruce Nissen, 236–63. Armonk, NY: M. E. Sharpe, 2002.

Katz, Alyssa. "Losing Home Run." *City Limits* 27, no. 3 (2002). http://www.citylimits.org.
———. "Second Helping." *City Limits* 24, no. 4 (1999): 24–29.
Katz, Michael B. *In the Shadow of the Poorhouse: A Social History of Welfare in America.* New York: Basic Books, 1986.
Katznelson, Ira. *City Trenches: Urban Politics and the Structuring of Class in the United States.* Chicago: University of Chicago Press, 1981.
Kaus, Mickey. *The End of Equality.* New York: Basic Books, 1992.
Klandermans, Bert. "The Social Construction of Protest and Multiorganizational Fields." In *Frontiers in Social Movement Theory,* edited by Aldon D. Morris and Carol McClurg Mueller, 77–103. New Haven, CT: Yale University Press, 1992.
Knoke, David. "The Sociopolitical Construction of National Policy Domains." In *Interdisziplinare Sozialforschung: Theorie und Empirische Andewendungen,* edited by C. H. A. Henning and C. Melbeck. Frankfurt: Campus Verlag, 2004. In English at http://www.soc.umn.edu/~knoke/pages/Knoke_Constructing_National_Policy_Domains.pdf.
Koopmans, Ruud, and Paul Statham. "Political Claims Analysis: Integrating Protest Event and Political Discourse Approaches." *Mobilization* 4, no. 2 (1999): 203–21.
Kornbluh, Felicia. "Class Dismissed: Welfare Recipients Fight to Stay in College." In *These Times,* October 5, 1997, 18–20.
Krinsky, John. "ACORN." In *Poverty in the United States: An Encyclopedia of History, Politics, and Policy,* edited by Gwendolyn Mink and Alice O'Connor, 107 (Santa Barbara, CA: ABC–CLIO, 2004).
Krinsky, John, and Ellen Reese. "Forging and Sustaining Labor-Community Coalitions: The Workfare Justice Movement in Three Cities." *Sociological Forum* 21, no. 4 (December 2006): 623–58.
Kruger, Daniel. "Moody's Upgrades NYC GOs to A3, Citing Fiscal Prudence." *Bond Buyer,* February 25, 1998.
Lafer, Gordon. *The Job Training Charade.* Ithaca, NY: Cornell University Press, 2004.
Lakoff, George. *Moral Politics: How Liberals and Conservatives Think.* 2nd ed. Chicago: University of Chicago Press, 2002.
Langemeyer, Ines. "Changing Everyday Culture: The Contradictory Formation of 'Active Subjects.'" In *Proceedings of the Eleventh Annual Conference on Alternative Futures and Popular Protest,* vol. 3, edited by Colin Barker and Mike Tyldesley (Manchester, UK: Manchester Metropolitan University, April 2006).
———. "Contradictions in Expansive Learning: Towards a Critical Analysis of Self-Dependent Forms of Learning in Relation to Contemporary Socio-technological Change." *Forum: Qualitative Social Research/Qualitative Sozialforschung* 7, no 1 (2006), art. 12. http://www.qualitative-research.net/fqs-texte/1-06/06-1-12-e.htm.
Lave, Jean, and Etienne Wenger. *Situated Learning: Legitimate Peripheral Participation.* Cambridge: Cambridge University Press, 1991.
Lawson, Ronald. "Tenant Responses to the Urban Housing Crisis, 1970–1984." In *The Tenant Movement in New York City, 1904-1984,* with the assistance of Rueben Johnson III, edited by Ronald Lawson with the assistance of Mark Naison. Philadelphia: Temple University Press, 1986.
Lee, Carol D., and Peter Smagorinsky. *Vygotskian Perspectives on Literacy Research: Constructing Meaning through Collaborative Inquiry.* Cambridge: Cambridge University Press, 2000.
Leontiev, A. *Activity, Consciousness, and Personality.* Moscow: Progress Publishers, 1978. http://www.marxists.org/archive/leontev/works/1978/.

Lewis, David. "Poor Squeezed Out of Day Care." *Daily News*, March 1, 1998.
———. "Welfare Boss: Work Is the Way," *Daily News*, March 11, 1998.
Lewis, Dillona C. "School's Out for Welfare Recipients: College Students Forced to Abandon Studies by Welfare Reform." National Association of Social Workers, New York Chapter, 1999. http://www.naswnyc.org/welfare.html.
Lewis, Justin. "Reproducing Political Hegemony in the United States." *Critical Studies in Mass Communication* 16, no. 3 (1999): 251–67.
Lieberman, Robert C., and Gregory M. Shaw. "Looking Inward, Looking Outward: The Politics of State Welfare Innovation under Devolution." *Political Research Quarterly* 53, no. 2 (June 2000): 215–40.
Liff, Bob, and Russ Buettner. "City Expanding Workfare for Single Parents." *Daily News*, March 19, 1996.
Lipton, Eric. "Rejecting Favoritism Claim, Court Upholds a City Welfare Contract." *New York Times*, October 25, 2000.
Lopez, Steven Henry. "Overcoming Legacies of Business Unionism: Why Grassroots Organizing Tactics Succeed." In *Rebuilding Labor: Organizing and Organizers in the New Union Movement*, edited by Ruth Milkman and Kim Voss, 114–32. Ithaca, NY: Cornell University Press, ILR Press, 2004.
———. *Reorganizing the Rust Belt: An Inside Study of the American Labor Movement*. Berkeley and Los Angeles: University of California Press, 2004.
MacDonald, Heather. "Wimping Out on Welfare." *City Journal*, Autumn 2003. http://www.city-journal.org/html/13_4_sndgs01.html.
MacLeod, Gordon, and Martin Jones. "Reregulating a Regional Rustbelt: Institutional Fixes, Entrepreneurial Discourse, and the 'Politics of Representation.'" *Environment and Planning D: Society and Space* 17 (October 1999): 575–605.
Maier, Mark. *City Unions: Managing Discontent in New York City*. New Brunswick, NJ: Rutgers University Press, 1987.
Main, Thomas. "Hard Lessons on Homelessness: The Education of David Dinkins." *City Journal*, Summer 1993. http://www.city-journal.org/html/issue3_3.html.
Maxwell, Terrence. "After Welfare: A Study of Work and Benefit Use after Case Closing." Albany, NY: Nelson A. Rockefeller Institute of Government, 1999.
McAdam, Doug, Sidney Tarrow, and Charles Tilly. *Dynamics of Contention*. Cambridge: Cambridge University Press, 2001.
McCann, Michael W. *Rights at Work: Pay Equity Reform and the Process of Legal Mobilization*. Chicago: University of Chicago Press, 1994.
McCarthy, John, Clark McPhail, and Jackie Smith. "Images of Protest: Dimensions of Selection Bias in Media Coverage of Washington Demonstrations, 1982 and 1991." *American Sociological Review* 61 (1996): 478–99.
McFadden, Robert D. "Union Chief Calls Workfare 'Slavery.'" *New York Times*, April 19, 1998.
McFadyen, Deidre. "At 1549, Members Call Fraud Typical." *Chief/Civil Service Leader*, December 4, 1998.
McFadyen, Deidre, and Mark Daly. "DC 37 Urges Jobs Program Reprieve." *Chief/Civil Service Leader*, January 25, 2002.
McGowan, Kathleen. "The Welfare Estate." *City Limits*, June 1999. http://www.citylimits.org.
McGowan, Kathleen, and Jarrett Murphy. "Contractus Maximus." *City Limits*, January 2000. http://www.citylimits.org.
McKinley, James C. Jr. "Dinkins Shifts on Fiscal Plan Under Pressure." *New York Times*, November 13, 1991.

McMahon, E. J., and Fred Siegel. "Gotham's Fiscal Crisis: Lessons Unlearned." *Public Interest* 158 (Winter 2005): 96–110.

McMillan, Tracie. "The Big Idea: TANF Taketh Away." *City Limits*, January–February 2005. http://www.citylimits.org/content/articles/articleView.cfm?articlenumber=1220.

———. "Bloomberg Balks on Bills." *City Limits Weekly*, July 25, 2005. http://www.citylimits.org/content/articles/weeklyView.cfm?articlenumber=1755.

———. "Ending Workfare as We Know It?" *City Limits*, July–August 2005. http://www.citylimits.orgcontent/articles/articleView.cfm?articlenumber=1263.

———. "Stamping Out Hunger." *City Limits Weekly*, May 2, 2005. http://www.citylimits.org/content/articles/weeklyView.cfm?articlenumber=1715.

———. "Welfare 101: More Education Allowed." *City Limits Weekly*, April 25, 2005. http://www.citylimits.org/content/articles/weeklyView.cfm?articlenumber=1709.

Mead, Lawrence M. *Government Matters: Welfare Reform in Wisconsin.* Princeton, NJ: Princeton University Press, 2004.

———. *The New Paternalism: Supervisory Approaches to Poverty.* Washington, DC: Brookings Institution Press, 1997.

———. *The New Politics of Poverty.* New York: Basic Books, 1992.

Meyer, David S. "Social Movements and Public Policy: Eggs, Chicken, and Theory." Center for the Study of Democracy. Paper 03-02. January 15, 2003. http://repositories.cdlib.org/csd/03-02.

Meyer, David S., and Nancy Whittier. "Social Movement Spillover." *Social Problems* 41, no. 2 (May 1994): 277–98.

Mink, Gwendolyn. *Welfare's End.* Ithaca, NY: Cornell University Press, 1998.

Mische, Ann. "Crosstalk in Social Movements: Reconceiving the Culture-Network Link." In *Social Movements and Networks: Relational Approaches to Collective Action,* edited by Mario Diani and Doug McAdam, 258–80. Oxford: Oxford University Press, 2003.

Mische, Ann, and Philippa Pattison. "Composing a Civic Arena: Publics, Projects and Social Settings." *Poetics* 27 (2000): 163–94.

Mische, Ann, and Harrison White. "Between Conversation and Situation: Public Switching Dynamics across Network-Domains." *Social Research* 65, no. 3 (Fall 1998): 695–724.

Mohr, John W. "Introduction." *Poetics* 27 (2000): 62–64.

———. "Measuring Meaning." *Annual Review of Sociology* 24 (1998): 345–70.

———. "Soldiers, Mothers, Tramps and Others: Discourse Roles in the 1907 New York City Charity Directory." *Poetics* 22 (1994): 327–57.

Mohr, John, and Vincent Duquenne. "The Duality of Culture and Practice: Poverty Relief in New York City, 1888–1917." *Theory and Society* 26, no. 2–3 (1997): 305–56.

Mollenkopf, John H. *A Phoenix in the Ashes: The Rise and Fall of the Koch Coalition in New York City Politics.* Princeton, NJ: Princeton University Press, 1992.

Mueller, Carol. "Media Measurement Models of Protest Event Data." *Mobilization* 2, no. 2 (1997): 165–84.

Naples, Nancy A. "The 'New Consensus' on the Gendered Nature of the Welfare State." *Signs* 22, no. 4 (Summer): 907–45.

Nardi, Bonnie A. *Context and Consciousness: Activity Theory and Human-Computer Interaction.* Cambridge, MA: MIT Press, 1996.

Needleman, Ruth. "Building Relationships for the Long Haul: Unions and Community-Based Groups Working Together to Organize Low-Wage Workers." In *Organizing to Win: New Research on Union Strategies,* edited by Kate Bronfenbrenner, Sheldon Friedman, Richard W. Hurd, Rudolph A. Oswald, and Ronald L. Seeber, 71–86. Ithaca, NY: Cornell University Press, 1998.

Ness, Immanuel. *Immigrants, Unions, and the New U.S. Labor Market.* Philadelphia: Temple University Press, 2005.

New York State Office of the Governor. "Governor Pataki Announces Historic Welfare Reforms." Press release, June 29, 1997. http://www.state.ny.us/.

Nightingale, Demetra Smith, Nancy Pindus, Fredrica D. Kramer, John Trutko, Kelly S. Mikelson, and Michael Egner. "Work and Welfare Reform in New York City During the Giuliani Administration: A Study of Program Implementation." Report. Urban Institute, Washington, DC, 2002. http://www.urban.org/url.cfm?ID=410542.

Nissen, Bruce. "The Effectiveness and Limits of Labor-Community Coalitions: Evidence from South Florida." *Labor Studies Journal* 29, no. 1 (Spring 2004): 67–89.

Norkus, Zenonas. "Mechanisms as Miracle Makers? The Rise and Inconsistencies of the 'Mechanismic Approach' in Social Science and History." *History and Theory* 44, no. 3 (October 2005): 348–72.

O'Connor, James. *The Fiscal Crisis of the State.* 2nd ed. New York: St. Martin's Press, 2002.

Olick, Jeffrey K., "Genre Memories and Memory Genres: A Dialogical Analysis of May 8th, 1945 Commemorations in the Federal Republic of Germany." *American Sociological Review* 64 (June 1999): 381–402.

Oliver, Pamela E., and Gregory M. Maney. "Political Processes and Local Newspaper Coverage of Protest Events: From Selection Bias to Triadic Interactions." *American Journal of Sociology* 106, no. 2 (2000): 463–505.

Oliver, Pamela E., and Daniel J. Myers. "How Events Enter the Public Sphere: Conflict, Location, and Sponsorship in Local Newspaper Coverage of Public Events." *American Journal of Sociology* 105, no. 1 (1999): 38–87.

Pacenza, Matt. "Bloomie: May Tempforce Not Be With You?" *City Limits Weekly*, January 21, 2002.

Padilla, Mercedes. "Estudiantes de Hostos Protestan Medidas." *El Diario/La Prensa*, September 11, 1998.

Parrott, James A. "Bolstering and Diversifying New York City's Economy." In *Rethinking the Urban Agenda*, edited by John Mollenkopf and Ken Emerson, 46–53. New York: Century Foundation Press, 2001.

Parrott, Sharon, Wendell Primus, and Shawn Fremstadt. "Administration's TANF Proposals Would Limit-Not Increase-State Flexibility." Report. Center for Budget and Policy Priorities, Washington, DC, 2002. http://www.cbpp.org/2-26-02tanf.htm.

Pear, Robert. "Governors Unite to Fight Medicaid Cuts." *New York Times*, February 27, 2005.

———. "Study by Governors Calls Bush Welfare Plan Unworkable." *New York Times*, April 4, 2002.

Peck, Jamie. "New Labourers? Making a New Deal for the "Workless Class." *Environment and Planning C-Government and Policy* 17, no. 3 (1999): 345–72.

———. *Workfare States.* New York: Guilford Press, 2001.

———. *Work-Place: The Social Regulation of Labor Markets.* New York: Guilford Press, 1996.

Peck, Jamie, and Nik Theodore. "Beyond 'Employability.'" *Cambridge Journal of Economics* 24 (2000): 729–49.

———. "Commentary, 'Work First': Workfare and the Regulation of Contingent Labour Markets." *Cambridge Journal of Economics* 24 (2000): 119–23.

Peck, Jamie, and Adam Tickell. "Neoliberalizing Space." In *Spaces of Neoliberalism: Urban Restructuring in North America and Western Europe*, 33–57. Malden, MA: Blackwell, 2002.

Perez-Pena, Richard. "Transit Union Agrees to Allow Workfare Plan." *New York Times,* September 19, 1996.

Pinker, Steven. *The Language Instinct: How the Mind Creates Language.* Cambridge, MA: MIT Press, 1994.

Piven, Frances Fox, and Richard A. Cloward. *Poor People's Movements: How They Succeed, Why They Fail.* New York: Pantheon, 1977.

———. *Regulating the Poor: The Functions of Public Welfare.* 2nd ed. New York: Vintage Books, 1993.

Pixley, Jocelyn. *Citizenship and Employment: Investigating Post-Industrial Options.* Cambridge: Cambridge University Press, 1993.

Polletta, Francesca. *Freedom Is an Endless Meeting: Democracy in American Social Movements.* Chicago: University of Chicago Press, 2002.

———. "'It Was Like a Fever . . .' Narrative and Identity in Social Protest." *Social Problems* 45 (1998): 137–59.

Powell, Roslyn, and Mia Cahill. "Nowhere to Turn: New York City's Failure to Inform Parents on Public Assistance about Their Child Care Rights." *Georgetown Journal on Poverty Law and Policy* 7, no. 2 (Summer 2000): 370–71.

Pred, Allan. "The Locally Spoken Word and Local Struggles." *Environment and Planning D: Society and Space* 7 (1989): 211–33.

Quadagno, Jill. *The Color of Welfare: How Racism Undermined the War on Poverty.* New York: Oxford University Press, 1994.

Raspberry, William. "Protesting Up the Wrong Tree." *Washington Post,* July 28, 1997.

Ray, Raka. *Fields of Protest: Women's Movements in India.* Minneapolis: University of Minnesota Press, 1999.

Reese, Ellen. *Backlash against Welfare Mothers, Past and Present.* Berkeley and Los Angeles: University of California Press, 2005.

Reich, Robert B. "Working But Not 'Employed.'" *New York Times,* January 9, 2001.

Rhodes, R. A. W., and David Marsh. "New Directions in the Study of Policy Networks." *European Journal of Political Science* 21 (1992): 181–205.

Rich, Andrew. *Think Tanks, Public Policy, and the Politics of Expertise.* Cambridge: Cambridge University Press, 2004.

Richie, Brooke, and Robin Epstein. "Day Carelessness." *City Limits* 22, no. 7 (August–September 1997): 12–13.

Robinson, Gail. "Private Money for Public Needs." *Gotham Gazette,* February 15, 2003. http://www.gothamgazette.com/article/20030922/200/524.

Rossi, Peter H. *Down and Out In America: The Origins of Homelessness.* Chicago: University of Chicago Press, 1989.

Roth, Roland. "New Social Movements, Poor People's Movements and the Struggle for Citizenship." In *Urban Movements in a Globalising World,* edited by Pierre Hamel, Henri Lustiger-Thaler, and Margit Mayer, 25–44. London: Routledge, 2000.

Sabatier, Paul A. "The Need for Better Theories." In *Theories of the Policy Process,* edited by Paul A. Sabatier, 3–18. Boulder, CO: Westview, 1999.

Salamone, Gina. "DC 37 Votes for Bloomberg." *Chief/Civil Service Leader,* July 22, 2005.

Sassen, Saskia. *Globalization and Its Discontents: Essays on the New Mobility of People and Money.* New York: Free Press, 1998.

Sassoon, Anne Showstack. *Gramsci's Politics.* Minneapolis: University of Minnesota Press, 1987.

Saunders, Lee. "Fighting for Our Future Means Returning to Basics." *Public Employee Press,* February 12, 1999.

Savner, Steve. "Welfare Reform and Racial/Ethnic Minorities: The Questions to Ask." *Poverty and Race* 9 (July–August 2000): 3. Poverty and Race Research Action Council, http://www.prrac.org.

Schleichler, Bill. "Making Workfare Work." *Public Employee Press* 37, no. 1 (January 26, 1996): 10-11.

Schram, Sanford F. *Praxis for the Poor: Piven and Cloward and the Future of Social Science in Social Welfare.* New York: New York University Press, 2005.

———. *Words of Welfare: The Poverty of Social Science and the Social Science of Poverty.* Minneapolis: University of Minnesota Press, 1995.

Schwartz, Anne. "Parks Opportunity Program," *Gotham Gazette,* April 2004 http://gothamgazette.com/article/parks/20040420/14/956.

Sclar, Elliot. *You Don't Always Get What You Pay For: The Economics of Privatization.* Ithaca, NY: Cornell University Press, 2000.

Sengupta, Somini. "City Hall to Use $54 Million To Add Day Care Subsidies." *New York Times,* April 18, 2000.

Sewell, William H. Jr. "Space in Contentious Politics." In *Silence and Voice in the Study of Contentious Politics,* edited by Ronald R. Aminzade, Jack A. Goldstone, Doug McAdam, Elizabeth J. Perry, William H. Sewell Jr., Sidney Tarrow, and Charles Tilly, 52–88. Cambridge: Cambridge University Press, 2001.

———. "Three Temporalities." In *The Historic Turn in the Human Sciences,* edited by Terrance McDonald, 245-80. Ann Arbor: University of Michigan Press, 1996.

Shinn, Marybeth, Jim Baumohl, and Kim Hopper. "The Prevention of Homelessness Revisited." *Analyses of Social Issues and Public Policy* 1, no. 1 (December 2001): 95-128.

Simmel, Georg. "The Metropolis and Mental Life." In *The Sociology of Georg Simmel,* edited and translated by Kurt Wolff. Glencoe, IL: Free Press, 1950.

———. "The Web of Group Affiliations." In *Conflict and the Web of Group Affiliations,* by Georg Simmel, edited by Kurt Wolff. Glencoe, IL: Free Press, 1951.

Sirico, Robert. "Work Is Moral and So Is Welfare." *New York Times,* July 27, 1997.

Sites, William. "The Limits of Urban Regime Theory: New York City under Koch, Dinkins, and Giuliani." *Urban Affairs Review* 32, no. 4 (March 1997): 547–58.

———. *Remaking New York: Primitive Globalization and the Politics of Urban Community.* Minneapolis: University of Minnesota Press, 2003.

Smith, Neil. "Homeless/Global: Scaling Places." In *Mapping the Futures: Local Cultures, Global Change,* edited by J. Bird, B. Curtis, T. Putnam, G. Robertson, and L. Tickner, 87–119. London: Routledge, 1993.

Snow, David A., and Robert D. Benford. "Clarifying the Relationship between Framing and Ideology in Social Movement Research: A Comment on Oliver and Johnston." *Mobilization* 5, no. 1 (2000): 55–60.

———. "Ideology, Frame Resonance, and Participant Mobilization." In *From Structure to Action: Comparing Social Movement Research Across Cultures,* 197–218. Greenwich, CT: JAI Press, 1988.

Snow, David A., E. Burke Rochford Jr., Steven K. Worden, and Robert D. Benford. "Frame Alignment Processes, Micromobilization, and Movement Participation." *American Sociological Review* 51, no. 4 (1986): 464–81.

Solomon, Gavriel, ed. *Distributed Cognitions: Psychological and Educational Considerations.* Cambridge: Cambridge University Press, 1993.

Somers, Margaret R. "The Narrative Construction of Identity: A Relational and Network Approach." *Theory and Society* 23, no. 5 (October 1994): 605–49.

Soss, Joe, Sanford F. Schram, Thomas P. Vartanian, and Erin O'Brien. "Setting the Terms of Relief: Explaining State Policy Choices in the Devolution Revolution." *American Journal of Political Science* 45, no. 2 (April 2001): 378–95.

Stark, David. "Recombinant Property in East European Capitalism." *American Journal of Sociology* 101, no. 4 (1996): 993–1027.

Starr, Roger. "Making New York Smaller." *New York Times Magazine*, November 14, 1976, 32–33, 99–106.

Steier, Richard. "Bloomberg Lands a Big One." *Chief/Civil Service Leader*, July 22, 2005.

———. "DC 37 Sues on WEP's Growth in Parks Dept." *Chief/Civil Service Leader*, February 12, 1999.

———. "Dispute on HHC Deal Leads to Layoff of 585." *Chief/Civil Service Leader*, May 22, 1998.

———. "National Union Ousts Hill as DC 37 Head." *Chief/Civil Service Leader*, December 4: 1998.

———. "Roberts Wins, DC 37 Loses." *Chief/Civil Service Leader*, February 6, 2004.

———. "Say Breakdown by Hughes Led to Wrongdoing." *Chief/Civil Service Leader*, December 4, 1998.

———. "Targets: 'Friends of Rudy.'" *Chief/Civil Service Leader*, October 30, 1998.

Steinberg, Marc W. *Fighting Words: Working-Class Formation, Collective Action, and Discourse in Early Nineteenth Century England*. Ithaca, NY: Cornell University Press, 1999.

———. "The Talk and Back Talk of Collective Action: A Dialogic Analysis of Repertoires of Discourse among Nineteenth-Century English Cotton Spinners." *American Journal of Sociology* 105, no. 3 (1999): 736–80.

———. "Tilting the Frame: Considerations on Collective Action Framing from a Discursive Turn." *Theory and Society* 27, no. 6 (1998): 845–72.

———. "Toward a More Dialogic Analysis of Social Movement Culture." In *Social Movements: Identity, Culture, and the State*, edited by David S. Meyer, Nancy Whittier, and Belinda Robnett, 208–25. Oxford: Oxford University Press, 2002.

Stetsenko, Anna. "Activity as Object-Related: Resolving the Dichotomy of Individual and Collective Planes of Activity." *Mind, Culture, and Activity* 12, no. 1 (2005): 70–88.

"Strategies for College Access and Human Capital Development." *WRI Update* 4, no. 1 (Spring 1999): 1–6.

Swarns, Rachel. "Mothers Poised for Acute Lack of Daycare." *New York Times*, April 14, 1998.

Swyngedouw, Erik. "Neither Global nor Local: 'Glocalization' and the Politics of Scale." In *Spaces of Globalization: Reasserting the Power of the Local*, edited by Kevin R. Cox, 137–66. New York: Guilford Press, 1997.

Tabb, William K. "The New York City Fiscal Crisis." In *Marxism and the Metropolis: New Perspectives in Urban Political Economy*, 2nd ed., edited by William K. Tabb and Larry Sawers, 322–45. New York: Oxford University Press, 1984.

Tait, Vanessa. *Poor Workers' Unions*. Boston: South End Press, 2005.

Tarrow, Sidney. *Power in Movement*, 2nd ed. Cambridge: Cambridge University Press, 1998.

Thompson, Tommy G. *Power to the People: An American State at Work*. New York: Harper Collins, 1996.

Thrush, Glenn. "In a Giving Mood." *Newsday*, July 6, 2005.

Tilly, Charles. "Contentious Conversation." *Social Research* 65, no. 3 (1998): 491–510.

———. *The Contentious French*. Cambridge, MA: Harvard University Press, 1986.

———. *From Mobilization to Revolution*. Reading, MA: Addison-Wesley, 1978.

————. "Parliamentarization of Popular Contention in Great Britain, 1758–1834." In *Roads from Past to Future*. Lanham, MD: Rowman and Littlefield, 1997.

————. "Regimes and Contention." Working paper. Lazarsfeld Center at Columbia University, May 6, 1998. http://www.ciaonet.org/wps/tic09/.

————. *Stories, Identities and Political Change*. Lanham, MD: Rowman and Littlefield, 2002.

————. "The Time of States." *Social Research* 61, no 2 (1994): 269–95.

Tilly, Chris, and Charles Tilly. *Work under Capitalism*. Boulder, CO: Westview Press, 1998.

Tomasello, Michael. *The Cultural Origins of Human Cognition*. Cambridge, MA: Harvard University Press, 1999.

Tuchman, Gaye. *Making News: A Study in the Construction of Reality*. New York: Free Press, 1978.

Turner, Jason A. "Testimony, Hearing on TANF Reauthorization, 2002." Reprinted in *Welfare: A Documentary History of U.S. Policy and Politics*, edited by G. Mink and R. Solinger, 767–74. New York: New York University Press, 2003.

————. "'Universal Engagement' of TANF Recipients: The Lessons of New York City." *Heritage Foundation Backgrounder* 1561. Heritage Foundation, Washington, DC, 2003. http://www.heritage.org/Research/Welfare/bg1651.cfm.

Turner, Lowell. "Globalization and the Logic of Participation: Unions and the Politics of Coalition Building." *Journal of Industrial Relations* 48, no. 1 (2006): 83–97.

"Union Hits Abuse of Workfare." *Public Employee Press*, April 19,1996.

Van Ryzin, Gregg G., and Andrew Genn. "Neighborhood Change and the City of New York's Ten-Year Housing Plan." *Housing Policy Debate* 10, no. 4 (1999): 790–838.

Vogel, Carl, and Neil DeMause. "Jason's Brain Trust." *City Limits*, December 1998. http://www.citylimits.org/content/articles/articleView.cfm?articlenumber=508.

Volo_inov, V. N. *Freudianism: A Marxist Critique*. Edited by Neal H. Bruss, translated by I. R. Titunik. New York: Academic Press, 1976.

————. *Marxism and the Philosophy of Language*. Translated by L. Matejka and I. R. Titunik. Cambridge, MA: Harvard University Press, 1973.

Vygotsky, L. S. *Mind in Society: The Development of Higher Psychological Processes*. Edited by Michael Cole, Vera John-Steiner, Sylvia Scribner, and Ellen Souberman. Cambridge, MA: Harvard University Press, 1978.

————. *Thought and Language*. 2nd ed. Edited and translated by Alex Kozulin. Cambridge, MA: MIT Press, 1986.

Wagner, David. *The Poorhouse: America's Forgotten Institution*. Lanham, MD: Rowman and Littlefield, 2005.

Wagner-Pacifici, Robin. *Theorizing the Standoff: Contingency in Action*. Cambridge: Cambridge University Press, 2000.

Wasserman, Stanley, and Katherine Faust. *Social Network Analysis: Methods and Applications*. Cambridge: Cambridge University Press, 1994.

Waterman, Peter, and Jane Wills, eds. *Place, Space and the New Labour Internationalisms*. Cambridge, MA: Blackwell, 2002.

Watts, Duncan J. "The 'New' Science of Networks." *Annual Review of Sociology* 30 (2004): 243–70.

Weaver, R. Kent. *Ending Welfare as We Know It: Context and Choice in Policy Toward Low-Income Families*. Washington, DC: Brookings Institution, 2000.

Weikart, Lynn A. "The New Public Management and the Giuliani Administration in New York City." *Urban Affairs Review* 36, no. 3 (2001): 359–81.

Welfare Law Center. "Another Court Victory in *Reynolds v. Giuliani*." *Welfare News*, December 2000. http://www.nclej.org/contents/reynolds_another_victory.htm.

———. "New York City Admits Monitoring Insufficient to Establish Proper Processing of Applications for Food Stamps, Medicaid, and Cash Assistance: Court Bars Opening of More Job Centers" *Welfare News*, September 1999. http:// www.nclej.org/contents/ monitoring.htm.

———. Summary of *Matthews v. Paoli*. http://www.nclej.org/contents/docket/docket2001 .htm.

———. "Welfare Law Center Claims That NYC Job Centers Deter Food Stamps, Medicaid and Cash Assistance Applicants: Court Grants TRO." *Welfare News*, December 1998. http://www.nclej.org/contents/jobctr.htm.

Williams, Timothy. "Report Assails Poor Upkeep in City Parks." *New York Times*, June 16, 2006.

Wood, Lesley J. "Breaking the Bank and Taking It to the Streets: How Protesters Target Neoliberalism." *Journal of World Systems Research* 10, no. 1 (2004): 69–89.

Wright, K. "Food Stamp Hurdles." *City Limits Weekly*, September 23, 2003. http://www .citylimits.org/content/articles/weeklyView.cfm?articlenumber=1313.

Zedlewski, Sheila R., and Donald W. Alderson. "Before and after Reform: How Have Welfare Families Changed?" Urban Institute, Washington, DC, 2001. http://new federalism.urban.org/html/series_b/b32/b32.html.

TESTIMONY BEFORE NEW YORK CITY COUNCIL GENERAL WELFARE COMMITTEE
Diamond, Seth. September 29, 1999.
Dulchin, Benjamin. October 20, 1998.
Hughes, Charles. March 26, 1996.
Laurie, Rebecca. October 20, 1998.
McLaughlin, Brian. April 22, 1999.
Power, Michael. October 20, 1998.
Saunders, Lee. September 28, 1999.

UNPUBLISHED MATERIAL
Abramowitz, Mimi. "Workfare and Nonprofits, Ten Myths." Pamphlet, Workfare Campaign of Resistance, New York, 1997.

ACORN WEP Worker Organizing Committee. "Year End/Year Beginning." Report, January 1998.

"Agenda: WEP Strategy Meeting." Communications Workers of America, Local 1180, October 1997. Meeting materials from WWT files, in the author's possession.

Barker, Colin. "A Modern Moral Economy? Edward Thompson and Valentin Volosinov Meet in North Manchester." Paper presented to the conference on Making Social Movements: The British Marxist Historians and the Study of Social Movements, Edge Hill College of Higher Education, London, June 26–28, 2002.

Child Care, Inc. "Welfare to Work and Child Care: Pathways to Success (Helping Families on Public Assistance to Make Good Child Care Arrangements)." Report, Year I Preliminary Findings, August 1997.

City of New York Department of Parks and Recreation. "Eight Seasons Report, 1996–1997: A Report to the People." Report, 1997.

City of New York Office of the Mayor. "Mayor Giuliani Calls on City Council Not to Undermine Welfare Reform." Press Release 380-99, 1999.

Collins, Chik. "Discourse in Cultural-Historical Perspective: Critical Discourse Analysis, CHAT, and the Study of Social Change." Typescript, May 2006.

Community Service Society of New York. "Public Assistance: New Shelter Allowances." Newsletter, Advocacy, Counseling, and Entitlement Services Project, Retired Senior Volunteer Program, Community Service Society, New York, 2003.

Community Voices Heard. "Community Jobs Concept Paper." Typescript, 1997. CVH files, New York.

Davenport, Christian, and Marika F. X. Litras. "Rashomon and Repression of the Black Panther Party: A Multi-Source Analysis of the Truth(s) within Our Data." Paper presented at the annual meeting of the American Sociological Association, Washington, DC, August 2000.

Dehavenon, Anna Lou. "From Bad to Worse at the Emergency Assistance Unit: How New York City Tried to Stop Sheltering Homeless Families in 1990." Report, Action Research Project on Hunger, Homelessness, and Family Health, New York, December 1996.

———. "Out of Sight! Out of Mind! Or, How New York City and New York State Tried to Abandon the City's Homeless Families in 1993." With Margaret Boone. Report, Action Research Project on Hunger, Homelessness, and Family Health, New York, October 1993.

Dennis Rivera to Lee Saunders, Trustee of District Council 37, AFSCME. December 28, 1998. Fifth Avenue Committee files.

DiBrienza, Steven. "How Much Would the Transitional Jobs Program Cost?" Typescript, 1999. New York City Council General Welfare Committee files.

District Council 37, AFSCME, AFL–CIO, "Federal Welfare Reform and Governor Pataki's Proposed New York State Implementation Plan: A Brief Overview and the Union's Position." Green Paper, 1997.

Fording, Richard, Sanford F. Schram, and Joe Soss. "The Color of Devolution: The Politics of Local Punishment in the New World of Welfare." Paper presented at the annual meeting of the American Political Science Association, Washington DC, September 1–4, 2005.

Guild, Kristin. "The New York State Taylor Law: Negotiating to Avoid Strikes in the Public Sector." Restructuring Local Government Series. Paper, Cornell University Department of City and Regional Planning, Ithaca, NY, May 1998.

Jessop, Bob, and Jamie Peck. "Fast Policy/Local Discipline: The Politics of Time and Scale in the Neo-Liberal Workfare Offensive." Paper presented at the meeting of the International Sociological Association, Montreal, July 1998.

Krinsky, John, and Sarah Hovde. "Balancing Acts: The Experience of Mutual Housing Associations and Community Land Trusts in Urban Neighborhoods." Report, Community Service Society, New York, 1996.

Krueger, Liz, Liz Accles, and Laura Wernick. "Workfare: The Real Deal II: An Update on the Current Reality in New York City for Welfare Recipients Participating in a Mandatory Work Experience Program (WEP)." Report, Community Food Resource Center, New York, 1997.

Mahoney, James. "Tentative Answers to Questions about Causal Mechanisms." Paper presented at the annual meeting of the American Political Science Association, Philadelphia, August 28, 2003.

McCall, Carl H. "New York City's Economic and Fiscal Dependence on Wall Street." Report, Office of the State Comptroller, August 13, 1998.

National Employment Law Project. "New York City's Workfare Program Fails to Move Welfare Recipients to Work: The Facts Behind the Rockefeller Institute Report." Report, September 23, 1999.

New York City Coalition Against Hunger. "Breadlines in Boomtown." Report, NYC-CAH, New York, June 1997.

New York City Independent Budget Office. "Governor Wants Remaining Welfare Surplus to Help Close Budget Gap." *Inside the Budget NewsFax*, February 25, 2002.

———. "New York's Increasing Dependence on the Welfare Surplus." Fiscal brief, 2001.

———. "Use of Work Experience Program Participants at the Department of Parks and Recreation." *Inside the Budget NewsFax*, November 1, 2000.

———. "With Welfare Surplus Shrinking, City Could Face $80 Million Aid Loss." Fiscal brief, April 2004.

New York City Welfare Reform and Human Rights Documentation Project. "Hunger Is No Accident: New York and Federal Welfare Policies Violate the Human Right to Food." Report, July 2000.

Office of the Mayor [of New York City]. Mayor's Management Reports, 1997–99.

Pavetti, LaDonna. "The Challenge of Achieving High Work Participation Rates in Welfare Programs." WR&B Brief 31, Brookings Institution, Washington, DC, 2004.

Peter Laarman to Rev. John Blackwell, December 4, 1997 (draft). Pledge of Resistance files, Urban Justice Center, New York, 1999. In the author's possession.

Pledge of Resistance Files. Urban Justice Center, New York.

Public Advocate for the City of New York. "Welfare and Child Care: What about the Children?" Report, June 1997.

Rohatyn, Felix. "New York's Fiscal Crises, 1975–2002." M. Moran Weston II Distinguished Lecture in Urban and Public Policy, Columbia University School of International and Public Affairs, February 26, 2002.

Swyngedouw, Erik. "The Socio-spatial Implications of Innovations in Industrial Organization." Working Paper 20, Johns Hopkins European Center for Regional Planning and Research, Lille, 1986.

Tilly, Chris. "Workfare's Impact on the New York City Labor Market: Lower Wages and Worker Displacement." Russell Sage Working Paper 92, Russell Sage Foundation, New York, March 1996.

Turetsky, Doug. '"We are the Landlords Now . . .' A Report on Community-Based Housing Management." Report, Community Service Society, New York, 1993.

Vedres, Balázs, and Péter Csigó. "Negotiating the End of Transition: A Network Approach to Local Action in Political Discourse Dynamics, Hungary 1997." Working paper, Columbia University, Institute of Social and Economic Research and Policy, 2002.

WEP Workers Together. "Why We Are Marching in the Labor Day Parade." Flyer, September 1996.

Wernick, Laura, John Krinsky, Paul Getsos, and Community Voices Heard. "WEP: New York City's Public Sector Sweatshop." Report, Community Voices Heard, New York, June 2000.

INTERVIEWEES

All interviews were recorded on audiotape and were conducted at the organization's offices in New York City, except those marked by †, which were recorded but conducted off-site, or by *, which were not taped and were conducted while trailing organizers and subsequently recorded in field notes.

Liz Accles, organizer, Welfare Made a Difference Campaign, Community Food Resource Center, October 1999

Gail Aska, director of public relations and founding member, Community Voices Heard, April 2000

Deborah Bell, executive director, Professional Staff Congress, January 2004†

Ilana Berger, codirector, Families United for Racial and Economic Equality (FUREE), September 2003

Richard Blum, staff attorney, Legal Aid Society, December 2003

Dominic Chan, executive director, Jobs with Justice, November 1997

Marc Cohan, director of litigation, Welfare Law Center, October 1997

Peter Colavito, chief of staff for city councilmember Bill DiBlasio, December 2003†

Heidi Dorow, director, Urban Justice Center Organizing Project, November 1997, October 1999†

Benjamin Dulchin, director of organizing, Fifth Avenue Committee(FAC)/WEP Workers Together (WWT), April 1997, November 1997, October 1999

Eugene Eisner, partner, Eisner and Hubbard, November 1999

Maurice Emsellem, staff attorney, National Employment Law Project (NELP), May 2000

Daniel Esakoff, organizer, New York State United Teachers, August 2003†

Andrew Friedman, codirector, We Make the Road by Walking, September 2003

Don Friedman, policy analyst, Community Food Resource Center, October 1999

Paul Getsos, lead organizer, Community Voices Heard (CVH), June 2000

Bill Henning, second vice president, Communications Workers of America, Local 1180, October 1999

Jon Kest, director of organizing, New York ACORN, September 2003

Elaine Kim, organizer, Community Voices Heard (CVH), June 2000

Liz Krueger, associate director, Community Food Resource Center, October 1999

Peter Laarman, senior minister, Judson Memorial Church, November 1997

Maureen Lane, codirector, Welfare Rights Initiative of Hunter College, August 2003

Dilonna Lewis, codirector, Welfare Rights Initiative of Hunter College, August 2003

Mary O'Connell, assistant general counsel, District Council 37, AFSCME, March 2000

Lionel Ouellette, organizer, ACORN WEP Worker Organizing Committee, April–June 1998*

Elana Ripps, organizer, Fifth Avenue Committee(FAC)/WEP Workers Together (WWT), October 1999

CeOtis Robinson, organizer, Fifth Avenue Committee(FAC)/WEP Workers Together (WWT), October 1999

Catherine Ruckelshaus, staff attorney, National Employment Law Project (NELP), May 2000

Tyletha Samuels, organizer, Community Voices Heard (CVH), July 2000

Milagros Silva, lead organizer, ACORN WEP Worker Organizing Committee, November 1997

Brenda Stewart, organizer and founding member, Families United for Racial and Economic Equality (FUREE), August 2003

Jim Williams, executive director, National Employment Law Project (NELP), February 1999

Karen Kithan Yau, Skadden Fellow, National Employment Law Project (NELP), November 1997

Sondra Youdelman, director of public policy, Community Voices Heard (CVH), August 2003

Keren Zolotov, organizer, ACORN WEP Worker Organizing Committee, April–June 1998*